5-22-63   (63-8310)

lliam

The Liberator

WILLIAM LLOYD GARRISON

John L. Thomas is an Assistant Professor of History at Harvard University and is recognized as one of our foremost young historians. His study of William Lloyd Garrison has been awarded the 1961 Allan Nevins Prize in American History by the Society of American Historians.

The Liberator

WILLIAM LLOYD GARRISON

A Biography

by John L. Thomas

With Illustrations

Little, Brown and Company · Boston · Toronto

Published simultaneously in Canada
by Little, Brown & Company (Canada) Limited

PRINTED IN THE UNITED STATES OF AMERICA

In Memory of
MY FATHER

Contents

Illustrations

(Between pages 246 and 247)

The Liberator

WILLIAM LLOYD GARRISON

Prologue

"I WILL BE as harsh as truth, and as uncompromising as justice." So William Lloyd Garrison warned the American people in 1831 in the first number of the *Liberator*, his abolitionist newspaper and for thirty-five years the strident voice of his anti-slavery conscience. "On this subject, I do not wish to think, or speak, or write, with moderation. No! no! Tell a man whose house is on fire to give a moderate alarm; tell him to moderately rescue his wife from the hands of the ravisher; tell the mother to gradually extricate her babe from the fire into which it has fallen; — but urge me not to use moderation in a cause like the present. I am in earnest — I will not equivocate — I will not excuse — I will not retreat a single inch — AND I WILL BE HEARD."

Garrison was as good as his word. Until Lee's surrender at Appomattox brought an end to slavery in America he made himself heard, at first with hatred, then with grudging admiration, and finally with respect. He hated slavery because it denied God to black and white men alike. This hatred he preached to a whole generation of Northerners and made the central theme of his life. He was an irascible man, irresponsible and often vindictive, but he was also single-minded and courageous. If too often his moralizing seemed empty and pretentious, the moral values he taught were real

and compelling. More than any other American of his time
he was responsible for the atmosphere of moral absolutism
which caused the Civil War and freed the slave.

The contradictions in the man found their reflection in the
dominant mood of ante-bellum America. The American
people proclaimed the virtues of the free individual and
regularly elected military men for presidents. They professed
a hatred of privilege and thought of themselves as a chosen
people. They feared the power of institutions and proceeded
to organize societies and institutions of every conceivable
kind. They boasted of their secular Enlightenment heritage,
yet remained profoundly Christian. They talked like prag-
matists and acted like idealists. They preached equality and
practiced slavery. And finally, they believed in peace but
went quickly and dutifully to war. This was the generation
which began by vilifying Garrison and ended by honoring his
courage and foresight.

When he died in 1879 few Americans doubted that he had
been the founder and chief prophet of the abolitionist crusade. In the eighty-four years since his death, however, the
Garrison legend, which he deliberately constructed, has
crumbled beneath the repeated hammerings of historians who
have questioned his primacy, minimized his effectiveness,
emphasized his fanaticism, and challenged his premises. Some
of his critics have discovered new anti-slavery heroes to replace him. Others have singled out his turbulent career as
proof of the dangers of moral abstractions and the need for a
pragmatic approach to politics.

Because he belonged to a deeply religious age Garrison
would not have understood a view of history which ignored
the hand of God in the affairs of men. The dates of his lifetime, 1805–1879, serve as the terminals of the age of American religious reform; those of the *Liberator*, 1831–1865, mark

the life span of anti-slavery. In his mind the energies of religious reform and the forces of abolition were one and the same. He only knew that he and his followers were Christian soldiers doing God's work in the world.

The American abolitionists constituted a religion, and Garrison the leader of a schismatic sect within that religion. He took the formula for salvation of the religious revivalists of his day and applied it directly to slavery. "Immediate emancipation" as he taught it was not a program but an attitude, an urgent warning that shut out thoughts of expediency or compromise. Applied to politics, it fostered an apocalyptic view of the world and released in him hidden desires for perfection. Christian perfection, in turn, offered the comforting ideal of the perfect society, harmonious, self-regulating, free from the demonic aspects of power. Garrison's experiment in practical piety carried him out of the anti-slavery camp, beyond the Jacksonian compass to the very borders of Christian anarchy. It took secession and the coming of a war he had predicted to recall him to the realities of institutionalized slavery and the task of abolishing it. For the failure of his generation to achieve the racial democracy which the Civil War made possible he must be held accountable. He made the moral indictment of slavery which precipitated the war, but he lacked the understanding and sustaining vision to lead his countrymen toward the kind of democratic society in which he believed. Both in his great achievement and in his tragic failure he spoke for his age.

1

Newburyport Boyhood

O N A MARCH DAY in the year 1873 William Lloyd Garrison sat in his study drafting a formal reply to friends who urged him to write his autobiography. "There are innumerable battles yet to be fought for the right," he wrote in his neat and careful script as though for the eyes of posterity, "and those who shall hereafter go forth to defend the righteous cause . . . cannot fail to derive strength and inspiration from an intelligent acquaintance with the means and methods used in the Anti-Slavery movement."[1] He was not sure he was up to the job himself. Now nearing seventy and in failing health, he knew his work was finished. The prospect of compiling a history of American abolitionism — for such he believed his life story to be — seemed uninviting. He would need time, he told his friends, to consider the project.

Sitting erect at his desk, his blunt features crowned by a massive bald head, cold blue eyes peering over square, steel-rimmed spectacles, Garrison looked the very embodiment of moral reform. There was a righteousness in his face which no one could mistake for humility. For thirty-five years he had been loved by only a handful of people and fiercely hated by many more who saw nothing but his fanaticism and pursuit of notoriety. Now he was a legend, hailed throughout the North as the genius of the anti-slavery movement by a

Union all too willing to represent the Civil War as a triumph of justice and to name him one of its heroes. Much as he craved recognition, he could not accept this praise, for he knew that not long ago many of these same admirers had denounced him as a traitor to his country. He was not so jealous of his reputation as to accept fame on such easy terms. Admiration without assent to his principles left him unmoved. In his mind the emancipation of the slave had been a simple case of cause and effect: the moral energy of the abolitionists finally roused a conscience-stricken nation to action. He and his followers were God's instruments. Through them God had made a civil war and freed the slave.

Garrison's faith in the moral regeneration of mankind grew out of his belief in an infinitely merciful God who offers eternal salvation from sin. It was a religion of the heart rather than the head, a complex of emotional impulses defying analysis and testifying only to the will to believe. The true Christian, once assured of divine aid, purged himself of sin and put on Christ. Then, seeking out and joining with fellow converts, he might unhinge the immoral governments of this world and usher in a reign of true holiness. It was this militant Christianity which was the driving force of abolitionism.

The climate of post–Civil War America was not congenial to such Christian idealism. A new and alien science was beginning to challenge Garrison's belief in preordained progress. Even as he sat at his desk contemplating his life's work, he sensed that he had lived beyond his time, and that his faith held little appeal for the new generation. All the more reason, perhaps, to tell the true story of American anti-slavery. To those who believed still in the perfectibility of man he would offer the evidence of his life. The story of his life, like the history of the reform movement for which it was expended, has its beginnings in the religious ferment of the Great Awakening as it made itself felt in the frontier revival in eighteenth-century Nova Scotia.

The Garrison story begins in Nova Scotia one day in the year 1763 with the arrival from England of Joseph Garrison, the grandfather of William Lloyd Garrison. Here on the frontier along the Saint John River, which cuts through the deep forests of New Brunswick, Joseph Garrison met a group of settlers from the Merrimack Valley whose names had figured regularly if not prominently in the history of the colony for over a hundred years. These Massachusetts families were part of the first migration of adventurous New Englanders drawn to the frontier by the promise of cheap lands and an urge to spread the Great Awakening. The movement was mostly a communal enterprise: groups of families and neighbors hired agents to purchase the lands, settled the tracts together, and quickly organized themselves into transplanted New England townships. Such was the arrangement which led to the founding in 1764 of Maugerville, some fifty miles up the Saint John. One of the lots was given to Joseph Garrison, who was already exploring the surrounding country with an eye toward establishing a lumber business.

Nothing is known of Joseph's former life in England. Apparently he was just one of a great number of his countrymen who took advantage of the return of peace to try their fortunes in the New World. He soon joined the New Englanders and in the summer of 1764 married Mary Palmer, daughter of Deacon Daniel Palmer, one of the leaders of the community. Thereupon he received a grant of land from his father-in-law on an upriver tributary where he settled to the task of clearing five hundred acres and raising a family of nine children.[2]

Slight of stature, with a scarlet birthmark and a congenital limp, Joseph was an unprepossessing man who lacked both the physical and temperamental qualities of the pioneer. In him optimism ran unchecked by the more sober virtues of shrewdness and hard work. Along the river, even in his grandson's day, the Garrisons were known for their easygoing ways and sanguine views. Joseph simply lacked the industry to make his ideas work for him. He was full of schemes for exploiting the new country. He discovered coal deposits along nearby Grand Lake, but his plan for mining them proved impractical. When he contracted to make barrel staves for New England distilleries in 1772, the Revolution soon put an end to his hopes for a fortune in the lumber trade.[3]

In the years after Lexington, when his father-in-law plunged the town into revolutionary ferment, Joseph stood aloof, refusing to sign town resolutions supporting the New England colonies or to throw his lot in with the Loyalists. Neither before nor after the Revolution did he join in the political life of the settlement, but remained on its edges, an amiable but enigmatic figure, untouched by its lively religious interest or its spirit of enterprise. He died in 1783, a disappointed man, leaving a widow, nine children and a rundown farm.

Abijah, the fifth child of Joseph and Mary Garrison and father of William Lloyd Garrison, was born in 1773. The pleasures of farming which eluded his father appealed even less to the boy, who shared Joseph's penchant for dreaming and longed to go to sea. After his father's death Abijah stayed on the family place just long enough to acquire a rudimentary education and then shipped aboard a schooner in the carrying trade, learned his seamanship from a cousin, and eventually became a sailing master. The ships Abijah sailed made leisurely runs to Newburyport, often stopping to take on cargo at the fishing villages and lumber ports along the coast. Abijah liked the unattached life of a sailor and marveled at the cosmopolitan atmosphere of Newburyport, which made the river towns in the province seem like lonely backwashes in a flood tide of commercial prosperity. He also came to enjoy the company of cronies in waterfront taverns and developed a taste for the rum which his ship brought back from New England.

Abijah Garrison was a maverick. Tall and fair, he was a handsome man despite his prematurely thinning hair and a birthmark like his father's. His full reddish beard and lively blue eyes gave him the romantic look of a wanderer, and his boisterous spirits made him a choice companion. He had a ready tongue and a keen sense of humor along with a broad sentimental streak. Yet Abijah, like his father, was a born failure — genial, weak-willed and unlucky. He dreamed of the day when he could sail his own schooner and meanwhile played the errant son, ascribing to misfortune his failure to get ahead in the world. As he approached manhood his relations with his family grew steadily less cordial, an apparent reluctance to pay his debts more than once straining the parental bond. More than once, too, his genial manner gave way to dark suspicions of plots against his good name. He resented criticism of his free and easy life, and in moments of despair saw himself as a tragicomic victim of fate. For all his irresolution and occasional ill-natured outbursts, Abijah easily won friends among his landbound neighbors, who listened to his tales of adventure that linked their drab lives with the bustling world of New England. To them he seemed a strange man, oddly likable in spite of his taste for rum and fear of hard work.

This was how he impressed Fanny Lloyd when, on one of his stops at Deer Isle in Passamaquoddy Bay in the year 1798, he wandered into a Baptist prayer meeting, spied the handsome "Miss Blue Jacket," introduced himself and boldly escorted her home. Frances Maria Lloyd was the daughter of Irish immigrants who settled on Deer Isle just prior to the Revolution. The Lloyds were not like the Garrisons. Fanny's father, Andrew Lloyd, was a narrow and hard-bitten Anglo-Irishman who had left the grinding poverty of Ireland for apprenticeship in America.[4] Hard work paid off and Lloyd made a success of pioneering. At the time of Abijah's visit he was a pilot in the coastal trade and a sheep farmer on the windswept island. A man of moderate means, he was a stanch Anglican and the iron-willed patriarch of a sizable family, admired and respected by his neighbors. His daughter never forgot the esteem which her father enjoyed in the island community, for Andrew Lloyd was everything that his future son-in-law could never be — proud, ambitious, unyielding and righteous.

Fanny herself was a tall willowy girl with features too severe to be pretty, snapping black eyes and raven-black hair. Unlike her people, she was a devout Baptist, the child of a religious revival which swept across Nova Scotia in the last years of the eighteenth century.

Many of the New England émigrés brought to the frontier the same "New-Light" enthusiasm which Jonathan Edwards kindled in the Connecticut Valley in the 1740's. The New-Lights were religious emotionalists who demanded direct and visible proof of divine grace as the test of salvation. The redeemed were expected to dramatize their struggle for sanctification publicly, and in gatherings which were often marked by excesses to put on Christ and declare themselves blessed. Carried to the frontier by impassioned converts, this new religious spirit spread like a flash fire across the province, engulfing whole congregations and leaving in its wake hundreds of "burned-over" communities of the newly saved. For twenty-five years Nova Scotia was torn by the same dissension and controversy which Edwards's Great Awakening had fomented in New England. The result was religious revolution. On the eve of the American War for Independence a majority of the settlers in the province were Congregationalists. Twenty-five years later only two Congregational churches were left, the Anglican establishment had crumbled, and a militant Baptist Church stood everywhere unchallenged.[5]

Fanny Lloyd was won over by a Baptist evangelist who roamed the province in the last years of the century. Hers was the classic frontier tale of the worldly young woman who came to scoff and stayed to pray. The effects of Baptist preaching on her strong will were mixed. At first she succumbed to an obsessive concern with self and agonized over her unworthiness. But the urge to proselytize — to bring others to salvation — proved too strong and hardened her will. She could, and usually did, profess humility, but she could not practice it. Try as she might to repress them, pride and a driving ambition always managed to betray her essentially compulsive nature. Fanny was caught between a yearning for personal holiness and a longing for power over other people. Above all, she wanted to reach out to other sinners, convince them of their infinite guilt, and save them. Though she toyed with the notion of renouncing the world and its snares, she was never able to relinquish this hold on other people.

Her decision to abandon a comfortable Anglicanism for the soul-searching rigors of the Baptists had cost Fanny her home and family. Andrew Lloyd, outraged at the "vulgar enthusiasms" of itinerant preachers, pleaded with his daughter, then threatened, and finally turned her out of his house. She was living with an uncle when Abijah met and courted her. Her life was lonely after she left her father, and Abijah offered the security of marriage and a home of her own. She thought she saw in him a good and generous man who could be tamed of his irregular habits by a religious experience like her own. What Abijah thought he was getting is less clear. What he did get was more than he bargained for. Fanny's determination overawed the easygoing seaman, and her quick tongue proved more than a match for his. The impressionable Abijah soon fell in love and married Fanny sometime in the year 1798.

Their marriage did not flourish. Abijah's carefree manner and lack of steady income vexed his proud wife. As he grew increasingly unmanageable Fanny retreated to the solaces of her religion. Recalling the "rude blast of misfortunes" that followed her marriage, she confessed that "had it not been for an over-ruling Providence, I must have sunk under their pressure. I was taught to see that all my dreams of happiness in this life were chimerical; the efforts that we make here are all an imbecility in themselves and illusive, but religion is perennial. It fortifies the mind to support trouble, elevates the affections of the heart, and its perpetuity has no end."[6] Fanny was never so happy as when she could forget the problem of keeping her husband on the straight and narrow path and, with her mind "engaged in religion," contemplate her heavenly reward.

Abijah, in his turn, was amazed and then a little frightened by his wife's righteousness. Life at home became a battle of wills in which he soon knew he was fairly beaten. He turned for comfort to waterfront cronies and drink. For the next few years their life together was one long and dreary succession of removals, first to the Garrison farm on the river, where Fanny lost her first child; then to Saint John, where a daughter Caroline Eliza and a son, James Holley, were born; and then on to Granville. With them each time went Abijah's dream of success.

As her family increased Fanny found her unsettled life more and more difficult. Abijah suffered from periodic attacks of rheumatism which kept him at home dependent on the support of his mother and stepfather, whose care he acknowledged with a due sense of gratitude but with little intention of repayment. His wife worked hard at converting him to Baptist ways, and Abijah even confessed a desire, no doubt half sincere, to "enjoy a Ray of Divine Light from the Throne of God and Lamb." At sea he would write Fanny of his yearning to be at home with his family "Free'd from a Tempestuous Sky and Enraged Ocean, with Just Enough (Good God) to supply our Real Wants and Necessities."[7] He had no real intention of leaving the sea, however, for he was a skilled seaman if a poor provider. Reluctantly Fanny admitted that she could not change him.

By 1805 it was time once more for Abijah to be moving on. Renewed hostilities between France and England and the prohibition of the American trade hit the Maritimes hard, and work as a sailing master became difficult to find. After months of indecision Abijah determined to take his family to New England, where a hazardous neutral trade was still profitable. He admitted that he had been following "the Rule of false Position, or rather permutation, these Last Seven Years" and promised to mend his ways. Perhaps a change of scene would help. "Not that I am dissatisfied towards Government," he wrote to his parents, "but the barrenness of these Eastern Climes rather Obliges me to seek the welfare of my family in a more hospitable Climate, where I shall be less exposed to the Ravages of war and stagnation of business, which is severely felt in Nova Scotia."[8] Appended to her husband's excuses was a brief note from Fanny asking God's blessing in all things temporal and spiritual.

A few weeks later, in the early spring of 1805, Abijah and his family sailed for Newburyport. There they settled in a small frame house on School Street next door to the Presbyterian vestry where the famed revivalist George Whitefield had died thirty-five years before. In this house on December 10, 1805, William Lloyd Garrison was born.

In 1805 Newburyport was a thriving seaport town of five thousand people which the Revolution had transformed from a patrician village into one of the busiest ports on the Atlantic Coast. Huddled at the foot of a long ridge at the mouth of the Merrimack River, the town was the shipbuilding center of New England and the hub of the profitable West Indian trade. From its yards brigs and sloops sailed out to Guadeloupe and Martinique, and fishing fleets left regularly for the Grand Banks, returning with cod and pollock for reshipment to Baltic and Mediterranean ports. Recently citizens of the town had dredged the harbor and dug a canal linking the 'Port with the lumber country upriver; in 1805 they were busily reinvesting their profits in local distilleries, tanneries and iron foundries. On the eve of the renewed war between France and England, Newburyport enjoyed the benefits of a neutral trade which flourished as it never did again.

North of the town along the river lay the shipyards, where master builders turned out the ships that swelled the town's merchant fleet. To the south toward open sea was "Joppa," the village of fisherman's shanties with their racks of salted cod. But the heart of Newburyport was its waterfront and commercial houses. Here stood the huge warehouses at the foot of the docks which looked out on the masts of coasters and West Indian traders in the harbor.

Just above the docks lay Market Square, from which wide,

elm-shaded streets ran up the rising ground to High Street and the long ridge that overlooked the town. High Street, where according to local legend "retired merchants do congregate," was second in prestige only to Salem's Chestnut Street. Here lived the wealthy merchant families — Jacksons, Lowells, Tracys and Cushings — in hip-roofed mansions set in exotic landscaped gardens. High Street was a world of Stuart portraits and Adam parlors, dress balls and liveried footmen. To the newly arrived Garrisons, as to the rest of the town, it presented the imposing view of a conservative if not completely closed society of first families who cultivated the virtues of decorum and good taste in an atmosphere of quiet elegance. The opinions of High Street gentlemen were decidedly Federalist, and in the year 1805 they continued to dominate local and state politics, confronting the rest of the country with the model of rule by the Wise, the Just and the Good. The future rebel against these Federalist principles of moderation and good sense grew up in the conservative stronghold of Essex County North and began his career as a defender of the interests and family influence of High Street.

Abijah and Fanny Garrison joined the "middling ranks" of Newburyport society — as the families on the hill somewhat patronizingly called them — a class of artisans, mechanics, small merchants, shopkeepers and clerks. If High Street cherished the authority of wealth and manners, School Street, where the Garrisons settled, stood for the homelier values of piety and integrity. Its aim was not sophistication but respectability. The High Street families took their pleasure in soirées and oyster suppers; Abijah and Fanny Garrison's circle found fellowship in prayer meetings and evening hymn sings. Although they tended to follow the political direction of the Federalist coterie and shared its belief in benevolence and charity, the tradesmen and artisans of Newburyport displayed a more strenuous temper and formed a society at once cruder and more energetic. Abijah dreamed of some-day joining the carriage set on the hill; his son, possessed of a more sensitive conscience, would live to reject and finally condemn that world.

The Garrisons shared the frame house on School Street with David Farnham, a captain in the coastal trade, and his wife Martha. With Farnham's help Abijah soon found work, and "Aunt Martha" became a mainstay of the Garrison house-hold in the stormy years ahead. She too was a devout Baptist, and many an evening the parlor was filled with the old hymn tunes interwoven with discourses on total depravity and the atoning blood of Christ. With his father so often away from home, Lloyd — as his mother chose to call him — grew up in an atmosphere of female piety.

For two years after Lloyd's birth Abijah shipped as sailing master aboard coasters and appeared periodically between long slow voyages to Virginia and the West Indies, meanwhile sending word of himself in letters that complained of hard work and poor provisions. Back on shore he found his dream of domestic bliss shattered and hard luck dogging him once more. Even as he arrived in Newburyport neutral trade was already beset with formidable hazards, for both French and English cruisers were taking heavy toll of American mer-chantmen. In 1807 Jefferson's Embargo ended the prosperity which Abijah and his fellow townsmen were beginning to take for granted. Newburyport plunged into a depression from which it never fully recovered. Shipyards and wharves grew silent, soup kitchens sprang up along the waterfront as hundreds of seamen suddenly found themselves without prospects of work. Some of them drifted into the provinces, but most of them, like Abijah, hung on in Newburyport and joined their employers in open defiance of a policy they believed intentionally devised to ruin New England.

On the first anniversary of the signing of the Embargo flags flew at half-mast in the town, and a crowd of seamen, Abijah among them, marched to the old Customs House to cheer inflammatory speeches against the administration. Newburyport took the lead in denouncing the "terrapin" policies of Virginia's lordlings. In 1808 Massachusetts, following the example of the town's Essex Junto, entered a period of outright resistance to the national government which lasted until the return of peace eight years later. Lloyd Garrison's childhood years were bitter ones for New England. As the boy grew older he listened eagerly to High Street explanations of "Mr. Madison's War" and learned to share the Federalist gentlemen's mortal hatred of the party of Jefferson.

Meanwhile Abijah's enforced idleness provoked a domestic crisis. His wife's ways had never been his and a life of churchgoing and prayer services depressed him. Without work and apparently disinclined to find it, he again took refuge in waterfront taverns where he and his cronies indulged in the inexpensive pleasures of damning Jefferson and consuming quantities of local rum. Fanny's muttering only aggravated the trouble. If she would not tolerate his carousing, he for his part saw little sense in swapping conviviality for dubious promises of salvation. In the early summer of 1808 tragedy struck the household — Caroline, Lloyd's eight-year-old sister, died suddenly. The birth of another daughter, Maria Elizabeth, a few weeks later did little to assuage Fanny's grief. When she gave way to a sudden fit of temper and disrupted one of Abijah's social evenings at home by breaking the bottles and forcibly ejecting his companions, her husband had had enough. He walked out and never returned. Years later he reappeared on the Saint John, a lonely schoolteacher telling

his relatives of his "whirl about the world."[9] Bitter and unrepentant, Fanny seldom mentioned his name again.

With three children and no money, Fanny needed all her
iron determination to keep her family together. But she was
young and strong — her friends said that only a cannon ball
could kill Fanny Garrison. Leaving the children with Aunt
Martha Farnham, she found work as a practical nurse in the
homes of the well-to-do families of the town. Domestic service involved a loss of status that stung her pride. In spite of
her professed contempt for the opinions of the world she bitterly resented her reduced circumstances. Her relations with
her employers were frequently marred by the injustices, real
or imagined, she felt in working for people more fortunate
than herself. On one occasion she provoked a quarrel with a
Mrs. Gardner, wife of a Salem doctor, to whom she gave a
piece of her mind, "Drawing the picture of a true bred Lady
and a Country ignorant Bred lady who aspired after Dignity
and sunk in impertinence and ostentation[.] I told her for all
she was Dr. G['s] Wife I had seen the day that I would not
set her with the Dogs of my fathers flock."[10] Fanny would
court no one's favor.

She also worried lest Abijah's weakness appear in his sons
and they too fall into evil ways. Anxiety drove her to dominate them. Only constant vigilance, she believed, could exor-
cise Abijah's curse. "Your good behavior," she wrote to young
Lloyd in one of her endless directives, "will more than compensate for all my troubles; only let me hear that you are
steady and go not in the way of bad company, and my
heart will be lifted up to God for you, that you may be kept
from the snares and temptations of the evil world."[11]

Her control over Lloyd was nearly complete. Only three
years old when his father left home, he easily fell under his
mother's sway and grew up a model child and dutiful son.

As companion, teacher and protector of her son Fanny left an indelible mark on the boy's mind. All his life Garrison was happiest in the company of women most like his mother, strong-minded women with repressed maternal instincts. Although he became a champion of women's rights, the Victorian ideal of the "new woman" remained repugnant to him. The image of his mother, stern and righteous yet loving and compassionate, dominated the man just as the real Fanny ruled his childhood.

With his brother James, who was six years older than Lloyd and remembered his father well, Fanny had no success. Resentful of his mother's domination yet dependent on her love, James ended by making a confused and tragic bid for independence. The atmosphere in School Street was redolent with maternal solicitude and soul-searching as Fanny strove to teach her younger son a Christian asceticism which was not properly hers. One of the boy's earliest memories was that of his mother bent in prayer with her "Dear Christian Friends" in the parlor. Years later, when he abandoned the church, charging it with sectarian exclusiveness, Garrison instinctively reverted to the image of this small group of communicants as embodying the true spirit of Christianity.

Lloyd grew up in extreme poverty; without the help of devoted friends Fanny Garrison would never have been able to provide even the necessities for her family. As a man he always boasted of making his way from obscurity to recognition "unaided and alone," and in fact the hardship of these early years made a lasting impression on him. The child of five stood on street corners around the town peddling home-made molasses candy and was often detailed to collect scraps from the table of "a certain house in State Street," trudging back home accompanied by the taunts of playmates. Although these childhood scenes left no apparent trace of bitterness at the time, Garrison was to be greatly impressed with the power of wealth and position all his life and secretly vexed by his failure to achieve them. The young boy, however, inheriting the easy optimism of the Garrisons, confidently assumed that somebody would always look out for him. Somebody usually did.

In 1810 after a visit with her family in Nova Scotia, Fanny returned to Newburyport looking for work once again. Within a year the town was razed by fire and slipped even further into the doldrums. Soon after this — sometime in the year 1812 — Fanny, taking James with her, moved to Lynn, where she placed him with a local cordwainer while she took a position as housekeeper. Lloyd went to live with a Newburyport neighbor, Ezekiel Bartlett, a poor woodcutter and deacon of the struggling Baptist Church. Here he remained for three years.

Lloyd found life with Deacon Bartlett tolerable if lonely. After the daily chores of splitting and delivering cordwood to the houses on High Street, he explored the back country and the waterfront in long solitary excursions. In the summer there were swimming in the harbor and furtive raids on the barrels of molasses piled on the wharves; in the winter he skated on the mall and engaged in snowball skirmishes with the "Northenders." He was a slight and fragile boy, small for his age, and though never intractable, inclined to obstinacy like his mother. Once he ran away after a quarrel with the deacon and was finally discovered halfway to Lynn headed for his mother. For the most part the Bartletts' spartan household and Fanny's frequent letters of advice ensured his model behavior. If he received a thorough religious training, he was less fortunate in acquiring an education. Deacon Bartlett undertook to provide what he could for his schooling, but after three months of the luxury of grammar school he was withdrawn to help his foster parent earn his living.

Fanny disliked Lynn — only "necessity compels me to stay in it," she admitted. She missed Lloyd, and James was proving more than a handful. In the company of fellow apprentices he had discovered rum. His revolt, like his father's, began and ended in the grogshop: at the age of fourteen he was well on the way to becoming an incurable alcoholic. Fanny, seeing the handiwork of Satan in his misbehavior, scolded and prayed over him but only succeeded in alienating him further. James found in blackstrap and the laughter of wild companions the recognition he craved. "I took a drink, it was sweet, and from that fatal hour I became a drunkard." So runs James's confession of his fall from grace. "I soon got so I could take my glass as often as the master," he recalled, "and in a little while it required double that quantity to satesfy [*sic*] my appetite."[12] From this point James's life became one long cycle of drinking bouts, brief periods of repentance, and the inevitable fall.

Fanny never stopped trying to save her older son and meanwhile tightened her grip on Lloyd. "O Lloyd," she once wrote to him, "if I was to hear and have reason to think you was unsteady, it would break my heart. God forbid! You are now at an age when you are forming character for life, a dangerous age. Shun every appearance of evil for the sake of your soul as well as the body."[13] James rebelled against this compulsive righteousness, but Lloyd, secure in his mother's absence as well as her love, never felt the need to revolt.

With the coming of peace in 1815 Lloyd joined his mother and brother in Lynn. Soon after he arrived she apprenticed him to a Quaker shoemaker in Market Street, Gamaliel Oliver. Customers entering Oliver's shop in the year 1815 saw a frail, undersized boy of ten perched on a high stool and enveloped in a huge leather apron, his legs dangling beneath the heavy lapstone. Lloyd did not take readily to this new regimen. Pounding the leather into shape and stitching heavy boots seemed a poor kind of work. He had hardly finished his first pair of shoes, however, when Fanny packed up the family and moved to Baltimore, where another Lynn shoemaker, one Paul Newhall, had decided to establish a factory. Newhall agreed to hire the boys and board the family at his house, an arrangement that seemed a godsend to the desperate Fanny. In the autumn of 1815 the Garrisons sailed from Salem, and while Fanny busied herself with a nautical journal and the seasick Lloyd was confined to his cabin, James befriended the crew and assured himself of a full quota of rum.

No sooner had the family settled in Baltimore than New-hall's ambitious project collapsed and Fanny took a position in the home of a local merchant to whom she apprenticed James. She fought all James's battles for him and refused to believe the reports of his frequent misbehavior. His own stories of ill-treatment at the hands of his employer filled her with indignation, yet when he brought his friends home, she lectured them peevishly on the evils of strong drink and loose living. But James was already a hopeless case. Dissatisfied with his job and fed up with his mother's preaching, he left Baltimore for Frederick, where he tried clerking in a store, quarreled with the owner, threatened the son with a knife, and was fired. He crawled back to Baltimore and his mother, who gave him her last fourteen dollars and a final lecture. "I promised to do better," James wrote of this last painful scene, "and left my parent in tears for the wellfare [sic] of her ruined son. I shall never forget that parting. It seemed my heart would burst, but I could not shed a tear."[14] James left for Lynn with the intention of returning to the shoe trade, but within a few years quit his work and went to sea. Lloyd did not meet him again until twenty-five years later when, worn out by drinking and a life of debauchery, James came home to die.

Garrison remembered little of this period of his life. The darkly romantic Baltimore of slave coffles and whipping posts was the product of his life there fifteen years later. The boy of ten was closely supervised by his mother and seldom strayed beyond her view. Life with the exacting Fanny must have been difficult, for he thought of nothing but returning to "Uncle Bartlett's." "He is so discontented," complained Fanny to Martha Farnham, "that he would leave me to-morrow and go with strangers to N.P.; he can't mention any of you without tears."[15] Reluctantly she submitted to his pleas to rejoin the Bartletts' and go back to school. In the summer of 1816 he was back in Newburyport for what proved to be the last of his formal education in the local grammar school. As a young newspaperman Garrison admitted to a "very inferior education" and complained that he did not know "one single rule of grammar."[16] His reading at this time consisted of such sermons and religious tracts as the pious deacon could afford; his social life was confined to the children's singing school and Sunday pilgrimages to church.

The problem of placing him in a trade became more urgent when Fanny's health suddenly failed and she realized that soon she would be wholly dependent on her younger son. Finding a position to his liking was not easy. He flatly refused to clerk in a store and explained that without capital he could never set up for himself. Hopefully Fanny and Deacon Bartlett apprenticed him to a Haverhill cabinetmaker, but at the end of six weeks, lonely and unhappy, Lloyd ran away. Despairing of teaching the headstrong youngster a trade he clearly disliked, his master released him. Then the deacon noticed an advertisement of a position with the *Newburyport Herald*, and Lloyd dutifully applied. The editor, Ephraim W. Allen, took an immediate liking to the keen but stubborn boy, and on October 18, 1818, Lloyd was apprenticed to Allen for the term of seven years. Garrison never tired of affirming the providential nature of his choice, which put into his hands "the great instrumentalities for the final overthrow of the slave system. . . . Had I not been a practical printer — an expert compositor and able to work at the press — there would have been no Liberator."[17] Divine presence aside, his real education had begun.

2

The Young Conservative

FROM 1818 to 1825 Lloyd Garrison went to school to New England conservatism in the offices of the *Newburyport Herald* and graduated an expert printer and a loyal Federalist. Along with a mastery of the mechanics of printing he acquired principles and prejudices which he kept all his life.

The printing trade fascinated the thirteen-year-old boy from the beginning. So small at first that he had to perch on top of a fifty-six-pound weight to reach the compositor's box, he nevertheless learned easily, and it was not long before he could handle the composing stick better than any of Allen's apprentices. The editor taught him the importance of clean copy, and soon he could set a thousand ems an hour without a mistake.

He boarded with his employer. Editor Allen, recognizing the boy's voracious appetite for learning, fed it as best he could. Lloyd read constantly and indiscriminately — Shakespeare and the sentimental novelists, Pope, Byron, the Waverly novels and Mrs. Felicia Hemans, and the polemics of Federalist scribblers. The *Herald* office opened a new world of politics and literature to the young apprentice, who began to dream of entering that world as a man of letters in his own right. Under Allen's tutelage he developed a keen interest in the management of the paper and the Federalist politicians of the town. Midway in his apprenticeship, when Lloyd was seventeen, Allen advanced him to shop foreman with the responsibility for making up the paper.

Lloyd found his friends among the other apprentices in Newburyport, poor boys like himself who could not afford an education and approached the business of self-improvement in deadly earnest. His closest friend was William Goss Crocker, an ardent Baptist and later a missionary to Liberia. Toby Miller was working at the *Herald* to earn his tuition at Andover Seminary. Isaac Knapp, another member of the circle, was a companionable but ineffectual young man who also hungered for fame. He and Lloyd became fast friends and eventual partners in the *Liberator*. The liveliest of Lloyd's acquaintances was Thomas Bennett, an adventurer and amateur classicist who was preparing a translation of Cicero's orations.

Along with these friends Lloyd accepted the narrowing horizons of Newburyport. He joined the Franklin Club, a local debating society, and spent evenings arguing whether mixed dancing injured the morals of young females or whether democracy fostered the arts. The friends met regularly in a room over Gilman's bookstore to read poetry and compose pale imitations of the saccharine verses of Mrs. Hemans. Lloyd attended church regularly and sang in the choir. Although he never became a member, he delighted in weighty sermons, studied the Bible and pondered the doctrines of plenary inspiration and the second blessing. He was nearly the "complete Baptist" his mother had predicted, a "devout legalist" with all the orthodox persuasions.

To his friends he seemed something of a prig, for they found his uncommon gravity amusing. "He was an exceedingly genteel young man," one of them remembered, "always neatly, and perhaps I might say elegantly dressed, and in good taste, and was quite popular with the ladies."[1] Another recalled him as a "handsome and attractive youth, unusually dignified in his bearing for so young a man."[2] Already he saw himself as a man of probity. Oblivious to the charges of prudery, he fashioned an image of the young man of sentiment to whom all things mattered deeply. In time this image grew into a public role which he learned to play with consummate skill. The Garrisonian myth sprang from this carefully cultivated notion of himself which the eighteen-year-old apprentice offered to his friends — the figure of the true Christian gentleman who is in but not of the world. It was not just a pose: Lloyd was self-righteous but he was not a hypocrite. Despite his apparent freedom he was still his mother's son raised on her twin convictions that virtue is its own reward and that piety is the final test of character. Fanny Garrison bequeathed to her son an obsession with purity and her own secret craving for power and respect. Like her he thirsted for recognition — he would be admired, though for what he did not yet know. But it was wrong, he suspected, not to take life seriously, and this meant first of all being serious with oneself. Once he found a cause he would have fame soon enough. Meanwhile he wore the look of dedication that puzzled his friends as they wondered just what it was he sought.

After the return of peace with England the *Newburyport Herald* continued to offer its readers the same wholesome Federalist fare it had supplied for twenty years. As the organ of the party in Essex County North it had changed little since the days when its first editor lauded the "free and valuable" administration of John Adams. Ephraim Allen had arrived in town about the turn of the century and during New England's long night of opposition to the Virginia dynasty had served the cause faithfully with jeremiads on

democracy and appeals to the good sense of propertied gentlemen. When Lloyd Garrison entered his office in 1818, Allen
was still busy trying to rejuvenate a moribund Federalism that
had barely survived the Hartford Convention. In this un-
rewarding work he soon had occasion to enlist the editorial
talents of his apprentice.

/ Young Garrison's education was no mere flirtation with
the spirit of conservatism but a thorough indoctrination in
Federalist legend and lore. The files of the *Herald* held a
whole library of party history, from the secessionist schemes
of Timothy Pickering to the ill-fated deliberations of the
Hartford Convention. All the spoils of a thirty-year war of
words lay at Lloyd's fingertips. He studied the dire prophecies of Fisher Ames, lingered over the oratorical flourishes
of Harrison Gray Otis, relished the caustic phrases of Timothy
Pickering, and thrilled to the harangues of free-swinging
Federalist editors of an earlier day. The epic of New England's struggle against Democracy and Infidelity was charged
with all the drama and suspense, the histrionics and the pag-
eantry needed to capture the loyalty of a high-principled
young blood. From these Federalist stalwarts Lloyd learned
both the art of dramaturgy and the difficult science of fighting impossible odds.

The archpriest of Federalist journalism was Benjamin Russell, who in announcing the advent of a new "era of good
feelings" in 1815 admitted only to the willingness of Massachusetts to forgive an errant Republic its mistakes. In thus
proclaiming the magnanimity of New England, Russell put
the official Federalist seal on the truce with the rest of the
country as well as on the party's admission of defeat. Repudiated at the polls again in 1816, the spirit of Federalism
retired to the chill libraries of Essex County mansions where
elderly admirers of Timothy Pickering reminisced over the

lost greatness of the Junto. As he read the partisan accounts of the battles against democracy, Lloyd Garrison concluded that Federalism still lived. What the party needed, he convinced himself, was a new editor cut to the pattern of Benjamin Russell, whose hammer-like blows struck sparks of truth. Who knew but that someday Russell's mantle might fall on him? It was a dream worth cultivating. While New England joined the rest of the country in opening the New West, Lloyd turned back to the lost engagements of Federalist history and learned his lessons so well that soon he could recall with the best of High Street gentlemen the evil days when "the ghost of democracy stalked through our towns, carrying desolation and death to the rights and liberties of the people."[3]

Newburyport had been the home of Federalism even before John Adams coined the term Essex Junto for its knot of discontented and obstinate conservatives. Not many cities on the seaboard could match its roster of distinguished Federalists — Congressmen Theophilus Parsons, Stephen Higginson, and Tristram Dalton, Judge John Lowell, and the merchant princes Jonathan Jackson and Nathaniel Tracy. Joined to Salem's Chestnut Street and Boston's State Street, the elm-shaded walks along High Street formed the backbone of Massachusetts Federalism. Boston boasted of the wealth of newly arrived Essex County émigrés, but Newburyport and Salem, where aristocratic discontent cooled the Indian summer of the party, were the real centers of conservative opinion in America.

In the Federalist view the future of the country lay not in the West with its wild notions of equality and license but in settled coastal villages like Newburyport where people lived sober and decent lives. To aid them in their struggle against the New West the New England Federalists invoked a myth as old as John Winthrop's City on a Hill — the myth of New

England's mission to civilize the wilderness. The New England mission, preached by politicians and clergymen alike, reinforced a sectional pride that lived on after the death of the Federalist Party into a new age when the slavery controversy gave it the appearance of fact.

This faith in the peculiar destiny of New England was the intellectual heritage of Lloyd Garrison. He came to believe in the superiority of his section as firmly as in the stern God of the Baptists. In Fisher Ames and Timothy Pickering he discovered the naturally appointed leaders of the nation. As he studied the history of the secessionist movement in New England it seemed to him that never had Massachusetts been so glorious as when, outmaneuvered by a hostile administration, she refused to support an unjust war and retreated into splendid isolation. The lofty ideals in which the Junto enveloped their plots seized the imagination of the budding Federalist. In 1845, at the height of the slavery controversy in Massachusetts, he would argue for separation from the Union in terms which were essentially those of his spiritual guide and mentor, Timothy Pickering.

As the captain of New England secessionism Pickering always identified his cause with righteousness. "I am disgusted with the men who now rule and with their measures," he wrote to Rufus King in 1804. ". . . I am therefore ready to say 'Come out from among them, and be ye separate.' "[4] When corruption, he went on, was the object and instrument of the President and the tendency of his administration, what was left but to withdraw? Pickering foresaw nothing but peace and harmony resulting from secession. The South would need the naval protection of the North, which in turn would require agricultural products from the Southern Confederacy. Pickering's real reasons for advocating secession, however, were political. "I believe, indeed," he argued with

the precise logic of the unworldly, "that, if a Northern confederacy were forming, our Southern brethren would be
seriously alarmed, and probably abandon their virulent measures."⁵

Forty years later Garrison proposed Northern secession in
almost identical terms. He never read Pickering's correspondence and would have denied the similarity of their arguments.
The parallel is nonetheless striking. As a self-appointed judge
of American life, Pickering displayed the same unbending
rectitude and disregard of consequences that marked Garrison's anti-slavery views. Pickering, to be sure, expressed no
very strong opinions on slavery — his opposition to the system
extended no further than an objection to the three-fifths
clause. In 1812 he was perfectly willing to unite with Southern slaveholders in detaching the West. In pursuing his
version of truth he was no more consistent than Garrison.
Pickering would have abhorred the doctrines of the *Liberator*,
and Garrison lived to disown both the Revolutionary generation of which Pickering was a member and the Constitution
he helped to ratify. Yet both men, each in his own time, tried
to capture the revolutionary tradition, the first in defense of
minority privilege, the other in support of human rights.

Only as the last-ditch stand of a repressed minority can
New England Federalism and Garrisonian abolitionism be
compared. Still, Pickering's plots contained the ingredients
for martyrdom as his pupil was quick to see. There was just
enough tenacity in young Garrison for him to recognize his
hero's dedication and reckless determination. Narrow and
pharisaical Pickering certainly was, but when he stood forth
as the champion of sectional interests in the face of national
hostility, he appeared the personification of virtue, a man of
"unsullied reputation."⁶ It was no coincidence that Lloyd
Garrison made his debut on the political stage in the role

of a young Galahad rescuing a languishing Federalism and burnishing the tarnished reputation of its spokesman.

Lloyd noticed as he worked at the compositor's desk that most of the communications from readers that crossed Allen's desk eventually found their way into print. A perennial source of native American humor and no doubt a favorite topic in the Franklin Club was the blessings of bachelorhood. Lloyd made his first appearance in print at the age of eighteen in a letter defending this time-honored institution and warning against "Hymen's silken chains" and brawling and contentious females.[7]

From domestic tyranny, "An Old Bachelor," as he styled himself, turned to adventure — a fictional account of a shipwreck less significant for its complete ignorance of nautical matters than for its unconscious religious and sexual symbolism. Sailing from Bermuda to Liverpool, the narrator is awakened in the middle of the night by a crash which "precipitated me out of my birth [sic] against the opposite side of the room." Groping his way to the deck, he finds that the vessel has struck a reef and "bilged." Quickly he clambers into a lifeboat filled with the members of the crew and pushes off into the storm. There is a terrifying glare of lightning, but a dead silence surrounds the lifeboat. Suddenly a giant wave swamps the fragile longboat, and the narrator, "being an expert swimmer," seizes an oar and strikes off alone.

I heard the groans of my expiring companions re-echo over the vast expanse of waters, fainter and more faint, and then — all was silent! An awful and most horrible stillness reigned: I murmured against that Providence who had so wonderfully preserved my life before — it was a moment of despair; — I thought, or fancied I thought, that one of my dying companions was grasping me with the strength of a giant, and endeavoring to draw me under

with him — or that some terrible monster of the deep was swallow-
ing me up in his terrific jaws — a cold tremor pervaded my whole
frame — my head grew dizzy, and my senses were completely
worked up to a frenzy — I uttered a piercing shriek, and swooned
away.

He awakes to find himself miraculously cast up on a
sandy beach with his oar "grasped firmly" in his hands.[8]
This thinly disguised drama of salvation prefigures the pattern of Garrison's adult life. The anxiety and self-alienation,
the overwhelming sense of guilt and total reliance on God's
grace disclose a personality less concerned with the claims of
people than with the awesome commands of a father. Like
his narrator in the tale, Garrison would be ready to abandon
his comrades in his struggle for salvation. Already Fanny
Garrison's convictions were hardening into a protective au-
thoritarianism over the insecurity of her eighteen-year-old
son.

With pardonable pride Lloyd wrote to his mother of his
astonishment "at the different subjects which I have discussed,
and the style in which they are written." He assured her that
he was successfully cultivating "the seeds of improvement"
and developing his intellectual powers.[9] In fact, his was a
mediocre literary talent. He lacked a feeling for the sound
and shape of words as well as a natural sense of rhythm. As
he modeled his work on the accepted journalistic style of the
day he came to depend on an Addisonian rhetoric that always shackled his prose. James Russell Lowell once observed
that there is death in the dictionary, that true vigor does not
pass from page to page, but from man to man. It is just this
absence of human contact that mars Garrison's mature style.
At best in a handful of *Liberator* editorials his words, though
inspired by passion, are rhetorical and impersonal. More often

they are simply turgid and monotonous. These youthful attempts, like so much of his later writing, betray the failure of feeling in a shallow and unimaginative mind. They may have kept him from wasting time, as he told his mother, "in that dull, senseless, insipid manner which generally characterizes giddy youths," but they hardly justified the "signal success" he claimed for them with readers of the *Herald*.

Lloyd's obvious need for new ideas was supplied by Caleb Cushing, whose return to Newburyport in 1821 helped widen his young friend's intellectual horizons. Cushing was the son of a wealthy local merchant and a recent graduate of Harvard, where first as a student and then as a tutor he had discussed politics with Harvard's young scholars, George Bancroft, Jared Sparks, and Edward Everett. He had even written an article for Everett's *North American Review* denouncing slavery, which he traced to prejudices of the whites "with regard to the minds of the blacks whom we desired to believe incapable of elevation, order and improvement."[10] He condemned slavery as unchristian and unrealistic but added significantly that emancipation posed insoluble problems. In 1821 Cushing came home to practice law as a first step toward entering politics. Cosmopolitan and urbane, he brought a new tone to the *Herald*, whose staff he joined first on a part-time basis and then, in Allen's absence, as temporary editor.

It was Cushing who first called young Garrison's attention to slavery. To be sure, New England had disapproved of the institution ever since the Revolution, and for years the three-fifths clause of the Constitution had been a stormy issue in Congress and the subject of much debate back home. A serious student of Federalism like Lloyd could hardly have avoided the pronouncements of his heroes on the evils of slavery. Even the *Herald* carried occasional accounts of abolition in England and news of the American Colonization

Society. From his mother he had learned that slavery and true Christian spirit were incompatible. During a nearly fatal attack of consumption Fanny wrote him of her colored nurse, "so kind no one can tell how kind she is, and although a Slave to Man, yet a freeborn soul, by the Grace of God."[11] This Lloyd knew well enough, but absorbed in the fascinating business of acquiring a reputation, he did not regard slavery as a serious problem until Cushing opened his eyes. Cushing's scruples mirrored the confusion of a growing opinion in New England that condemned slavery in the abstract but hesitated for political reasons to meddle with it.

Slavery was not the only topic which Lloyd discussed with his new friend. Cushing lent him books and urged him to undertake other challenging subjects. Revolutions in South America, rebellions in Greece, uprisings in Verona and Naples all seemed to forecast the eventual triumph of the people over the forces of reaction and repression. Lloyd's investigation of the South American revolts led him to denounce American foreign policy in ringing tones. If the new republics could not rid themselves of "the dross of superstition and tyranny" on their own, they must be taught to enforce justice and pay due respect to the American flag. Coercion held the answer. "The only expedient to command respect and protect our citizens will be to finish with the cannon what cannot be done in a conciliatory manner, where justice demands such proceedings."[12] The appeal to force came easily to young Garrison. Christian nonresistance lay far in the future, a cause to be fervently embraced until war promised to accomplish what moral suasion alone could not. Forty years later Garrison would return to this youthful conviction that since the right is mighty, one must not cavil at the just use of force.

In 1823 Massachusetts Federalists chose Harrison Gray Otis as their candidate for governor. The campaign of one of his heroes gave Lloyd his first real chance to defend the principles of Federalism and the reputation of an idol which had been severely damaged by the Hartford Convention. A new cause required a new nom de plume. On March 14, 1823, the *Herald* ran the first of a series of letters signed "One of the People" extolling the "superior intellect" of Harrison Gray Otis and the Federalists. Otis may have been Lloyd's ideal statesman, but as a gubernatorial candidate he proved a distinct liability. Unable to explain the "deep lethargy" into which the Federalist Party had fallen, Lloyd prepared for the worst by warning of the "tremendous evils" that would accompany Otis's probable defeat.

. . . then it is that we are forced, however reluctantly, to cast back our recollections to those destructive measures which were adopted by our oponents by which the liberties of our people were hazarded with impunity, as the friendly beacon for every true Federal Republican to remain in the course he has strictly pursued, which carries him safe from the shoals of delusion, upon which his enemies are wrecked.[13]

Delusion prevailed: Otis carried Newburyport but lost Essex County and the rest of the state. "One of the People" retired into editorial limbo.

These early editorials evidence more passion than political acumen. Slowly the young man was mastering the difficult art of avoiding argument. Temperamentally unfitted for the work of logical exposition, he simply was not happy with ideas. His effectiveness as a Federalist propagandist and later as an anti-slavery agitator depended less on an analysis than a total disregard of other people's ideas. Already he disdained to treat his adversaries seriously: convinced that only malice could explain the wanton attacks on Otis, he refused to investigate them. This studied contempt for his opponents furnishes the key to his peculiar use of language. Beneath the invective and the vituperation lay a belief in the moral depravity of those who disagreed with him. He accepted the Federalist myth at face value — to him the Republicans really were a "turbulent faction" rallying around a "rebellious standard." Violence to fact troubled the neophyte Federalist no more than it did the abolitionist editor. Even now he viewed the American political scene as the stage for a morality play and politicians as Bunyanesque symbols of good and evil. These editorial experiments written with a conviction worthy of a better cause show the hardening mind of a zealot.

By the summer of 1823 Fanny Garrison was dying of consumption and longed to see her younger son once more. Reluctantly he agreed to come to Baltimore since he disliked leaving home just when he was becoming a success. His determination to become an author stiffened his mother's resistance. "You have no doubt read," she warned him in a last letter before his arrival, "of the fate of such characters, that they generally starve to death in some garret or place that no one inhabits; so you may see what fortune and luck belong to you if you are of that class of people."[14] Lloyd found her weak and bedridden and was strangely moved by their reunion. "You must imagine my sensations," he wrote to Allen, "on beholding a dearly loved mother, after an absence of *seven* years. I found her in tears — but O God, so altered, so emaciated, that I should never have recognized her, had I not known there was none else in the room."[15] Early in September, 1823, Fanny died, and after attending to her burial Lloyd returned to Newburyport.

It was not to the solaces of his mother's religion that Lloyd turned in the next year but to the forthcoming presidential election. Nowhere did the tides of partisan political feeling run higher in the spring and summer of 1824 than in Essex County, where diehard members of the old Junto plotted to sabotage the campaign of John Quincy Adams, that "rank apostate" from true Federalism, and throw the state to William H. Crawford. As the campaign neared its climax Garrison, now an open champion of Pickering and the Junto, deserted the columns of the *Herald* for those of the *Salem Gazette* to lambaste Adams and loudly proclaim the little-known merits of Crawford. With the first of a series of editorials entitled "The Crisis" and signed "Aristides" he was back in the political arena again offering his dubious talents in the service of another lost cause.

In Crawford, he discovered the son of a humble farmer struggling against the adversities of life; in Adams, the son of an ex-President rolling in wealth and supported by his sire's popularity. Scarcely more accurate was his characterization of Andrew Jackson, who by the late summer had begun to outdistance his rivals. Open letters to Jackson from irate Federalists flooded the New England press, and Garrison, not to be outdone, devoted two columns to apprising the general of his unfitness for the exacting duties of public office. Jackson, he warned, possessed the "savage and domineering spirit" of one "born and bred up in the field." As for the people — the same electorate presumably intelligent enough to elect Crawford — they were not to be trusted. Here speaks the true Federalist:

Sir, republics are always in danger; aspiring and designing men can easily cheaply purchase the tools of faction, to consummate their wishes. The views of the people, however pure and upright they may first be, are nevertheless shuffling and fickle when these insidious agents are let loose upon the community. Flattery judiciously disposed, can lull them into the by-paths of error, and prejudice will warp and mislead them.[16]

With a final warning to the freemen of Massachusetts to look to their liberties and elect Crawford, "Aristides" retired from the conflict. Massachusetts guarded her freedom by voting solidly for John Quincy Adams. To all but the credulous Lloyd Garrison it was clear that the Federalist Party was dead. He would make one last attempt to raise the spirit of conservatism before joining the ranks of Adams's supporters in 1828. By then he was four years too late.

The year 1825 saw Lloyd back on the *Herald* for his last year of apprenticeship. His life for the next twelve months was uneventful, for Newburyport still slumbered untouched by the currents of reform that were gathering in New York and the Ohio Valley. The Franklin Club met regularly, and he rehearsed his speeches in the solitude of the local cemetery, practicing for the time when he could deliver his maiden political address. His appetite for literature involved him in a heated exchange with John Neal, the Yankee humorist, in the first round of an editorial scrap which lasted for years. Neal surveyed the American literary scene for the readers of *Blackwood's* and pronounced it a barren waste. His dismissal of such worthies as Joel Barlow and Thomas Fessenden brought Garrison charging to their defense in a long and belligerent essay in which he dismissed Neal as a madman "fitter to be confined for real downright insanity and clothed in a straight jacket, than obtruding his pestiferous productions upon the public."[17] America, he admitted, still required the finishing hand of time, but there was a rich harvest of fame shortly to be gathered in. He might have added that he meant to share in that harvest.

Lloyd celebrated his twentieth birthday with the end of his

apprenticeship. His had been an education in sentiment: he had learned to pay lip service to the conservative principles of Federalism though as yet he scarcely understood them. What appealed to him most was the romantic spirit of revolt in the last stand of the old seaboard aristocracy. The fact that Pickering's rebellion had been a war of revenge, that the Junto acted from personal hatred only added the color of personalities to a moral issue. High-mindedness and self-deception make an inflammable mixture. In time the secessionist impulse of the Federalists fused with the most temperate of social philosophies would produce that peculiar compound which another generation called "Garrisonism." For all their bellicose spirit, however, these editorial experiments were the work of a fledgling reformer still casting about for a cause.

In December, 1825, Garrison left the *Herald*. More than anything else now he wanted a newspaper of his own and a chance to be a force outside politics. He knew that words would be his means to power and that he could manipulate them to make himself the fearless crusader he wanted to be — they were his instruments for transforming a private vision into a public role. Three months after leaving the *Herald* he had established himself as sole owner, editor and printer of the *Newburyport Free Press*.

Allen advanced him the money for his venture, which turned out to be a poor risk. The small-town newspaper at this time served as the handmaiden of the politician and shared his fate when the election returns came in. Six months before an important national election local party members would rent a room, hire an editor on a one-year contract, and buy a press with just enough type to print a serviceable party bulletin. After the election, depending on the success of their candidate, they might continue the sheet as a party organ or sell it to the next adventurer for a song. The latter was the case with the *Free Press*, or *Northern Chronicler*, as it was originally called by the Jacksonian clique which founded it in 1824. The next year they sold it to Isaac Knapp, Lloyd Garrison's earnest friend; but Knapp had neither a nose for news nor a head for figures, and six months of struggling with his creditors convinced him that the town could not or would not support two newspapers. Accordingly, on March 16, 1826, he announced his retirement for reasons of health and the transfer of his paper to "MR. WILLIAM L. GARRISON, a young gentleman who possesses a thorough knowledge of the business, and of known talent and integrity."[18] It took the new owner just six months to realize he had made a bad bargain.

To set his paper on the proper course Garrison rechristened it the *Free Press*, a title, he explained, "sonorous and politically more appropriate."[19] In the very first issue he announced his independence of all parties and factions. Readers' doubts as to the new editor's political views, however, were quickly dispelled when they discovered on the masthead the old Federalist slogan *Our Country — Our Whole Country — And Nothing But Our Country*. There could be no doubt as to which was the side of the angels: the *Free Press* trumpeted its editor's militant Federalism.

Now an enterprising young man stepping into the political scene in 1826 might have ensured his own future and that of his newspaper in one of two ways. He could offer his services to the followers of John Quincy Adams or he could join the liberal insurgents in the administration party who were chafing under the leadership of Boston "nabobs" and contemplating a new political party. In all the confusion of shifting party alignments one fact was clear — the old Federalist Party was dead. To ignore its demise was to indulge in fantasies; to attempt to perpetuate the ideals and aspirations of the Essex Junto was to court political suicide. Yet Lloyd Garrison, neglecting the example of wiser men, determined to hold fast to the spirit of Fisher Ames. He would rake the ashes of sectionalism until, phoenix-like, the Party of the Wise and the Good rose again in all its pristine glory.

He opened his revival by presenting Massachusetts' war claims to the national government, a shopworn Federalist article that had been retailed without success in Washington for ten years. The Old Colony, he admitted, would no longer threaten secession; but it was folly to deny that her confidence had been weakened — "that her faith in the integrity of government has become speculative; that her rights have been invaded; and, finally, that she feels deeply and sensibly the glaring insult to her character."[20] The citizens of Newburyport expressed their indifference to the question of their integrity by canceling their subscriptions. In three weeks' time he had purged his list of all but a few stanch Federalists. Undismayed by this wholesale desertion, he fired off an editorial at the defectors accusing them of plotting against freedom of the press. "The gag shall be applied only when we are helpless," he declared.[21]

His editorials showed only a meager understanding of American politics. With his propensity for hero-worship he idealized the system as a machine originally designed to produce the great man but badly operated by scheming politicians for their own corrupt purposes. Compromise — politics as the art of the possible — he could not understand. The more he studied politics the more convinced he became of its utter wrongfulness. There was something vicious about backstairs conferences, secret bargains and haggling over votes. Even party organization seemed sinister. Political decisions, he felt, ought to be made openly in public view by upright men with correct principles, and parties should function as open markets for moral axioms. In the public arena, in full view of the citizenry, the great man would emerge and, using the force of his superior judgment, rise to immediate leadership. The fate of American democracy, he concluded, hinged on its use of such leadership.

Garrison distrusted politics not simply because he feared power but because he wanted it. Although he showed few of the outward signs of a child of adversity, he hungered for recognition. His father had been a ne'er-do-well. He had a drunkard for a brother. His mother had died an abandoned and bitter woman. He had been denied an education and a chance to enter a profession. If it took perseverance to make himself known, he had plenty of that. As he looked about him at the giants of New England — Daniel Webster, Harrison Gray Otis, Lyman Beecher — he gathered that character was the key to success. All of his idols were public figures with powerful personalities that lifted them above the crowd. Webster's beetled brows and flashing eyes matched the thunderous tones of his speeches and lent personal force to the grandeur of his American dream. Lyman Beecher, the emblem of Puritan righteousness, hammered his pulpit as if it were an anvil striking sparks of divine zeal. Harrison Gray Otis, another of the New England titans, also used the spoken word to advertise his genius. All three of Garrison's heroes were spellbinders who inspired awe by the sheer force of their personalities. It seemed to him that the secret of their power lay in a union of virtue and strength. Ironically, all three would soon disillusion him by disclosing the very lack of moral fiber he credited them with. Meanwhile the editor of the *Free Press* decided to follow their example and cast himself into a role which would give full play to his driving ambition.

Thus personalities rather than politics determined the course of the *Free Press*. Without a sturdy political platform Garrison could only stand on the conviction that controversy would sell newspapers and earn him a reputation as a crusader for truth. He perfected a high moral tone and studied abuse, dubbing Henry Clay "our immaculate Secretary of State" and William B. Giles a "jewel in the tarnished crown of the Old Dominion." Rival editors he dismissed as political brawlers and mountebanks, political opponents as insignificant politicians with paltry artifices. Soon this calculated belligerence provoked a quarrel, and significantly, his first editorial dispute involved his benefactor and now rival editor, Ephraim Allen.

When Jefferson and Adams died on the fiftieth anniversary of the signing of the Declaration of Independence, Allen treated his readers to a panegyric. Garrison decided to catch his former employer out. The editor of the *Herald*, he complained, was guilty of indecorum and language both rhapsodical and offensive, since everyone knew that Jefferson's deist views inculcated a loose morality. Allen countered with a reminder of his rival's youth and inexperience and recommended a more charitable tone. This "mock dignity" was too much for the thin-skinned Garrison, who let loose a volley of invective at Allen:

He has flattered himself too highly to imagine that we are ambitious of breaking a lance with him. We shall look for a better antagonist. Here, the victory would not be the equivalent to our condescension. — We disclaim having made, at the beginning, any 'attack' — he alone has provoked it. But in our plenitude, we have already been too prodigal of favors. Every word, which we have bestowed upon the caterer for the Herald, has come from us with

the same reluctance that we should sacrifice so many U.S. Bank-
notes. He has therefore the sum of our generosity.[22]

If he hazarded Allen's friendship in his haste to get ahead,
he gained two new friends at this time in John Greenleaf
Whittier and William Ladd. Whittier and Ladd were harbingers of a season of Christian reform that came to Newburyport in the spring of 1826. They represented a kind of
religious zeal which was new to Garrison, and their ideas
led him to the doorstep of the evangelical reform movement.
The story of his discovery of Whittier and his part in establishing him as a poet was one Garrison never tired of telling.

One morning in the late spring of 1826 he entered his office
to find slipped under the door a letter from Haverhill written
in violet ink in a spidery feminine hand. Enclosed he found
a poem, "The Exile's Departure," signed "W," which Whittier's eighteen-year-old sister had secretly copied and sent to
Garrison for his comments. Garrison fancied himself a critic
of discernment as well as a poet, and he took great pride
in the literary column of his paper. His aesthetic creed, drawn
from the precepts of New England theocrats, was both rigid
and narrow. He demanded subjects selected with "skill and
judgment," poetic themes spotlessly pure, "lofty emotion"
and "deep pathos," verse heavily freighted with "that darling
figure," personification. The reigning queen of Garrison's
world of fancy was Mrs. Felicia Hemans, that "wonderful and
extraordinary woman," whose syrupy concoctions blended
chaste passion and female virtue in just the right proportions.
He commended her works to his readers with the assurance
that they would find them "pure as the cloudless skies of an
Italian summer." Whittier's poem, which drew heavily on this
sentimental tradition, met every test in the Garrisonian canon.
He printed it in his next issue accompanied by the following

invitation: "If 'W,' at Haverhill, will continue to favor us with pieces beautiful as the one inserted in our poetical department for to-day, we shall esteem it a favor."[23]

Once he learned the young poet's identity, he wanted to meet him. He hired a buggy and, accompanied by a young lady, drove to the Whittier farm and introduced himself. Whittier, he remembered, entered the parlor "with shrinking diffidence, almost unable to speak, and blushing like a maiden."[24] Warming to his role of patron, Garrison gave him fatherly encouragement and lectured his parents on the need to cultivate genius. "We endeavored to speak cheeringly of the prospects of their son," he later explained, "we dwelt upon the impolicy of warring against nature, of striving to quench the first kindlings of a flame which might burn like a star in our literary horizon — and we spoke too of fame." Whatever the effects of this harangue on the taciturn John Whittier, his son responded to Garrison's encouragement by sending him sixteen more poems, all of which he published.

Whittier set Garrison thinking. In these poems Whittier was beginning to give artistic form to his Quaker beliefs. The poems developed the themes of the inner light, renunciation of pride, and service to Christ, not as mystical visions of another world but as practical guides to action. This piety and quiet intensity challenged Garrison to examine his ideas. Whittier's faith in the goodness of men — his passionate conviction that God dwells in every soul — conflicted sharply with Garrison's orthodox persuasions. Fanny Garrison's God had been a stern and righteous judge of human sin, and her son grew to manhood secure in the belief in innate depravity and original sin, the atoning blood of Christ, and the divinity of the Sabbath. His conservative political bias was reinforced by the conviction acquired from the New England clergy that only the moral force of orthodoxy could save a democratic people from drifting into atheism and degeneracy. The *Free Press* joined in denouncing the cardinal American sins of Sabbath-breaking, free thought, dueling, prostitution, theater-going, and tippling. By the time he met Whittier his religious sentiments had hardened into a joyless and militant puritanism.

Whittier's poetry revealed a militancy of a different sort, a sympathy for the downtrodden that Garrison had yet to experience. His poems denounced war and violence, condemned wealth and fame as "mad'ning zeal" and "earthly pride." His Quaker prophecy of a world of endless bloom "far beyond the reach of time" suddenly seemed more appealing than Fanny's dire predictions. If Whittier's practical simplicity still eluded Garrison, he understood his young friend's appeal to conscience and was touched by it. Whittier showed him that a Christian life was not an impossibility. Temperamental opposites they certainly were: Whittier, shy, painfully self-conscious, introspective; Garrison, ebullient and aggressive. Yet each possessed a moral ardor that the other recognized and respected. Whittier became firmly attached to his benefactor and followed him into the antislavery camp in 1833. Although he grew increasingly critical of Garrison's aims and methods thereafter and finally broke with him altogether, he continued to defend him against critics long after their close friendship died. In him Garrison found that rarity among reformers — a man as dedicated and strong-willed as himself with whom he could not quarrel.

Soon after his meeting with Whittier he discovered William Ladd, the Yankee pacifist and founder of the American Peace Society, whose visit to Newburyport in the summer of 1826 launched him on his career of Christian reform. The handful of parishioners who gathered in the Congregational Meeting-House in Newburyport on a June evening in 1826 expecting

another pious sermon on the "peace question" found William
Ladd something of an anomaly. A huge mountain of a man,
carelessly dressed, with an easygoing manner that belied his
enormous energy, Ladd was no religious ascetic but a retired
sea captain with a Falstaffian wit. To Garrison, who listened
carefully as Ladd took the measure of his subject in the salty
phrases of a seaman, he seemed a huge compound of fat, good
nature and benevolence. Who was this strange man whose
earthy humor carried a Christian message?

William Ladd was one of the legendary race of Yankees in
whom there mingled freely the shrewdness of a Down East
peddler and the visionary zeal of a crank. He was born just
before the Revolution, in Portsmouth, New Hampshire, the
son of a well-to-do merchant. In 1797 he graduated from
Harvard and then shipped aboard one of his father's merchant-
men for a year. In 1806 he returned to the sea, this time as
supercargo on the Negro sloop captained by the famous Paul
Cuffee, in order to study the Negro character. Then, sick of
the sea and dissatisfied with his aimless life, he retired to his
father's farm in Minot, Maine, where he discovered for the
first time "that Name which is above every name," became
converted and joined the church. Henceforth his life was
given over to experiments in scientific farming and conducting
evangelical forays among his neighbors.

Ladd discovered the peace cause at the bedside of the
Reverend Jesse Appleton, president of Bowdoin College and
a founder of the Massachusetts Peace Society. Appleton gave
him Noah Worcester's *Solemn Review of the Custom of War*
to study; and a quick perusal of the tract convinced Ladd
that finally, at the age of forty-one, he had found a way to
be useful. In 1826 he was tramping all over New England
lecturing wherever he could find a hall and collect an audience. Like the rest of the reformers who were soon to claim

Garrison's attention, he preached instant repentance and total dedication. "He who does not give his prayers, his influence, his talents, and, if necessary, his purse," he told his Newburyport listeners, "fails in his duty as a Christian and a man." Garrison was struck by this plain reasoning. Here in the person of a rustic reformer was a vital religious force that could change the world. Ladd's argument was simple and practical. Americans were politically free – why could they not become morally free? Cleanse America of evil by converting the sinner to righteousness, the warmonger to a man of peace. Bring him to Christ, show him the error of his ways, give him salvation as a cure. What this homely Yankee proposed, Garrison suddenly realized, was a blueprint of the perfect society. In Ladd's proposition lay the seeds of a great Christian movement.

Enthusiastically he reported Ladd's speech in his paper. No one, he wrote, could doubt that the pacifist was destined to prove the foremost philanthropist of his age, a man of "noble efforts."[25] Thus began a friendship which despite prolonged and bitter disagreement lasted until Ladd's death in 1841. Ladd, like Whittier, was too sure of his cause and too amiably disposed toward mankind to harbor grudges. He remained to the last a man of peace who practiced what he preached.

In September the *Free Press* collapsed under the weight of its editor's unpopular opinions, and Garrison found himself in financial straits. There was nothing left but to cut his losses by selling the paper and seek work as a journeyman printer in Boston. He announced that "influenced by considerations important only to himself," the editor had decided to offer his entire establishment for quick sale. In a valedictory more caustic than his usual tone he announced the sale of the paper to one John Harris. He admitted that the *Free Press* had startled many readers, offended others. "This is a time-serving age and he who attempts to walk uprightly and speak honestly, cannot rationally calculate upon speedy wealth or preferment."[26] He confessed to no regrets and made no apologies. His conscience was clear.

Failure could not dull the excitement of new ideas. Newburyport hardly qualified as a sink of corruption, but his certainty of having been victimized by its cliques and cabals made his departure seem less of a retreat. Now that he was setting out for Boston it simplified his mistakes to explain them as the work of a petty conspiracy against his good name. Such was his mood when he plunged into a last squabble, as if to show his fellow townsmen that nothing became his life in the town like leaving it. This time his victim was Caleb Cushing.

Since leaving the *Herald* Cushing had divided his time between literature and politics. His popularity with the manufacturers of the Merrimack Valley led to his nomination for the Congressional seat for Essex County against the incumbent John Varnum of Haverhill. The campaign reached new heights of personal animosity: Cushing was accused of loose morals and Varnum was denounced for alleged shady dealings with the Junto. Garrison, apprised of Cushing's views on the tariff, remained loyal to the old Federalist principles and supported Varnum against Cushing's "coalition of interests and family influence."[27] Yet when he announced the sale of the *Free Press* to Harris, who was a close friend of Cushing's, and Harris promptly came out for his friend, rumors circulated concerning a deal between young Garrison and the wily Cushing. As soon as Garrison learned of the rumors he rushed to the attack. First he fired off a letter to the *Haverhill Gazette*, Varnum's sheet and the source of the story, denying the accusation and offering as proof of his fidelity to Federalism a six-month record unblemished by even a hint of Republican heresy. Then, still smarting at the injustice, he marched into a Cushing rally, strode to the platform, and delivered a tirade against his former friend accusing him of cowardice and the intent to deceive. Cushing lost the election by a wide margin, and neither man ever forgave the other. For his part Cushing grew convinced of his protégé's dangerous fanaticism, while Garrison, once he became an abolitionist, denounced Cushing for every sin he could think of.

In December, 1826, Garrison left for Boston, an unemployed journalist with six months' stormy experience. Not until after the Civil War did he enjoy his return visits to Newburyport. During the lean anti-slavery years ahead he explained his dislike of the town as a product of its conservative opposition to his cause. A better reason perhaps was that it had witnessed his first failure.

3

Boston

To the young provincial from Newburyport, Boston
seemed vast and forbidding in the cold gray light
of December, 1826. Hurrying through crooked streets to his
boardinghouse in the North End, he remembered earlier visits
to the city. Once on an errand to a printing house near the
waterfront he had lost his way and wandered for hours
through these same winding streets homesick and frightened.
A second trip the previous summer had also ended unhappily
when his twenty-mile hike in new shoes left him so crippled
with blisters and aching feet that he rushed to catch the first
stage home. Now he was back a third time, not the successful
young journalist he fancied himself but a lowly journeyman
printer seeking a second chance.

Formidable as it may have appeared to him, Boston in 1826
was a small city of some fifty thousand people which still
wore its colonial heritage with pride. Mayor Josiah Quincy
with the blessing of Boston's first families was just beginning
to modernize the city, paving the streets, building a new city
market, and providing police and fire protection. Lloyd Garrison caught the unmistakable air of paternalism blowing
down from Beacon Hill, where merchant families preserved
their conservative opinions as carefully as their fortunes.

Wealthy Bostonians, he knew, were as fully aware of their

duty to lead the civilization of the country as the High Street
gentlemen of Newburyport. By the middle of the third decade
of the nineteenth century they had settled to the task and were
enjoying what the good Dr. Bowditch called "the best days of
the Republic." Secure in their beliefs, conservative Bostonians
applauded the sentiments of Daniel Webster, discussed the
sermons of William Ellery Channing, and kept a sharp eye on
the earnings of A. & A. Lawrence & Company. In the "un-
adorned good sense" of Unitarianism and the *North American
Review* they found a metaphysic for their Whiggery.

That wealth and position carried responsibilities towards
their less fortunate townsmen, the leading families of Boston
never doubted. Most of the city's social services were furnished by private charity. Many a Sunday afternoon Garrison
strolled through the Common to the strains of a brass band
hired by the Society for the Suppression of Vice in the vain
hope of emptying the grogshops. Wives and daughters of
leading citizens devoted leisure hours to such benevolent societies as the Boston Fatherless and Widow's Society and the
Penitent Female Refuge. By the time Lloyd Garrison arrived,
charitable associations had become a habit with Boston's well-
to-do: between 1810 and 1840 they averaged at least one new
benevolent institution a year, most of them founded for the
dual purpose of attending to the needy and repairing public
morals. The logic of Boston paternalism posited social control
as well as Christian charity, and the art of using their wealth
wisely was one which these families had fully mastered.

It was not to the Boston of Beacon Hill or to the fashionable West End that Garrison went on his arrival, but to the
Scott Street boardinghouse of his friend Thomas Bennett,
himself a newcomer from the 'Port. Bennett's boardinghouse
lay in the heart of another and different society of the middle
classes. This was the Boston Emerson meant when he spoke

of the city as a moving principle, "a living mind, agitating the mass and always afflicting the conservative class with some odious novelty or other." Middle-class Boston consisted of professional people, small merchants, artisans, and shopkeepers, many of them, like Garrison, recent arrivals from Essex North and the Old Colony. They brought with them a seaboard conservatism and social aspirations which they shared with the patricians, but they wore their conservatism with a difference. In the first place, they disliked the proprietary manner of the old families and resented their institutionalized snobbery. Coming from country strongholds of orthodoxy, they mistrusted the "icy system" of Unitarianism with its cool lucidities that replaced the majesty of God with the tricks of human reason. The benevolence of the Boston merchants stemmed from a recognition of their declining political power, while the religious impulse of middle-class Boston sprang from the rocky soil of Christian zeal.

Garrison's orthodox friends in his adopted city assumed that only Christianity could save the nation from infidelity and licentiousness. They viewed the renovation of American morals as a crusade which could never be won by local contingents of philanthropists dispensing charity and advice but demanded a revolutionary army organized into missionary, tract, and Bible societies captained by the great religious leaders of the day. One of these leaders was their own Lyman Beecher, recently made pastor of the Hanover Street Church. If the spiritual center of Unitarian Boston was Channing's Federal Street congregation, evangelical Boston made its headquarters in the home of Lyman Beecher in the North End next to the old burying ground on Copp's Hill, whither he was known frequently to retire to pray for those whose feet stumbled on the dark mountain. Hanover Street Church became Garrison's spiritual home and Beecher his mentor.

Beecher had also come to Boston in 1826 in response to a challenge. As an organizer and what another age would call a public-relations expert he had few peers. Earlier he had organized the Connecticut Society for the Reformation of Morals to protect the Standing Order against "Sabbath-breakers, rum-sellers, tippling folk, infidels, and ruff-scuff" who made up the ranks of democracy. He wrote tracts, held revivals, established a magazine, lectured on temperance, lobbied for Sunday blue laws, and fought manfully to preserve the establishment at every turn. When he finally lost the battle against disestablishment in Connecticut in 1817, he admitted that "it was as dark a day as ever I saw."[1] Presently, however, he saw the light: far from destroying Christian order, disestablishment had actually strengthened it by cutting the churches loose from state support. With missions, revivals, and voluntary associations Christians could exert a far stronger influence than ever they could with shoe buckles, cocked hats, and gold-headed canes. To prove his point Beecher threw himself into the work of Christian reform, fashioning Bible and tract societies, supporting home missions, the temperance cause and all the other benevolent associations which sprang up in the East after 1812. Under his aegis these vast interdenominational societies formed a benevolent empire run by an interlocking directorate of lay and clerical figures whose avowed aim was the engineering of mass American consent to Christian leadership.

As the democratization of American church polity proceeded apace, the need for a major theological reorientation grew urgent. This need Beecher and his old Yale classmate, Nathaniel Taylor, attempted to meet with a doctrine of their own. "Beecherism," or "Taylorism" as it was more commonly called, took for its central theme the primacy of reason over the letter of revelation. Men are punished for their sins, Beecher and Taylor argued, only because they freely and willingly choose to sin. Without free agency there could be no sinful act; men are truly free agents. Saving grace lies within the reach of any man who will but try to come to Christ. Sin is selfishness, and regeneration simply the act of will which consists of the preference of God to every other object, that act being the effect of the Holy Spirit operating on the mind. "Whosoever will may come" — this was the real import of their new doctrine which furnished the rationale for the revivals and the benevolent crusade of the Second Great Awakening. In Beecher's new formula piety and ethics, severed in the First Great Awakening, were reunited in a democratic evangelical puritanism.

Beecher's connection with this theology was not always clear or consistent. Taylor was a speculative thinker and a reformer; Beecher was neither. Deep down in his soul he was a trimmer, and he refused to jeopardize his plans for a great American church by getting embroiled in doctrinal dispute. In 1826, however, when Garrison first heard him preach, he stood foursquare behind the new theology for which he claimed partial credit. More important, he brought to Boston an experience in organizing religious enterprises which few of his colleagues could match. Once established in Hanover Street, he inaugurated a series of revivals, using a new "soft persuasion" adapted to city congregations. It was not long before he noticed that the evangelical people of Boston lacked political influence. Quickly he organized the Hanover Association of Young Men and sent its members into the city primaries with instructions to outvote the "smoking loafers," remove the liquor booths from the Common, and stop the Sunday steamboat excursions to Nahant. This they promptly did, and soon Beecher was a commanding figure in Boston society.

To Garrison, who went regularly to hear him preach, there seemed something majestic in this stocky figure with his untidy robes flying behind him as he strode to the pulpit to do battle for the Lord. Beecher was a dynamo. Both the muscularity of his sermons and his devotion to the strenuous life revealed a man of prodigious energy, impatient of all restraint and aching to get on with the business of Christianizing the country. His conversation abounded in military figures — plans of battle, shot and shell, victorious charges, and routing the enemy. Beecher had the kind of Christian belligerence which young Garrison understood. "As a divine," he noted enthusiastically, "Lyman Beecher has no equal." What was it that gave Beecher his strength? "Truth — TRUTH — delivered in a childlike simplicity and affection."[2] Sitting in the back pews of Hanover Street Church, Garrison did not realize yet the full import of Beecher's message or the lengths to which it would carry him. He only knew that Beecher offered revealed religion as a guide; but for a young man intent on directing the lives of other people that was enough.

More than a month went by before he found work. The next year he spent migrating from one printing job to another before joining the *Massachusetts Weekly Journal*, a new Whig paper edited by David Lee Child. In his leisure he surveyed his adopted city, strolling through Beacon Hill, exploring the wharves, and standing with the crowd on the Common to watch the militia march on training days. He went to hear Beecher's archenemies, Channing and John Pierpont, the flinty pastor of the Hollis Street Unitarian Church and grandfather of J. Pierpont Morgan. Much as he disapproved of the "icy system," he was impressed with Channing's low-keyed sermons, and from Pierpont he learned that works were more important than doctrine. Slowly Boston cosmopolitanism began to tell, and a new note of sophistication appeared in the verses he scribbled off for his own amusement.

> I think if our first parents had been driven
> From Paradise to Boston, their deep woe
> Had lost its keenness — no place under heaven
> For worth of loveliness, had pleased them so;
> Particularly if they had resided
> In that fine house for David Sears provided.[3]

His hunger for recognition was partially assuaged by an incident in the summer of 1827. When Daniel Webster moved up to the Senate, he left a vacancy in the House of Representatives. A party caucus duly assembled in July and was presented with the candidate of the Central Committee, Benjamin Gorham. Gorham's nomination was just about to be put to a vote when out of the audience and onto the platform strode Garrison, primed with a lengthy speech in support of his perennial favorite, Harrison Gray Otis. The Central Committee had already rejected Otis because of his antiquated views on the tariff, but when Garrison launched his panegyric, it was clear that the action of the committee had been premature. An acid reminder from the chairman that he was out of order failed to dampen the enthusiasm of the fledgling orator, who was beginning to enjoy himself. Unfortunately, halfway through his oration his memory failed him and he had to take recourse to a copy of the speech tucked in his hat. Still, when he finished and returned to his seat, he found that he had upset the carefully laid plans of the steering committee, who decided to consult Otis once more. He left the meeting in triumph. A few days later one of the Federalist gentlemen who had attended the caucus wrote a letter to the *Courier* demanding to know the name of the young upstart who had disrupted the proceedings. In his reply Garrison sympathized with his critic for the trouble he had experienced in learning his name. "Let me assure him, however, that if my life be spared, my name shall one day be known to the world, — at least to such an extent that common inquiry shall be unnecessary. This, I know, will be deemed excessive vanity — but time shall prove it prophetic."[4]

The editorial opportunity he sought came in the person of the Reverend William Collier, who ran a boardinghouse on Milk Street. Collier was a Baptist city missionary and the editor of a struggling temperance newspaper, the *National Philanthropist*. His boardinghouse served as a haven for missionaries, visiting clergymen, itinerant evangelists and Christian reformers of all kinds; his paper exposed the evils of drink and denounced gambling, prostitution, dueling, and theatergoing, and extolled the virtues of Bible societies, home missions, and Sabbath observance. In its pages each week could be found the evangelical prescription for a better world.

At Collier's Garrison met the printer of the *National Philanthropist*, Nathaniel White, who hired him as a typesetter sometime late in 1827. When Collier, discouraged by the anemic circulation of his paper, decided to sell out to his printer, White made Garrison his new editor. On January 4, 1828, the *National Philanthropist* appeared for the first time under new editorial direction, although Garrison's name did not appear on the masthead until March.

Once again he set out to refashion a newspaper according to his notions of popular journalism. He increased the number of columns, enlarged the format, and cleaned up the typography. Collier's motto, *Moderate Drinking is the Downhill Road to Drunkenness*, he decided to keep, but for Collier's sermons he substituted stinging editorials. His experiences with the *Free Press* had taught him the need for a platform. In an editorial entitled "Moral Character of Public Men" he expounded his new philosophy of reform. "Moral principles should be inseparably connected with political; and the splendid talents of the dissolute must not be preferred to the competent, though inferior, abilities of the virtuous of our land." Americans, he continued, had never understood the need for a moral influence sufficient to control party intemperance and enhance the value of public opinion. It therefore behooved Christians especially to guard against "the common partialities and obliquities of political strife." Political parties should henceforth be subject to Christian control. No longer would the duelist, the gambler, the debaucher, or the "profane swearer" be elected simply because he was a Federalist or a Republican. Political morality must be raised to the level of Christian behavior. "It is due to our principles, our civil, social and moral institutions, that men whose characters are notoriously bad should be deprived of the control of our political destinies."[5]

There was nothing new in Garrison's plea for religious influence in politics; it had been the stock-in-trade of evangelicals and their benevolent societies for fifteen years. Behind its seemingly nonpartisan appeal lay the conservative opinions of clericals who sought to defend the established order from onrushing democracy. One of the most striking of the many ironies that studded Garrison's career was the fact that his anti-slavery radicalism evolved out of a literal interpretation of these principles of Christian conservatism.

The professed aim of the benevolent societies which sprang up after 1812 in response to the challenge of democracy was the extension of the Christian faith and the reformation of public morals. The American Bible Society, the Sunday School Union, the American Tract Society, home and foreign missionary societies all shared the common goal of educating the citizen for participation in a Christian America. The publications of the Bible Society urged its members to scrutinize voting lists and elect only Christian candidates. The Society for the Preservation of the Sabbath discredited any office-seeker who failed to keep the Sabbath. The Temperance Society withheld its support from any politician known to imbibe. And so it went. Denied entrance to the halls of state through the main portals, the ministers availed themselves of the back door. If they could not make the laws themselves, they could see to it that the laws recognized their influence. By the time Garrison joined them, the benevolent societies were busy as never before operating a gigantic political lobby, publicity bureau, and propaganda machine in the interests of the new puritanism.

When it came to defining the Christian statesman the evangelical formula grew blurred. It was all well and good to insist on honesty, trust, duty, and uprightness, but what did these words really mean? Granted that the unregenerate politician could be identified by his sins — tippling, gambling, and general licentious behavior, but the positive content of the ideal of Christian statesmanship remained unexplored. The evangelical argument ran like this: A "professing Christian" is one who is regenerate (i. e., has received saving grace) and is thus free from selfishness, hypocrisy, and dishonesty. Once in office he is bound to make the right decisions. His views on the tariff, land grants, or the Bank hardly matter since he can *always* be trusted to reach a Christian solution. On the theory that it takes a Christian to recognize and elect a fellow communicant, the evangelicals argued that social reform really begins with the moral reform of individuals. Not until everyone is purified can the problem of Christian government be solved. Poverty, slavery, capital punishment, im-

prisonment for debt, extension of the franchise, all the major
social problems await the regeneration of the individual. Once
the saints are legion they will make their righteousness felt,
and their moral omnicompetence will ensure a reign of peace
and justice.

Thus the problems of social and political reform were reduced in the evangelical equation to elements of personal
morality. By reforming the individual and bringing him to
Christ the preachers would mysteriously change his heart
and thereby qualify him for leadership. Piecemeal reforms,
especially those favored by political parties and disaffected
minorities, they dismissed as pernicious half-measures based on
compromise rather than the rock of universal love.

Such in all its essentials was the doctrine of moral reform
as Garrison understood and accepted it, an equation of duties
and rewards. "If we have hitherto lived without reference
to another state of existence," he wrote in one of his new
editorials, "let us do so no longer." The fruits of earth are
bitter. Christians must lay up treasures in heaven "where
change and decay have never entered, and the ardent aspirations of the soul are satisfied in the fulness of God." The balm
of Gilead alone can restore peace to the troubled, health
to the wounded, and happiness to the suffering: "its application will make men the heirs of joyous immortality; and thanks
to the Great Physician of souls, this sovereign balm can be obtained without money and without price."[6] Faith without
works, however, was not enough. The very certainty of
Christian truth dictated the need for an immediate reform of
the evils of the world.

If I were an atheist and expected to perish like the ox — or a deist,
and rejected God's glorious and exalted revelation — or if I dis-
believed the doctrine of rewards and punishments in a future

life — or professed to receive all my happiness on earth — neither my interest nor my pleasure would lead me to squander away existence upon the unproductive things of the world. I could not be so selfish (with my present feelings) as to remain an idler here, or a passive spectator of the contest between right and wrong — virtue and vice — truth and error — which must continue to the end of time. . . . While there remains a tyrant to sway the iron rod of power, or chain about the body or mind to be broken, I cannot surrender my arms. While drunkenness and intemperance abound, I will try to reclaim the dissolute, and to annihilate the progress of vice. While profanity and sabbath-breaking, and crime wound my ear and affect my sight, I will reprove, admonish and condemn. While the demon of war is urging mankind to deeds of violence and revenge, I will 'study the things that make for peace.' While a soul remains unenlightened, uneducated, and without 'the glorious gospel of the blessed God,' my duty is plain — I will contribute my little influence to the diffusion of universal knowledge.[7]

From now on, he promised, his methods would be those of Christian example and enterprise. "The gospel of Christ breathes peace to men," he explained, "its language is full of the mildness of God. . . . This gospel is not to be propagated by fire and sword, nor nourished by blood and slaughter. It must go forth under the banner of the cross."[8] Beneath that banner in the years to come he would collect a band of militant Christian rebels who cared less for the mildness of God than for their freedom of conscience.

If it was true that politics and morals were indistinguishable, how could the religious reformer avoid the pitfalls of party politics? It was one thing to point out, as he did, the "inutility, the folly, the slothfulness and bane of party spirit." Still, the notion that opinions and habits could be changed without votes and laws, he admitted, was both "visionary" and "highly dangerous." Private example might influence a household, but only public effort could convert a nation. "Hence it has seemed to me," he wrote, "that the readiest way to operate on the mass of society is to begin with the opulent." The manners of fashionable people soon become law to an otherwise "lawless multitude" — "its enactments go into immediate operation; it is a stream, winding through the innumerable channels of community, transparent, gentle, fructifying — or turbid with pollution, and pernicious in its circulation." Thus he saw in the General Union for Promoting the Observance of the Christian Sabbath, supported by wealthy businessmen, "the most efficient instrument in the cause of religion and public morality ever put into practice in any age and country."[9] To the Jacksonian critics who complained that such groups were cancerous growths on the body politic he replied with the warning that "unless societies are formed to operate upon public sentiment, to sound the trumpet of alarm over a slumbering land, to give adaptation and strength to the hands of the people, the tide of desolation will continue to swell till neither ark nor mountain will be able to save us from destruction."[10]

At this point Garrison was fairly caught in the evangelical contradiction, for if the urgency of the American political situation was clear, so was the necessity of choosing sides. He could not avoid political choice any more than the evangelicals could mask their Whiggish prejudices. He took care to remind his readers that he was not permitted to indulge in political dispute, that "it does not become us to advocate particular candidates for office." All he could do was to urge them to seek out "Christian and moral men" worthy of their confidence. Yet when Daniel Webster was criticized by the Boston merchants for his about-face on the tariff question, Garrison rushed to the defense of that "star in the galaxy of

American worthies."[11] As to the tariff, he admitted to strongly favoring protection which would help supply the domestic market "with cheaper goods than England can possibly do."[12]

The *National Philanthropist* was strictly prohibitionist. To dramatize the dangers of alcohol Garrison resorted to every sensational trick he knew — lurid tales of spontaneous combustion, stories of starving families victimized by the drunkard's curse, and reams of homiletic verse.

> What is the cause of every ill?
> That does with pain the body fill?
> It is the oft repeated gill
>   Of Whiskey. . . .
>
> What makes chill penury prevail,
> Makes widows moan and orphans wail,
> And fills the poor house and the jail?
>   'Tis Whiskey.[13]

Patiently he distinguished for readers the absolute evil of alcohol from lesser sins like gluttony. "If my companion swallow a turkey or masticate a small pig, or demolish a sirloin of beef, he does not whet my appetite nor induce me to follow his example."[14]

To expand the circulation of the *National Philanthropist* he wagered that all tipplers who subscribed to it would save at least the cost of the paper in six months' time. He also enlisted the support of women and expressed surprise that "assimilated as is domestic enjoyment with a temperate household," appeals to the weaker sex were so few. With all due allowance for their retired habits, it was essential to capitalize on the "immense influence which the females of our country are capable of exerting over our habits and manners as a people."[15] Thus began his lifelong liaison with "female influence," the evangelical practice which Hawthorne and then James deplored as the cause of an insidious feminizing of the American character. Eventually the Zenobias, the Olive Chancellors and Miss Birdseyes became the mainstays of Garrisonian reform.

Garrison relished the role of public censor. His paper advertised projects like the Penitent Female Refuge to "bring back the abandoned from the path of lewdness and moral death" and the Society for the Promotion of Morality and Piety in Boston. As a self-appointed guardian of American morals, he set out to purify the national literary taste. First to fall beneath his censorious eye were the "vile outpourings" of Tom Moore, those "unholy emanations of lewdness and intemperance." He recommended as a corrective to the Irish Anacreon the "comprehensive and masterly" sermons on intemperance of Lyman Beecher.[16]

His campaign for purity involved him in a skirmish with Boston culture — with the "indelicate" offerings of Mrs. Knight at the Federal Street Theater and the "bill of licentiousness" offered by an Italian dance troupe at the Tremont. Even the Immortal Bard, whose plays caused every virtuous man to "veil his face," failed to meet his exacting standards of decency. Lotteries, Sunday mails, and Sabbath-breaking loomed large as sins of huge dimensions. The sight of "profligate coxcombs and dissipated dandies" enjoying a Sunday stroll sent him straight to his desk to demand rigid enforcement of blue laws. Behind the lumbering Sunday mail coaches he saw "skepticism and depravity" stalking abroad. In dark moments like these he wondered why Christians wasted their lives in fruitless doctrinal quarrels "while infidelity is seeking to subvert the purity of our institutions and the permanency of our liberties."[17]

He did not really believe all of his predictions of impending doom. Though he scarcely realized it, his belief in moral progress harmonized completely with the confident outlook of the Jacksonian age. In 1828 Senator Richard M. Johnson, spokesman for the New West and archenemy of the New England clergy, delivered an oration on the Senate floor in which he prophesied unlimited progress as the American destiny. Reading Johnson's speech, Garrison was moved to add an editorial comment of his own. He examined and rejected the romantic notion of the mortality of civilizations. "The idea has obtained in all ages that there must be a constant succession of empires, like waves of the ocean, and that the oblivious hand of time must blot out with the lapse of centuries. Nothing can be more erroneous."[18] America's future, he concluded, was unlimited, with population expanding, a government based on equality of rights, humanity and justice blended with religious principle. Why should the Republic crumble or dissolve?

Garrison's hymn to progress formed part of the liturgy of evangelicalism. For all their jeremiads and professional pessimism the American evangelicals were the unwitting carriers of the Revolutionary heritage. Their faith in the efficacy of voluntary associations revealed a deep commitment to the doctrine of progress. They believed that they could convert a wicked nation to goodness simply by organizing and directing public opinion, that is, by the judicious use of Christian pressure groups. But who could say where this process might end? In stressing the importance of public opinion they gave their own meaning to the ideal of democratic association, but their vision of progress and their ideal of the free individual were fundamentally similar to the perfectionist image of the Jeffersonians. True, they cried down natural reason and the Enlightenment world view. Nevertheless, their acceptance of the principle of free association and their certainty of the power of revealed truth to win in the open market sustained and carried forward the optimism of the Revolutionary generation. In perfecting their scheme for a stable society strong in religious habit and united in the Protestant faith they discovered the very democratic techniques which were soon to be turned against them. The whole benevolent apparatus — open societies, public meetings, free literature, propaganda — which they used to impose a conservative Christian pattern on American society might as easily be appropriated by another group of reformers with a more explosive cause. Tracts, newspapers and placards, so effective in fighting Sabbath-breaking and the Sunday mails, could also be used to free the slaves. In the principle of voluntary association they had found an effective method for agitating causes which could divide as well as unify the country. Had they but known it, the evangelicals had fashioned an engine of national self-destruction. All that logic required was a man who practiced the Christian zeal they preached.

Gradually Garrison began to distinguish between complaints of irreligious behavior and major social evils. He continued to lash out at profane language and licentiousness, at habits like "the present rage of sporting huge mustaches," but he was slowly discovering that there were certain questions to which the evangelicals had no easy answers. One of these was William Ladd's peace question and the problem of defensive war. Indifference to principle nettled him. If war was morally wrong, how could defensive war be right? If slavery was un-Christian, why did Christians practice it? What could be more reasonable than the attempt to live by the all-sufficient word of God? The more he pondered the gospel of Christ the closer he was drawn to its simple message —

"Go ye and do likewise." The theological implications of Christian perfectionism were not yet clear to him. Just how truth could be gleaned from the chaff of Biblical contradictions he did not as yet know. He was satisfied to consult his conscience and then act.

In this mood of self-examination he approached the problem of American apathy. What but "indifference" explained the reluctance of Christians to undertake the work of reform? "There are, in faith, few *reasoning* Christians," he wrote; "the majority of them are swayed more by the usages of the world than by any definite perception of what constitutes duty."[19] Was there not enough Christian influence in the country to reform it?

By the "duty of reasoning Christians" he did not mean simply the common-sense adaptations of religious precepts to daily life, but a purer and more personal belief in the superiority of the righteous man. Slavery and war, vices "incorporated into the existence of society," could only be corrected by refashioning America according to the word of God. The errors of the evangelicals, he saw, lay not in their ideals but in their failure to live up to them. It was a question of fundamentals — spiritual principles were levers for moving the world, social action a form of personal atonement. Slowly he was learning that evangelical passion logically ends in radicalism; further, that perfectionism and radicalism are similar states of mind. In the consistency with which he pursued his discovery lay the profound unity of his life.

The radical in American politics, like his counterpart the true evangelical, stands outside the community, his isolation defined by his ideals. To his less excitable fellows he is something of an anomaly, admirable perhaps, but irritating. Since his actions are dictated by conscience alone they are usually predictable. He combines steadfastness of purpose with an almost reckless disregard of self-interest. He will not compromise his beliefs and prefers to suffer, indeed to court, martyrdom rather than give in to the majority. His distrusts politics and relies instead on a direct appeal to the moral sense of other people. He views society as a collection of individuals to be rededicated by his teachings — as a pool of water whose placid surface is broken by single pebbles tossed upon it, each one radiating concentric circles of right conduct. Because he rests his case on emotion rather than reason, the radical is wary of subtleties which he calls hairsplitting. Something of an anti-intellectual, he mistrusts the doctrinaire yet is often guilty of ex cathedra pronouncements himself. Consistency is not his forte: in his search for a better vantagepoint from which to analyze the evils of society he frequently and often abruptly shifts his ground. His motives are mixed and not always harmonious. He often wavers between the compulsion to be right and the urge to make others right. This tension between the demands of self and the claims of other people is both a weakness and a strength — a weakness because it often blinds him to the realities of political change; a strength because it makes conscience the touchstone of all behavior. This outline of the American radical temperament is also the profile of Garrison's personality.

One of the myths that attach themselves to the American radical is that of rugged independence. The image of the lone figure struggling against overwhelming odds is a naturally appealing one to an age that enjoys chiefly the nostalgia of the history of American radicalism. Garrison was the willing perpetrator of just such a myth. He liked to tell how, unaided and alone, he found his way to abolition and formed the crusade that eventually freed the Negro. This legend, carefully nurtured by his followers, ensured his fame but obscured the debts he owed to others. Beecher and Boston supplied him with most of the causes and techniques he used in the anti-slavery cause. Long after he denounced Beecher and the evangelicals he remained obligated to them for the convictions which led him to racial equality. He came to Boston a brash young man without a cause; he left eighteen months later sure that he had found one. The year 1828 was his *annus mirabilis* for which the evangelicals had prepared him. In March of that year Benjamin Lundy arrived in Boston.

4

Benjamin Lundy

O N THE EVENING of March 17, 1828, Benjamin Lundy
gathered a group of Boston ministers in William Collier's boardinghouse to discuss the means of forming a local
anti-slavery society. The meeting was hardly a success. Of
the handful of clergymen assembled only Samuel Joseph May,
the young pastor of the Unitarian Church in Cambridgeport,
evinced the slightest interest in Lundy's project. The rest,
while stoutly maintaining their dislike of slavery, opposed
anything so rash as a society to abolish it. If he hoped to
change their minds, Lundy might as well have been talking
to the cobblestones in Milk Street.

As he lectured the group Lundy noticed a young man
with a balding head and steel-rimmed glasses who sat on the
edge of his chair, eyes fixed intently on Lundy, following
every word and nodding his head vigorously in agreement.
After the meeting Lundy spoke to his admirer, whose name
he understood to be Garrison, the twenty-two-year-old editor
of Collier's paper. Garrison told him of his high regard for
Lundy's own newspaper, the *Genius of Universal Emancipation*, and showed him an editorial he had written denouncing
slaveholders for trying to "seal up the mind and debase the
intellect of a man to brutal incapacity." "Our boasted
liberty," he had written, "is a paradox. We have warmed in

our bosom a serpent, the poison of whose sting is felt through every vein of the republic; we have been industriously creating mines of irremediable destruction, gathering materials for a national catastrophe."[1] Reading this bombast, Lundy may have noticed Garrison's confession that he lacked information "by which to form an accurate statement of what has been done and the means now in operation to redeem the oppressed and degraded sons of Africa in our land." When he finished chatting with Garrison, Lundy realized that he had only to supply this information to make a convert. Little did he know that his facts were the keys to Pandora's box and that he was about to release a scourge of God.

Benjamin Lundy was born a Quaker in Sandwich, New Jersey, in 1789. His great-grandfather had been one of the original settlers of Bucks County, Pennsylvania, and a founder of the Society of Friends there. As a Quaker, Lundy inherited a long tradition of uncompromising resistance to slavery, a tradition that emphasized the moral wrong of slaveholding and reduced the problem to the dimensions of individual conscience. The opinions of the Quakers were not always moderate and inoffensive. Their belief in the immediacy of the Holy Spirit and their trust in the informed conscience freed them from institutional prejudices and the need to compromise. Lundy's forebears bequeathed to him a concern with personal worthiness and soul-searching, an unyielding hostility to slavery, the militant views and blunt language of Christian zealots. He found this same spirit reborn in his young friend.

Lundy was a slight, stoop-shouldered, brittle man with thinning reddish hair — quiet, unassuming, and absolutely fearless. His initiation into the anti-slavery movement came on a trip to Wheeling, West Virginia, which was a regular stop for the slave coffles headed from the Tidewater over the mountains into the Old Southwest. As he watched the procession of manacled slaves driven through the dusty streets, he was filled with revulsion and the iron entered his soul. In Ohio, where he settled after the war of 1812, he formed the Union Humane Society, an abolitionist organization that numbered five hundred members at the end of its first year. During the Missouri crisis he went to St. Louis and witnessed the defeat of the free-state forces there before returning to Ohio penniless and discouraged. There were two Quaker anti-slavery newspapers in the Mississippi Valley at this time — the *Philanthropist*, edited by Charles Osborne, and the *Emancipator*, published by Elihu Embree. When Embree died suddenly and Osborne's sheet was sold to a printer who did not measure up to Lundy's anti-slavery standards, he decided to print a paper of his own. Accordingly, he moved to Mt. Pleasant, Ohio, where he brought out the first number of the *Genius of Universal Emancipation* in January, 1821. When he first met Garrison, he was still printing his paper between trips to the West Indies and lecture tours in New England.

Lundy drove himself mercilessly. He usually carried his type with him on his travels, stopping to print an issue of his paper whenever he found the time and the money. His travels took him into Quaker meetings on Nantucket and in the hill towns of North Carolina, the drawing rooms of wealthy Philadelphia Friends and the shacks of free Negroes in Baltimore. A pioneer in the field of anti-slavery lecturing, he was not, as Garrison soon realized, an effective orator. His weak voice and halting delivery made him much more effective in small gatherings than in the lecture hall. Yet he was accustomed to mobs and brickbats. Six months before he met Garrison he was accosted in a Baltimore street by an irate slave-trader named Austin Woolfolk who had been the target of one of his more caustic editorials. Woolfolk challenged him, knocked him flat, and then, discovering that he had no intention of defending himself, proceeded to administer a brutal beating. Lundy picked himself up and marched to the nearest police station to swear out a writ against his assailant. After a seemingly endless delay he had the satisfaction of receiving damages to the amount of one dollar.

Until he met Lundy, Garrison had felt no immediate concern for the slave. To be sure, slavery was a national wrong which would someday have to be corrected. He had discussed the slave insurrections in South Carolina with Caleb Cushing and followed the progress of the Missouri debates with interest. His religious upbringing and his mother's possessive grip had taught him to hate the idea of holding property in human beings. No doubt he sincerely believed slavery the "curse" he named it in the pages of his papers. Its effects, however, were little felt in New England where it had been abandoned fifty years before. Lundy may have argued that the people of the free states carried the blood of the slave "on every finger," but most New Englanders thought otherwise. Except for the childhood interlude in Baltimore, Garrison had seen nothing of slavery and knew little of its extent and political power. His meeting with Lundy was thus a turning point in his life, for it was Lundy's facts and figures which persuaded him that here was a cause more important than temperance and Sabbath observance.

He promptly reported Lundy's meeting at Collier's as a clarion call for "a strong and extensive interest in the cause of emancipating the slaves in our country."[2] Lundy's spell still held him, for he announced that the clergymen had given "their entire approbation" to his ideas. He praised Lundy and described the *Genius of Universal Emancipation* as "the bravest and best attempt in the history of newspaper publications." He cited Lundy's figures on the number of anti-slavery societies as proof of the great advance of Southern humanitarian sentiment. Even the American Colonization Society came in for its share of the plaudits along with Lundy's Haitian colonization scheme. He noted that over one thousand free Negroes had already been sent back to Africa while over seven thousand were now established in Haiti. "This number may appear insignificant, when contrasted with the rapid increase of slaves in the southern States, during the same period; but this very multiplication magnifies the extent of the relief which has been given; for if these immigrants had remained, how long would it have taken to redouble their number?" Soon he would draw from the same set of figures an entirely different conclusion as to the worth of the Colonization Society. Now he saw only the rapid progress of Christian spirit: the prejudices of the South were gradually yielding to the dictates of humanity and justice; anti-slavery societies were being formed; and public opinion against slavery was gathering a force which in time would become irresistible.

Had Garrison bothered to examine Southern opinion carefully he would have discerned a far different temper. Under the pressure of declining prices and a revived Northern humanitarianism the South was abandoning the Jeffersonian ideal of a free society for a defense of slavery as a positive good. The "positive good" defense of slavery preceded Garrison's entrance into the anti-slavery movement by nearly a decade. At a time when he first began to think about slavery, Southern intellectuals had already discovered a divine sanction for their way of life. In the years to come many of them protested that their defense was a reaction against the irresponsible attacks of Garrison and his fellow fanatics, but the truth was that their rationale of slavery had been completed long before the first number of the *Liberator* appeared.

With the arrival of the Missouri question in Congress, Southern liberalism entered upon a period of decline. The assertion of federal power to regulate slavery in the territories, no matter how dangerous a usurpation of the powers of the states, was a debatable issue which Southern statesmen felt competent to discuss. When Northern restrictionists injected the question of "higher law," however, the debates rose to the rarefied plane of moral philosophy where the defenders of slavery felt distinctly uncomfortable. The natural law argument, as expounded on the Senate floor by Rufus King of New York, was deceptively simple. If it was wrong for individuals to hold property in other men, King reasoned, it was wrong for groups of men to own slaves; and all compacts or laws imposing slavery were void because they violated the law of nature which is the law of God and paramount to all human control.[3]

There were several ways of dealing with the natural law argument, the most extreme of which was to reject it out of hand. This course John Randolph took when he pronounced the Declaration of Independence, the restrictionists' chief authority, "a fanfaronade of metaphysical abstractions." William Pinkney of Maryland submitted a modified version of Randolph's indictment by declaring that Jefferson's "self-evident truths" were, properly construed, neither self-evident nor truths. As a counterweight to the hazy abstractions of the Declaration he offered the seemingly more substantial prescriptive rights of Edmund Burke.

King and his Northern contingent were most vulnerable to Southern shafts when they identified natural law with the law of God. The Southerners knew their Bible quite as well as the New Englanders, and the Old Testament provided them with all the ammunition they needed. They put their case in

the form of a syllogism: Whatever God sanctioned for the
Hebrews He intended for all times; God gave the Hebrews
the institution of slavery; therefore slavery bore the stamp
of divine approval. It followed that slavery was "natural" in
the only intelligible sense of the word; that is, it was a natural
possession of all civilizations and a natural part of God's plan.
In the measured terms of Burke's reinterpretation of natural
law Southern congressmen announced their desertion of the
Enlightenment camp for the fortress of romantic conservatism.

Garrison, in imputing to the South an enlightened conscience, could not have been more wrong. If he had troubled
to study the Missouri debates, that "title page to a great tragic
volume," as John Quincy Adams called them, he might have
read a speech by Senator William Smith of South Carolina
which would have changed his mind. In the course of his
long and turgid oration Smith invoked the Bible, history, and
science in support of slavery. There had always been slaves,
he said, ever since the Flood. Christ tacitly approved slaveholding and so did the Holy Fathers. Criticism of slavery
proceeded from the heated brains of fanatics whose misguided
zeal disrupted the pattern of Christian living. As for Jefferson's disturbing ideas in *Notes on Virginia*, they were simply
the "effusions of speculative philosophy of his young and
ardent mind, and which his riper years have corrected."
Let Northerners, he warned, think twice before interfering
with Southern institutions.

Smith's devious route to "higher ground," Garrison soon
learned, marked the trail for many a Southern pamphleteer
in the next few years. Already new groups of propagandists
were urging Southerners to quit apologizing for slavery.
The South Carolinians Thomas Cooper, Whitemarsh B.
Seabrook, and Edward Brown attempted to prove the merits

of the slave system with Biblical and historical precedents. "Slavery," Brown wrote, "has ever been the stepping ladder by which countries have passed from barbarism to civilization."[4] As the decade progressed these sentiments were echoed throughout the lower South until, in 1829, the Governor of South Carolina could announce to the legislature, "Slavery *is not a national evil; on the contrary, it is a national benefit*."[5] Soon Thomas R. Dew, James Hammond, William Harper, and Albert Taylor Bledsoe would embroider this argument with their own distinctive rhetoric, but with the exception of George Fitzhugh, later pro-slavery thinkers added little to this premise. Arguments from Scripture and history sufficed for some years to come to hold the line against Northern humanitarians.

Garrison was so impressed with Lundy's "unconquerable spirit of reform" that he decided to join his crusade. Henceforth slavery took precedence over all the other moral causes with his decision "to spread the light of knowledge and religious liberty wherever darkness and superstition reign." But the *National Philanthropist* proved a poor medium for his new cause. Its circulation was none too healthy, and besides, as the owner reminded him, it was a prohibition paper which supposedly eschewed political controversy. Yet politics were crowding in on Garrison until his self-imposed restraints on editorial opinion suddenly seemed hypocritical. He examined the tariff question again and found New England's demands for protection perfectly just. When South Carolina publicly weighed the value of the Union, he could not refrain from offering a word of warning to her "blustering demagogues" with their "rebellion mania." "Now all this bombast and bullying will accomplish nothing. The tariff may be oppressive and unproductive, but it cannot be altered till another session of Congress. If THE PEOPLE are dissatisfied, let them wait in quiet submission till December, and then let petitions for redress pour in. . . . But to declaim about open resistance — !!"[6] Thus spoke the future secessionist in 1828.

On the Fourth of July he submitted his resignation with the announcement that his new convictions forced him to seek "a different though perhaps not more honorable or beneficial employment." In August Lundy returned to the city for a second attempt to crack Boston's "icy reserve." Everywhere in New England he found Yankees rather "cool calculators" on the subject of slavery. His meeting in Boston was held in the vestry of the Federal Street Church despite the vehement protests of its pastor, the Reverend Howard Malcolm. Quietly yet forcefully Lundy outlined his program of voluntary manumission and criticized the American Colonization Society's policy of purchasing slaves, which, he argued, employed the wealth but not the will of the people. When he finished, up jumped the Reverend Malcolm and proceeded to excoriate Lundy's scheme and any other plan for interfering with slavery. As slavery moved farther south, he pointed out, it was gradually declining and soon would be excluded from all but the southernmost states. Meanwhile it behooved Christians to refrain from agitating this vexing subject.

Garrison was incensed by Malcolm's bold apology for slavery; he dashed off a letter to the *Boston Courier* blasting Malcolm and calling on all "high-minded, spirited and philanthropic men" to join him in petitioning Congress for the abolition of slavery in the District of Columbia. Next he drew up a plan for circulating petitions throughout the state. At a second meeting with Lundy he suggested exploring the possibilities of a local abolition society, but both he and Lundy knew how slim their chance of success really was. He was getting a taste of the opposition anti-slavery would provoke in the future, and he liked it.

Lack of money and the importunings of politicians ended this first experiment in agitation. Late in August a group of town fathers from Bennington, Vermont, came to Boston in search of an unemployed editor with a spirit sufficiently adventurous to publish an Adams campaign sheet in their state. Directed to Garrison, they were desperate enough by this late date to accept all of his terms, including the right to discuss slavery and other moral reforms in the projected newspaper. As for Garrison, the lingering appeal of politics and the hope of a steady income for at least six months were strong inducements to return to the free-wheeling partisan journalism of the *Free Press*. He accepted on the spot. With a single timid anti-slavery petition and an unfinished plan for an abolitionist society to show for his conversion he set out for Bennington.

Horace Greeley remembered the *Journal of the Times* — the name of Garrison's new venture — as one of the liveliest newspapers in the history of Vermont journalism. More accurate was the editor's description of it as "a very singular kind of political paper."[7] Its uniqueness lay, first of all, in its belated appearance: on the evening of October 2, 1828, when Garrison put the paper to bed for the first time, Andrew Jackson had all but won the election. By September, Old Hickory had been accepting the congratulations of well-wishers in the parlor of the Hermitage, and only the unduly pessimistic thought the honors premature. Adams was cheerfully conceded all of New England, but the rest of the country was expected to go for Jackson. All that could be rightfully demanded of the *Journal of the Times* was to confirm this sad prediction by holding Bennington and Vermont for the administration against the Jacksonian tide.

Garrison's employers must have doubted their wisdom when they picked up the first issue of the *Journal of the Times* to read that their paper would be "trammelled by no interest, biased by no sect, awed by no power." The new editor defined his objectives as the suppression of intemperance, the emancipation of the slave, and the perpetuity of national peace. Far down the list came the re-election of John Quincy Adams, which somehow was calculated to "supply the wants of the people." Unaccountably the rumor had spread that his paper was an Adams sheet. "The blockheads who have had the desperate temerity to propagate this falsehood have yet to learn our character. . . . *We* conduct a hireling press! — we shall see."[8] What Bennington subscribers saw was a spiritless campaign for Adams.

In timeworn Federalist clichés he warned of dangers greater than at any time since the formation of the Republic. The "dregs" of society — "the vulgar, the profane, the intemperate" — had been foolish enough to choose a conservative Tennessee landowner "with the most aristocratical propositions" to serve their selfish ends. "Unlettered presumption" threatened the country with "universal corruption." Garrison even suggested that British gold was at work buying votes for Jackson, though for purposes apparently unknown. He summoned Vermont to her duty, but his heart was not in it — he simply could not warm to the task of fending off the indiscriminate charges hurled at Adams by the Jacksonians. Publicly he anticipated the time when the election was over and "our literary and moral departments will exhibit a fulness and excellence commensurate to their importance."[9] When the election returns reached Bennington, he hurried to put a decent face on the rout by describing it as a victory of turbulence over order, ignorance over knowledge. He was happy to be free of his political obligation, and was just turning to weightier matters when a final quarrel between Adams and the Federalist Old Guard erupted as if to vindicate his lackluster performance.

Adams's troubles began when William B. Giles, an apostate Federalist, released a letter to the press stating on the authority of Jefferson that Adams had known of the secessionist plots of the New England Federalists as early as 1808 and had communicated them to Jefferson himself. Giles's letter not unnaturally roused the ire of the Massachusetts Federalists, who issued a denial and demanded an explanation from Adams. The ex-President was in no mood to renew the quarrel and replied carefully, admitting the general truth of Giles's allegation but refusing to name names. But the Federalists were not to be thus mollified; in their rejoinder they raised the ghost of Adams's apostasy and added new charges. Garrison rushed to the aid of Otis and the Federalists. "We gave Mr. Adams our ardent and entire support till the close of the Presidential election," he explained. But Adams had made aspersions on New England which presented him in a new light. He had instigated a needless quarrel and then retreated from the fray with "neither the frankness of sincerity, nor the manliness of independence." If citizens had to choose, "it were better . . . that one man should be sacrificed, than that a large majority of the people of New England should be implicated in a charge of once harboring designs hostile to the Union."[10] Not until he saw the crusty old warrior battling singlehanded for the right of petitions in the House of Representatives ten years later did Garrison realize that he had misjudged his man.

Bennington did not take kindly to the voluble visitor from the Bay State nor to his multifarious projects for its civic improvement, which included a lyceum, a local temperance society, a new heating plant for the church, and bigger and better Sunday schools. The sight of his angular figure loping across the green while he lectured a lagging companion, or poised like a stump orator on the edge of a group of loiterers, afforded the townspeople no end of merriment and quickly earned him the sobriquet " My Lloyd Garrulous." "He is, withal, a great egotist," wrote the rival editor of the *Gazette*, "and when talking of himself, displays the pert loquacity of a blue jay." He brought with him all the graces of a Boston dandy. One week his paper sported Horatian odes to the Green Mountains, "those stupendous monuments to God's right hand," the next, effusions of the poet who declared himself "immersed to the eyes in love" with a Boston belle. Then what were the plain citizens of Bennington to make of lines like these?

> Happy is he who disdains the earth,
> And plumes his hopes for a heavenly birth, —
> Whose treasures are wisely laid above,
> Seal'd by the bond of eternal love. — 11

No one could doubt his promise to agitate the slavery question. He followed the parliamentary debates on West Indian emancipation and combed the speeches of Thomas Fowell Buxton and Henry Peter Brougham for new ideas. Slowly it dawned on him that the English abolitionists had much to teach him. In 1828, after years of planning, they had finally combined into a single society for the emancipation of slavery throughout the Empire. He hailed their achievement as "the most stupendous scheme of benevolence that has ever been devised for the good of mankind" and recommended the immediate formation of a similar society in the United States. Americans had leaders similar to William Wilberforce and

Thomas Clarkson — they had their Websters and Clays who could "unquestionably put a new aspect on Europe and America." The fate of his first anti-slavery petition quickly taught him that nothing like the parliamentary strength of the English abolitionists was to be found in Congress.

Two weeks after his arrival in Bennington he printed a notice of a meeting for the purpose of preparing a petition to Congress demanding the abolition of slavery in the District of Columbia. Without waiting for the approval of the meeting he hastily printed a petition and mailed it to every postmaster in the state together with the request that it be returned with as many signatures as possible before the middle of December. The petition stated that the signers deemed it unnecessary to prove in detail the inconsistency of slavery with the principles of American government and the spirit of Christianity, and that while they admitted that Congress had no power to legislate on slavery in the states, they earnestly prayed that it might remove the cancer "from the vitals of the republic." On January 26, 1829, Garrison's petition, bearing the names of two thousand three hundred and fifty-two citizens of Vermont, appeared before the House Committee for the District of Columbia.

Meanwhile, on January 6, 1829, Representative Charles Miner of Pennsylvania took the floor with resolutions that instructed the Committee for the District of Columbia to consider the feasibility of abolishing the slave trade in the District. Garrison followed the subsequent debates closely, even scrutinizing the voting lists, and when he discovered that three New Englanders — James W. Ripley of Maine, Jonathan Harvey of New Hampshire, and Rollin C. Mallary of Vermont — had opposed the resolution, he opened fire with one of the bitterest attacks of his editorial career. Who were these poltroons, he asked, these sanctimonious hypocrites who

quoted the Bible to prove that might makes right and that it
was right to destroy the souls of their fellow men?

Are we — in the Fifty Third Year of the Independence of the
United States — are we to gravely discuss the question, whether
all men are born free and equal as if it were a new doctrine? Are
we to learn, whether the *colored* of our race are really brutes
or human beings? Whether they have bodies capable of suffering,
or souls which can never die? Whether it is consistent with the
principles of our government to shackle some of our species with
galling chains, and to mar their image by applying the whip and
the brand? Or whether it is criminal to traffic in human flesh, or
degrading to buy and sell in a national capacity?[12]

Garrison chose the phrases "colored of our race" and "some
of our species" to show that his case for universal brotherhood
rested on the belief in a single creation. God had created all
men at the same moment, and they were all equally His
children. From this faith in equality he never retreated, even
when nineteenth-century science lent its support to the theory
of the multiple creation of races.

Ripley and Mallary, the "dough-faces" who stood accused,
protested against such uncivil treatment; but he refused to give
an inch and sneered at their contention that Northern agitation of the slavery question would merely destroy Southern
good will. "So! we must continue to traffic in human flesh,
and multiply our victims, and perpetuate the damning stain
of oppression, in a national capacity, because an attempt to
remove the disgrace would again rouse up the advocates of
slavery! Good God! is this the language of a representative
from New England — this his humanity, his moral courage,
his sense of duty?"[13]

Presently there were other complaints about his harsh

language, the *New York Journal of Commerce* taking the lead in censuring him. He fought back gamely against these "timid, half-minded, shivering-in-the-wind" editors, all of them "contemptible animals." "Your dependent, calculating editor is a wretched tool in the hands of designing men," he thundered. "He sacrifices principle to interest."[14] Actually, his language had changed no more than his attitude toward wrongdoing. He had been calling his opponents harsh names and imputing evil motives to them ever since he started writing for Ephraim Allen. Jefferson had been a "criminal" and John Neal a "buffoon." Unitarians were "infidels" and Sabbath-breakers "vicious degenerates." He did not need the example of British abolitionists to teach him how to call a spade a spade — he simply applied the old words to a new sin. Privately he likened himself to the Old Testament prophets Isaiah and Jeremiah, who hurled imprecations like thunderbolts to awaken a sleeping nation. His motives were not unmixed — strong language advertised both the sin and the man brave enough to name it. But one who feared "the terrible judgment of an incensed God" as much as he did worried only that his words might not be strong enough.

Lundy came North again in January, 1829. In his talks with Garrison he proposed a merger of talents: he would continue his work with Haitian colonization, traveling and lecturing while Garrison replaced him as resident editor of the *Genius*. Garrison readily agreed. His contract was due to expire in March, and now that the election was over his employers had grown noticeably cool toward his abolition activities. Besides, anti-slavery promised to be a full-time job and Lundy an excellent teacher. The two men parted, agreeing to join forces as soon as both were ready. On March 27, 1829, Garrison published his third valedictory.

To my apprehension the subject of slavery involves interest of a greater moment to our welfare as a republic, and demands a more prudent and minute investigation, than any other which has come before the American people since the Revolutionary struggle — than all others which now occupy their attention. . . . It is true, many a cheek burns with shame in view of our national inconsistency, and many a heart bleeds for the miserable African; it is true examples of disinterested benevolence and individual sacrifices are numerous, particularly in the Southern States; but no systematic, vigorous and successful measures have been made to overthrow this fabric of oppression. I trust in God that I may be the humble instrument of breaking at least one chain, and restoring one captive to liberty: it will amply repay a life of severe toil.

Now there could be no turning back. In April he returned to Boston to await Lundy's call.

5

The Road to Prison

IN BOSTON ONCE MORE Garrison found himself in "somewhat of a hobble, in a pecuniary point of view" and
made straight for Collier's, where he was sure of free room
and board. No sooner had he settled there than his financial
embarrassment grew acute — he was served with a warrant
for failing to attend the annual muster of the Newburyport
militia. Five years before in a sudden burst of patriotism he
had joined the local company, although he had never bothered
to train. Now, with his newly acquired pacifist scruples, he resolved to pay the fine. But with what? He sat down and wrote
to his friend Jacob Horton in Newburyport confessing that
he hadn't so much as a farthing and asking Horton for eight
dollars to rescue him from his "unpleasant dilemma."[1] Thus
began the habit of indiscriminate borrowing which marked
his financial dealings for the next forty years, most of them
spent just one jump ahead of his creditors. He spent money
freely; when it was gone, he sent his pride "on a pilgrimage to
Mecca" and touched his friends for loans. Sometimes he paid
them back, but just as often they wrote his debts off as good
investments in reform. He never mastered the intricate finances of the *Liberator*, whose accounts finally became so
jumbled that it took a committee of unusually patient friends
to unsnarl them. Eventually his colleagues came to recognize

in him the reformer bent on directing other people's lives but requiring no small amount of managing himself.

He discovered that the *National Philanthropist* was being edited by William Goodell, the hard-eyed evangelical reformer from Providence destined to be first an invaluable ally and then a dangerous enemy. Garrison helped with the presswork, and in the evenings, after a day at the composing desk, took his friend on long walks through Boston, talking all the while about Lundy and slavery. In conversations lasting long into the night they swapped ideas for organizing anti-slavery in New England. Their ignorance helped to reduce the question to the manageable proportions of Christian conduct. If the gospel spelled equality before God, if the Declaration of Independence proclaimed equality before the law, then how could slaveholders be both Christians and democrats? If Christianity and Infidelity were incompatible, where was the middle ground between democracy and slavery?

From the outset Garrison's hatred of slavery was an abstract concern centered exclusively on the contradiction of bondage in a free society. He did not need to know how slavery worked in order to condemn it. Slavery was evil, and evil could never produce good — it was that simple. He won Goodell over to this view just as Lundy had converted him. When the *National Philanthropist* folded in August, 1829, Goodell returned to New York to spread his friend's ideas and help form a national anti-slavery society.

In June, 1829, Garrison accepted an invitation from the American Colonization Society to deliver the annual Fourth of July address in Park Street Church. Here was what he had been waiting for, his first chance, at twenty-three, to reach a wider audience than the handful of reformers who gathered at Collier's. Carefully he drafted his speech, revising it again and again until it satisfied him. It was a long address — too long, he admitted, for easy listening but barely sufficient to do justice to his momentous subject. He trembled at the thought of speaking before an audience that "bids fair to be overwhelming." John Pierpont had composed an ode for the occasion, and Whittier and Goodell promised to attend; but most of his listeners would be members of the staid Congregational Society prepared to accept colonization as an unpleasant duty but not even remotely interested in abolition. For these fainthearted he promised some "severe animadversions" that might offend "though not reasonably."[2]

His sponsor, the American Colonization Society, symbolized the confusion of American thinking on slavery before 1830. The philosophy of the colonizationists developed logically out of the equivocal views of the Revolutionary generation and its chief spokesman, Thomas Jefferson. Jefferson hated slavery both in principle and in fact. He believed that even if it were proven that Negroes were inherently inferior to whites, it did not follow that slavery was either just or right — "*whatever be their degree of talent, it is no measure of their rights.*" Yet he was by no means sure that the Negro was inferior. He set out to study the race carefully, observing their actions and accomplishments, seeking information wherever he could find it on the mental capacities of both slaves and freedmen. The further he pursued his investigations, however, the more certain he grew of the inferiority of the Negro. He was convinced that "the whole commerce between master and slave is a perpetual exercise in the most boisterous passions, the most unremitting despotism on the one part and degrading submission on the other," and that "the blacks, whether originally a distinct race, or made distinct by time and circumstances, are inferior to the whites in endowments of both mind and body."[3] It was impossible for both races to live together. The only solution lay in educating the Negro, preparing him for self-government, and then returning him to his native Africa. In Jefferson's mind, as in the view of the American Colonization Society of which he approved, benevolence and expediency joined hands.

Jefferson's opinion of the Negro was widely shared by the churchmen of his generation, who in general displayed more concern for the sensitivity of slaveholders than for the condition of their slaves. They agreed with the Jeffersonian humanitarians that the Negro was totally unfit for democratic society and feared lest an ignorant and vicious colored population destroy white freedom. They thought of colonization as a kind of national blood purge, drastic therapy to restore the health of the body politic. The American Colonization Society was an offspring of the mating of these vague Christian sentiments with the instinct for national self-preservation, a sickly child of eighteenth-century philanthropy. Jefferson's generation could never bring itself to believe in the "self-evident truths" of racial equality proclaimed in the Declaration of Independence, and the American clergy had never troubled themselves with such a pernicious abstraction to begin with. It was left to another age — the ante-bellum generation of Garrison and his abolitionists — to apply the truth of equality literally.

Efforts in behalf of colonization dated from 1800, when the Virginia Assembly in secret session passed a resolution empowering the governor to correspond with the President of the United States "on the subject of purchasing lands without the limits of this State, whither persons obnoxious to the laws or dangerous to the peace of society may be removed." Jefferson responded enthusiastically to the Virginia proposal and suggested that in the event that no suitable haven could be found on the North American continent, "Africa would offer a last and undoubted resort."[4] He corresponded with the British government and the governors of Sierra Leone, and even considered the newly purchased Louisiana territory as a possible asylum for the blacks. There the matter rested, however, until 1816, when General Charles Mercer, one of the original architects of the Virginia plan, pledged himself to revive the secret resolutions of 1800 and set colonization in motion.[5]

On January 1, 1817, the American Colonization Society held its first election of officers. Bushrod Washington was elected president, and vice-presidencies were scattered among twelve members from nine states. Lest there be any misunderstanding among the members as to the purpose of the Society, Henry Clay, a charter member and vice-president, reminded his colleagues at the first session that "it was not proposed to deliberate upon or consider at all, any question of emancipation, or that which was connected with the abolition of slavery." Upon that condition alone, he continued, the many gentlemen present from the South and West had attended and could be expected to cooperate.[6] John Randolph quickly echoed Clay's admonition, adding that "it had not been sufficiently insisted on with a view to obtain the cooperation of all the citizens of the United States, not only that this meeting does not in any wise affect the question of Negro Slavery, but, as far as it goes, must materially tend to secure the property of every master in the United States over his slaves."[7] The Society at the outset limited itself to the removal of the "idle, vicious and degraded blacks" who "sally forth from their coverts, beneath the obscurity of night and plunder the rich proprietors of the valleys" or "infest the suburbs of towns and cities."[8] The Northern clergy joined in declaring the free Negro a national menace, and these opinions soon received the official sanction of the society. At the seventh annual meeting of the society in 1823 Robert Goodloe Harper summarized the objects of colonization as first, the relief from a population "pregnant with future danger and present inconvenience," second, the removal of "a great public evil," and finally, the diffusion of "the blessings of knowledge and freedom on a continent that now contains 150 millions of people, plunged in all the degradation of idolatry, superstition, and ignorance."[9] Just how the degraded freedman would Christianize a dark continent and enlighten its inhabitants neither Harper nor his fellow colonizationists cared to say.

Despite the roseate predictions of its founder the achievements of the Colonization Society in its first dozen years were not impressive. Between 1820 and 1830 only 1420 Negroes were returned to Africa. Until 1827 all the emigrants were free Negroes; after that date the number included slaves who had received their freedom on condition that they be deported. The expenditures of the society for this decade amounted to $106,367.72, or roughly seventy-five dollars for every Negro deported. The Upper South led in the number of emigrants, Virginia sending 580 and North Carolina, 400. South Carolina, Georgia, and Mississippi, where slavery was most profitable, sent a combined total of 73 deportees. Of the first consignment of 84 blacks expatriated in 1820, 24 died. The mortality rate for Negroes transported during the rainy season continued to be one in four, while for those lucky enough to be deported in the dry season it was one in six.[10] By 1829 Southerners were justly complaining of the cruel absurdity of the scheme and Northerners of its effects in strengthening slavery. Both were right. In trying to be all things to all men the Colonization Society had succeeded only in entangling its members in a monstrous contradiction: their humanitarianism had fashioned an inefficient and inhuman system. This was the institution that requested Garrison's services on July 4, 1829.

The Park Street address contained the germ of almost every argument Garrison ever used. The occasion was a colonization meeting but the speaker was already an abolitionist. He began by defining slavery as a national sin and turned immediately to an indictment of American religion. What was Christianity doing for the nation? It explored the isles of the seas in search of converts but ignored the slave languishing in misery at home. It formed charities into golden links of benevolence but allowed the black man to perish in iron chains. Could Christians contend with cannibals and yet be conquered by their own children? "I will say, finally, that I despair of the Republic while slavery exists therein. . . . our destruction is not only possible but almost certain."[11]

Suppose, he went on, that by a miracle all the slaves were suddenly made white? What would his audience do then? "Would you shut your eyes upon their sufferings, and calmly talk of constitutional limitations?" To keep men in chains because of their color was beneath contempt. "This is their country by birth, not by adoption. Their children possess the same inherent and unalienable rights as ours, and it is a crime of the blackest dye to load them with fetters." The occasion was the fifty-third anniversary of the signing of the Declaration of Independence and a time to remind Americans of the glaring contradiction between their creed and their actions. "In view of it I am ashamed of my country. I am sick of our unmeaning declaration in praise of liberty and equality, of our hypocritical cant about the unalienable rights of man."

This was not the language of moderation so dear to the Colonization Society, but an appeal to higher law that could prove fatal to the spirit of good will it celebrated. When he spoke of "sacred principles," Garrison meant nothing less than a body of moral truths so distinct and compelling as to need no proof. Far from being a philosopher, he was not even a very logical thinker: his habit of avoiding intellectual complexities was already deeply ingrained. All of his ethical ideas, grounded as they were in a profound anti-intellectual bias, proved impervious to analysis, but as he explained them now they seemed simple and self-evident.

The foundation of his moral system was an unshakable faith in a supreme law of God binding everywhere and at all times. He believed that this same divine law manifested itself in the revelations of the Bible and in the reason of men. Since all law began in the immutable will of God it followed that divine law and the law of nature were really one and the same command. In the final judgment all man-made law — all human conduct — had to be tested by the divine standard. It mattered little, therefore, whether slavery was measured by Biblical precept or the "self-evident" truths of the Declaration of Independence. In either case it failed of God's approval. All men, individually and collectively, could judge when their actions harmonized with higher law, but the best guide to the moral life was the individual conscience. In appealing directly to this moral sense in each of his listeners Garrison was in effect inviting them to practice a kind of philosophical anarchy. He was aware only of making piety rather than utility the standard of human conduct, but those of his listeners who were wiser than he recognized his words for what they were — a plea for Christian perfection.

As a child of light he conceived of the religious sense as the universal property of mankind. This religious sense, which he thought of simply as an awareness of divine presence, directed men through their consciences. It was conscience alone that gave men their unique dignity, defined them as humans and determined their worth. Once they understood the divine purpose they could carry out God's promises of a final triumph of righteousness over sin, life over death, spirit over matter. Slaveholders, by refusing to acknowledge this human quality in the Negro, denied the fundamental religious sense of mankind. They were practicing atheists. Slavery could thus be explained as the willful repudiation of God's commands by unbelievers. For the flouting of divine law Garrison held the slaveowner directly responsible; in his view the master was an evil man who had closed his heart to the word of God. The sinner embodied the sin. It was just this identification of the sinner with the sin that troubled his colonization audience, who saw slavery as an incidental social evil best cured by removing the Negro. They were not prepared to grant his cardinal principle — that slavery was "inhumane" because it denied to Negroes the dignity of men — nor could they accept his reading of the Declaration of Independence.

As he produced it for the examination of his audience the Declaration of Independence emerged not as an elaborate metaphysical discussion but as a simple, common-sense approximation of the law of God. He was oblivious to the dangers of identifying reason with revelation or Scripture with natural rights. He only knew that the rights of life, liberty, and the pursuit of happiness spoke to the rational faculties of men just as God's word appealed to the universal religious sense. Somehow — he was not sure how — the Bible and the Declaration fused into a mystical corpus of higher law, the "injunctions of Holy Writ" upheld "the common dictates of humanity."

In citing Scripture as the final authority against slavery he did not mean to include all of the Old Testament or even those parts of the New which appeared to sanction slavery. The trouble with plenary inspiration, he had discovered, was that it solved nothing. To every passage exhorting Christians to proclaim liberty to the captives, slaveholders could counter with Paul's injunction to treat one's slaves mercifully. The truth was that Garrison was launched on a process of interpretative reading of the Bible that could only end in the rejection of all Scripture except the gospel of Jesus. The Park Street address took an advanced position against the pro-slavery forces from which there was no retreat.

He closed his two-hour performance with an appeal to the churches. "Let them pour out their supplications to Heaven in behalf of the slave. Prayer is omnipotent: its breath can melt the adamantine rocks, its touch can break the stoutest chains." In years to come his bitter and unreasoning hatred of the American churches puzzled and offended his more moderate followers who never understood how great had been his initial belief in their efficacy. In 1829 he was certain that once Christian opinion was brought to bear on slavery it would not survive another day. Let Christians awake, therefore, and arm for a holy contest. "I call upon the churches of the living God to lead this great enterprise. If the soul be immortal, priceless, save it from remediless woe."

Most of Garrison's audience thought this note of alarm ill-considered and premature. What was it this young man said about disunion — "the fault is not ours if a separation eventually take place"? If, as they devoutly believed, the American political genius was most perfectly expressed in the art of accommodation and compromise, then here was the kind of misguided zeal the society could well do without. As for his wild notions of inaugurating a mass movement against slavery, they could do without this too. The Park Street address, though it excited misgivings among the colonizationists, scarcely stirred the millpond surface of Boston society. Goodell dutifully reported the speech in the failing *National Philanthropist*, but before Garrison realized how little he had

impressed the city, Lundy's call came and he hurried off to
Baltimore.

Lundy had already announced the new partnership and
recommended his colleague as a man "in every way qualified"
as an anti-slavery crusader. No sooner did Garrison appear,
however, than he began to object to colonization, explaining
to Lundy that since July he had had some sobering second
thoughts on the justice of exporting the Negroes either to
Africa or to Haiti. The whole scheme, he announced, looked
like a fraudulent device for stamping the Negro with the mark
of inferiority. He was sure now that nothing short of total and
immediate emancipation would satisfy the demands of Christian behavior. Would this opinion obstruct Lundy's Haitian
project and could the two men consent to disagree? "Well,"
Lundy replied, "thee may put thy initials to thy articles, and
I will put my initials to mine, and each will bear his own
burden." "Very well, that will answer," Garrison rejoined,
"and I will be able to free my soul."

He boarded with Lundy at the home of two Quaker ladies
in Market Street, where he met with a new kind of religious
reformer. Most of Lundy's friends and associates were Quakers and free Negroes — John Needles, a devout Friend who
had helped Lundy and would help Garrison in the future,
William Watkins, Jacob Greener and his sons, free Negroes
and bitter enemies of the Colonization Society. The atmosphere in Market Street differed sharply from the professional
air in Collier's nest of reformers, for Lundy's friends exhibited
little of the studied benevolence and organizational zeal of
the Boston evangelicals. Their practical piety and simple ways
contrasted markedly with the smugness and self-assurance of
the new arrival. It was not long before Garrison saw that
these quiet people with their apostolic ideas of love and sense
of personal commitment had much to teach him.

In September the two editors set to work supplying the
Genius of Universal Emancipation with a new face. The
paper, enlarged and expanded, now appeared every week.
Beneath an American eagle perched on the masthead stood
Garrison's motto, the quotation from the Declaration of Independence proclaiming the equality of all men. For the first
time in his career he was free from the arduous work of type-
setting and proofreading. The *Genius* was commissioned to
the Baltimore firm of Lucas and Deaver, printers obliging
enough to accept the work on credit.

From the beginning it was clear that the two men had
agreed to go their own ways. Lundy launched a series of
articles on Haiti describing in radiant terms the condition of
the expatriates there. He explained that the situation was much
improved over the three years previous: Haitian proprietors
were gradually becoming reconciled to granting emigrants
land, and the government was beginning to take an active
interest in their welfare. "There the *color of their skin* will
not be looked upon as a mark of degradation," Lundy wrote.
Happily surveying the cloudless skies over Haiti he ignored
the storm his young associate was busy brewing right in
Baltimore. Garrison had elected to settle his accounts with
the Colonization Society in his opening editorial.

He approached his subject by the devious route of praise.
No one, he declared, was a truer friend to the Colonization
Society than he. But the work of colonization was exceedingly dilatory and uncertain. "Viewed as an auxiliary, it de-
serves encouragement; but as a remedy it is altogether inadequate." The results of ten years' work were far from
encouraging. "For my own part, I do not believe that the
removal of the great body of the blacks can be effected by
voluntary contributions or individual sacrifice; and if we depend alone upon the efforts of colonization societies, slavery

will never be exterminated." In place of the ambiguous phrases
of the society he offered the following propositions:

1. That the slaves are entitled to immediate and complete
   emancipation: consequently, to hold them longer in bondage is both tyrannical and unnecessary.

2. That the question of expediency has nothing to do with
   that of right, and it is not for those who tyrannise to say
   when they may safely break the chains of their subjects. . . .

3. That, on the ground of expediency, it would be wiser to
   set all the slaves free to-day than tomorrow — or next
   week than next year. To think of removing them all out
   of the land is visionary. . . . Hence, the sooner they receive the benefits of instruction, the better for them and
   us. We can educate two millions of slaves, now, with
   more facility and success than four millions at the expira-
   tion of twenty-five years. Give them liberation, and every
   inducement to revolt is removed; give them employment
   as free laborers, and their industry will be more productive and beneficial than mines of gold; give them religious
   and secular instruction, restrict them with suitable regulations, and they will make peaceable citizens. . . .

4. That, as a very large proportion of our colored population
   were born on American soil, they are at liberty to choose
   their own dwelling place, and we possess no right to use
   coercive measures in their removal.[12]

As with so many of Garrison's later pronunciamentos the
editorial clarity was more apparent than real. "Immediate and
complete emancipation" — what did it mean? In spite of his
temerity he did not know. Thus the phrase "suitable regulations," which signified that he had no plan, that all plans were
matters of mere "expediency" with which he need not concern himself. He was concerned solely with the abolition of

the *status* of slavery. What followed then, whether apprenticeship, forced labor, copyhold, progressive enfranchisement,
mattered little. Let Americans admit that slavery was a sin,
he seemed to be saying, and they would find a solution. Behind all his radical statements lurked the old evangelical argument that God in His infinite mercy and wisdom would find
a way if only men believed in Him. But this was mere equivo-
cation. Did Garrison mean to raise the slaves to full citizen-
ship in one bold stroke? Or did he contemplate an indefinite
period of education and preparation? How were Negroes to
be trained for "productive" labor and the duties of freemen?
How long would they be second-class citizens? Would they
be the wards of the state or the responsibility of the federal
government? As yet these questions were hypothetical; some-
day they would become real and need answers. "Immediate
emancipation" followed by "suitable regulations" was not
freedom but slavery under another name. Yet without some
plan or method immediate emancipation was only a cruel
joke. In his haste to disown the Colonization Society he failed
to recognize this dilemma. It seemed to him that only the
principle mattered. "If justice requires instant abolition, then
surely it is proper to obey its mandates. Don't talk of *expediency* as an offset; as if it were expedient to persevere in crime,
year after year! Never . . . do evil, that good may come."[13]
Beyond this Christian precept he was not prepared to venture.

Garrison was not the first of the American abolitionists to
espouse immediate emancipation. Probably the first American
advocate of immediatism was George Bourne, an English
emigrant who settled in New York City after seven years of
observing slavery at first hand in Virginia. Bourne's chief
work, *The Book and Slavery Irreconcilable*, which appeared
in 1815, was an uncompromising indictment of slavery which
even Garrison's could not surpass. Bourne leveled his argu-

ments directly at the personality of the slaveholder. "Every man who holds Slaves and who pretends to be a Christian or Republican," he protested, "is either an incurable Idiot who cannot distinguish good from evil, or an obdurate sinner who resolutely defies every social, moral and divine requisition."[14]

Beside this fiery arraignment Garrison's declaration in the *Genius of Universal Emancipation* seems like pale copy. Although Garrison never admitted a debt to Bourne's pamphlet, it would be strange indeed if a convert with his literary tastes who pored over Congressional and Parliamentary debates and studied the works of abolitionist pioneers had not read it by 1829. Another argument for immediate emancipation with which Garrison may have been familiar was James Duncan's *Treatise on Slavery*, printed in Indiana in 1824. Duncan condemned gradual manumission as "moral turpitude," and, like Bourne before him, prescribed immediate emancipation as the only sure remedy for "heinous sin."

If by "immediate emancipation" Garrison meant only the *immediate adoption of laws providing for gradual emancipation*, priority is even less his due. There were a host of antislavery pioneers before his entrance into the field who had advocated one form or another of immediate anti-slavery legislation. In 1812 Amos Stoddard strongly urged the passage of laws for freeing the *post nati*. A few years later Estwick Evans proposed that the federal government purchase all slaves and grant them their freedom when they had worked out their purchase price. Various other plans for immediate action were offered after 1815 by John Adams, John Jay, Daniel Raymond, Edward Bettle, and Samuel Sewall. Thus by 1829 immediate emancipation, though by no means a widely shared doctrine, had been propounded in some form a number of times by men every bit as zealous as Lundy's assistant.

Without stopping to examine his new principle in the light of the actual conditions of slavery in Baltimore, he turned to perfecting his techniques for agitating immediate abolition. Soon he discovered a set of simple rules for indoctrinating the American public, which he taught to a whole generation of anti-slavery radicals. The first and most important of the Garrisonian axioms was his command not to explain but to denounce. "Slavery is a monster," he taught the readers of the *Genius*, "and he must be treated as such — hunted down bravely, and despatched at a blow." Next inculcate a sense of guilt, collective and individual, by emphasizing the barbarity of slavery. "We read of the dark ages, and wonder at the depravity of mankind; yet we now defend practices, and nourish vices which throw as disastrous an eclipse over our land, as any that brooded over the earlier period of our world." Then stress the disparity between American profession and American practice. "We panegyrize our freedom and equality, as a knave boasts of his honesty, or a courtezan of her chastity. Our Declaration of Independence declares, that 'all men are born equal' — but it lies, in the face of heaven and earth, if our practices are defensible; and the lie is repeated annually, all over the land, by a multitude of men who make high pretensions to the truth."[15] Spare neither North nor South in your censures. "It is a solemn truth, that in New England the free blacks have fewer privileges, and are treated more contemptuously than those in the slave states."[16] Chide the people for their failure to perform their duty as citizens by voting down slavery. "How have they met their responsibility? By undutifully absenting themselves from the polls! by sinking into a culpable and despairing apathy! by surrendering their arms without a show of resistance! by refusing to co-operate at a time when every thing valuable is at stake."[17] Finally, reprobate the lack of Christian zeal in the

American churches and denounce the ministers responsible for this moral laxity.

With reverence, and in the name of God, we ask what sort of religion is now extant among us? Certainly not such as cheered the prophets through the gloom of the old dispensation . . . not such as Jesus laid down his life to vindicate. . . . It is a religion which complacently tolerates open adultery, oppression, robbery, and murder! seldom or never lifting up a wavering voice, or a note of remonstrance, or propitiatory sacrifice! — a religion, which is graduated by the corrupt, defective laws of the State, and not by the pure, perfect laws of God! — a religion, which quadrates with the natural depravity of the heart, giving license to sin, restraining no lust, mortifying not the body, engendering selfishness and cruelty! — a religion which walks in 'silver slippers,' on a carpeted floor, having thrown off the burden of the cross, and changed the garments of humiliation for the splendid vestments of pride! — a religion which has no courage, no faithfulness, no self-denial, deeming it better to give heed unto men than unto God! Verily, this generation will have a solemn account to give in the great and terrible day of judgment.[18]

It was no accident that his formula for anti-slavery agitation contained the ingredients of martyrdom complete with crown of thorns. In the autumn of 1829 the brig *Francis* out of Newburyport cleared Baltimore harbor bound for New Orleans with a cargo of slaves for the Louisiana sugar plantations. The *Francis* was owned by one Francis Todd, a well-to-do Newburyport merchant with considerable prestige and, as it turned out, a very thin skin. Her captain was Nicholas Brown, a Yankee skipper with a long and creditable record in the coastal trade and a reputation as an honest and humane skipper. The slave cargo of the *Francis* was part of a total of fifty thousand Negroes transported annually either over the mountains or down the coast to the Gulf States. The principal

effect in the United States of the prohibition of the international slave trade had been to increase the demand for slaves
from Virginia and Maryland. As the price of slaves rose
precipitously so did the number of slave-dealers and merchants
in the domestic trade who were not above making an occasional slave voyage when business was slow. Todd was only
one of a number of New Englanders engaged in the domestic
slave trade on a part-time basis, and his cargo of eighty-eight
blacks was not particularly noteworthy. But he had the double
misfortune of hailing from Newburyport and arousing the
curiosity of his fellow townsman.

One of Garrison's innovations in the *Genius of Universal
Emancipation* was the "Black List," a forerunner of the "Refuge of Oppression" column in the *Liberator*, in which he
printed examples of the barbarities of slavery — kidnappings,
whippings, murders. In the issue for November 13, 1829,
there appeared a notice of the departure of the *Francis* with
the editor's caustic reminder that the ship was owned by a
New England man. "So much for New England principle!"
he scoffed and promised to allude to "this damning affair"
more particularly in his next number. True to his promise, he
returned to the Todd incident determined "to cover with
thick infamy all who were concerned in this nefarious business."[19] Todd and Captain Brown he denounced as "highway
robbers and murderers," "enemies of their own species." "I
recollect," he continued, "that it was always a mystery in
Newburyport how Mr. Todd contrived to make profitable
voyages to New Orleans and other places, when other merchants, with as fair an opportunity to make money, and sending to the same ports at the same time, invariably made fewer
successful speculations." Now the mystery was unraveled.

Any man can gather up riches if he does not care by what means
they are obtained. The *Francis* carried off *seventy-five* slaves,

chained in a narrow place between decks. Capt. Brown originally intended to take *one hundred and fifty* of these unfortunate creatures; but another hard-hearted shipmaster underbid him in the price of passage for the remaining moiety.

He sent a copy of the article to the *Newburyport Herald*, hoping that Allen would reprint it, and another to Todd himself.

Lundy knew that Garrison's article veered dangerously near the shoals of libel. A pungent stylist in his own right, Lundy had nevertheless acquired the journalist's habit of sticking closely to the facts, and Garrison's easy appropriation of hearsay discomfited him sorely. This was not the first time he had received complaints about the junior editor's language. With not a little apprehension they waited to see what Todd would do. He soon obliged them by filing a suit for libel. A month later, in February, 1830, they were presented with another action by the State of Maryland for "contriving and unlawfully, wickedly, and maliciously intending to hurt, injure, and vilify" the Massachusetts shipowner. Todd's civil suit was postponed pending the outcome of the state's action at law.

The trial in which Lundy and Garrison were co-defendants was held on the first day of March, 1830, before Judge Nicholas Brice in the Baltimore City Court. The editors were fortunate in securing the counsel of an able young lawyer of liberal sympathies, Charles Mitchell, who offered his services without charge. Witnesses for the prosecution included Todd's Baltimore agent, the pilot of the *Francis*, a customs officer, and the printers of the *Genius*. Attempts by Lundy and Garrison to limit the indictment to specific counts and their demands for articles of proof of libelous intent were unavailing. Garrison's editorial was admitted just as he had written it. The prosecution showed that whereas there were eighty-eight, not seventy-five, slaves aboard the *Francis*, none of them had been chained, but all of them allowed their freedom below decks, and that they had received humane treatment and had even been permitted to hold daily prayer meetings. Further evidence was offered to show that Captain Brown enjoyed a reputation for kindness in the trade, and that Todd, disliking the business of carrying human cargo, had only agreed to the contract because, as he put it, "freights were dull, times hard, and money scarce." The prosecuting attorney closed his case by pointing out that no law had been broken by Todd and Brown and that only Garrison's fanaticism and virulence could explain his attack.

Now if Garrison had possessed the instincts of a true reporter, he might have checked the real story of the loading of the *Francis* and uncovered the facts which could have cleared him. Subsequent investigation revealed that the Negroes, terrified at the prospect of joining slave gangs in Louisiana, had escaped to the nearby woods, where they were finally recaptured and driven half naked and panic-stricken back to the ship. Without this damaging evidence Mitchell could only defend his clients in terms of higher law and attempt to play on the sympathies of the jury. Eloquence was not enough: it took the jury just fifteen minutes to return a verdict of guilty. A motion for a new trial was denied, and a judgment rendered fining Garrison, now identified as the sole author of the offending editorial, fifty dollars and costs. Since he lacked the money to pay his fine and the usually resourceful Lundy failed him, he had no choice but to accept a jail sentence of six months. On April 17, with the inmates' cries of "Fresh fish!" ringing in his ears, he strode into the Baltimore Jail calmly prepared to exploit his imprisonment to the fullest.

Lundy had been forced to suspend the *Genius* while he helped his friend fight the libel suit. He defended Garrison

to the end, insisting that while there were many of his editorials that had not met with his approval, Garrison had never
deliberately flouted his wishes. As for their personal relationship, "we have ever cherished for each other the kindliest
feelings and mutual personal regard. It would be superfluous
in me to say that he has proven himself a faithful and able
coadjutor in the great and holy cause in which we are engaged. — Even his enemies will admit it."[20] Garrison apolo-
gized neither to Lundy nor to his readers. His only regret, he
announced, was that so far his views on immediate emancipation had been "imperfectly developed" and that, concerned
with the "cares and perplexities of the establishment," he had
not succeeded in making his position absolutely clear. "I have
used strong, indignant, vehement language, and direct, scorch-
ing reproof. I have nothing to recall."[21]

Life behind bars began pleasantly enough, as the following
bit of calculated playfulness written to Harriet Farnham Horton clearly shows:

Baltimore Jail
May 12, 1830

. . . I am as meek as any occupant of a ten-foot building in
our great Babel. . . . It is true, I am not the owner of this huge
pile, nor the grave lord-keeper of it; but then, I pay no rent —
am bound to make no repairs — and enjoy the luxury of independence divested of its cares. . . . I sing as often, and quite as
well as I did before my wings were clipped.

To change the figure: here I strut the lion of the day, and, of
course, attract a great number of visitors, as the exhibition is
gratuitous — so that, between the labors of my brain, the conversation of my friends, and the ever changing curiosities of this
huge menagerie, time flies away astonishingly swift. Indeed, so
perfectly agreeable is my confinement, that I have no occasion
to call upon my philosophy or patience. . . .[22]

Given the freedom of the huge jail, he spent much of his time wandering about the corridors and chatting with the other prisoners. His meals he took with the warden and his family. Lundy came often to discuss plans, bringing with him Isaac Knapp, Garrison's old friend, who had arrived from Boston to help Lundy until Garrison was released. One of the daily occurrences in the jail was the visit of the slave-traders to buy Negroes, slave or free, who had been collected overnight. On one occasion Garrison confronted a master who came to reclaim his slave and spent an enjoyable hour arguing the merits of Noah's curse as proof of the divine sanction of slavery. He won the debate but lost the case. It was satisfying to give his return address as Baltimore Jail, and though he now and again gave way to his longings to return to New England — "that paradise of our fallen world" — his chief worry was that he might be released before he had time to publicize his "incarceration."

First on the promotional agenda came an account of the trial itself, an eight-page pamphlet entitled *A Brief Sketch of the Trial of William Lloyd Garrison, for an Alleged Libel of one Francis Todd, of Massachusetts,* which he dashed off in the space of a week to call the attention of the world to Maryland justice. After expatiating on the unfairness of the proceedings and the vindictiveness of the prosecutor at length he arrived at his central theme — himself. If Judge Brice thought he had stifled a public nuisance, he was wrong. "So long as a good Providence gives me strength and intellect, I will not cease to declare that the existence of slavery is a foul reproach to the American name. . . . I am only in the *alphabet* of my task; time shall perfect a useful work." He cited in his defense the civil rights guaranteed in the Constitution, stalking horses he would ride for thirty-five years. "I think it will appear," he concluded in a sudden shift to understatement, "that freedom of the press has been invaded, and that power and not justice, has convicted me."

When he tired of letter-writing and moral strictures, there was the Byronic gesture of inscribing a sonnet on the walls of his cell exalting the "immortal MIND" and its victory over massive bolts and iron grates. Meanwhile Lundy attended to the distribution of the pamphlet, and by June was able to report that over one hundred newspapers and periodicals had praised the dauntless young editor who dared to tell the truth about slavery.

One day early in June, Lundy appeared at the jail with the money for Garrison's fine and a letter from Arthur Tappan, the New York philanthropist. Tappan had read Garrison's sketch of the trial with a deepening hatred of slavery. He paid the fine and donated another hundred dollars to help revive the *Genius*, which he said was much needed "to hold up to American freemen, in all its naked deformity, the subject of slavery."[23] On June 5, forty-nine days after he first entered the jail, Garrison walked serenely out of the yard, pleased with the thought of returning to Boston but even more satisfied with his first small offering on the altar of freedom.

6

Launching the *Liberator*

GARRISON HEADED NORTH in June, 1830, with a letter of recommendation from Lundy and just enough pocket money to get to Boston. He was determined to organize an anti-slavery society as soon as possible, but that took money and friends. Thanks to advance publicity his name was already known in reform circles in Boston and New York. Riding the lumbering coaches northward from Baltimore, he decided to capitalize on his stroke of good luck in winning the notice of the influential Arthur Tappan by calling on his benefactor in person.

Arthur Tappan, the man who paid Garrison's fine and helped finance the *Liberator*, dominated the American reform movement in 1830 as no single individual after him. A native of Northampton, Massachusetts, he had been raised on the Yankee precepts of holiness and thrift. In 1815 at the age of twenty-nine he established a dry-goods emporium at No. 162 Pearl Street in New York City. When a sudden influx of Manchester cottons flooded the market and swept the new firm into bankruptcy, Tappan turned his reputation for probity to good account by shifting to French silks and quickly built a thriving business on the untried policy of low prices and cash payments. With the sizable profits from his venture he began to finance the American millennium — Bible and tract societies, the free church movement, schools for Negroes, a female rescue league, the temperance cause, and Christian journalism. In an age of associations he was the prince of joiners — a member of the United Domestic Missionary Society, the Young Men's Missionary Society, an honorary director of the New York Evangelical Missionary Society, a liberal supporter of the American Tract Society, to which he gave the initial sum of twenty thousand dollars at its formation, a patron of the American Bible Society, in whose name he established one hundred scholarships at Yale. Another of his projects was the Magdalen Society of New York, an "Asylum for Females who Deviated from Paths of Virtue," and still another, the *Journal of Commerce*, a newspaper run on Christian principles with which to fight the liquor traffic, prostitution, circuses, and the theater. As a strict Sabbatarian he always made sure the presses stopped running promptly at midnight on Saturday.[1]

When Garrison first called on him Tappan was already famous as the patron saint of the evangelical crusade, a sharp critic of slavery, and the adviser of religious reformers all over the country. The machinery of New York's "Great Eight" was powered largely by funds supplied by Arthur Tappan & Company. From his cubicle in the center of the store he kept the wheels of his numerous engines of reform turning by drafting the necessary money orders and consulting with the host of Christian workers who came to him for advice. He kept no records of his donations and seldom mentioned them to others. Each morning he opened his store with a prayer meeting, and at noon when his clerks put down their bolts of cloth for lunch, he retired to his desk to munch a soda cracker and sip a glass of water while contemplating his weightier tasks in the vineyard of the Lord. Behind his grave exterior, his formal courtesy and self-effacing manner there lurked the passion of a true believer.

Tappan had supported the American Colonization Society for several years until he learned that rum and gunpowder were being shipped to the settlers in Liberia, whereupon he indignantly withdrew his aid. These doubts soon led to others, and when he read Garrison's attacks on the society in the *Genius* he was converted to abolition. He told Daniel Webster, who sought his help in founding a state colonization society in Massachusetts, that he was no longer interested in colonization, "for I see that it originated in a plan to get rid of the free negroes in order to render slavery more secure, and I will have nothing more to do with it."[2] Once he abandoned colonization he was determined to destroy it. It was he who urged Garrison on to a war of extermination against the society, writing to him of his desire to see more argument in the *Liberator* "to show THE IMPOSSIBILITY *of the Colonization Society's ever effecting the entire removal of our colored slave population*."[3] Yet with characteristic humility Tappan credited Garrison, "that distinguished and fearless philanthropist," with converting him to immediate emancipation.[4]

Arthur Tappan and his choleric brother Lewis, an equally devoted abolitionist, were surprised and favorably impressed with the meekness of the stormy petrel from Baltimore. "His appearance and deportment at that time," Lewis recalled, "were not likely to be forgotten. His manly form, buoyant spirit, and countenance beaming with conscious rectitude, attracted the attention of all those who witnessed his introduction to Mr. Tappan."[5] Garrison recounted his experiences in jail and confided to the brothers his hope of winning the forthcoming civil suit with Todd by uncovering new evidence in Newburyport. Arthur promised his help, and the next day Garrison set out for Boston. Although he succumbed to the

young editor's infectious zeal, Tappan was by no means convinced of Garrison's fitness for publicizing the anti-slavery
cause. He had read those blazing editorials in the *Genius*
signed "W.L.G." and did not like their severity. Who knew
what this firebrand might do once he was free from Lundy's
chastening influence? He decided to wait and see.

Meanwhile Garrison, heartened by his interview with Tappan, returned to Newburyport to find the town nearly as cold
on the subject of slavery as Baltimore. Ephraim Allen and his
other friends urged him to give up his dream of reviving the
Genius and settle to a less dangerous occupation. He could
not possibly win the libel suit, they argued, so why not admit
failure and come home? Their proposals fell on deaf ears —
in July, after scouring the town in vain for new evidence, he
was back in Baltimore awaiting the trial.

During this flying trip to New England he toyed with the
idea of establishing his own newspaper. Working for Lundy
cramped his form — what he wanted was a paper whose
editorial policy would be his alone. One evening in August he
sat down at his desk in the boardinghouse and put his thoughts
on paper. Since his primary object would be the abolition of
slavery, Washington seemed the obvious place to establish
the paper, for there he could examine slavery from every
angle. "In its investigation, I shall use *great plainness of
speech*," he paused to underscore the phrase, "believing that
*truth can never conduce to mischief and is best discovered by
plain words.*"[6]

So pleased was he with his prospectus that he made several
copies, one of which he mailed to Arthur Tappan, who sent
back a favorable reply and a check. Thus began a relationship which, despite Tappan's growing misgivings as to Garrison's competence, helped support the *Liberator* and its editor
through the first years of a troubled career.

In August, Garrison found that Todd's suit had been postponed and Lundy had given up hope of reviving the *Genius*,
a decision which concerned him less now that he had his own
paper to consider. While awaiting release from jail he had
written three lengthy exposés of colonization, and these he
now decided to deliver on a lecture tour throughout the
Northeast to raise funds for the *Liberator*. After failing to
find a hall in Baltimore he said good-by to Lundy and started
for Philadelphia and a meeting with a second group of
abolitionists who would soon form an outpost of "Garrisonism" in the City of Brotherly Love.

In 1830 the anti-slavery center of the Philadelphia Friends
was the home of James and Lucretia Mott in South Fourth
Street. Lucretia was a heavy-featured woman with a gentle
mouth and deep-set gray eyes that masked her enormous
energy and strong will. At school in Poughkeepsie she had
met James Mott, a tall, shy, excessively grave young man who
taught the boys' classes; and in 1811, when she was nineteen
and he twenty-three, they married and settled in Philadelphia,
where Mott entered a cotton commission house. Their first
experience with slavery came in 1815, when a South Carolina
planter willed his slaves to the Philadelphia Meeting to be
manumitted, a request which James recognized as involving
"considerations of no small magnitude to civil society." Three
years later Lucretia accompanied the Quaker preacher Sarah
Zane on a tour of Virginia, where the sight of slave coffles
shuffling through Harpers Ferry affected her much as a
similar view had startled Benjamin Lundy. Prodded by her
conscience, she began to examine the free produce movement
and soon concluded that it was her duty to boycott all products made by slave labor. Henceforth the groceries in the
Mott household came from Lydia White's Requited Labor
Grocery and Dry-Goods Store, although James continued to

accept commissions for slave cotton. Their family ate only free rice and free sugar and wore clothes made from free cotton. Even their candies were "free sweets" stamped with anti-slavery couplets:

> If slavery comes by color, which God gave,
> Fashion may change, and you become the slave.

After struggling with his conscience for five years James abandoned the cotton for the wool business, a decision, Lucretia admitted, that made them "happy in the final freedom" though "quite unsettled with regard to the future."

In 1828, just as Lucretia was beginning to take a more active part in Quaker affairs, Elias Hicks split the Society of Friends in America into two warring factions. As a Quietist, Hicks objected to the growing worldliness of the Quakers and their eagerness to cooperate with other churches in promoting Bible and missionary societies. Especially did he disapprove of the increased institutionalizing of Quakerism, the excessive use of Quaker forms of speech and behavior, the arbitrary power of the elders, and the infiltration of "evangelical" beliefs in the Bible as the word of God. Not all the books ever written, he told his followers, could communicate God to His children, who needed only the guidance of the Inner Light.[7]

The Motts joined the Hicksites because they too disliked "oppressive authority" and sought a practical Christianity. Lucretia particularly deprecated controversy over creedal differences and held that the "gloomy dogmas of the schools" mattered less than the heavenly light within. "Men are to be judged by their likeness to Christ rather than by their notions of Christ," she announced in one of her sermons not long before she met Garrison. She was even more critical of dictatorial practices among the elders that kept men and women from thinking for themselves. "The veneration of believers," she complained, "has been strengthened by their not being allowed to think."[8] She worried lest the fear of being called an infidel keep too many Friends from striking out on their own in reforming the world. "I care not for charges of verbal infidelity; the infidelity I should dread, is to be faithless to the right, to moral principle, to the divine impulses of the soul, to a confidence in the possible realization of the millennium now." *The millennium now* — here was the key to the Motts' faith and the goal of their practical Christianity.

At first the Motts' religious liberalism shocked Garrison, who still prided himself on his orthodoxy. Gradually, however, as their friendship deepened, he was won over by their tolerance and simplicity. Looking back at their first meeting from the height of his career, he admitted that their friendship had been a decisive influence in his life. "Though I was strongly sectarian in my religious sentiments (Calvinist) at that time, and hence uncharitable in judgment touching theological differences of opinion . . . yet they manifested a most kind, tolerant, catholic spirit, and allowed none of these considerations to deter them from giving me their cordial approbation and cheering countenance as an advocate of the slave. If my mind has since become liberalized in any degree, (and I think it has burst every sectarian trammel,) — if theological dogmas which I once regarded as essential to Christianity, I now repudiate as absurd and pernicious — I am largely indebted to them for the change."[9]

A lecture hall and an audience willing to hear a tirade against colonization proved hard to find in Philadelphia in 1830. After importuning nearly every church leader in the city, Garrison was about to leave for New York in despair when he was finally given the Franklin Institute for three successive nights beginning on August 31. The small audience composed of the Motts and their Quaker circle of Shipleys, Pughs, and Davises and a handful of free colored people listened attentively if not with entire approval to his impeachment of the Colonization Society. Even Lucretia thought his speech somewhat severe, although she could not help agreeing that his principles were correct. She and her husband invited him to their home, where spirited and earnest conversation soon thawed the young lecturer's reserve. They talked of Lundy and his work, and Lucretia inquired about his own plans, the state of anti-slavery opinion in New England, and his hopes for the *Liberator*. He left Philadelphia in buoyant spirits, assured of the interest of many of the Quakers there and anxious now to test the doctrine of immediate emancipation in Boston.

Garrison's doctrine of immediate emancipation was an import from England. In May, 1830, while he still sat in his Baltimore cell planning his strategy, across the Atlantic, in London, there occurred an event that marked the turning point in the history of anti-slavery. On May 15 English abolitionists, members of the Anti-Slavery Society, met in Exeter Hall for their annual convention. With the diminutive William Wilberforce, now at seventy-one ill and shrunken, presiding on a platform filled with elder statesmen in the cause, his protégé Thomas Fowell Buxton rose ponderously to offer a resolution calling for the abolition of slavery throughout the Empire "at the earliest possible period." Buxton's carefully worded resolution was backed by the authority of the veterans Wilberforce, Zachary Macaulay, Thomas Clarkson and James Stephen, men who knew the wisdom of moderation and had practiced it for forty years in their campaign against the West Indian planters. By 1830, however, the leadership of the abolitionist party outside Parliament had fallen into the hands of younger men with less patience and

more militancy. Before the May meeting they had agreed to
demand immediate emancipation as the sole remedy for
slavery. To the consternation of the Old Guard they amended
Buxton's resolution to provide for immediate action and the
formation of an Agency Committee to convert all England.

Following up their unexpected success, the advocates of
immediate emancipation decided to go straight to the country
without waiting for elections to provide them with a more
tractable ministry. The success of their agents was astounding: in twelve months' time the number of anti-slavery
societies rocketed from two hundred to thirteen hundred, and
petitions with hundreds of thousands of signatures flooded
Westminster. Their new techniques — the lecture, pamphlet,
handbill and poster — gave English abolition a momentum
which it never lost. In 1832 Parliament passed the long-over-
due Reform Bill, and in April of the next year, when three
hundred delegates marched in a body to present an address to
the Prime Minister, the government realized that thanks to the
Agency Committee the delegates spoke the demands of the
majority of Englishmen. Before such strength it could only
bow by passing the West India Emancipation Act on August
29, 1833.

Garrison was impressed with the English indictment of
the West Indian planters and with the emphasis on slavery as a
sin. If Clarkson and Wilberforce, the wisest and best men of
their age, agreed on immediate emancipation as the only hope,
then Americans had best accept it as the terms of divine
justice.

In his belief that the British anti-slavery model was ex-
portable Garrison was wrong on two counts. In the first place,
the power of Parliament to legislate for the colonies far sur-
passed congressional authority over the states. The English
abolitionists demanded that Parliament put a definite terminus

to slavery by legislative fiat — this was all that "immediate emancipation" really meant. Nothing like a general law abolishing slavery in the South could be expected from Congress. Little as he knew of constitutional law, Garrison admitted that Congress had no power to regulate slavery in the states, and this hard fact should have prevented him from making any such easy assumptions as his British friends might afford.

The second factor which Garrison overlooked in his haste to copy British methods was the obvious prestige of the anti-slavery movement in England. When it was formed in 1823 the Anti-Slavery Society boasted a royal duke for its president, five peers and fourteen members of Parliament for vice-presidents. Where were the likes of these to be found in America?

Yet for all his ignorance of the actual machinery of British anti-slavery, Garrison rightly sensed an affinity stemming from the religious dedication common to Englishmen and Americans. The soul of abolition in England was Evangelicalism, the religion of the Clapham Sect of "Saints," as they were called because of their piety and high seriousness, their air of self-condemnation and their accent on Christian conduct. Evangelicalism in England, unlike the more diffuse religious sentiment in America, was a movement, and the Clapham Sect a distinct *set* of people who shared the same belief in the power of the regenerated will to shape society to its own image.

Evangelicalism was thus a practical religion, and the Claphamites, like the Tappans and Motts, were practical people. The Saints, whose solid town houses ringed Clapham Common, were men of the world who enjoyed the amenities of life and knew the value of money as a power for good. Theirs was no closed sainthood — they practiced no initiatory rites, professed no rigid code. Unable to ignore worldly opinion, they were nonetheless happiest in their own community of shared values, admonishing one another in plain language and organizing projects for improving society, chief among them the abolition of slavery. Theirs were feelings which Garrison could understand, a sense of consecration overriding all doubts, a moral rather than mystical faith in divine purpose, the kind of assurance that had sustained his mother through the dark days of her marriage and driven him to take up the cause of the slave. In the spirit of English Evangelicalism he set out to organize American abolitionists and form a Clapham Sect of his own.

On October 12, 1831, the *Boston Courier* printed this notice:

> WANTED. — For three evenings, a Hall or Meet-inghouse (the latter would be preferred), in which to vindicate the rights of TWO MILLION of American citizens who are now groaning in servile chains in the boasted land of liberty; and also to propose just, benevolent, and constitutional mea-sures for their relief. As the addresses will be gra-tuitous and as the cause is of public benefit, I cannot consent to remunerate any society for the use of its building. If this application fails, I propose to ad-dress the citizens of Boston in the open, on the Common.
>
> WM. LLOYD GARRISON
> No. 30 Federal Street, Oct. 11, 1830

It was not a church or religious society that answered his appeal but Abner Kneeland's group of freethinkers who of-fered their rooms in Julien Hall. Accordingly on Friday evening, October 15, he rose before a "small but select audience" of "the virtuous and high minded portion of the community" (already favorite Garrisonian phrases) to deliver what was perhaps the most important speech of his life. Lyman Beecher was there, all smiles and benevolence, and so was John Tappan, the hardheaded brother of Arthur and Lewis. Samuel Joseph May, the Unitarian minister who had attended Lundy's meeting at Collier's two years earlier, brought along his cousin Samuel Sewall and his brother-in-law Bronson Alcott.

Garrison began his talk by thanking Kneeland's "infidels" for the use of their hall. It was indicative of the depths to which the New England conscience had descended that he was forced to accept the charity of the very men whose atheistic opinions he had censured in the pages of the *National Philanthropist*. Abolition properly belonged to the churches, and if they refused to act, they must be purified by true Christians. Slaveowners were not and never could be Christians — "God, and the angels, and the devil, and the universe know that they are without excuse." He charged colonizationists with playing a cruel joke on an unsuspecting public. He himself had been their dupe until he discovered their diabolical purpose, but now duty demanded that he denounce their plot. Were statistics needed to prove the futility of colonization, or quotations to confirm the cunning of its leaders? If so, here they were in abundance. . . .

His speech was a masterpiece of destructive argument. When he finished May and Sewall knew that they had been called to a holy war. After the lecture Beecher, Alcott, May and Sewall approached the platform, and their reactions to Garrison were as varied as their personalities. Beecher seemed visibly disturbed. Once before he had been approached by this brash young man who wanted to convert him to abolition, and he had put him off by saying that he already had too many irons in the fire. "Then you had better let all your irons burn rather than neglect your duty to the slave," Garrison had retorted. But this evening Beecher was upset by the ardor with which Garrison argued his dangerous ideas. "Your zeal is commendable," he told him, "but you are misguided." If he would only forget his fanatical ideas, Beecher said, he could make him the Wilberforce of America. But Garrison only smiled his disagreement and turned to accept the congratulations of May and Sewall. For some time now he had doubted Beecher's conviction, and his remarks that evening only confirmed the great man's lack of moral fiber. An idol had fallen.

Far different were the responses of Sewall and May. The two Samuels shared more than progressive Unitarian homes and a Harvard education. They were kindred souls who cared less for polity and forms of worship than for diffusing a nondenominational faith based on the idea of moral self-improvement. They were ready for abolition just as Garrison was ready for the affection and good sense they offered. "That is a providential man!" May remembered telling his cousin. He told Garrison that though he could hardly endorse all of his views, he was convinced that his was a divine calling. Alcott invited them to his home, where they sat till long past midnight listening to the endless flow of Garrison's arguments. "That night," May admitted, "my soul was baptised in his spirit, and ever since I have been a disciple and fellow-laborer of William Lloyd Garrison."[10]

Both May and Sewall remonstrated with Garrison for his violent and abusive language. They disliked his journalistic slang and his habit of calling slaveholders thieves and robbers and accusing everyone who disagreed with him of willful blindness. May tried to warn him of the dangers of excessive heat: "Oh, my friend," he entreated, "do try to moderate your indignation, and keep more cool! why, you are all on fire!" "Brother May," Garrison snapped, "I have need to be

all on fire, for I have mountains of ice about me to melt."[11]
The cousins continued to hope that somehow they might
channel Garrison's godly energy. In this they were mistaken.

His decision to publish the *Liberator* in Boston did not
come immediately, but after audiences in New Haven, Hartford and Newburyport spurned his lectures on colonization
he decided that there was a greater need for a revolution in
public opinion in the North — "*and particularly in New
England*" — than in the South. Printing an unpopular newspaper in a strange and hostile city was more than even he
could contemplate. Let Lundy attend to Washington. In
Boston he had a reputation that he could turn to good account
in getting credit and patronage. Isaac Knapp, who had come
north with him, agreed to a partnership, and Sewall and May
promised to find subscribers. Thus his seemingly bold resolve
to launch the paper "*within the sight of Bunker Hill and the
birthplace of Liberty.*"[12]

He had difficulty naming his paper. Sewall thought the
Liberator altogether too provocative a title and suggested the
Safety Lamp, but Garrison would not agree. The actual
printing of the paper proved to be the worst of their troubles,
since they had neither a press nor the means to buy one. They
solved the problem temporarily by inducing their friend
Stephen Symonds Foster, the foreman of the *Christian Examiner*, to lend them his type in exchange for a day's work
at his press. The first three numbers of the *Liberator* were
printed with type hurriedly set in the middle of the night
and returned the next day. For his fourth number Garrison
succeeded in locating a lot of secondhand type and a small
hand press.

On Saturday morning, January 1, 1831, four hundred
copies of the *Liberator* carried Garrison's declaration of
principles to the Boston public. His famous manifesto, squeezed

into four closely printed columns, sat askew on a front page measuring exactly fourteen by nine and a quarter inches. "I am aware that many object to the severity of my language," he wrote in a pointed allusion to the strictures of May and Sewall, "but is there not cause for severity?"

I will be as harsh as truth, and as uncompromising as justice. On this subject, I do not wish to think, or speak, or write, with moderation. No! no! Tell a man whose house is on fire to give a moderate alarm; tell him to moderately rescue his wife from the hands of the ravisher; tell the mother to gradually extricate her babe from the fire into which it has fallen; — but urge me not to use moderation in a cause like the present. I am in earnest — I will not equivocate — I will not excuse — I will not retreat a single inch — AND I WILL BE HEARD.

The words if not their spirit were new. He had said the same thing before and would repeat it countless times again. But he never succeeded in saying it as well.

7

Fanning the Flames

THE OFFICE OF the *Liberator* was located in Merchants Hall, first in No. 6, and then after a few weeks in No. 10 under the eaves. It was a small dingy room with tiny, ink-spattered windows. In one corner stood the press opposite the battered composing desk; in the center of the room a long roughhewn mailing table littered with copy ran from wall to wall and next to it Garrison's bed for visitors to step around. In this room the editor worked sixteen hours every day but Sunday, setting type, running off copy, compiling mailing lists, answering letters with painstaking deliberation, and as midnight approached dashing off the editorials that soon made him notorious. The partners lived chiefly on water and stale bread from a nearby bakery. In February they took on a colored apprentice to help with the manual work.

Visitors were welcome at No. 10 Merchants Hall, and they began coming in increasing numbers, some out of sheer curiosity, but more with real interest and the desire to help. May and Sewall were frequent callers and so was Arnold Buffum, the taciturn Quaker hatter from Rhode Island. Here too came Ellis Gray Loring, the proper Bostonian lawyer; David Lee Child, the liberal Unitarian editor who remembered Garrison from the days of the *National Philanthropist;* and Amos Phelps, the energetic Congregational minister, first an

admirer and then a bitter enemy of the *Liberator*. Oliver
Johnson, a devout young evangelical who used the *Liberator*
type to print his fly-by-night *Christian Soldier*, often wandered in, drawn by Garrison's apostolic manner. To Johnson
the editor seemed a divinely inspired leader; and in the years
to come he served his master as chore-boy, loyal and unquestioning for thirty-five years, his carbon-copy mind reproduc-
ing faithfully the Garrisonian gospel.

Here in No. 10 his visitors would sit dispersed about the
crowded and stuffy room listening to Garrison, who sat tipped
back in his editorial chair, stroking a stray cat in his lap and
pausing in the midst of his endless monologue to wipe an ink-
stained hand across his balding head. He thrived on the interest
and admiration of these new friends with whom he talked
simply and candidly. The contrast between the incendiary
editor of their imagination and the mild, gentle-humored man
behind the desk disconcerted more than one of his visitors.
Instead of a dark-visaged desperado — "something like a pi-
rate" — they found a scholarly-looking gentleman. Nothing
pleased the twenty-six-year-old editor more than to be described as a man of tender sensibilities and courtly manners.

So demanding was the manual work of printing the
Liberator that Garrison hardly found time for composition.
"My worthy partner and I complete the mechanical part,"
he explained to May in apologizing for some editorials he
regarded as slipshod, "that is to say, we compose and distribute, on every number, one hundred thousand types, besides
performing the presswork, mailing the papers to subscribers
&c., &c."[1] The editorial fraternity may have received the
Liberator "with acclamation" as he joyfully reported to May,
but the public, which knew the paper chiefly through the
reputation of its editor, greeted it with apathy and then with
downright hostility.

In an age of mass communication it is difficult to understand how the *Liberator* acquired the reputation it did. It is a mistake to imagine smudged copies clandestinely passed from hand to hand on the Charleston waterfront and in the back streets of Richmond, or even widely read among Northern reformers. At the end of its first year, the *Liberator* had gained only fifty white subscribers, and two years later they numbered less than four hundred. Garrison enjoyed the distinction unique among editors throughout the country of addressing his message to white philanthropists and his appeals for funds to the free Negroes. By his own admission the *Liberator* belonged not to the whites — "they do not sustain it" — but "emphatically to the people of color — it is their organ."[2] Its chief source of revenue in its first difficult year was the pathetic contributions from the underprivileged colored communities in Philadelphia, New York and Boston. Garrison announced that his paper had acted on the free Negroes "like a trumpet call." By the middle of February he had ninety new subscriptions from Philadelphia and over thirty from New York. "This then," he wrote to May, "is my consolation: if I cannot do much, in this quarter, toward abolishing slavery, I may be able to elevate our free colored population in the scale of Society." But already rumblings in the South indicated that the *Liberator* was destined for a greater role than this.

The secret of Garrison's rapid ascent to notoriety lay in his ingenious use of his list of exchanges, which numbered over a hundred periodicals at the end of the first year. These he manipulated skillfully to set off chain reactions of public opinion. Southern editors received the *Liberator*, found it highly offensive, and quoted it to show their readers the lengths to which diabolical Yankees were prepared to go in stripping the South of her birthright. Next, Northern editors,

neutral or openly hostile to abolition but sensing good copy
here, reprinted the Southern editorials and added comments
of their own. Then both the original editorial and the commentary appeared in the *Liberator* together with more Garrisonian invective, and the process began all over again. In
September, 1831, for example, Garrison proclaimed his undy-
ing friendship for Southern planters in these words: "I would
not, wittingly, harm a hair on their heads, nor injure them
in their lawful property. I am not their enemy, but their
friend. It is true, I abhor their oppressive acts; nor will I
cease to denounce them in terms of indignation. They will
surely be destroyed if they do not repent. MEN MUST BE
FREE."³ When the volatile editor of the Tarboro', South
Carolina, *Free Press* read this, his righteous anger boiled over
and he replied with the charge that Garrison was employing
"secret agents" in the Palmetto State to incite a slave rebellion,
and suggested, further, that all such traitors apprehended by
loyal sons of the South should be roasted alive. Gales and
Seaton's *National Intelligencer* picked up the Tarboro' editor's rabble-rousing and printed it with an editorial warning
Garrison against "poisoning the waters of life" of the whole
American community. "We know nothing of the man," the
editors admitted, "we desire not to have him unlawfully dealt
with: we can even conceive of his motive being good in his
own opinion," but Bostonians who love the Union must inter-
vene to "vindicate the cause of humanity, as it is outraged by
the publication to which we refer." All of which appeared in
the *Liberator* a few weeks later as proof of "Southern mendac-
ity and folly." "My contempt of it is unutterable," Garrison
remarked. "Nothing but my own death, or want of patronage,
shall stop the *Liberator*."

Angry letters piled up on the mailing table. He answered
as many of them as he could, patiently explaining his terms

of opprobrium but refusing to alter his style. Publicly he announced, "My language is exactly such as suits me; it will displease many, I know — to displease them is my intention." Further advice would be considered intrusive. "I do not want it. I want more leisure from manual labor, in order to do justice to the cause — I want a larger periodical that will enable me and my correspondents to appear before the public without crowding each other."[4] Still the letters filled with fear and contempt kept coming. "You d——d scoundrel. Hell is gaping for you! the devil is feasting in anticipation." A Washington slaveholder wrote, "Your paper cannot much longer be tolerated. . . . Shame on the Freemen of Boston for permitting such a vehicle of outrage and rebellion to spring into existence among them."[5] Such complaints simply added fuel to the fire of Garrison's incendiary glee. "Foes are on my right hand and on my left," ran one self-congratulatory editorial. "The tongue of detraction is busy against me. I have no communion with the world — the world none with me."[6] Privately he confided to Henry Benson, a new agent for the *Liberator* in Providence and his future brother-in-law, that he was vastly pleased that "the disturbances at the South still continue. The slaveholders are evidently given over to destruction. They are determined to shut out the light — to hear none of the appeals of justice and humanity. I shudder when I contemplate their fate."[7]

Critics of the *Liberator* accused it of inciting violence. It was one thing, they declared, to protest pacific intentions, but what were readers to make of verses like the following that appeared immediately beside the editor's disavowal of force?

> Though distant to be the hour, yet come it must —
>   Oh! hasten it, *in mercy*, righteous Heaven!
> When Afric's sons, uprising from the dust,
>   Shall stand erect — their galling fetters riven . . .

Wo if it come with storm, and blood and fire,
    When midnight darkness veils the earth and sky!
Wo to the innocent babe — the guilty sire —
    Stranger and Citizen alike shall die!
Red-handed Slaughter his revenge shall feed,
    And Havoc yell his ominous death-cry,
And wild Despair in vain for mercy plead —
While Hell itself shall shrink, and sicken at the deed![8]

Suddenly, in August, 1831, came Nat Turner's Rebellion in Southampton County, Virginia, as if to give the lie to Garrison's irenic declarations. A month later the *Liberator* was on trial for its life.

On August 21, 1831, a band of slaves variously estimated between fifty and seventy in number marched through Southampton County killing and looting. Their leader was Nat Turner, a thirty-one-year-old fanatic who believed himself divinely commissioned to free his fellow slaves and who had been plotting this uprising with the help of heavenly voices for some time. When the sign came he fell into a trance but recovered in time to begin butchering every white man in Virginia. His army of the Lord was easily routed, though not before he and his followers had killed sixty-one whites. Turner was hanged along with all of his confederates, and an aftermath of reprisals began in which over a hundred Negroes were killed, many of them after inhuman torture.

In the midst of this six-month reign of terror many Southerners were forcibly reminded of another black prophet, David Walker, whose *Appeal* calling on the slaves to revolt had been published in Boston less than two years before. David Walker was a free Negro of almost legendary fame and one of the first heroes of the anti-slavery movement. The son of a slave father and a free mother in Wilmington, North Carolina, he had wandered all over the South for years before settling in Boston, where he opened a secondhand clothes shop. In September, 1829, just as Lundy and Garrison were organizing their joint enterprise, Walker published his pamphlet, *Appeal in Four Articles Together with a Preamble to the Colored Citizens of the World, but in Particular, and Very Expressly, to those of the United States of America,* an extraordinary piece of malevolence based on a belief in the superiority of the black race. In the course of his travels Walker had acquired a rudimentary education that somehow accounted for his crude cyclical philosophy of history in which God regularly intervened on the side of downtrodden races. In his role of prophet he foresaw a war of extermination that would kill off the whites "like rattlesnakes." "Let twelve good black men get armed for battle and they will kill and put to flight fifty whites. Get the blacks started, and if you don't have a gang of tigers and lions to deal with, then I am a deceiver of the blacks and of the whites. If you commence make sure work of it: don't trifle, for they will not trifle with you. Kill or be killed."[9]

Walker's *Appeal* went through three editions in six months, each more bloodthirsty than the last. Just before his death in 1830 under mysterious circumstances, he visited Richmond, Virginia, where he circulated thirty copies of his pamphlet, only twenty of which were recovered when he was arrested. Thus, when the black prophet Nat Turner attacked his white masters a year later, it seemed to many a Virginian that the blood bath was the result of Walker's devilish *Appeal.*

Garrison emphatically condemned both the *Appeal* and Turner's hair-raising conspiracy. Yet his attitude toward violence, indeed, his allegiance to the peace cause remained curiously ambiguous. Reviewing the *Appeal* for readers of the *Genius,* he had criticized it as "a most injudicious publication" while admitting that its incitement to violence was "warranted by the creed of an independent people." Although he "deprecated its circulation," he was forced to admire its "impassioned and determined spirit" and "the bravery and intelligence" of its author.[10] When Southern editors clamored for his punishment as an apologist for the Southampton revolt, Garrison was correct in replying that he had never preached anything to the slaves but submission. Yet his disavowal of violence was something less than unequivocal. A month after the revolt, he wrote, "I do not justify the slaves in their rebellion: yet I do not condemn *them*, and applaud similar conduct in *white men*. I deny the right of any people to fight for liberty, and so far am a Quaker in principles. Of all men living, however, our slaves have the best reason to assert their rights by violent measures, inasmuch as they are more oppressed than others."[11] Thirty years later he would soon dispose of the incident at Harpers Ferry in nearly identical terms. Then it appeared to many Southerners, just as it did to the Virginia legislature in the aftermath of Nat Turner's revolt, that the editor of the *Liberator* was not the man of peace he pretended to be. They saw only a misguided fanatic who called slaveowners "beasts" and "criminals" and denounced their measures as "atrocities." They proposed to deal with him accordingly.

In October the city of Georgetown in the District of Columbia passed an ordinance prohibiting free Negroes from receiving the *Liberator*. Then a vigilance committee in Columbia, South Carolina, offered a reward for the apprehension of any person caught circulating Garrison's paper or Walker's *Appeal*. Town meetings in Bethesda, Maryland, and Savannah, Georgia, voted similar measures. The Grand Jury of Raleigh, North Carolina, found a true bill against Garrison and Knapp for distributing their paper in the county contrary to the laws of the state. In December, Governor James Hamilton of

South Carolina forwarded to the legislature a special message together with copies of the *Liberator* and Garrison's
speech to the Free People of Color delivered the previous
June in Philadelphia. In his message Hamilton referred to a
letter from the governor of Virginia which he said "leaves no
doubt that the spirit of insubordination in that State was
excited by the incendiary newspapers and other publications,
put forth in the non-slaveholding States, and freely circulated
within the limits of Virginia." At Hamilton's suggestion, South
Carolina's Senator Robert Y. Hayne wrote a letter of protest
to his old colleague Harrison Gray Otis, now mayor of
Boston, asking what measures might be taken to suppress the
Liberator immediately. Only after making several inquiries
could Otis unearth enough information to allay his suspicions.
"I am told," he reported to Hayne, "that it is supported
chiefly by the free colored people; that the number of subscribers in Baltimore and Washington exceeds that of *those in
this city*, and that it is gratuitously left at one or two of the
reading rooms in this place." As far as he could ascertain, Otis
said, the editor was a disgruntled ne'er-do-well who had lived
for a while in Baltimore, "where his feelings have been
exasperated by some occurrences consequent to his publications there." Atrocious and detestable as his sentiments were,
his newspaper had yet to stir even a teapot tempest and was
not likely to win converts among the more respectable classes
of Boston. It would be hasty and imprudent, Otis concluded,
to take any immediate action.[12]

Nevertheless, he dispatched police officers to No. 10 Merchants Hall to establish the truth of Hayne's complaint that
Garrison regularly supplied him with the *Liberator*. The visit
proved to be just what the editor wanted — a chance to
defend the freedom of the press.

The Hon. Robert Y. Hayne, of Columbia, S.C. (through the medium of a letter), wishes to know of the Mayor of Boston who sent a number of the *Liberator* to him, a few weeks ago? The Mayor of Boston (through the medium of a deputy) wishes to know of Mr. Garrison whether he sent the aforesaid number to the aforesaid individual? Mr. Garrison (through the medium of his paper) wishes to know of the Hon. Robert Y. Hayne, of Columbia, S.C., and the Mayor of Boston, what authority they have to put such questions?[13]

He never received an answer.

In November came the strongest protest yet against the *Liberator* — an open invitation to kidnapping. The upper house of the Georgia legislature passed a resolution providing "that the sum of five thousand dollars be, and the same is hereby appropriated to be paid to any person or persons who shall arrest, bring to trial and prosecute to conviction, under the laws of this State the editor or publisher of a certain paper called the *Liberator*."[14] Secretly pleased with the welcome publicity, Garrison professed himself shocked at this "monstrous proposition."

Where is the liberty of the press and of speech? where the spirit of our fathers? where the immunities secured to us by our Bill of Rights? Is it treason to maintain the principles of the Declaration of Independence? Must we say that slavery is a sacred and benevolent institution, or be silent? — Know this, ye Senatorial Patrons of kidnappers! . . . The *Liberator* shall yet live — live to warn you of your danger and guilt — live to plead for the perishing slave — live to hail the day of universal emancipation.[15]

To Henry Benson he wrote of the "perilous times" ahead for the *Liberator* and the Negroes. "So infuriated are the whites against them since the Virginia and North Carolina insurrection that the most trifling causes may lead to a war of extermination."[16]

These prophecies seemed premature and even ludicrous in 1831. Not for another five years would Southern statesmen in league with Northern business interests mount a full-scale counterattack on abolition. If his bid for recognition as the leader of American anti-slavery led Garrison intentionally to overestimate the dangers to the *Liberator,* his analysis of the issues nevertheless proved correct. The events of the next decade would show that the defenders of slavery were bent on destroying abolition even if it meant the annihilation of American civil liberties. By standing on their constitutional rights, Garrison, James G. Birney, Theodore Weld, Elijah Lovejoy and the other "martyrs" of the anti-slavery movement had largely won this fight by 1840. In attaching to their cause the rights of free speech, free press, and free assembly they won over to their side new recruits who were less concerned with slavery as a sin than with the loss of basic freedoms, and who gradually came to see in the struggle between the anti-slavery and the slavery forces the choice between an open society with its free intellectual market and a closed community afraid of ideas. Then, as in its first year, the *Liberator* upheld its editor's belief that "the triumph of truth is as sure as the light of heaven."

Not Southern opposition alone but a lack of patronage threatened the life of the *Liberator* in its first year. Garrison organized groups of free Negroes in Boston and lectured in Providence, New York and Philadelphia to raise money for his paper; but he knew that it could not survive indefinitely on these slender contributions. Desperately he called for "a concentration of moral strength" in Boston, an anti-slavery society to save the *Liberator.*[17] His call was soon heeded.

On Sunday afternoon, November 13, 1831, fifteen men met in the offices of Samuel Sewall in State Street to hear Garrison expound on the need for a New England anti-slavery society.

He had announced in advance that if the apostolic number of twelve could be found in agreement on principles, they would form a society forthwith. Now he spoke long and earnestly on the merits of the British anti-slavery model and the virtues of immediate emancipation. When it came time to vote, however, only nine of the group could bring themselves to agree with the editor; six others, including Sewall, Loring and Child, feared the repercussions in Boston society of such radical doctrine. The meeting ended without any action on Garrison's project.

A month later he tried again, this time with only nine disciples — Sewall, Loring, Child, Knapp, Johnson, and four others. A committee headed by Garrison was appointed to draft a constitution which was to be reported at the first general meeting of the new society on January 1, 1832. The *Liberator* gave an account of these proceedings and issued an immediate call for membership. At the meeting on the first day of the new year Garrison's constitution was adopted with only a few minor alterations. New recruits appeared at this meeting, among them Dr. Gamaliel Bradford, soon to be made superintendent of the Massachusetts General Hospital, and the Reverend Abijah Blanchard, an anti-Masonic editor of local fame. The question of a preamble to the constitution was postponed for a second meeting a week later at the African Baptist Church in Belknap Street in the heart of Boston's "Nigger Hill." The preamble bore the Garrisonian stamp and provoked strong disagreement. After prolonged debate in which Sewall, Loring and Child objected strenuously to the language of the preamble and the principles of the majority, the constitution was signed by Garrison and eleven others, none of whom, it was observed, could have put a hundred dollars into the treasury without bankrupting themselves. The opposition of his three friends did not prevent Garrison from indulging in the histrionics he so enjoyed. "We have met tonight in this obscure school-house," he told the gathering, "our members are few and our influence limited; but, mark my prediction, Faneuil Hall shall ere long echo with the principles we have set forth. We shall shake the Nation by their mighty power."[18]

The New England Anti-Slavery Society elected as its first president Arnold Buffum, the Quaker hatter from Providence. Garrison was appointed corresponding secretary, an arrangement that satisfied both Garrison, who wanted to be free to edit his paper, and the members, who feared that his radical ideas might prejudice their organization in the eyes of New Englanders. Buffum supplied the driving force of the society in its first year. The son of a farmer in Smithfield, Rhode Island, he was a self-educated man, an amateur inventor and educational reformer as well as a stanch abolitionist. Not long before the formation of the society he had returned from England, where he discussed slavery with Clarkson and educational theory with leading Quakers whose system of "infant schools" he was anxious to try out in this country. Garrison's call found him already active in Quaker circles preaching emancipation and Elias Hicks's free-produce ideas. Buffum and the faithful Oliver Johnson immediately took to the field as agents of the society, traveling throughout southern New England, organizing local societies, challenging colonizationists, and defending Garrison and the *Liberator* from charges of fanaticism. Meetings of the society were held on the last Monday of each month, and standing committees were appointed to prepare petitions, improve conditions in Negro schools, and repeal the Massachusetts law preventing intermarriage of blacks and whites. The *Liberator* was declared the official organ of the society, a policy terminated to the satisfaction of all parties by the publication of a new paper, the *Abolitionist*, at the end of the year. "Our little society is gradually expanding, and begins already to make a perceptible impression upon the public mind," Garrison wrote his friend Ebenezer Dole in June, 1832. "Scarcely has the good seed been buried in the earth, and yet even now it is sending up shoots in every direction."[19]

The "good seed" of New England abolitionism was its founder's belief that emancipation could be accomplished only by the moral rebirth of every American citizen. As the New England Anti-Slavery Society grew, it sprouted branches of "Garrisonism" in every direction. It was marked with many of the virtues and all of the deficiencies of its leader's personality. In the first place, Garrison was not an organizer. Much as he admired the efficiency of the English abolitionists, he distrusted political maneuvering, particularly in large organizations where power might be ranged against him. He was not above the tricks of manipulating blocs of votes himself, but he preferred open debate and the rough-and-tumble exchange of opinions. He believed that right decisions resulted from the deliberation of enlightened individuals who instinctively arrived at a simple solution and proceeded to carry it out. He was further convinced that emancipation would become a reality only when a majority of Americans had been converted in free and open discussion. Thus he saw his society simply as a forum for individuals to bear their testimony against slavery.

The New England Society grew into just this kind of organization. Visitors at its annual meetings who were accustomed to the orderly business procedure of more centralized societies were shocked by the lack of system, the chaotic financial condition, and the general absence of direction in Garrison's society. They entirely mistook the dispositions and intentions of the delegates for whom the annual trek to Boston was in the nature of a pilgrimage rather than a business meeting, and from which they returned refreshed with literally hundreds of hours of talk. Eloquence was a penny a bushel at these meetings, it is true, but eloquence was what the members required. Along with Garrison they believed that "moral suasion" meant collecting one, two, or a half-dozen people and peppering them with arguments for immediate emancipation. Although the society printed and distributed pamphlets and tracts, it was far less effective than the New York and the Western societies at this type of propaganda. Its forte was the spoken word — it furnished the best of the anti-slavery orators and evangelists. Evangelism thrives on community spirit, and this the annual conclave of the New England abolitionists provided in abundance: two-hour speeches, endless motions, resolutions, amendments, and marathon personal testimonies of delegates each trying to outdo the others in depicting the horrors of slavery and the depravity of the planters. If it did nothing more, the annual meeting of the society furnished a release for pent-up emotions and sent members back to their homes prepared to disrupt church services, badger their neighbors, and wander the countryside in search of a martyrdom which was the aim of the society and its founder.

While the new agents of the society opened their lecture tour early in the spring of 1832, Garrison returned to his paper and the unfinished campaign against colonization. "Every Monday evening an animated discussion is held in this city on the principles and tendencies of the American Colonization Society," he reported. "The friends of this pernicious combination, having no ground on which to stand, are routed in every debate."[20] These discussion groups ceased to satisfy him when he discovered that Boston's leading colonizationists refused to be drawn into debates with him, but following the example of their New England agent, the Reverend Joshua N. Danforth, went methodically about the city infiltrating the churches. Their obvious disdain irked Garrison. "Mr. Danforth and his coadjutors cannot be induced to defend their cause. They affect to belong to the 'good society folks,' and therefore cannot stoop to the canaille. Miserable pride! It is destined to have a mighty fall."[21]

For some time now he had been weighing Tappan's suggestion that he write an anti-colonization tract. He sent for the files of the *African Repository*, the organ of the Colonization Society, and collected the reports of auxiliary societies, speeches by leading colonizationists and dispatches from the colony in Liberia. The longer he studied the society's meager achievements, the more important it seemed to tear off its mask of respectability. By April he had compiled an indictment that answered, and a month later *Thoughts on African Colonization: or An Impartial Exhibition of the Doctrines, Principles and Purposes of the American Colonization Society* was ready for the press. He was doubtful at first of his success in discrediting the society and claimed only that his pamphlet was "calculated to make a salutary impression."[22] When no effective rebuttal from the colonizationists appeared, however, he dropped his modest pose and announced that it behooved every lover of truth and friend of humanity to read it carefully. His boast contained a measure of truth, for despite its severe limitations *Thoughts* stands as a major contribution to the theory of racial democracy which, a century after Appomattox, is still striving for recognition.

By the time he left Baltimore for Boston he had concluded that the greatest obstacle to emancipation was the complacency of Northerners who would not accept his principles. Gradually the evil of slavery became identified in his mind with the lack of Christian ideals. The real enemy, he now

saw, was not the slaveholder, culpable as he was, but the
great mass of indifferent people all over the country. Just as
the twentieth-century Communist discovers his chief enemy in
the middle-class liberal, so Garrison singled out as his victim
the well-meaning but morally uncommitted citizen who made
up the ranks of the American Colonization Society. Not content with presenting his case for immediate emancipation, he
was driven to destroy the society and incriminate its members.

The significance of his vendetta against colonization lay in
the new perspectives it furnished him. It was easy enough to
label his enemies "hard-hearted incorrigible sinners" and "piti-
ful, pale-faced usurpers," but what was his alternative to a
program he denounced as inadequate in design and injurious
in its operation? He needed to define his plan for freeing the
slave with a precision he had not yet shown. Since the founding of the American Colonization Society in 1817 its most
effective critic had been the Northern free Negro. Garrison's
first contact with this body of opinion came in Baltimore,
where he met Lundy's friend William Watkins, whose trenchant criticism of colonization principles he published in the
Genius. Why, asked Watkins, should Negroes be forced to
leave their home for certain death in Africa? Why leave a
land of gospel light for one enshrouded in pagan gloom?
These questions set Garrison thinking.

At this time, too, Garrison first read Walker's *Appeal,* one
section of which was devoted to "Our Wretchedness in Consequence of the Colonizing Plan." Walker leveled his sights
on the false friends of the Negro who, he said, did not care
"a pinch of snuff" either for Africa or the slave. To them he
said simply, "We must and shall be free, I say, in spite of
you." Reading Walker's impassioned pages or listening to the
heated discussion of Watkins and Lundy's other colored
friends, Garrison wondered how the colonizationists had

duped Americans into believing the Negro unfit for civilized life. That there were thousands of them huddled into slums in Northern cities and living in crime and squalor he would not deny. Yet once given education and proper Christian training might not the whole race rise to the level of Watkins and Walker or even — secretly he believed it possible — to that of white Americans? Then he realized that the answer hinged on the fate of the American Colonization Society.

In its first crucial year the *Liberator* pressed the attack on colonization to the limits of sensationalism. An editorial for April 23, 1831, announced the editor's decision to unmask the society as a group of Negro-haters "who have entered into this CONSPIRACY AGAINST HUMAN RIGHTS." Hard on the heels of this accusation came others: the Colonization Society was founded on "Persecution," "Falsehood," "Cowardice," and "Infidelity"; it conspired to strengthen slavery; it libeled the Negro race; it betrayed the American heritage of freedom.[23]

In June, 1831, he was invited to address the Free People of Color in Philadelphia, where he was the guest of Robert Purvis, the son-in-law of Negro leader James Forten. Talking with these colored families and visiting in their homes made him realize how much emancipation meant to them. They flattered him, sought his advice, and openly courted his approval. He, in his turn, lectured them endlessly, advising them to make Jesus their exemplar and refuge, and counseling them against hatred and violence. He clearly enjoyed playing their father confessor, and there was a good deal of spurious humility in his posture. He could hardly meet these Negroes on their own terms without betraying a habitual sense of superiority, but he could learn to respect if not to understand them. Even then he was driven to ritualize his initiation by a formal act of contrition. "I never rise to address a colored audience," he told them, "without feeling ashamed of my own color; ashamed at being identified with a race of men who have done you so much injustice. . . . To make atonement, in part, for this conduct, I have solemnly dedicated my health, and strength, and life, to your service."[24] Though he spoke of love, forgiveness and compassion, what emerged most clearly from this confession was his own overriding sense of guilt.

Back in Boston he prepared to dispose of colonization once and for all. He had to prevent the society from poisoning the minds of the people, for until Americans were willing to admit the Negro to an equality of rights there could be no Christian society. "They do not wish to admit them to an equality," he confessed to Henry Benson, "they tell us we must always be hostile to the free people of color, while they remain in this country. If this be so, then we had better burn our bibles, and our Declaration of Independence and candidly acknowledge ourselves to be incorrigible tyrants and heathens."[25] The only other course open to Christians lay in a holy war of extermination of prejudice, and this course he now determined to take.

Thoughts on African Colonization is a bulky pamphlet of two hundred and forty pages which opens with the familiar dispassionate announcement of the author's "unbiassed mind" and "lively sense of accountability to God."[26] So far, his reward for disinterested benevolence had consisted solely of persecution and abuse. "I have been thrust into prison, and amerced in a heavy fine! Epithets, huge and unseemly, have been showered upon me without mercy. . . . Assassinations have been threatened me in a multitude of anonymous letters. Private and public rewards to a very large amount . . . have been offered to any person who shall abduct or destroy me."[27] Of his supposed recusancy to the cause of colonization he says only that "whereas I was blind, now I see," and seeing, has decided to tell all.

The main section of the pamphlet containing the mass of damaging quotations against colonization is divided into ten headings, each of them compiled about a core of quotations designed to establish the truth of the allegation. To support his first claim that the society is pledged not to interfere with slavery he cites the second article of its constitution defining its purpose as "exclusively" colonization. To this he adds Henry Clay's periodical disclaimers of any intention to meddle with slave property. Then follow quotations from John Randolph, G. W. Custis, Francis Scott Key, quotations from a dozen annual reports of the society, quotations from colonization tracts, from auxiliary societies, memorials, and addresses — quotations *ad nauseam*. "Out of thine own mouth will I condemn thee," warns the frontispiece, and so it proves.

In his resolve to ruin the Colonization Society whatever the cost, Garrison did not scruple to use dishonest methods. His promise to discuss the society as a whole counted for nothing. Individual opinions of its members he treated as official declarations of policy; he held the society responsible for all the editorial views of the *African Repository*. But his most serious editorial transgression was the sin of omission, his unfair practice of quoting out of context. From a speech of Dr. E. B. Caldwell, one of the founders of the society, he took the following excerpt:

The more you improve the condition of these people, the more you cultivate their minds, the more *miserable* you make them in their present state. You give them a higher relish for those privileges *which they can never attain*, and turn what you intend for a blessing into a *curse*. No, if they must remain in their present situation, *keep them in the lowest state of ignorance and degrada-*

tion. The nearer you bring them to the condition of *brutes,* the better chance do you give them of possessing their apathy.[28]

Actually Caldwell had gone on to add: "Surely Americans ought to be the last people on earth to advocate such slavish doctrines — to cry peace and contentment to those who are deprived of the blessings of civil liberty." This qualification Garrison found it convenient to omit. There were other examples of quotations similarly doctored with italics, sentences truncated and meanings twisted. He distorted ideas because at bottom he did not really respect them. Concerned with the immediate impact of opinion and unable to follow other people's thoughts to their logical ends, he felt no misgivings about appropriating only what he needed at the moment, whether it was a paraphrase of a Biblical quotation or a fragment of reasoned argument. When colonizationists complained of this willful misrepresentation, he retorted that however much he altered the structure he had not changed the meaning — the devil's altar-rail needed not his polishing. Such specious arguments aside, it was true most of his quotations required no accommodation. Even without these fraudulent tactics the Colonization Society stood condemned.

The text of *Thoughts* shows every sign of having been hastily compiled from earlier editorials and speeches in the attempt to lend fervor to the exposition. Yet seldom does the forced eloquence rise above the commonplace. It is rather in its appeal to the spirit of religious orthodoxy that the tract attains its object in disclosing the revolutionary power latent in the evangelical formula. The argument rests on Garrison's assumption that sin, far from being solitary, springs from communal roots. Slavery is the sum of interlocking and mutually sustaining sinful acts and can be wiped out only by collective repentance. Just as the lone sinner is cured by regeneration, so a whole people can purify themselves under the convenant by refusing to sin any longer. Their reward is God's approval evidenced in a flourishing and holy community. "I appeal to those who have been redeemed from the bondage of sin by the precious blood of Christ, and with whom I hope to unite in a better world in ascribing glory, and honor, and praise to the Great Deliverer for ever. If I can succeed in gaining their attention, I feel sure of convincing their understandings and securing their support."[29] Regeneration, then abolition — the evangelical prescription for reform.

In closing their Bibles and ignoring God's command, he continued, Americans had forgotten that God made of one blood all nations to dwell on the face of the earth. For Garrison the words "one blood" expressed a biological fact as well as a spiritual truth. He believed that in a single creation God had made all races of men, who, however physically distinct, partook in common of the atoning blood of Christ. Christianity enjoined racial equality because God had placed his mark of infinite worth on all men. Some might argue that He had placed a special mark on the black man. "True: and he has also put a mark upon every man, woman and child, in the world; so that every one differs in appearance from another." To suppose therefore that races ought to be divided into self-enclosed communities each with its own exclusive culture was to misread the divine plan.

The difference between a black and a white skin is not greater than that between a white and a black one. In either case, the mark is distinctive; and the blacks may as reasonably expel the whites as the whites the blacks. To make such a separation we have no authority; to attempt it, would only end in disappointment; and, if it were carried into effect, those who are clamourous for the measure would be among the first cast out.[30]

The American Colonization Society, he went on, solemnly assured the people that Nature had played them falsely. Colored persons were born by mistake in this country; they should have been born in Africa. "There occur at least sixty thousand *mistakes* annually; while the Society has corrected only about two thousand in fourteen years! But — courage! men engaged in a laudable enterprise should never despair!"[31] What about the thousands of mulattoes, quadroons, octoroons? Was it really possible to define the precise shade of color which qualified a man for civilized life? If not, then Americans had better raise an army of whites to drive out *everyone* who could not produce vouchers that pure "English blood" flowed in their veins. He refused to grant that color was anything more than an incidental physiological difference like bone structure having no connection with a man's mental and moral proclivities. To be a thoroughgoing colonizationist one would have to be consistent. "I must be able to give a reason why all our tall citizens should not conspire to remove their more diminutive brethren, and all the corpulent to remove the lean and the lank, and all the strong remove the weak. . . . I cannot perceive that I am more excusable in desiring the banishment of my neighbor because his skin is darker than mine, than I should be in desiring his banishment because he is smaller or feebler than myself."

Nor were there any "impassable" natural barriers preventing racial intermarriage. Colonizationists argued that Nature forbade the lion to beget the lamb or the leopard the bear, but the "amalgamation" they so dreaded increased daily. The Southern planters had clearly shown that amalgamation was not only possible but eminently productive! Talk about the "barriers of Nature" when the land swarmed with living refutations of the statement. Miscegenation laws constituted a denial of our common humanity and a reproach to God. No man should be refused a share in the plenitude of creation which "presents to the eye every conceivable shape, and aspect, and color, in the gorgeous and multifarious productions of Nature." Like everything else in the universe the free mixture of races formed part of the divine plan.

Perhaps the gravest charge brought against the abolitionists is that of attempting to "white-wash" the Negro by making him like themselves. It is true that in his devotion to humanity Garrison forgot the Negroes as individual human beings, and that he wanted above all else to bring them to a state of grace. He believed that the nearer they approached the whites in their habits the better they were. He was continually searching for the signs of gentility and refinement which would prove them the equal of the whites, and when he thought he discerned such traits he rejoiced. "I wish you had been with me in Philadelphia," he wrote to Ebenezer Dole of his visit there in 1832, "to see what I saw, to hear what I heard, and to experience what I felt, in associating with many colored families. There are colored men and women, in that city, who have few superiors in refinement, in moral worth, and in all that makes the human character worthy of admiration and praise."[32] It is also true that his relationship with Negroes was always tempered by a sense of estrangement. For them he symbolized the humanitarianism of the white people, righteous but cold and impersonal, while in his eyes they appeared first and last as noble examples of an oppressed race. He admired but never really knew them or understood what it meant to be a Negro. They always seemed to him a social problem rather than simply people.

Still, if he thought only of "elevating" the race with the prayers and promises of a white man's religion, such was his prescription for all mankind. And if he continued to emphasize unduly the ability of the Negro to become like the white it was because few of his contemporaries were prepared to believe this was possible. The time when science would explode the myth of inherited racial characteristics lay far in the future. In 1832 Americans accepted the "depravity" and "corruption" of the colored people as established fact. What better way to prove equality, Garrison asked himself, than by making the Negro white? For the failure of perception and the habit of evading all genuine experience of the race his critics were right in condemning him. He never tried to understand people, black or white, but preferred to use them as counters in the grim business of reform. But at a time when it was generally agreed that the Negro race was inherently inferior Garrison's detachment — his ability to isolate people from the environmental forces that produce them — was an asset rather than a liability.

From the premise of Christian universalism *Thoughts* proceeded to a distinction between gradual and immediate emancipation. What was gradual emancipation — a gradual abstaining from cruelty and oppression? "Do colonizationists mean, that slave-dealers shall purchase or sell a few victims less this year than they did last? that slave-owners shall liberate one, two, or three out of every hundred slaves during the same period? that slave-drivers shall apply the lash to the scarred and bleeding backs of their victims somewhat less frequently?" *Immediate emancipation*, on the other hand, meant "simply declaring that slave-owners are bound to fulfill — now, without any reluctance or delay — the golden rule, namely, to do as they would be done by."[33] It did not mean that all slaves should immediately be given the right to vote or hold office or even be free from "the benevolent restraints of guardianship." Immediate emancipationists demanded only that the Negro be given the right to work as a free laborer along with education and religious instruction. Freedom would increase the value of Negro labor and augment the wealth of the South. The new freedmen would make good citizens: "they will not be idle, but avariciously industrious; they will not rush through the country firing dwellings and murdering inhabitants; for freedom is all they ask."[34]

The publication of *Thoughts* plunged the *Liberator* into temporary financial trouble, and soon Garrison was complaining that he must let the paper "die" or make public his embarrassment.[35] Happily, the tract began to sell. Arthur Tappan ordered one hundred copies for distribution among his friends. Copies found their way into the libraries at Lane Seminary and Western Reserve. Theodore Weld, a convert to abolition and a rising figure in Western anti-slavery circles, discussed Garrison's arguments with his followers. Within nine months it had sold 2750 copies — by anti-slavery standards an unprecedented number. Garrison was naturally pleased with his success and announced as early as June that "conversions from colonization are rapidly multiplying in every quarter."[36] The Colonization Society, after expressing the charitable hope that Garrison would modify his views, chose to ignore the work. Agents of the society made a few feeble attempts to defend colonization in open debate with the Garrisonians, only to be routed. Skirmishes between the two camps continued for a decade, but for all practical purposes the appearance of *Thoughts* ended the usefulness of the society. "The roads of Colonization and Abolition lead in different directions, but they do not cross each other," Henry Clay once said. In 1832, standing at the crossroads of reform, Northern opponents of slavery read Garrison's signpost and chose the road that led to emancipation.

8

Triumph and Doubt in 1833

IN APRIL, 1833, Garrison sailed for England on his first anti-slavery mission. In New York on the eve of his departure he discovered a "murderous design" to kidnap and deliver him to the authorities in Georgia, and he rushed off to Philadelphia to board the Liverpool packet before the conspirators realized their mistake. But he was too late — the ship had sailed and there was nothing to do but return secretly to New York and baffle the vigilance of his enemies by hiding aboard the pilot boat until it was far down the harbor. "My friends are full of apprehension and disquietude," he wrote to one of his female admirers, "but I *cannot* know fear. I feel that it is impossible for danger to awe me. I tremble at nothing but my own delinquencies, as one who is bound to be perfect even as my heavenly Father is perfect."[1]

As usual he had refurbished the facts to suit his purpose. His pursuers were not young bloods from Georgia intent on carrying him off, but the sheriff of Windham County, Connecticut, who had tried to serve him with five separate writs for his part in helping Prudence Crandall, the Quaker schoolmistress, establish a school for colored girls. The unhappy sheriff had caught sight of Garrison a few minutes after he left by stage for New York and had chased the coach for a few miles before giving up in disgust. Garrison was sure that the escapade was part of a plot to thwart his mission. "No doubt the Colonization party will resort to some base measures to prevent, if possible, my departure for England,"[2] he warned Knapp and instructed him to print the story in the *Liberator*. The more he considered the incident, the larger it loomed; and by the time he reached New York it had acquired the dimensions of a gigantic conspiracy. He enjoyed intrigue, and besides, cloak-and-dagger tales made good copy.

He was going to England as an agent of the New England Society to raise funds for a manual labor school for Negroes. The manual labor idea was an important part of the New England Society's program. The scheme originated in Switzerland and had been tried in several European countries before the Reverend George W. Gale brought it to the Oneida Institute in western New York. The plan provided that each student pay part of his expenses by working on the school farm, thereby reducing the costs of education and ensuring the health of the student, which, so the theory went, might be endangered by long hours of study. Such institutions, it was hoped, would provide rural havens of simplicity where young men could escape the wiles and snares of sophisticated society. Most of the theological schools in the country had already adopted a modified version of voluntary manual labor, but at Oneida work was compulsory. The Board of Managers of the New England Society were so impressed with the favorable reports from Oneida that they decided to combine the idea with Negro education in New England. In March, 1833, they appointed Garrison an agent to "proceed to England as soon as the necessary arrangements can be made, for the purpose of procuring funds to aid in the establishment of the proposed MANUAL LABOR SCHOOL FOR COLORED YOUTH."[3] Since the treasury lacked funds for the trip, Garrison spent six weeks making a series of farewell appearances in Boston, Providence, New

York, and Philadelphia dunning his colored friends. By April
he had nearly six hundred dollars, enough for traveling expenses, and on the first of May he embarked for Liverpool.

His own motives for undertaking the trip he kept to himself. He knew that Elliot Cresson, the agent of the Colonization Society, was conducting a fund-raising tour of the British
Isles. Using his reputation as the fearless editor of the *Liberator* and author of *Thoughts on African Colonization*, he
meant to unmask Cresson and his organization and establish
himself as the undisputed leader of American anti-slavery.
He also knew that Charles Stuart, a member of Tappan's
New York circle and an opponent of the Colonization Society, was already in England denouncing Cresson wherever
he went. Stuart was a retired British army captain who once
had been court-martialed for refusing to fire on a group of
East Indian natives. A bachelor with an effusive manner and
eccentric habits, he was also a spirited polemicist who would
have no difficulty in disposing of Cresson. Finally, Garrison
knew that the English abolitionists, already within sight of
their goal, needed no enlightenment on the American Colonization Society. Only a year ago Thomas Buxton had written
to tell him that it was wholly unnecessary for him "to set me,
or any of the true Anti-Slavery Party in this Country on our
guard against the delusive professions of the Colonization
Society or its Agent."[4] Still, if his newly acquired prestige
was to be of any help to him, he must make the pilgrimage to
London and personally receive the blessing of the English
anti-slavery veterans. Thus from the beginning his mission
took on the aspects of a publicity campaign to which the
intrigues surrounding his departure were a fitting prologue.

After a short passage of three weeks, most of which he
spent miserably seasick in his cabin, he stepped down the
gangplank at Liverpool wearied in "flesh and spirit." He did

not see the nearby slums that so appalled Melville, but reported that the city seemed "bustling, prosperous, and great" in its "commercial aspect." He rested a few days at Dingle Bank, James Cropper's country house, before continuing to London. He already spoke of Cropper as his "excellent friend," though he had yet to meet him, his host having proceeded to London before his arrival. Cropper more than fulfilled his description when Garrison joined him in London, for he more than anyone else was responsible for his American friend's remarkable success. Cropper was one of the group of wealthy Quaker merchants who supplied the cause of West Indian emancipation with new energy. Prudent and grave, given to weighty pronouncements but a shrewd judge of men, he knew everyone of consequence in the anti-slavery movement and himself was much admired by his colleagues.

On his arrival in London on May 27, Garrison discovered that almost every important English abolitionist had gathered in the offices of the society and the nearby Guildhall Coffee House to watch the passage of the West India Emancipation Bill through Parliament. Cropper took him to breakfast at the Coffee House and, much to Garrison's delight, introduced him as the distinguished agent of the New England Anti-Slavery Society. Realizing how timely his arrival was, he privately gave thanks to Providence for ordering events for him "in a manner so highly auspicious." Now came a round of visits to anti-slavery notables, beginning with a breakfast with Buxton. Presented to the great Parliamentary leader, he was not a little disconcerted when, instead of stepping forward to shake his hand, Buxton sat staring at him doubtfully. Finally, after a full minute of embarrassing silence, he asked, "Have I the pleasure of addressing Mr. Garrison, of Boston, in the United States?" Upon Garrison's assurance that such indeed was the case, Buxton again paused and then said in evident bewilderment, "Why, my dear sir, I thought you were a black man! And I have consequently invited this company of ladies and gentlemen to be present to welcome Mr. Garrison, the black advocate of emancipation from the United States of America." Whatever his private feelings, Garrison promptly replied that Buxton's was the only compliment he cared to remember.[5]

At Bath he spent five hours with the failing Wilberforce blissfully unaware of the old man's feeble condition. "I endeavored to communicate as briefly and clearly as possible, all the prominent facts relating to our great controversy," he reported to the Board of Managers. "I impressed upon his mind, tenderly and solemnly, the importance of his bearing public testimony against the American Colonization Society."[6] Wilberforce denied that he had ever considered colonization the sole remedy for American slavery, but agreed with his dogmatic young visitor that he should officially withdraw his support.

Thomas Clarkson, doddering and now almost totally blind, proved less tractable than his old friend and was not to be won over by the importunings of his uninvited guest. He was a good friend of Cresson's and knew many of the leading colonizationists in the United States well. Although he too believed that the society was only a first step toward emancipation, he was determined not to become involved in what seemed to him a foolish controversy. After four hours of fruitless argument in which Garrison "spared no pains to correct the erroneous views which he had formed," he left, lamenting that Clarkson should still feel it to be his duty to occupy neutral ground.[7]

On his return to London, Garrison found awaiting him a protest signed by Wilberforce and ten other English veterans denouncing the claims of the Colonization Society as "wholly

groundless." The protest, probably the work of Cropper and
Charles Stuart, came as a welcome surprise. Lest his American critics accuse him of intentional malice, he hastened to
disclaim all responsibility for the declaration. "In getting up
this protest," he explained to the New England Society on
his return, "I had no agency whatever. It was altogether unexpected by me."[8] The eleven signatures nevertheless represented a major achievement — the primary purpose of the
mission had been fulfilled. Now he had only to show himself
to the British public as the lion of American abolitionism by
devouring the Colonization Society's sacrificial lamb, Elliot
Cresson.

Upon reaching London in May he had written a letter to
Cresson accusing him of bilking the English public and challenging him to a public debate. Cresson naturally refused to
participate in such unseemly proceedings, whereupon Garrison sent an open letter to *The Times* of London charging
him with cowardice. In July, Charles Stuart, who had been
dogging Cresson's footsteps ever since his arrival, reported
that a meeting was being planned to organize a British
Colonization Society. Would Garrison attend and testify
against Cresson? Garrison would do more — he would contact the Duke of Sussex, Cresson's patron, and try to dissuade
him from supporting the project. Garrison failed to convince
the duke, but Stuart succeeded in collecting a group of
abolitionists including an ardent young agitator named
George Thompson to attend the colonization meeting and,
if possible, disrupt it. The Hanover Square meeting of the
English colonizationists barely escaped the fate which Garrison had prepared for it. Of the one hundred and twenty
present nearly one half were abolitionists rounded up by
Cropper, Stuart, and Thompson. The Duke of Sussex, who

presided, was bombarded with hostile questions. Finally, over
the fierce protests of the abolitionists the majority voted to
organize an English colonization society. Now there was
only one recourse left to the anti-slavery party — a meeting
of their own "as an offset," as Garrison put it, at which he
should be given free voice.

The Exeter Hall meeting on Saturday morning, July 13,
proved a resounding success. Garrison spoke for over two
hours. In his speech he adhered closely to his plan for posing
as the appointed agent of American anti-slavery reformers. "I
cherish as strong a love for the land of my nativity as any
man living. . . ." he told his audience. "But I have some
solemn accusations to bring against her." America was guilty
of "insulting the majesty of Heaven" by giving an open, deliberate and base denial to her boasted Declaration. She had
legalized licentiousness, fraud, cruelty and murder. In the
course of his diatribe he referred to the Constitution, a subject to which he returned a few days later in an article for
the *London Patriot* in an attempt to show that he had broken
all national ties.

I know [he wrote] that there is much declamation about the
sacredness of the compact which was formed between the free
and the slave States in the adoption of the National Constitution.
A sacred compact, forsooth! I pronounce it the most bloody and
Heaven-daring arrangement ever made by men for the continuance and protection of the most atrocious villainy ever exhibited
on earth. Yes, I recognize the compact, but with feelings of shame
and indignation; and it will be held in everlasting infamy by the
friends of humanity and justice throughout the world. Who or
what were the framers of the American government that they
should dare confirm and authorize such high-handed villainy —
such a flagrant robbery of the inalienable rights of man — such a
glaring violation of all the precepts and injunctions of the gospel

— such a savage war upon a sixth part of the whole population? It was not valid then — it is not valid now.[9]

Garrison's second object, to win acceptance as the official representative of American abolitionists, required a bit more ingenuity. In fact, he had approached Arthur Tappan and his friends for funds only to be refused. Tappan could not see that the British needed indoctrination in their own principles, and thought that any appeal for funds was premature. He even suspected that the real purpose of Garrison's mission was to inflate his own reputation, a shrewd guess as the Exeter Hall speech showed. "I have crossed the Atlantic on an errand of mercy," Garrison announced, "to plead for perishing millions and to discharge, in behalf of the abolitionists of the United States, a high moral obligation which is due the British public." He would not bore them with a "lachrymal display" of his losses and crosses in the cause, but it was well known in America that he had stood, "almost single-handed for a series of years, against and in the midst of a nation of oppressors." If anyone could rightfully claim the sympathy of the English reformers, it was a man who had endured the wrath of his country for righteousness' sake.

Near the end of his marathon performance he was interrupted by the arrival of the great Irish orator Daniel O'Connell, who had come to pay his respects. When he had finished, O'Connell strode to the platform and "threw off a speech as he threw off his coat," denouncing the Colonization Society and praising the wisdom of the New England Anti-Slavery Society in sending such an able advocate to English shores. Not since he printed the first number of the *Liberator* had Garrison been so well pleased with a day's work.

One final appearance and he could return home. On July 29, three days after the second reading of the West India

Emancipation Bill, Wilberforce died. In the endless funeral train to Westminster Abbey, behind princes of the blood, prelates of the Church, members of Parliament walked the grave bespectacled American with eyes piously lowered as if in a solemn recessional after the initiatory rites. When it came time to embark, he found he lacked the money for the return passage. Rather than approach Cropper and his friends, he borrowed two hundred dollars from Nathaniel Paul, a Negro minister and protégé of Tappan who was also collecting funds for a manual labor school. He promised to repay the loan to Tappan just as soon as he was able, but secretly he wondered how soon that would be. On August 18 he boarded the packet *Hannibal* and arrived in New York five weeks later.

Sitting in his cabin and reflecting on the summer's events, he had reason to be satisfied. Financially the trip had proved a failure, but he brought back with him the valuable protest, testimonials from Cropper and Thompson, and even a personal tribute from Zachary Macaulay thanking him for his "eminent services . . . rendered to the cause of humanity."[10] He had directed the rout of the colonization forces, paid a last tribute to the great Wilberforce, and made innumerable new friends. Most important, he returned with the recognition and good will he needed to build an American antislavery movement.

He stepped off the boat in New York to find the stage set for his entrance. While he was basking in the limelight of English flattery, the American reformers under the direction of Arthur Tappan were writing the script and casting the principals for the anti-slavery drama which played the American stage for the next thirty years. American abolitionism from its inception was the product of two distinct groups, one in New England under Garrison, the other in New York and the Ohio Valley under transplanted New Englanders like Theodore Weld, Beriah Green, Elizur Wright and Henry Stanton. As a patron of American reform with connections in both the East and the West, Arthur Tappan was a pivotal figure in the formation of a national anti-slavery society. His New York Committee served as a clearinghouse for abolition- ist projects, distributed information, and functioned as a di- rectory for reformers everywhere. It was Tappan's great achievement in the year 1833 to join together the Eastern and Western branches of the anti-slavery movement into a single national organ, an achievement which no amount of Garrisonian disparagement could ever undo.

Tappan's interest in the West dated from the autumn of 1829 and the appearance in New York City of the great revivalist Charles Grandison Finney. If Lyman Beecher served as the archpriest of the eastern half of the Benevolent Em- pire, the New West belonged to Finney. Just as Beecher's version of "immediate repentance" provided the theological underpinnings for Garrisonism, so Finney's Arminian doc- trine of the "new heart," at once simpler and bolder than Beecher's, supplied the rationale for Western anti-slavery.[11]

Tappan's lieutenant and the leader of the Western anti- slavery movement was a convert of Finney's, Theodore Weld, an unkempt, sad-eyed evangelical whose quiet intensity and natural shrewdness brought him quickly to the front of the movement. Modest and circumspect as he seemed, Weld was a natural leader of men, an astute judge of character, and an efficient organizer — all the things that Garrison was not. He had been lecturing on the temperance circuit when the Tap- pans, struck by his promotional talents and forceful presence, decided to have the sole use of so brilliant a lecturer and gave him the job of raising funds and selecting the site for a great theological seminary in the West based on the manual labor plan. In the fall of 1831, while Garrison was busy sending copies of the *Liberator* into the Ohio Valley, Weld set out on a tour of the West and South, addressing legislatures, colleges, churches and philanthropists on the subject of manual labor. His campaign took him as far south as Huntsville, Alabama, where he met James G. Birney, an earnest young country lawyer whose austere Presbyterian conscience had convinced him of the wrongfulness of slavery. Just as Garrison had first turned hopefully to the American Colonization Society for an answer to the problem, so Birney and Weld studied the society's program and weighed the justice of returning the Negro to Africa. Though Weld could not doubt the sinfulness of slavery, as yet he knew little about it, and Birney's searching questions and Scriptural arguments set him thinking. His effect on the Alabama lawyer was no less pronounced: when Weld started north after nearly a month in Huntsville, Birney abandoned a flourishing legal practice to become an agent of the American Colonization Society.

From now on Weld, like Garrison before him, occupied himself almost exclusively with the study of American slavery. The turning point in his career came with his visit to the wilderness campus of Western Reserve College in Hudson, Ohio, late in November, 1832. Here he met Elizur Wright and Beriah Green, two faculty members who had been converted to abolition by Garrison's *Thoughts*. "You will recollect," Wright admitted to Garrison soon after his talks with Weld, "that in a letter some time ago, I expressed some doubts with regard to the correctness of your views in respect to the African colony. Your 'Thoughts on African Colonization' have dispelled these doubts. I find that I was misinformed, as doubtless thousands are, in regard to your opinions."[12] Using Garrison's moral arguments, Wright and Green converted Weld to immediate emancipation and convinced him that "the very first business is to shove off the lubberly Colonization Society which is, at the very best, a superimposed dead weight."[13] Such was Garrison's message as the faculty at Western Reserve interpreted it. "The question now is, what shall be done?" Wright wrote to Weld in December. "We would put one hundred copies of the *Liberator* into as many towns on the Reserve, if we knew where to find the means." They planned to form a local anti-slavery society, he told Weld, but what was needed was a national organization along the lines of the other benevolent societies. "What would benevolent men in N. York think of a convention on this subject, about the time of the anniversaries next spring?"[14]

As he traveled east to New York City in January, 1833, Weld was pondering Wright's suggestion when he received a letter from Garrison inviting him to Boston to address the New England Society on the subject of manual labor. Weld refused, pleading prior engagements in New York City. "Besides, Sir," he went on, "I am ignorant of the history, specific plans, modes of operation, present position and ultimate aims of the N.E. Anti-Slavery Society. Residing in the interior of the state of New York, I have been quite out of range of its publications, have never seen any of them or indeed *any* expose of its operations, and all the definite knowledge of its plans and principles which I possess has been thro the perversions and distortions of its avowed opposers." Yet he could see by the *"expressive name"* of Garrison's organization that its sentiments agreed with his — that

Nothing but crime can forfeit liberty. That no condition of birth, no shade of color, no mere misfortune of circumstance, can annul that birth-right charter, which God has bequeathed to every being upon whom he has stamped his own image, by making him a *free moral agent,* and that he who robs his fellow-man of this tramples upon right, subverts justice, outrages humanity, unsettles the foundations of human safety and sacrilegiously assumes the prerogatives of God; and further, that he who retains by force, and refuses to surrender that which was originally obtained by violence or fraud, is joint partner in the original sin, becomes its apologist and makes it the business of every moment to perpetuate it afresh, however he may lull his conscience by the vain pleas of expediency or necessity.[15]

Reading Weld's letter, the very phrases of which were familiar, Garrison recognized his own arguments from the pen of a man who had never even heard of him. The *Liberator* had done its work well on the Western Reserve.

Garrison walked down the gangplank in New York to find the scene prepared for his arrival. In the spring of 1833, just as he had sailed for England, Arthur Tappan set his antislavery plans in motion. Elizur Wright came to New York to serve as secretary to the New York Committee, and Tappan dispatched him to Boston to scout out Garrison's society. In Boston, Wright met his old Yale classmate Amos Phelps, who gave him news of Garrison's successes in England. Wright found that New York lagged behind Boston and told the Tappan brothers so. As summer drew on and the New Yorkers waited for reports on the West India Bill, they accelerated their program of agitation by distributing copies of Garrison's *Thoughts* and launching the *Emancipator.* Then, hearing the news of the victory in Parliament, they decided to call a meeting of "The Friends of Immediate Abolition in the United States" on October 2 in Clinton Hall. On the day of the meeting posters were tacked up all over the city:

NOTICE

TO ALL PERSONS FROM THE SOUTH

All persons interested in the subject of a meeting
called by J. Leavitt, W. Green, Jr., W. Goodell,
J. Rankin, Lewis Tappan, at Clinton Hall, this
evening at 7 o'clock, are requested to attend at
the same hour and place.

MANY SOUTHERNERS

N.B. All Citizens who may feel disposed to manifest the *true* feeling of the State on this subject,
are requested to attend.

That same evening a mob of some fifteen hundred New
Yorkers stood in front of Clinton Hall yelling for the blood
of Arthur Tappan and William Lloyd Garrison. In their
midst stood Garrison himself, who had come to help organize the New York Anti-Slavery Society and was now wandering among them unrecognized.

Although Garrison was in no way responsible for the
Clinton Hall demonstration, a rumor had circulated that he
was back in the city and would attend the meeting. His
Exeter Hall address had jarred the nerves of patriotic New
York journalists, one of whom demanded that the "many-
headed Hydra" be "nipped in the bud." "He comes in the
flush of triumph," complained another, "and with the flatteries
still on his ear of those who wish *not* well to your country."[16]
Promptly at seven o'clock on Wednesday, October 2, he arrived at Clinton Hall only to find it locked and surrounded
by an angry crowd. Learning of the proposed demonstration,
the trustees had hastily withdrawn their permission to hold
the meeting there, whereupon Tappan and his friends adjourned to the Chatham Street Chapel uptown. Garrison, un-

aware of the change in plans and afraid that he might be recognized any moment by the mob shouting his name, turned on his heel and left.

Meanwhile the mob moved on to Tammany Hall for a meeting of their own. On the platform in the front of the dusty hall sat two of the city's well-known newspapermen, Colonel Webb and young James Gordon Bennett, who had brought along with them the Portland Yankee John Neal, Garrison's old nemesis. All three were hostile to the abolitionists and not averse to stirring up a mob if they could thereby upset Arthur Tappan's plans. Under the mistaken impression that Garrison was the real instigator of the meeting at Clinton Hall and was now somewhere in the audience, Neal stepped to the edge of the platform and demanded that he come forward and defend his views. Hearing no response, he plunged into a denunciation of anti-slavery. Suddenly word came that Tappan and his friends could be found in the Chatham Street Chapel, and with a roar the crowd poured out of Tammany headed for Chatham Street. There they found the huge iron gates to the chapel locked. Inside, the abolitionists were just completing the order of business. While the mob outside debated the best way of forcing their way in, the abolitionists hurriedly appointed a couple of committees, adjourned *sine die* and fled by the rear door just as a horde of rioters swarmed in the front entrance. Once in the chapel they held a mock meeting presided over by a frightened Negro whom they had collared on the way and dubbed "Arthur Tappan," and after an hour's frolic they dispersed.

Not until the next morning did Garrison learn he had been a part of the proceedings, whereupon he quickly slipped into the role of the coolheaded knight-errant who stood bravely by while a hysterical mob shouted for his head. Back in Boston he told his readers of his reception.

As soon as I landed, I turned the city of New York upside down. Five thousand people turned out to see me tarred and feathered, but were disappointed. As to the menaces and transactions of the New York mob, I regard them with mingled emotions of pity and contempt. I was an eye-witness of that mob, from the hour of its assembling at Clinton Hall to its final assault upon the Chatham Street Chapel — standing by it, undisguisedly, as calm in my feelings as if those who were seeking my life were my warmest supporters. . . . For myself, I am ready to brave any danger, even unto death.[17]

It was no wonder, he went on, that New York raged at his triumph — "the secret of their malice lies in the triumphant success of my mission. Had I failed to vanquish the agent of the American Colonization Society, or to open the eyes of the British philanthropists to its naked deformity, there would have been no excitement on my return."[18] Frustrated in their attempt to discredit him in England, the colonizationists resorted to violence at home: the Clinton Hall mob had been collected for the sole purpose of destroying William Lloyd Garrison.

Following his providential escape from the clutches of the colonizationists, he was more determined than ever to srtike for a national society while his reputation still glowed. The *Liberator* was bankrupt and he owed Arthur Tappan the two hundred dollars he had borrowed from Nathaniel Paul. If ever he needed organized support outside of Boston it was now. "I am more and more impressed with the importance of 'working whilst the day lasts,'" he wrote early in November. "If 'we all do fade as a leaf,' — if we are 'as the sparks that fly upwards' — if the billows of time are swiftly removing the sandy foundations of our life — what we intend to do for the captive, and for our country, and for the subjugation of a hostile world, must be done quickly."[19] In short, it was time to cash in on his reputation before it was too late.

The New York Committee was of a different mind, for the Clinton Hall affair indicated to them the need for moderation. Winter was nearly upon them and travel from the West would be expensive and hazardous. Better wait until spring when the delegates to the annual meetings of the benevolent societies would be congregating in New York. Then there would be a possibility of calling a real convention. Garrison refused to listen to these arguments and insisted that the call go forth at once. Postponing the meeting, he fumed, meant capitulating to the mob. Against their better judgment the committee gave way before his hectoring and drew up a circular inviting all the friends of abolition to a convention to be held in Philadelphia on December 4. They explained their change of plans by citing the urgency of the cause, which "must be injured by unnecessary delay" because "the public expectation is already excited. . . . We have before us numerous examples of similar organizations, which, though feeble and obscure, and condemned by public opinion in the outset, have speedily risen to great influence, and have been the means, under God, of immense benefit to the human race."[20] The reasoning sounded suspiciously Garrisonian. Privately Wright confided to Weld his own doubts as to the practicality of their decision, but admitted that "the most cool and collected friends of the cause here felt this to be a *necessity*, after a full view of the case."[21] Garrison had won his point.

His New England delegation assembled at New York's City Hotel on the first day of December and, accompanied by Tappan's deputies, proceeded to Philadelphia, where they joined Beriah Green and his small contingent from Ohio and a sizable deputation of Pennsylvania Quakers. At an informal meeting at the home of Evan Lewis on the eve of the con-

vention the delegates attempted to find a wealthy Phila-
delphian to preside over the meetings. Both Robert Vaux,
Cresson's friend, and another prominent citizen declined the
offer, at which point the laconic Beriah Green announced
that if there was not enough presidential timber among themselves, they would have to get along without such a figure
"or go home and stay there until we have grown up to be
men." Taking Green at his word, the delegates elected him
to preside over the convention which assembled the next
morning at Adelphi Hall of Fifth Street.

Garrison's spirit dominated the members of the convention,
but he himself did not. While they admired his dedication
and perseverance, the delegates were in no mood to be stam-
peded into hasty decisions. Many of them agreed with Lewis
Tappan that Garrison's name ought not to be "inserted prominently" lest it "keep away many professed friends of abolition."[22] Still, that name might be worth a good deal when it
came time to appeal to the English for help. Even if he was
notorious and overly concerned with his good name, he
stood for the Christian zeal they intended to foster. Thus he
found himself cast in a double role as the guiding spirit and
the wandering Jew of American abolition, constantly extolled but at the same time carefully prevented from leading
the convention into the wilderness of Scriptural quotation.

On the first day a committee was elected to draw up a constitution. He was excused from this task and placed instead
on a larger and less important committee heavily weighted
with moderates like Whittier, May, Jocelyn, and Green,
which was charged with composing a Declaration of Sentiments. This group promptly delegated the work to a sub-
committee consisting of May, Whittier, and Garrison, in the
hope that May's good sense and Whittier's Quaker humility
might blunt the shafts of Garrison's prose. Whittier and May

left him in the evening of the first day sitting at a table in his room drafting the document and returned the next morning to find him still bent over the manuscript. As they had feared, his Magna Carta contained a full-page diatribe on colonization which, if anything, outstripped his earlier exercises in invective. Fortunately, the full committee spent three hours pruning the declaration of its excrescences and the members insisted on excising the passage on colonization. Garrison fought hard to save it, arguing that colonization and slavery stood or fell together, and only reluctantly accepted the majority opinion. "All right, brethren," he finally agreed after all his objections had been disregarded, "it is your report, not mine."[23]

The Declaration of Sentiments of the American Anti-Slavery Society opens with a pointed reference to the meeting of the signers of the Declaration of Independence in the same city fifty-seven years before. "We have met together for the achievement of an enterprise without which that of our fathers is incomplete; and which, for its magnitude, solemnity, and probable results upon the destiny of the world, as far transcends theirs as moral truth does physical force." In view of its promises of liberty and equality the United States is the guiltiest nation on the face of the earth:

It is bound to repent instantly, to undo the heavy burdens, and to let the oppressed go free. . . . The right to enjoy liberty is inalienable. To invade it is to usurp the prerogative of Jehovah. Every man has a right to his own body — to the products of his own labor — to the protection of law — and to the common advantages of society. . . .

That all those laws which are now in force, admitting the right of slavery, are therefore before God, utterly null and void; being an audacious usurpation of the Divine prerogative, a daring infringement on the law of nature, a base overthrow of the very

foundations of the social compact, a complete extinction of all
the relations, endearments and obligations of mankind, and a
presumptuous transgression of all the holy commandments; and
that therefore they ought instantly to be abrogated.

Fully and unanimously recognizing the sovereignty of each
state, but maintaining the right of Congress to regulate slavery in the territories under its jurisdiction, the delegates
pledged themselves to rely on moral suasion and "spare no
exertions nor means to bring the whole nation to speedy
repentance."

The declaration reached the floor of the convention on
December 5. Thomas Shipley, the Quaker delegate from
Philadelphia, objected to the indiscriminate use of the word
"man-stealer" and suggested the qualifying phrase "according to scripture," which was accepted despite Garrison's
protest that the change appeared to make liberty dependent
on Biblical sanction. Lucretia Mott, who attended all the
sessions, offered a few verbal changes, but except for the
colonization branch which had already been lopped off in
committee, the declaration was accepted almost as it was
written. With a smile of obvious pleasure Garrison watched
as each delegate stepped gravely forward to sign his name.

Satisfying too was Lewis Tappan's eulogy placing him "in
the forefront of our ranks. . . . He has told the whole truth,
and put hypocrites and doughfaces to open shame. . . . He
has put the anti-slavery movement forward a quarter of a
century." Tappan could not deny his young friend's many
"imprudences," but it was clear, he said, that God had raised
just such a zealot to lead them. "Let each member present
feel solemnly bound to vindicate the character of Mr. Garrison," he concluded, scarcely realizing the awesomeness of
such a task. Dr. Abraham Cox then begged leave to read

Whittier's tribute, "W.L.G.," and sonorously intoned the six stanzas which began:

> Champion of those who groan beneath
>   Oppression's iron hand:
> In view of penury, hate, and death
>   I see thee fearless stand,
> Still bearing up thy lofty brow
>   In the steadfast strength of truth,
> In manhood sealing well the vow
>   And promise of thy youth.

The crown of laurels was not without its thorns. As the election of officers approached, the delegates were perplexed to know just what honor to distribute to their hero. The committee in charge of drawing up the constitution agreed that Elizur Wright should be the secretary of the society. The presidency obviously should go to Arthur Tappan, who, though unable to attend the meeting, was the man most responsible for its success. But what to do with Garrison? Would he accept a vice-presidency or a place on the Executive Committee — would he, in short, be willing to play second fiddle? The problem was solved temporarily when one of the delegates suggested that they create the office of secretary of foreign correspondence and ease Garrison into it. Accordingly, he was given the special post, which he held for six weeks before resigning in a huff after being told that all correspondence should be first submitted to the Executive Committee. His resignation gave the new society the answer to their question — Garrison would play second fiddle to no one.

There was one final problem for him to solve before he returned to Boston, and this was the matter of repaying Tappan the two hundred dollars borrowed from Nathaniel Paul.

At the moment he hadn't a penny. To make matters worse, the *Liberator* was still saddled with a thousand dollars' worth of unsold anti-slavery tracts. Unless he received some help — and that soon — the *Liberator* would surely go under. He therefore went to the new Executive Committee with a proposition. The society should undertake to buy four hundred and forty dollars worth of pamphlets (a large proportion of them his *Thoughts*). This, he explained, was the very least he required to save the *Liberator*. But the committee pointed out that the society lacked the funds to purchase so much as a single tract. At this point Arthur Tappan saved the day by offering to advance Garrison the money out of his own pocket and to let the society owe him. Whereupon Garrison announced that it would not be necessary to raise the whole amount since he already owed Tappan two hundred dollars. Now, after paying him his two hundred and forty dollar balance, the society could owe the remaining two hundred to Tappan, who in turn could owe it to Paul, and he, Garrison, would no longer owe anybody anything. To his own satisfaction if not that of the Executive Committee, he had saved his paper, paid for his return passage, and cleared his skirts of debt.[24]

In Boston once again he sat down to cast up his accounts of the last twelve months. In many ways it had been a gratifying year — his triumph in England, the organization of a national society, and a growing number of followers. "Almost every day brings some intelligence highly favorable to our cause," he wrote.[25] Beacon fires of liberty were beginning to burn all over the country. There was only one cause for dissatisfaction — despite the accolades heaped on him in Philadelphia, the American abolitionists had declined to accept his leadership. He had won their praises but not their support; a national society did not admit of the personal control he exercised over the New England Society. At Philadelphia he had met men every bit as devoted as he was, tough-minded and outspoken reformers who were not to be intimidated by belligerence however righteous. They wanted what Elizur Wright called "the right kind of fire," and they were prepared to build it themselves. He told his Boston partisans that "by dint of some industry and much persuasion, I succeeded in inducing the abolitionists in New York to join our little band in Boston in calling a national convention," but in his heart he knew that this was not so.[26] Already anti-slavery was growing faster than he had anticipated. To keep from being swallowed up in the national movement he must assert his control over his own followers.

With this object in mind he introduced a resolution at the monthly meeting of the New England Society in February, 1834, requesting the Board of Managers to call a convention of delegates from all the local groups in New England. "Our grand aim should now be to effect a complete concentration of all the anti-slavery strength we can muster that division may not weaken our efforts and that we may all see eye to eye."[27] His purpose, he said, was not to make the auxiliary societies subservient to the New England Society, but "to devise ways and means for the promotion of our glorious cause." Just what these means were New England abolitionists were to learn in the course of the next four years as one by one he produced them for their approval — woman's rights, nonresistance, and Christian perfectionism. Having failed to capture the national society, he began gathering his forces for a second assault.

9

Mobs and Martyrs

In September, 1834, Garrison married Helen Eliza Benson of Brooklyn, Connecticut. His marriage, a singularly happy one, afforded the additional advantage of allying his own Boston followers with the anti-slavery forces in southern New England. Helen's father, old George Benson, had been an abolitionist ever since he helped found the Providence Anti-Slavery Society back in 1792. At the time of his daughter's marriage the eighty-two-year-old Benson was president of the New England Anti-Slavery Society and the patriarch of a large family known for its austere moral code. A member of the prosperous Providence firm of Brown, Benson and Ives, he had retired in 1796 after a heated quarrel with his partners and withdrawn to his Brooklyn farmhouse, where he spent the rest of his life directing projects for Christian reform. To the Benson farm came Benjamin Lundy and William Ladd, young John Whittier, Samuel May, and finally Garrison himself to ask Benson's advice and the help of his two sons, George, Jr., and Henry.

Twenty-three-year-old Helen, her father's favorite, was a plain girl with heavy features and placid expression, self-conscious, shy, quick, practical and shrewd. Her sensitivity and quiet humor, hidden beneath a self-effacing manner, quite escaped her husband, whose very real devotion did not increase his power of perception. Helen's was a selfless love, the antithesis of Fanny's possessive worship of her son. Garrison still clung to the memory of his mother but married her opposite.

Helen first met Garrison on the eve of his departure for England when he spoke one evening at the African Church in Providence. Her brother George, an ardent abolitionist like his father, brought her along to hear the Boston Daniel bait the lions of College Hill, and after the lecture he introduced her to the great Garrison. Later they both testified to the fatefulness of this meeting, but within a week he was off to England, and nearly a year passed before he opened his campaign for her hand.[1]

A campaign it was, complete with Stendhalian strategies for trapping the unwary Helen. For one who boldly courted notoriety, Garrison was a timid lover as though fearful of bruising his ego in an open encounter. He knew just the kind of wife he wanted — a woman of "good sense" and "talent," given to no "unseemly familiarity of conduct" or "reckless disregard of all the rules of propriety." In short, a wife with a spirit exactly in unison with his own, who would provide home and family and submit to his mastery. Even when Helen Benson met all these demands, he was slow to declare himself. When his veiled hints and constant probing drove her to protest her unworthiness to be the wife of a great humanitarian, he replied peevishly that he had been "both vain and presumptuous" — "vain, in supposing that my letters can either amuse or interest you — presumptuous in thrusting them so frequently upon your notice."[2] Whereupon poor Helen confessed — if he might overlook her many deficiencies, "I see not why I may not gratefully acknowledge your attention in conferring so high an obligation upon me, and I sincerely respond to every tender expression of feeling. . . .

I have opened my heart to you."[3] Then followed his own
belated declaration. "Oh! generous, confiding, excellent girl!
Do you then reciprocate my *love?* Yes, my fears are dispelled, my hopes confirmed — and I shed delicious tears of
joy! . . . I did not dare to presume that you regarded me
with so much esteem."[4]

His own self-esteem intact and master of the situation once
more, he lectured poor Helen on the impropriety of flattering
him and apprised her of her duties. She must guard against
becoming "exalted in her mind" as well as against "excessive
humility." She should avoid "all tawdry and artificial aids to
the embellishment of her person." It was a wonderful favor,
he reminded her, to be a dutiful child of God, an obedient
disciple of the meek and lowly Jesus, and he prayed that she
be kept from the temptations and snares of the world, from
slothfulness and folly.[5]

Helen responded eagerly to his suggestions, anxious lest
Lloyd, as she now called him, think her "not sufficiently
grateful." She loved him, she admitted, "a thousand times
more than my tongue or pen can utter."[6]

Having carried his siege, Garrison wanted to be married
as soon as possible. Gallantly he addressed her as his "Charming Conqueror" but added the sobering reflection that their
contemplated union "gives universal satisfaction among my
friends both white and colored."[7] He gave precise instructions for the wedding: no "extravagance" or "eccentricity,"
no "showy kind" of wedding cake or expensive gifts. The
ceremony to be performed by May and held in the morning to allow the wedding party to reach Worcester by night-
fall. He had rented a small house in Roxbury which he
called Freedom's Cottage. Without consulting Helen he
furnished it and hired a housekeeper whom he assured her
was "modest" in her deportment and "genteel in her ap-

pearance." Helen applauded his new domesticity. "Do not fear but everything will suit me," she wrote. "I can assure you I am not difficult."[8]

Following a ceremony tailored to the bridegroom's specifications, the wedding party, including Garrison's Aunt Charlotte and Helen's companion Elizabeth Chace, set out for Freedom's Cottage and a well-chaperoned honeymoon. In Worcester, Garrison lost his baggage, and the cars made Aunt Charlotte violently ill. The party arrived in Roxbury to find Isaac Knapp and his sister, their new boarders, already comfortably installed. Even the irrepressible Garrison admitted that the arrival was "gloomy enough." Two days later his equanimity had returned, and he was able to report to Helen's sister Anna that the Garrisons eagerly awaited a visit from the Bensons. "I can hardly realize as yet, that I am married," he added, "although I have one of the best wives in the world." She fulfilled his every expectation. "Her disposition is certainly remarkable — so uniformly placid, so generous and disinterested, so susceptible and obliging, so kind and attentive."[9] Helen would need all these qualities in the years to come.

In October, Garrison returned to the urgent problem of saving his paper from complete collapse. The partners were now printing twenty-three hundred copies of the *Liberator* each week, only one quarter of which went to white subscribers, the rest going to editors on the exchange list, public officials, philanthropic societies, and free Negroes who could not or would not pay their bills. By 1834 the condition of the paper was growing desperate. Earlier in the year Garrison had enlarged the format and acquired six hundred new subscribers but "under such circumstances as to afford us no substantial aid: in fact, so remiss have they been up to this hour, in complying with the terms of our paper, that they have only increased our difficulties."[10] At the end of three years unpaid subscriptions totaled two thousand dollars. Allowing seven hundred dollars for the editor's salary (no princely sum, he assured readers) the *Liberator* showed an annual deficit of seventeen hundred dollars.

The partners, casting about for a solution to their financial problems, proposed a scheme whereby readers could buy shares in the paper payable to the New England Society which would then undertake to manage the accounts, but nothing came of their proposal. Arnold Buffum suggested that Garrison accept a salary from the society, which henceforth should direct the editorial policy of the *Liberator*, but Garrison bristled at this threat to his independence. Nor would he agree to discontinue the paper temporarily, as Elizur Wright advised, while he canvassed the countryside for funds. Henry Ware, May's old teacher, saw Garrison's embarrassment as an opportunity to put the editor in his place, and offered the support of Boston philanthropists in exchange for the power of censorship vested in a board of managers, "each of whom should, a week at a time, examine all articles . . . and induce Mr. Garrison to promise to publish nothing there which should not have been approved by them."[11] Ware's plan died quietly, and he himself admitted that he had been rash in proposing it since "all who know Mr. Garrison know that he is not a man to be controlled or advised."

Even Garrison's friends admitted that something must be done to soften his abusive tone. Elizur Wright complained of the difficulty of converting otherwise good men "who can not give up their grudge against Garrison."[12] Charles Stuart told Helen Garrison that the only "jangle of words" he had ever had with her husband "was when I cautioned him on the severity of his language" and asked her to remind Garrison "not to forget it."[13] Charles Follen, the aggressive Harvard professor who lost his job by joining the abolitionists, refused to become identified with the party of the *Liberator* because he distrusted its editor. Even Garrison's friend and patron Lewis Tappan admitted that several of his colleagues disapproved of the *Liberator* and refused to support it. His brother Arthur, for one, had become so dissatisfied with Garrison's policies that he was contemplating a new society in New England composed exclusively of anti-Garrisonian moderates.

Still worse was the reluctance of new men to join a society dominated by the "madman Garrison." Gerrit Smith, the reformer from New York, balked when Elizur Wright suggested he join the abolitionists and asked whether the *Liberator* more than any other paper was the favorite mouthpiece of the anti-slavery societies. Only when assured that the paper spoke solely for its editor did he agree to support the abolitionists. James G. Birney, another convert from colonization, wondered whether the *Liberator* would prove the fire ship of the anti-slavery fleet.

Even more ominous was the growing breach between Garrison and the New England clergy. At Andover Seminary professors warned their students against the imprudences of the *Liberator* party. Professor Sidney Willard, Ware's colleague at the Harvard Divinity School, joined in deploring Garrison's growing influence, and at Yale Leonard Bacon used faculty disapproval of the *Liberator* to strengthen the colonization forces on campus. In Boston the evangelical clergy, taking their cue from Beecher, approached Channing's followers with a plan for forming a society of moderates to "put down" Garrison. In the quiet of his Concord study Emerson summed up this growing resistance in a terse complaint. "The *Liberator*," he noted in his journal, "is a scold."

Garrison's critics had reason to worry about mounting opposition to anti-slavery in the North. Amos Phelps was hardly surprised to learn that as agent of the Massachusetts Society he was worth a ten-thousand-dollar reward in New Orleans. But when a Methodist minister was mobbed in the streets of Worcester in broad daylight and another clergyman arrested in Northfield, New Hampshire, as a common brawler, that was different! All over New England there were similar signs of growing protest. The president of Amherst College demanded the dissolution of the college anti-slavery society on the grounds that it was "alienating Christian brethren, retarding and otherwise injuring the cause of religion in the College, and threatening in many ways the prosperity of the institution."[14] In Washington, Connecticut, the principal of the local school was fired and driven out of town for expressing abolitionist opinions; and in New Canaan, New Hampshire, an experiment in biracial education at Northfield Academy ended abruptly when the townspeople hitched a hundred yoke of oxen to the school and dragged it off into a nearby swamp. Emerson and Horace Mann were hooted when they tried to speak on the subject of slavery. Whittier was roughly handled in Garrison's home town. Charles Burleigh, a recent addition to Garrison's staff, was mobbed in Mansfield, Massachusetts. To many of these men it seemed that as the clarion of anti-slavery the *Liberator* was not an asset but a liability and that the cause of their troubles lay in Garrison's intemperate and abusive language.

Garrison fought boldly for his editorial freedom. The hue and cry against his paper, he insisted, was itself a sign of progress. Four years ago there had not been so much as a peep or a mutter on the slavery question in the whole country. Now the subject was on every tongue.

Within four years, I have seen my principles embraced cordially and unalterably, by thousands of the best men in the nation. If God has made me a signal instrument in the accomplishment of this astonishing change, it is not for me to glory, but to be thankful. What else but the *Liberator* primarily, (and of course instrumentally,) has effected this change? Greater success than I have had, no man could reasonably desire, or humbly expect. Greater success no man could obtain, peradventure without endangering his reliance upon an almighty arm.[15]

Once again vanity obscured the truth: neither the New York abolitionists nor Weld's followers in the West unreservedly accepted the Garrisonian formula of immediate emancipation. The New York Society still felt it necessary to modify his phrase to "immediate emancipation, gradually accomplished." Weld and the Westerners, puzzled by the semantics of their New York brethren, inverted their motto to "gradual emancipation, immediately begun." All the abolitionists agreed with Garrison that slavery must be wiped out as soon as possible, but no one knew exactly what his formula meant. Nowhere outside his own bailiwick in New England was his notion of immediate emancipation unqualifiedly accepted. His flat assertion to the contrary convinced no one but himself.

Scarcely more convincing was his argument that language was, after all, a matter of taste — "and where is the standard of taste?" Though he admitted that his words were not always happily chosen, he explained that as an editor he necessarily wrote in great haste and could not remodel and criticize as he liked. Lest his critics seize on this as an admission of guilt, however, he proceeded to make a distinction between *principles* and *language* only to flout it with triumphant illogicality by proving that the "fallacy" of the moderates sprang from their erroneous principles.

When he examined the reaction of the American public to anti-slavery, he was on firm ground once again. What single abolitionist, he asked, had escaped the wrath of the people? "Are not all their names cast out as evil? Are they not all branded as fanatics, disorganizers and madmen?" Whittier's quiet manner did not protect him, nor did Beriah Green's vigorous tone make him popular. Phelps, Follen, Goodell, Birney, — all with styles superior, no doubt, to his own — were as cordially despised as he was. "Why are they thus maltreated and calumniated? Certainly not for the *phraseology* which they use, but for the *principles* which they adopted." The truth was — and here Garrison reached the heart of the issue — that an anti-slavery minority had collided with the conservative instinct of an American society determined to ignore the moral question of slavery. But he went further — he accused Northern businessmen and Southern slaveholders of conniving to destroy American freedom and plunge the country into barbarism. Both had a vested interest in corruption, and to protect this interest they were willing to proscribe and persecute. Against their dark conspiracy the abolitionists stood almost alone. "It is true, not many mighty have as yet been called to this sacred strife," he wrote to Channing. "Like every other great reform, it has been commenced by obscure and ignorant men. It is God's mode commonly, to choose the foolish things of the world to confound the wise; because his foolishness is wiser than men, and his weakness stronger than men." Like a tree planted by the water, the Saints would not be moved.

Ten years earlier Garrison's naïve conspiracy theory of history would have been discarded as the absurdity it was.

But in 1834 events in the North and the South were combining to give his convenient oversimplification the appearance of fact. Southern intellectuals were perfecting their theory of reactionary paternalism that utterly repudiated civil liberties. With its new "positive good" weapon the South was preparing an offensive against its critics which succeeded in silencing them at the cost of free institutions. Once apprised of the abolitionists' intentions Southern legislators reacted with near unanimity. Three years after the founding of the American Anti-Slavery Society every Southern state had passed laws prohibiting the organization of anti-slavery societies within their borders and preventing the dissemination of abolitionist literature. Even more effective than laws in securing uniformity were the vigilance committees, groups of prominent citizens in Southern communities entrusted with the execution of "justice" on those foolish enough to doubt the wisdom of slavery. These committees saw to it that local mails stayed closed to anti-slavery literature and that state laws prohibiting debate on slavery were duly enforced. By interrogating travelers and inspecting their baggage, by aiding local postmasters and offering rewards for the apprehension of notorious abolitionists like Garrison and Arthur Tappan they soon perfected all the inquisitorial techniques of a reign of terror. Typical of their efficiency was the work of the vigilance committee in Nashville, Tennessee, in 1835 in punishing Amos Dresser, a student from Lane Theological Seminary unlucky enough to be caught with a parcel of Bibles wrapped in a copy of the *Emancipator*. Although Tennessee had not yet passed a law under which Dresser could be prosecuted, the Committee solved the problem by confiscating his belongings, administering twenty lashes in the public square, and driving him out of town.

Not content with vigilance at home, Southern legislatures

mounted an attack on the right of petition and bombarded
Northern states with demands for action against abolitionist
publishers. To the abolitionists' dismay their demands drew
a sympathetic response from Northern legislatures. Only
Pennsylvania and Ohio flatly denied the constitutionality
of such controls. Bills to regulate anti-slavery publications
were introduced in Maine, New Hampshire, and Connecticut. In Rhode Island a similar measure passed through committee and was killed only by the efforts of the Republican
Thomas Dorr. Governor Marcy of New York promised to
use his upstate strength to bring the wild-eyed abolitionists
in the city into line. And in Massachusetts Garrison soon
found himself in mortal struggle with Governor Everett's
conservative Whigs, who dominated the legislature and were
determined to destroy him.

It was the reaction of the Northern public that most
disturbed the abolitionists. Everywhere there seemed to be
an agreement on the need to suppress anti-slavery, a view
which the Northern business community and the conservative
press manipulated all too easily. In Cincinnati James Birney,
who had abandoned colonization and was now a militant
abolitionist, set up his *Philanthropist* press only to have his
printing office torn apart and his home methodically wrecked.
His courage and persistence increased the hatred of his fellow townsmen until, plagued by lawsuits and hounded by
pro-slavery mobs, he left for New York to become the
secretary of the national society. When James Thome, one of
Weld's band, attempted to lecture in Granville, Ohio, citizens
of the town drove him off and burned the schoolhouse where
he was to speak. The indefatigable Amos Dresser was mobbed
in Marblehead, Massachusetts, less than a year after his
experience in Nashville. Utica, New York, made lecturing
a distinct hazard for the abolitionists, and from Weld came

periodic reports of violence in the West. Lecturing in the Presbyterian Church in the village of Circleville, Ohio, he was struck on the temple by a rock. While he sat down to clear his head, the audience hung cloaks and coats over the windows, and he managed to finish his talk. The next night the church was closed and he had to deliver his lecture in an abandoned storeroom while a mob outside pelted the shutters with rocks. Not far away in Berlin, Ohio, Marius Robinson was dragged out in the middle of the night, stripped, tarred and feathered, and driven into the woods.

For the most part undaunted, the abolitionists kept right on lecturing. John W. Alvord, another of Weld's "joyous warriors," kept up his spirits by retailing humorous accounts of the vicissitudes of his calling. "Last night Midd[l]ebury puked," he reported to Weld on one occasion. "Her stomach had evidently been overloaded. . . . Spasmodic heavings and wretchings were manifest during the whole day. Toward night symptoms more alarming." Warned off by the town fathers, Alvord and Thome insisted on holding their meeting.

All still until about 8 [o'clock] when in came a broadside of Eggs, Glass, Egg shells, white and yolks flew on every side. Br. Thom[e's] Fact Book received an egg just in its bowels and I doubt whether one in the house escaped a spattering. I have been trying to clean off this morning, but cant get off the stink. Thome dodged like a stoned gander. He brought up at length against the side of the desk, cocked his eye and stood gazing upward at the flying missiles as they stream[e]d in ropy masses through the house. . . . He apologizes to me this morning by saying he thought the stove was crackin!!!![16]

Eggs were one thing, the organized savagery of city mobs another. The climax to this early outbreak of violence came in the summer of 1835 in New York, when, in a sudden burst of race hatred mobs roamed the streets breaking up a meeting of the American Anti-Slavery Society, sacking Lewis Tappan's house, and invading the Negro section and methodically wrecking three churches, a school, and twenty homes.

Thus James Birney hardly exaggerated when he warned that the antagonist principles of liberty and slavery had been roused into action and only one could be victorious. Garrison turned his warning into a denunciation of the South. "And what has brought our country to the verge of ruin. . . . THE ACCURSED SYSTEM OF SLAVERY! To sustain that system, there is a general willingness to destroy LIBERTY OF SPEECH and of the PRESS, and to mob or murder all who oppose it. In the popular fury against the advocates of a bleeding humanity, every principle of justice, every axiom of liberty, every feeling of humanity — all the fundamental axioms of republican government are derided and violated with fatal success."[17] This histrionic identification of civil rights and the anti-slavery cause was to prove the most effective weapon in the Garrisonian arsenal, an argument which eventually turned back the pro-slavery assault on free society. In presenting the anti-slavery minority as the victims of a demonic slave power and, above all, by posing as their chief martyr, he dramatized the fundamental issues of freedom and won the grudging support of a number of Northern moderates who finally recognized the Southern threat to free institutions.

The first of Garrison's martyrs was Prudence Crandall, a fragile, birdlike zealot from Canterbury, Connecticut, who marched into the office of the *Liberator* in January, 1833. Two years before, she had bought a rambling house on the Canterbury green and opened a boarding school for young ladies. Her school prospered until she enrolled a young colored girl, whereupon the offended townspeople resolved to protect white womanhood by boycotting the school. Miss Crandall was ready to abandon her experiment in biracial education when she happened to read one of Garrison's editorials proposing a manual labor college for Negroes, which gave her the idea of opening her school to colored girls exclusively. She wrote to Garrison telling him of her plan and requesting an interview. "I do not dare tell any one of my neighbors about the contemplated change in my school," she added, "and I beg of you, sir, that you will not expose it to any one; for if it was known, I have no reason to doubt but it would ruin my present school."[18] Ten days later she appeared in Boston to discuss with him the best means of finding pupils. Garrison was convinced that the scheme was practicable, and on March 2, 1833, the *Liberator* carried the announcement that Miss Crandall was now accepting applications for her new school. The notice was accompanied by the editor's imprimatur assuring readers of his "pleasurable emotion" in contemplating the success of the venture and of his entire confidence in Miss Crandall. News of the proposed school was already abroad, however, and by the time Garrison sailed for England Miss Crandall was deep in trouble with the citizens of Canterbury incensed at the prospect of a "nigger school" on their doorstep.

A little opposition was all that the abolitionists needed to turn the affair into an anti-slavery *cause célèbre*. Arnold Buffum was dispatched by the New England Society to argue Miss Crandall's case in a Canterbury town meeting. Samuel May offered his services, and the Benson brothers hurried over from Providence. From New York came word that Arthur Tappan stood ready to meet all expenses. Meanwhile fifteen or twenty colored girls were recruited from

Providence, Boston, and New Haven, and classes at the school began. Then the townspeople discovered an old vagrancy law on the books and threatened to enforce it. Canterbury rallied in protest against Miss Crandall's experiment; grocers refused to sell to the school, doctors declined to attend the students, and town loafers added their bit by molesting Miss Crandall and the girls. Andrew Judson, the spokesman for the town, rushed up to Hartford, where he found a majority of the legislature willing to pass a law prohibiting the establishment of schools for out-of-state students without permission of the local authorities. Although the law was a clear violation of constitutional rights, it served its purpose. The school was closed, Miss Crandall arraigned, and her trial set for August. After a single night in jail spent in the cell of a recently convicted murderer she emerged to learn that overnight she had become the heroine of the anti-slavery movement. At the trial the jury was unable to reach a verdict, but a few weeks later a second jury convicted her on the charges of accepting nonresident pupils and teaching them. The case was appealed to the state supreme court, where about a year later the decision of the trial court was reversed on grounds of insufficient evidence. After twelve months of costly litigation Miss Crandall had won her case but lost her school: her fellow townsmen celebrated their legal defeat by breaking the windows of the school, filling the well with manure, and decorating the fence with dead cats. In the summer of 1834 Miss Crandall gave up the school, married a Baptist clergyman and moved West.

At first Garrison was impressed with the tenacity of the Quaker schoolmistress. "She is a wonderful woman," he wrote to Knapp, "as undaunted as if she had the whole world on her side."[19] He ordered Knapp and Johnson in his absence in England to make full use of her case, and when, just as he sailed, Canterbury committed its "outrageous crime," he urged them to make a prompt defense. "If we suffer the school to be put down in Canterbury, other places will partake of the panic, and also prevent its introduction in their vicinity. We may as well, 'first as last,' meet this proscriptive spirit *and conquer it*."[20] When he returned from England, however, the Canterbury cause was already lost and circumstances had changed. In the first place, Miss Crandall was not a reserved maiden lady but a spirited combatant who could trade epithets with the best of her opponents. With her own newspaper, the *Unionist*, she had conducted an able defense and given every indication of thoroughly enjoying her fame. Garrison noted that she was in danger of becoming "exalted above measure," in other words, a nuisance. He announced that her usefulness to the cause had ended and that though abolitionists should continue to "make the facts of this single case tingle in the ears of the people," it was best for Miss Crandall herself to move off "with flying colors" and leave him to cash in the depreciated currency of her reputation.[21]

To replace the chastened Miss Crandall as the star witness to the perfidy of New England he brought over the English agitator George Thompson in the fall of 1834. The two men had first met the previous year and struck up an immediate and deep friendship. A year older than Garrison, Thompson had risen in the English anti-slavery ranks only after years of adversity following a moral lapse that nearly ruined his life. Some years before, he had stolen a sum of money from his employer and been caught red-handed. He readily confessed his crime, and in exchange for a promise not to prosecute had finally made good the entire amount. Yet he was still paying for his mistake — despite his subsequent impeccable behavior and his services to the anti-slavery cause he was dogged by the story of his crime and new charges of misappropriation of abolitionist funds. Temperamentally he and Garrison were much alike. Both were self-made men driven by ambition; both tried to compensate for their unpopularity at home by seeking honor abroad. Thompson had a tall stately carriage and a formal manner to match. Where Garrison achieved at best only a blunt forcefulness on the platform, Thompson's resonant eloquence spun a kind of poetry of denunciation.

"He comes not as a foreigner but as 'a man and a brother,' feeling for those in bonds as bound with them." Thus Garrison announced Thompson's arrival in Boston. For all his charm and dedication to the cause Thompson, something less than a success in England, proved a distinct liability in America. He received a sample of the reception awaiting him in the United States when he stepped off the boat to learn that the proprietors of New York's Atlantic Hotel had canceled his reservations upon hearing of his anti-slavery designs. It was a measure of Garrison's reckless disregard of public opinion that in the midst of his own struggles with a hostile clergy he asked Thompson to bring the weight of English evangelicalism directly to bear on his New England cousins. Thompson arrived in Boston to find a conservative religious opposition preparing to deal with the *Liberator* and its editor once and for all.

The idea of an anti-slavery society composed of men of moderation and good sense proceeded from the fertile brain of Lyman Beecher. More than anything else Beecher feared disunion in church and society, and as he surveyed the work of the anti-slavery men in the year 1834, he was not encouraged by what he saw. The silken ties, those soft but mighty bands of love that united Christians in the North and South, were beginning to snap. Beecher had no trouble identifying the Atropos of the reform movement whose invective slashed the American lifeline. If Garrison were allowed to continue, he warned, abolitionism would not last two years. Something must be done immediately. Beecher spent the year 1834 as the first president of Lane Seminary trying to tame the reform impulses of his students and direct them into socially acceptable channels. For his pains he received nothing but their well-deserved rebukes. Led by Weld, the seminarians refused to be bridled and capped their series of protests by leaving the school. Back in Boston, Beecher's followers, heartened by premature reports of the master's success, went forward with their plans for a society based on "benevolent and enlarged feeling" whose first task would be to "put down" Garrison.

The American Union for the Relief and Improvement of the Colored Race — that "soulless organization with a sounding title," as Garrison dubbed it — was nearly stillborn. The handful of clergymen who met in Tremont Hall on January 14, 1835, were confronted with their archenemy accompanied by George Thompson and the rest of the Garrisonians who demanded to know the purpose of the new society. Receiving no answer and requested to leave, they opened a filibuster instead, whereupon Thompson was declared out of order and then "impertinent." The intruders next asked whether the American Union was to be open to "all friends of antislavery," as the first call had declared, or merely to those who "believe a new organization is necessary," as a subsequent announcement proclaimed. Once again they were asked to leave, which they finally did after hearing the ministers vote that slavery was not a sin and that the American Union contemplated "no designs of hostility in respect to any other institution." The abolitionists knew differently.

Garrison was correct in ascribing a sectarian spirit to the

American Union. The new society was dominated by the Congregational clergy who still found it difficult to work harmoniously with their more enlightened Unitarian brethren. The whole scheme might have collapsed had it not been for the arrival from New York of Arthur Tappan, bent on using the American Union to bring Garrison to reason. After meetings with both parties Tappan wrote an open letter to the *Boston Recorder* giving his blessing to the American Union but defending Garrison from the charge of atheism. No man, he pointed out, could be blind to Garrison's obvious faults, chief among which was "the severe and denunciatory language with which he often assails his opponents and repels their attacks," but these shortcomings need not obscure his "noble and disinterested efforts."[22] There was room in the movement for all good men: those who found it impossible to work with Garrison should strike out for themselves.

Lewis Tappan, in whom the milk of human kindness was slowly curdling, sensed the true purpose of the American Union from the beginning. He disapproved of Arthur's indulgent view of the new society and did not hesitate to assure Garrison of his continued support. "I have attentively read your remarks on the proceedings of the late convention in Boston," he wrote to Garrison, "to form what I should call AN ANTI-GARRISON SOCIETY, and, for one, I heartily approve them. They will meet with a hearty response from every true hearted emancipationist in the land. The times require decision and courage, and I feel thankful to God for your steadfastness at the post which providence has assigned you. Go on and prosper, thou friend of the oppressed! The Lord will be thy shield and buckler."[23] Without waiting for permission Garrison printed the letter, while Lewis quickly won back his brother's support for the *Liberator*. Arthur withdrew to a position of benevolent neutrality and meanwhile resumed his aid to the Garrison party. Back in favor with the president of the national society, Garrison opened fire on the American Union, which under his heavy salvos slowly sank into oblivion. The first threat to his hegemony in New England had ended.

The appearance of the American Union shattered Garrison's dream of leading a united church into the anti-slavery camp. He had always believed that abolition should be the work of the American churches, but here in Boston, the birthplace of American Protestantism, religious leaders were transgressing and lying against the Lord by refusing to denounce slavery. American Christianity had become a pillar of slavery, and ministers no longer preached the true word of God. From now on the drift of his thought toward anticlericalism was unmistakable as his obsession with conscience scattered before it questions of doctrine and polity. "To learn my duty," he warned his readers, "I will not consult any other statute-book than THE BIBLE: and whatever requirement of man I believe is opposed to the spirit of the gospel, I will at all hazards disobey."[24] Moral right, he declared, was ever paramount to legal right and should freely interrogate it. With George Thompson as his chief examiner he now took up the work of moral interrogation with renewed vigor.

At Freedom's Cottage the two men planned Thompson's itinerary for the summer of 1835, beginning with a tour of Maine and New Hampshire. Thompson found it rough going. In Augusta a mob smashed the windows of his hotel room and a committee of leading citizens urged his hasty departure. In Concord his meeting with the ladies' auxiliary ended precipitately in a shower of brickbats; and in Lowell a hail of refuse stopped the proceedings. Everywhere he went he was denounced as an itinerant "stirrer-up of strife" and an agent of "foreign interference." A man less sure of himself might well have admitted the unpalatable truth that Americans simply did not take to George Thompson, but Garrison, convinced of his visitor's curative powers, simply doubled the dosage. The disastrous tour dragged through the hot summer.

Elsewhere the national society was stepping up its offensive. In June the Executive Committee hit upon a new scheme for printing and distributing thousands of pamphlets and tracts. Then a circular went out to all its members calling for thirty thousand dollars to finance new periodicals and pay new agents. Until now most Northerners had looked upon the society as a collection of cranks and misguided meddlers well supplied with visions but lacking the common sense to effect any of their wild schemes. Two years had seen this unconcern give way to a real anxiety; and the announcement of a program designed to bring the anti-slavery message into every town and hamlet in the country roused the Northern public to action. Already there were mobs and riots aimed at the innocent free Negro. In Philadelphia gangs of toughs roamed the streets destroying Negro property and threatening the victims. In Utica rioters drove the delegates to a state anti-slavery convention out of town under a shower of mud and stones, and as soon as they were gone wrecked the offices of the city's abolitionist newspaper. In Hartford there were persistent rumors that a Negro church had been burned to the ground with the congregation locked inside it. Garrison thought he saw in these riots an "infallible sign" that Satan's time was short. "When tyrants increase the weight of the bondsmen's fetters, and threatens [sic] extermination to all who shall dare question their rights . . . it is pretty certain that they deem the hour of emancipation to be close at hand."[25] His followers who studied the explosive situation right in Boston more carefully did not share his optimism.

In July he sailed for Nova Scotia and a month's rest, leaving Thompson in the capable hands of Samuel May. He returned to find the city ablaze with anti-abolitionism. Negroes on "Nigger Hill" were being harassed by bands of thugs who turned out nightly to loot their homes and drive them off the street. The press was busy whipping up hatred for Thompson as the "paid agent" of the enemies of "republican institutions." In August, John Quincy Adams, back home between sessions of Congress, noted that a public meeting to silence the abolitionists was being planned and remarked acidly that "the disease is deeper than can be healed by town meeting resolutions." On Friday afternoon, August 21, Faneuil Hall was filled to capacity by Bostonians who came to hear Harrison Gray Otis argue the need to keep the abolitionists from scattering firebrands, arrows, and death.

Garrison considered attending the Faneuil Hall meeting to refute the charges against him, but at the last minute he was dissuaded from making what could only have been a dangerous gesture. Instead he took recourse to the columns of the *Liberator*. Linking the Faneuil Hall demonstration with the "popular fury" in the South, he lashed out at the "utter degeneracy" of Boston. How, he asked, had the abolitionists behaved under such provocation? "Have they, in a single instance, returned evil for evil? Who among them all, has given blow for blow? or who has girded on his sword, or who has recommended an appeal to force?"[26] He identified the source of this new proscriptive spirit as the *"sinful prejudices* in the high and educated classes." "Those classes do not compose the *active* portion of the mobs, but they do the passive, and that portion is the most numerous, and in our opinion the most to blame."[27] For the time being, however, it seemed better not to offer further provocation. Leaving his brother-in-law Henry Benson in charge of the paper, he spent September at the Benson farm in Brooklyn, partly to regain his health, which had broken down under the strain of Thompson's visit, and partly to avoid trouble. "There is yet too much fever, and too little rationality, in the public mind . . ." he wrote to Benson, "for . . . any of us to make addresses to the patient without having him attempt to knock us down. Write — print — distribute — this we may do with profit to our cause."[28] If he thought that the storm had blown over, he was quickly disillusioned on his return to the city. A few days earlier enterprising citizens had erected a gallows in front of his house and were now eagerly awaiting his arrival. Then they learned of a meeting of the Boston Female Anti-Slavery Society scheduled in Julien Hall at which George Thompson would speak.

Two facts are clear concerning the "Garrison mob" of October 21, 1835: it was instigated by the Boston press, and Garrison was not its intended victim. All during the summer the *Boston Atlas* and the *Gazette* had called for resistance to the "impudent bullying" of George Thompson, "not from the *rabble*, but from men of property and standing, who have a large stake in the community." A week before the riot Buckingham's *Courier*, which had defended Garrison in the past, joined the standing order in denouncing the Englishman as a "vagabond" and a "scoundrel" hired by the abolitionists to spread race hatred. On October 14 the anniversary meeting of the ladies' society was postponed for want of a hall, the proprietors of Julien Hall having withdrawn their permission. It took more than the timidity of property owners to stop Boston's intrepid feminists, led by Mary Parker, Theodore's iron-willed sister. They promptly arranged another meeting for the twenty-first at the society's rooms at 46 Washington Street.

By noon of that day five hundred handbills fresh from the printer's were circulating in State Street and in the hotels and business houses of the city.

THOMPSON

THE ABOLITIONIST!!!!

That infamous foreign scoundrel THOMPSON will hold forth *this afternoon*, at the Liberator Office, No. 48 Washington Street. The present is a fair opportunity for the friends of the Union to *snake Thompson out!* It will be a contest between the Abolitionists and the friends of the Union. A purse of $100 has been raised by a number of patriotic citizens to reward the individual who shall first lay violent hands on Thompson, so that he may be brought to the tar-kettle before dark. Friends of the Union, be vigilant!

Boston, Wednesday, 12 o'clock.

The handbill had been designed that morning at the office of the *Gazette* by two merchants, Isaac Stevens and Isaac Means, both of whom had signed the call for the Faneuil Hall meeting. To make sure of a mob sufficient for their purposes they sent one hundred of the handbills to the North End, where Irish mechanics could be counted on to treat the Englishman as fair game.

Promptly at two-thirty Garrison arrived at the Washington Street office, where he discovered over a hundred men milling about outside the building and an equal number lining the stairway to the hall on the third floor. Pushing his way through the crowd, which offered threats but no violence, he took his seat with the twenty-five ladies who comprised the

Boston Female Anti-Slavery Society. When he saw that his visitors showed no disposition to leave, he tried a bit of sarcasm. "If *gentlemen*, any of you are *ladies* — in disguise — why, only apprise me of the fact, give me your name, and I will introduce you to the rest of your sex, and you can take seats among them accordingly." This shaft wounded only the sensibilities of the Boston matrons — the crowd pressed forward calling for Thompson. Suddenly realizing that as the only man at the meeting (Thompson never showed up) he might well be chosen to fill the speaker's shoes, he retired behind the partition which separated the hall from the offices. Here he found Charles C. Burleigh, the Connecticut abolitionist and friend of Prudence Crandall, and together they sat calmly waiting for the mob to disperse. Meanwhile the ladies opened their meeting with a prayer.

Suddenly Mayor Theodore Lyman arrived, posted a handful of officers in the doorway, and mounted the stairs. Once inside the hall filled with shouting men, he tried to tell them that Thompson was not even in the city, but matters had already gone too far. The opening prayer was punctuated by fists banging on the door of the partition behind which Garrison sat writing an account of the "awful, sublime, and soul thrilling scene" which he could not see. Mayor Lyman turned to the members: "Go home, ladies," he pleaded, "go home."

> PRESIDENT [Miss Parker]: What renders it necessary we should go home?
>
> MR. LYMAN: I am the mayor of the city, and I cannot now explain; but will call on you this evening.
>
> PRESIDENT: If the ladies will be seated, we will take the sense of the meeting.
>
> MR. LYMAN: Don't stop, ladies, go home.

The sense of the meeting seemed to be that it would be wise to take the mayor's advice. The meeting was adjourned, and led by their doughty president, the ladies filed out "amid manifestations of revengeful brutality."

With the women gone and Thompson obviously nowhere on the premises, the mob began to shout for Garrison and meanwhile amused itself by tearing down the anti-slavery sign outside. As Burleigh strolled nonchalantly out of the office Lyman rushed in and ordered Garrison to leave by a back window which opened into a narrow lane. While the mob blockaded the front entrance, Garrison slipped out of the window, across the narrow way and into a carpenter shop where he climbed into the loft and hid behind a pile of lumber. But he had been spotted. Shouting "Lynch him!" and "Out with him!" the crowd poured into the shop and up the ladder. "On seeing me," Garrison recalled, "three or four of the rioters, uttering a yell, furiously dragged me to the window, with the intention of hurling me from that height to the ground; but one of them relented and said — 'Don't let us kill him outright.' So they drew me back, and coiled a rope about my body — probably to drag me through the streets." He made the best of his ridiculous posture. Bowing ironically from the loft to the men below, he begged their indulgence until he could back down the ladder. Once on the ground he was seized by three pairs of friendly arms and hustled out into State Street and up to the rear of the City Hall.

Here trouble began. Whatever its intentions up to this point — Garrison believed that he was headed for the Common and a coat of tar — the mob realized that once inside City Hall he was safe. In a rush on the doorway the rioters tried to snatch him and were beaten back by the police only after they had ripped the clothes off his back. Garrison re-

mained serene throughout, perhaps because he had lost his
glasses and could not see three feet in front of him. Later
he told friends that he felt "perfectly calm, nay very happy. . . .
It seemed to me that it was indeed a blessed privilege to
suffer in the cause of Christ." Mayor Lyman and his deputies,
less sure of divine interposition than their captive, decided
to whisk him off to the Leverett Street jail and lock him up
for safekeeping on the trumped-up charge of disturbing the
peace. Once again he was bustled out into the street, this
time to a waiting carriage. While the police officers beat off
attackers, the driver plied his whip and the hack careened
out of State Street and into Bowdoin Square headed for the
jail. Within an hour the mob had disappeared.

Garrison spent the evening behind bars in a suit of borrowed clothes chatting with the jailer and receiving his
friends. In the morning he re-enacted the ritual of the jail
by inscribing on the walls of the cell a message to posterity.
That afternoon he was released on condition that he leave
the city. The same evening, accompanied by Helen, he left
for Brooklyn.

From the Benson farm he sent orders to Burleigh and
Knapp to publish accounts of the riot, and within a few days
his own version appeared. When the Boston papers obliged
by blaming the abolitionists for the outburst, charges and
countercharges filled the press for weeks to come. Fanned
by regular blasts from the *Liberator*, the affair smoldered
throughout the winter.

Among his friends and followers Garrison's stock rose to
new heights. They marveled at his courage. "Joy to thee,
Son of Trial!" exclaimed an unidentified admirer whose
sonnet graced the columns of the *Liberator*. Knapp thanked
God for his partner's preservation "from the fury of a misguided and ferocious mob." Samuel Sewall congratulated

him on his escape, but he added that he did not believe the mob at any time meant to murder him. Maria Chapman thought otherwise. One of the doughty Weston sisters, she had married the abolitionist merchant Henry Chapman and become the guiding spirit of the Boston Female Anti-Slavery Society. It was she who led her companions "each with a colored friend" through the mob to her home. Now she praised Garrison for his coolness and bravery in the face of peril. But there were also rumors of his cowardice, of his begging for mercy on his knees, and of his precipitate flight from the city. Harriet Martineau, visiting Boston at this time and meeting Garrison on his return, thought she detected a "want of manliness" and an "excessive agitation" in him. By this time Garrison, who was enjoying his martyrdom, no doubt had embellished the facts to improve the drama. Burleigh, his companion for all but a few minutes of that afternoon, testified to his complete composure; and Mayor Lyman remembered that he had greeted him with a smile. However exaggerated his own accounts of behavior may have been, there is no reason to doubt that he followed his nonresistance precepts by refusing to escape or defend himself.[29]

It was Harriet Martineau who coined the phrase "Martyr Age" to describe Garrison's treatment by the Boston mob. He thought the phrase "reign of terror" more appropriate. "A cloud of infamy — a thunder-cloud of heaven's vengeance — a cloud of darkness and terror, covers the nation like a mighty pall," he wrote three weeks after the affair. "Rebellious, ungrateful and blood-thirsty land! how art thou fallen even to the lowest depths of degradation and sin."[30] It remained for a later generation to put the Boston mob in proper perspective. John Jay Chapman suggested the need for distinguishing between a "reign of terror" and "persecution." "The unpleasantnesses and injustices to which the Abolitionists were subjected," Chapman wrote, "never justified a literal application of the terms 'martyr,' 'reign of terror,' etc.; but the word 'persecution' is most aptly used to describe their sufferings, if we reflect that there are persecutions which do not result in death."[31] Prudence Crandall's discomfort at the hands of the people of Canterbury hardly qualified her as a martyr, nor were Birney's experiences in Cincinnati or Weld's treatment in the villages of Ohio part of a concerted reign of terror. The buffeting Garrison received from Irish workmen in State Street could hardly compare with Elijah Lovejoy's tragic defense of his press two years later in Alton, Illinois. But democratic society does not always resort to the coil of rope and the flaming cross to discourage unpopular opinions. Often a few well-aimed stones or a handful of efficient hecklers are more than enough. Almost all of the anti-abolitionist episodes had their antic aspects and their lunatic participants. Beneath the surface comedy, however, there lay in the silent hostility of the many and the compulsive hates of the few a major threat to free institutions. The Garrison mob was not simply a collection of pranksters; it was an irrational force capable of destroying democracy. It was the abolitionists' success in touching the consciences of their fellow citizens that ultimately saved them.

The Garrison mob brought about such an awakening of conscience in Boston. "Happily one point seems already to be gaining universal assent," the merchant Francis Jackson wrote to Samuel May in November, 1835, "that slavery cannot long survive free discussion. . . . As slavery cannot exist with free discussion — so neither can liberty breathe without it. Losing this, we too shall be no longer free men indeed, but little if at all superior to the millions we now seek to emancipate." Other men of property and standing in Boston were coming to the same conclusion. They had been made to see that however obstinate and shortsighted the abolitionists might be, their cause was inextricably woven into the fabric of free society. From his new law office in Court Street, Wendell Phillips, the young Boston patrician, looked down on the mob dragging Garrison through the streets and resolved then and there to join his cause. The twenty-four-year-old Phillips was the wealthy son of Boston's first mayor and a graduate of Harvard, where he had hobnobbed with the sons of Southern planters and joined all the best clubs. Tall, slim, with a ruddy complexion, Grecian features and wavy blond hair combed back over his high forehead, he was the picture of studied negligence, Boston's ideal of the aristocrat. At Harvard he had studied rhetoric with the famed Edward Channing, who taught him to hate purple prose and rely on the natural power of his magnificent voice and muscular mind. Along with money Phillips had inherited a strong social conscience, and it was this combination of wealth and moral commitment that drove him to play the patrician agitator, the reformer who could afford to throw himself into an unpopular cause and casually dismiss his notoriety. His acquisition was a godsend to Garrison. Serving his chief with loyalty and devotion until the very outbreak of war, he brought with him an energy and drive, a talent for agitation, and a voice that made him the greatest of the anti-slavery orators.

Henry Bowditch and George B. Emerson, sons of old families and beneficiaries of Boston's Golden Age, came over to anti-slavery. Even William Ellery Channing, finally convinced that he should speak out, hurried his *Thoughts on Slavery* into print. A plain Connecticut farmer, Henry C. Wright, who became Garrison's most devoted disciple, made his anti-slavery debut in a series of letters to the *Liberator* indicting the city officials and the business community. Orson Murray in Vermont and Nathaniel Rogers in New Hampshire promised to spread immediate emancipation in their states.

These new men represented different types of the New England character — the cultured Bostonian of old family whose conscience overthrew his sense of class, and the independent son of yeoman stock whose militant Protestantism drove him to abolition as the first step in the millennial experiment. But not even Garrison could unite Boston and the backwoods. The events of the next few years disclosed a rift in Garrisonism which piety and unction could not heal.

All this lay in the future. From the aftermath of the Boston riot there emerged a new attitude in New England which eventually created a Northern mind. Although there would be no more Garrison mobs, the conviction that slavery threatened democracy was not widely held in 1835, and in this sense Garrison's work was just beginning. But now he had new recruits who realized better than he that the anti-slavery cause transcended the personality of its leader.

10

"Our Doom as a Nation Is Sealed"

IN THE QUIET OF the Benson farmhouse, where he and his wife retired after his encounter with the Boston mob, Garrison took time to reflect on the progress of moral reform. "Much as my mind is absorbed in the anti-slavery cause," he confessed to his sister-in-law Anna, "there are other great subjects that frequently occupy my thoughts, upon which much light remains to be thrown, and which are of the utmost importance to the temporal and eternal welfare of man."[1] The peace cause, the status of women, the Sabbath question, temperance, home missions — all of these projects he had flung aside for the hectic work of organizing abolition in New England. It was time to pick up the loose threads once more in the hope of making a pattern of Christian reform. Of all his interests the nonresistance cause seemed most important now. His pacifist beliefs had been on trial that day in October as he stumbled along State Street towed by the mob. By refusing to fight back he had tested his principles, found them sound, and could recommend them now as a model of Christian behavior. "I am more and more convinced," he told Anna Benson, "that it is the duty of the followers of Christ to suffer themselves to be defrauded, calumniated, and barbarously treated, without resorting either to their own physical energies, or to the force of human law, for restitution and punishment." His clash with Boston's outraged sensibilities had put a new edge on his old hunger for holiness. Admittedly, slavery was only part of the problem of human evil — why not cure all sin by following the example of Christ? Peace and perfection — gospel truths and God's prescription for the sins of the world. A radical cure, no doubt, but certain. As he began collecting his anti-slavery forces scattered by the October riot, the image of the Master forgiving sinful man and offering peace remained deeply etched in his mind.

He had been reluctant to leave the city but there was no other choice. The house in Brighton Street, which he took in order to be nearer his office, was proving far more costly than Freedom's Cottage. Then, too, his health had suffered from irregular hours and jangled nerves, and Helen constantly worried about his safety in the streets. She was expecting her first child — a son born in February, 1836, whom they named George Thompson Garrison. Thompson himself was gone, smuggled out of the city on the Saint John packet. The *Liberator* undoubtedly would have to be suspended unless Knapp worked a miracle. Although the mob had not ventured near the office, the owners of Merchants Hall, unwilling to offer provocation, had ordered Knapp to clear out. Knapp and Burleigh withdrew, taking with them all of their stock and what little money there was, but not before their creditors, sensing the *Liberator's* end had come, flocked in.

Knapp managed to pay the debts, but an audit revealed a hopeless tangle in the accounts. The financial snarl caused raised eyebrows among some members of the society who undertook to reprimand Garrison for his laxity. "I am inclined to think," he complained in return, "that our friends, wholly ignorant as they are, generally respecting the losses and crosses of every newspaper concern, more or less, hardly do us justice as to our past management. I admit that we have not been methodical or sharp in keeping our accounts. . . . We have not squandered or misapplied, but, on the contrary, as a whole, been careful of our means."[2] Still, it was with relief that he learned of the decision to turn the financial responsibility for the paper over to Knapp and leave him free to manage the editorial work on a salary supplied by Loring and Sewall. He was happy to return to the more congenial task of baiting moderate abolitionists.

In November, 1835, William Ellery Channing's *Slavery* appeared in time to underscore the reaction of Bostonians to militant abolitionism, for Channing spoke with the authority of a veteran opponent of slavery. At the time of Lundy's first visit to Boston in 1828 he was already criticizing slavery while at the same time emphasizing the dangers of alienating the slaveholders. "It seems to me," he wrote to Daniel Webster in that year, "that, before moving in this matter, we ought to say to them distinctly, 'We consider slavery as your calamity, not your crime, and we will share with you the burden of putting an end to it.'" Ten years had scarcely altered this view. Although he subscribed to the *Liberator*, he had never approved of Garrison's "showy, noisy mode of action." His scholarly habits and aristocratic tastes led him to prefer the language of reason to the enthusiasm of agitators who seemed to him to display more will than brains. The Southern counteroffensive against civil liberties heightened his disapproval of slaveowners but did not moderate his opinion of the abolitionists. In 1835 he told a friend that were he to publish his criticisms of slavery, he would feel bound not only to defend the abolitionists' rights but to enlarge on what he deemed their errors.

True to his promise, Channing examined the positions of

slaveholders and abolitionists in his essay and found both of them wanting in common sense and Christian charity. He began by establishing "a first, fundamental truth — a human being cannot rightfully be held and used as property." From this principle he proceeded to other natural rights — the right to seek knowledge, to better one's condition, to live as a member of a community under the equal protection of the law — rights violated by slavery. The initiative in removing slavery, however, he was prepared to leave to the slave-owner, who alone "has the intimate knowledge of the character and habits of the slave." Abolitionists he thought culpable on two counts: first, for hastily adopting the unworkable formula of immediate emancipation, and secondly, for indulging in irrational propaganda. The abolitionists, he said, had done great mischief, nor was this mischief to be winked at simply because it had been done with the best of intentions. The anti-slavery party had fallen into the common error of enthusiasts of taking a too narrow view and believing that there was no other sin than the one they denounced. The cause of the slave required zeal, but also the wisdom of moderation. The abolitionists had only stirred "bitter passions and a fierce fanaticism" which shut every ear and every heart against the voice of conscience.

Many of the abolitionists, though "grieved at some few censures," as Ellis Gray Loring explained, agreed with him in pronouncing "nineteen twentieths" of Channing's book sound in principle. A private dissenter was John Quincy Adams, who objected to the "jesuitical complexion" of Channing's arguments. "The wrong or crime of slavery is set forth in all its most odious colors," Adams noted in his diary, "and then the explanation disclaims all imputation of criminality upon the slaveholders." Adams's doubts were echoed loudly in the *Liberator*, which dismissed the author as an "Ishmael-

ite" and the pamphlet as "an inflated, inconsistent and slanderous production. . . . a work in active collision with itself."[3]
After appropriating every one of the abolitionists' arguments,
Garrison complained, Channing neutralized their force by
impugning their methods. "He modestly asks us to give up
our watchword 'Immediate Emancipation,' to disband our
societies, and to keep our publications from slaveholders."
What sort of give-and-take nonsense was this? The source
of Channing's heresy, he argued, was his foolish belief that
men were not always to be judged by their acts or institutions.
From this delusion it followed that slaveowners, far from
being the miserable sinners they appeared, might be thought
to act from disinterested motives of benevolence! The cardinal point in immediate emancipation, on the other hand, was
its identification of slavery as *sin*. Sin allowed of no degrees;
no plan was needed to stop sinning. But Channing exonerated
the sinner — he divorced the sinner from his sin. His work,
therefore, was "utterly destitute of any redeeming, reforming power," "calumnious, contradictory and unsound." Such
timeservers the abolitionists could well do without.

Garrison recognized Channing's pamphlet for what it was
— a threat to the continued control of the pioneer anti-slavery
men. As a liberal Channing was unable to remain silent any
longer; as a moderate he was unwilling to swallow immediate
abolition. To the Garrisonians his moderation seemed at best
a shuffling policy. "The plain English of the whole of it,"
Amos Phelps, Garrison's choleric friend, complained, "is this,
that he — *and he is but one of a hundred such* — can't keep still
any longer on the subject, but cannot bear to come out on
the subject without taking sundry exceptions, just to 'save
their skins' from the kicks we have had to take, as well as to
seem to have some justification for their long and guilty
silence."[4] The real issue, however, lay deeper than Phelps

realized. It was this: Could anti-slavery, born in religious radicalism and nurtured by the New Theology of Beecher and Finney, withstand an accession of the moderates? Could it relinquish the notion of slavery as a sin and retain its purity? Could the abolitionist sect become a church without endangering its principles, let the unregenerate in without undermining its holy work? In short, could abolition survive success? Garrison thought not. Channing cried for moderation and understanding, but the Declaration of Sentiments of the national society branded slavery a sin. Channing proposed reflection and study, and meanwhile the slave languished in chains.

Channing represented a way of life that was hostile to evangelicalism. A man of breeding, he was first and last an intellectual who distrusted undirected moral energy. He believed in intelligence and leisure, education, good taste and social poise — all that was most suspect in the view of one who had been raised on the meager intellectual fare of the evangelists. Moreover, status meant more to Garrison than he would admit. The reverse side of his myth of the self-made man showed a sense of social inferiority tinged with envy. Although he worked closely with Boston patricians in the next few years — with Wendell Phillips, Edmund Quincy, Ellis Gray Loring, Henry Bowditch — the alliances were not of his making and the terms were always his own. Such a surrender could not be expected from Channing, in whose work Garrison sensed a note of social superiority. To Channing the Garrisonians were pious fools with violent impulses which sprang from too much goodness and too little lucidity. They were men who chose passion instead of reason which was the mark of a true morality. Garrison, on the other hand, viewed Channing as the potential Judas of Christian reform, a timid closet-philosopher half afraid of his own beliefs. He seemed

to personify in his passivity the dangers of too much thinking. Of the two, Channing was perhaps the better judge of
character and certainly the more magnanimous, for it was
he who made the first tentative gesture of friendship. In
March, 1836, he attended the hearings of the Lunt Committee, which had been appointed by the Massachusetts legislature to investigate the need for a gag law against the abolitionists, and in front of the assembled legislators approached
Garrison and took his hand. Only the most sanguine of the
anti-slavery men, however, believed that the gesture symbolized a new alliance between the Garrisonians and an emergent
Northern liberalism.

The Lunt Committee was the Massachusetts answer to
Southern clamor against the abolitionists. At the suggestion
of Governor Everett a joint committee was appointed to
consider a law curtailing anti-slavery publications and meetings. Immediately the Massachusetts Anti-Slavery Society (as
the old New England Society was now called) requested a
hearing, which was held on March 4, 1836. At their briefing
sessions the society chose their speakers carefully. The burden of their case was carried by Loring, Sewall, and Follen,
the first two respectable if not brilliant speakers, the last an
eloquent and persuasive lecturer. The gallery of the Chamber
of Representatives was packed with members of the society
and anti-slavery sympathizers. All went well at the first hearing as long as Loring and Sewall held the floor, but when
Follen mounted the rostrum and unleashed an attack on the
"mobocrats" of Boston and their "blood-hounds" who made
the streets of Boston unsafe, Chairman George Lunt lost patience. "Stop sir! You may not pursue this course of remark.
It is insulting to the committee and to the Legislature which
they represent." Forbidden to continue, Follen sat down, the
abolitionists flatly refused to proceed, and the hearing was

adjourned. Next day the society drew up a memorial to the legislature complaining of the uncivil treatment they had received and demanding a free and open hearing, which demand was granted and a second hearing arranged. At the new hearing the Garrisonians fared little better. William Goodell, Garrison's waspish companion in the days of the *National Philanthropist*, arrived from New York and was quickly added to the list of speakers. Goodell had lost none of his bite since he and Garrison, seven years before, had argued the merits of colonization; and he immediately took the offensive by charging the committee with a "foul conspiracy" to subvert American freedom, only to be shut off by Lunt. Unnerved by its encounter with professional agitators, the committee adjourned never to meet again. Though it censured the anti-slavery party, the Lunt Committee failed to recommend measures for controlling their activities. Free speech had won a notable victory.

Garrison's remarks at the hearing, sandwiched in between the heavy arguments of Loring and Sewall, went almost unnoticed in the ensuing uproar. Those who troubled to listen caught a new note of sectionalism in his reference to American civil liberties. "Sir, we loudly boast of our free country, and of the Union of these States. Yet I have no country! As a New Englander, and as an abolitionist, I am excluded by a bloody proscription from one-half of the national territory. . . . Where is our Union? . . . The right of free and safe locomotion from one part of the land to the other is denied to us, except at the peril of our lives! . . . Therefore it is, I assert, that the Union is now *virtually* dissolved."[5]

Virtually but not *actually*. Garrison was not a disunionist yet: although he indulged freely in propaganda and prophecy, he was not ready to admit that the Constitution was a pro-slavery document. Like most of the abolitionists, he had veered with the winds of political change, first denouncing the Constitution as a "heaven-daring compact" and a "corrupt bargain" and then discovering in the Congressional power over the District of Columbia a beacon for Southern states. Reluctantly he had come to accept the best abolitionist opinion that Congress had no power to regulate slavery in the states. As hope for effective state action receded in the Thirties, however, and the abolitionists began to doubt their ability to convert the South, they recognized the need for capturing the Constitution. How much more effective their campaign would be, how much more important the petition and the vote, if they could prove that the Constitution was really an anti-slavery document. If it encompassed the abolition of slavery throughout the Union, then abolitionists in agitating for immediate action were only demanding due enforcement of fundamental law. A tidy syllogism, simple, unhistorical, and unrealistic. It was a measure of his deep concern with politics in an election year that despite his predictions of disunion Garrison recognized the importance of an anti-slavery interpretation of the Constitution and tried to achieve one.

The task he set himself — that of producing a consistent reading of the Constitution — was beyond his powers, for it required the kind of reasoned historical method which he had always disparaged. In the next few years other abolitionists, better equipped and more persevering, worked out dozens of theories of the unconstitutionality of slavery, all of them ingenious, none of them convincing. In 1836, however, Garrison was pioneering in a juridical wilderness with no compass to guide him. That he soon lost his bearings is hardly as surprising as that he should have attempted the discovery at all.

He found his clue to the anti-slavery character of the Constitution in the preamble, which, he announced, "presupposes oppression and slavery, in any and every form, wholly unwarrantable, and consequently is a warrant for a general emancipation of the slaves." Emancipation as implied in the preamble ought to be the work, not of Congress nor yet of the state legislatures, but of "the people of each State, and of the several States," presumably gathered in special convention. As for Article IV, Section 2, which provides for the return of persons held to service and labor, this clause does not apply to slaves because by law slaves are not "persons" but "things." By the Constitution American slavery is a thing unknown — every bondsman is therefore a freeman! "The conclusion, then, to which people of the free States must come, is this — that southern slavery is a violation of the United States Constitution, that it must be resisted as such."[6] He granted that this new reading of the Constitution marked a departure from his initial views. "We have often had occasion to speak of the wickedness of the national compact," he conceded but added quickly that his denunciation had been "extorted in view of the construction which has been put upon certain articles in the Constitution of the United States, by the supreme and inferior courts — by the physical cooperation of the free States to keep the slaves in bondage — and by the tacit recognition of slavery which was made on the adoption of the Constitution, between the several States." Now with a proper understanding of the Constitution, the abolitionists had only to uphold the fundamental law of the land. In a single stroke he had legitimized abolition and committed his followers to political action.

First and most important in his program of constitutional action was the vote with which abolitionists could organize a Christian party in politics "not made up of this or that sect or denomination, but of all who fear God and keep his commandments and who sincerely desire to seek judgment and relieve the oppressed." Politics was admittedly a dirty business and weak men might be tempted to sell their principles for political gain. But changing the world meant accepting the realities of political power. "I know it is a belief of many professedly good men," he had written in 1834, "that they ought not to 'meddle' with politics; but they are cherishing a delusion, which, if it do not prove fatal to their own souls, may prove the destruction of the country."[7] However logical the use of the ballot now seemed to him, there were those abolitionists in 1836 to whom it was a snare. They argued that from its inception the anti-slavery movement had been a *moral* crusade, and they cited Garrison's own Declaration of Sentiments of the American Anti-Slavery Society, which nowhere mentioned the duty to vote, as proof that the founders had not meant to rely on the whims of mere politicians. Impatiently Garrison brushed these objections aside with the remark that since he had drawn up the declaration, he might be assumed "competent to give an exposition of its doctrines."[8] The founders had clearly intended that both moral suasion and the franchise be brought to bear on slavery. Arguments without votes, he insisted, accomplished nothing.

To show the extent of his political commitment he supported Amasa Walker, the Democratic candidate for a Congressional seat, against the conservative Whig, Abbott Lawrence. "Ordinarily, I perceive little intelligence, and scarcely any conscience, or honesty, or fear of God, at the polls," he admitted to Boston's Negro voters. "The politics of this nation, at the present time, are corrupt, proscriptive, and even ferocious."[9] The Whig cause, which he used to think "essentially a good one," had fallen to the trimmer Clay; and Jacksonian Democracy, conceived in iniquity and unbelief, was slavery's behemoth. Nevertheless, it behooved abolitionists to study the Southern stratagem and, as he explained, "to be

competent fully to unravel its political relations and hearings.
... Although we may not, in the technical sense of the term,
become politicians ourselves, yet it is vastly important that
we should watch, and expose mere politicians — such men as
Van Buren, Calhoun, Pinckney, and the like — and the latest
movements of the State and National Governments, in their
opposition to inalienable human rights should be made manifest before all the people."[10]

As the Presidential campaign entered the summer of 1836
and the election in Massachusetts narrowed to a choice between the Little Magician and the trimmer Daniel Webster,
Garrison understood for the first time the nature of the abolitionist dilemma. "Political abolitionists are now placed in an
awkward predicament," he admitted to his friends.[11] Both
candidates had come out against abolition and had tried to
check the spread of anti-slavery influence. How could an abolitionist vote for either of them? "To this I reply," Garrison
wrote a week before the election, "it is not necessary that they
should cast their votes in favor of any Presidential candidates,
nor do we see how they can properly do so."[12] True abolitionists belonged to no party or sect; they had emancipated
themselves once and for all from political shibboleths and
sectarian fetters. Abolition alone claimed their loyalty, and
"this cause they can never abandon, or put in peril, on any
pretext whatever." Since both parties had officially declared
their hostility to anti-slavery, reformers must be wary "lest
they be seduced from their integrity of character by political
intrigue" even if it meant relinquishing their right to vote.
Such was the origin of the revolution in the Garrisonian attitude which was to end a few years later in the doctrine of
disunion. Faced with a decision that involved choosing the
lesser of two evils — a cardinal rule in democratic politics —
Garrison refused to take the step which he believed an aban-

donment of principle. In thus committing his followers to a boycott of elections he was in effect challenging the democratic process. His theory of disunion did not appear in all its splendid simplicity for two years, but the decision to "come out" from a corrupt society was the result of his disillusionment with the Presidential campaign of 1836. Henceforth the main avenue of political reform remained closed to Garrison and those like him who preferred righteousness to success.

For a while during the election year it seemed that an alternative political route lay through Congress, where petitions might do the work of ballots. Garrison had pioneered in the organized use of the anti-slavery petition in Vermont back in 1828 and was well aware of its advantages. In the first place, the right of petition was guaranteed in the Constitution: Congress was obliged to receive petitions and to take some kind of action, however unfavorable, which meant invaluable publicity for the abolitionists. Then, too, petitions were cheap, easy to circulate, and effective in bringing the slavery question before the country. Garrison's first petition campaign in 1828-1829 had provoked a lengthy and acrimonious debate in the House before the members rejected abolition of slavery in the District as inexpedient and dangerous. The advantages of a petition flood were too obvious to be ignored.

He was not alone in recognizing the possibilities of the petition. The national society, disappointed by the meager results shown by the anti-slavery pamphlet, was turning to what everyone agreed was a more economical and effective propaganda device. By the middle of the decade pamphlets had proved a costly failure. To be sure, they had won the support of a few liberals chiefly concerned with civil liberties, but this gain had been more than nullified by the problems of cost and waste. No pamphlet paid for itself, distribution was haphazard, and agents seldom knew whether the thousands of tracts they scattered over the countryside were even read. Petitions, on the other hand, were economical and effective. As local and state societies took up the strategy in earnest, the number of petitions forwarded to Congress, twenty thousand in 1836, jumped to over three hundred thousand two years later. Petitions against the foreign-slave trade, petitions for the abolition of slavery in the District of Columbia, petitions against the admission of new slave states, even petitions asserting the right of petition. A deluge of signatures poured into Congress in a steadily increasing volume until the Senate and House of Representatives finally found a way to divert the flood they could not shut off.

At first Garrison supported the petition campaign with enthusiasm. He gave orders to Knapp "to make everything give way (communications, editorials, and all) to the debates in Congress upon the petitions."[13] Feverishly he directed their distribution and collection, and gloated over the increasing number of signatures. "Send me your petitions to Congress," he ordered George Benson in January, 1836. " 'Keep the mill a-going,' as the saying is. The blustering of the southern members in Congress is ludicrous enough. The knaves and cowards!"[14] In April, when a bill for the admission of Arkansas stalled in the House, he hastily collected and forwarded petitions to keep it there. His enthusiasm waned, however, when the Southern caucus in Congress rallied to retaliate. As early as January, John C. Calhoun, sensing the need for a countermeasure against petitions, urged his colleagues to meet the danger now before it was too late. Thereupon he moved to table all anti-slavery petitions as "a foul slander on nearly one-half of the states of the Union." After a heated debate Calhoun's motion was replaced by a compromise offered by

James Buchanan of Pennsylvania which avoided outright denial of the right of petition by providing for the reception of
all anti-slavery petitions coupled with a rejection of their
contents. Buchanan's rule became standard Senate procedure
for dealing with the abolitionists. The House had John
Quincy Adams to contend with, and Adams waged a one-
man war against the "gag rule." Over his protests a special
committee of the House reported three resolutions drawn up
by its chairman, Henry Laurens Pinckney of South Carolina.
The first denied the power of Congress to abolish slavery in
the states; the second declared that slavery in the District of
Columbia should be left alone; and the third provided that
"all petitions, memorials, resolutions, propositions, or papers
relating in any way to any extent to the subject of slavery
shall, without being printed or referred, be laid upon the
table and that no further action whatever be taken thereon."
The Pinckney gag became the first of a series of gag rules
designed to meet the abolitionist challenge. Not even Adams's
parliamentary skill could prevent this biennial infringement
of civil liberties: a gag rule was passed at the beginning of
each new session until finally, in 1845 at the height of the
Mexican crisis, the last of them was repealed. By that time
Garrison was well down the road to disunion in his retreat
from politics — a withdrawal that began with the Pinckney
resolutions in 1836.

From the White House, where Demon Democracy was to
rule for four more years, and from a Congress dominated
by apostate Pinckneys and Calhouns, Garrison turned hopefully to the church only to find theocratic conservatism in
the person of Lyman Beecher in the pulpit. In 1836 Beecher
still dreamed of a Christian America united in a single Protestant church, and he was still determined to ignore any social
issue too thorny to be settled by love and charity. Beecher's

difficulties proceeded from his bland assumption that no differences were too great to be reconciled by a strong and
united church. He easily identified the chief dangers to the
country — "political atheism," "power-thirsty politicians,"
"the corrupting influence of preeminent prosperity," and
"universality of the suffrage." To combat these unwholesome
influences he invoked the power of church institutions, an
educated clergy, and, above all, the authority of the Bible.
In the summer of 1836 he delivered a ringing defense of the
divinity of the Sabbath as the moral sun of the universe and
God's instrument for man's salvation. The fourth command-
ment, as he explained it, emerged as the sublime ordering
principle of Christian life, a moral law enforced by a learned
clergy and offering the only permanent solution to the problems of democratic society. Beecher's sermon sounded the
call to the conservative clergy to meet the challenge of Garrison and his race of "impudent young men" whose defiance
of church law and clerical authority presaged a new age of
barbarism.

Garrison seized on Beecher's sermon as a lever with which
to pry open the whole question of slavery and the church.
It was not just that the good doctor's language was "extrava-
gant and preposterous," he complained. Beecher offered no
Scriptural authority for the divinity of the Sabbath. Even
more serious was Beecher's hidebound conservatism drawn
from the letter of the law rather than the spirit of Christ, his
program to make "the outward observance of one day of the
week . . . of paramount importance to every thing else in
the moral and spiritual world, instead of being subordinate
and cooperative."[15] True Christianity required the "service
of God, who is a spirit, and must be worshipped in spirit and
in truth," but Beecher and the theocrats believed that law
might do the work of spirit. They were loud, earnest, and

eloquent in behalf of the sanctity of institutions, yet timid and apprehensive on the question of human rights. "Let men consecrate to the service of Jehovah not merely one day in seven, but *all* their time, thoughts, actions and powers." Not outward observance but inner light. "If men will put on Christ," Garrison concluded, "they may be as free as their Master, and he is Lord even of the Sabbath day."

These strictures not unnaturally stirred the New England clergy to wonder and protest. "Free as their Master" — did Garrison mean freedom from sin, the attainment of perfection? Letters poured into the *Liberator* office complaining of the editor's veiled language and deploring his apparently heretical notions. "As I anticipated, my remarks upon the sanctity of the Sabbath, in the *Liberator,* are subjecting me to much censure, particularly among the *pious* opposers of the anti-slavery cause," Garrison remarked acidly. The *New Hampshire Patriot, Vermont Chronicle, Christian Mirror*, and *Boston Recorder* denounced him as a "monster" and an "infidel," simply because he held that *all* time should be devoted to the service of God and the good of mankind, because he believed that "the real children of God 'do enter into rest' here on earth, without being necessitated to wait for a respite until eternity dawns."[16] Under fire from a hostile press and the conservatives in the Massachusetts Society, he agreed to leave the Sabbath question alone and return to anti-slavery. It was a promise he could not keep: his investigation of "that pernicious and superstitious notion" had precipitated a conflict with the churches that lasted his lifetime.

His estrangement from the church, like the retreat from politics, was the result of a profound disillusionment. He was convinced that the country needed more practical righteousness, more benevolent societies and good works. Instead of attacking slavery, capital punishment, the land problem, and the other social evils of the day, the churches and the clergy were indulging in doctrinal disputes, endless polemics and theological hairsplitting. As the Great Revival smoldered out there arose a new spirit of sectarian exclusiveness and denominationalism. The years after 1835 saw a clerical reaction to revivalism which produced rifts in all of the major Protestant denominations as the conservatives seized control of their churches once more. In 1837 after a series of heresy trials, the Old School Presbyterians finally succeeded in driving out over half of their membership for doctrinal deviation. The General Conference of the Methodist Church voted in 1836 to prohibit the discussion of slavery on the grounds that the only "safe, Scriptural and prudent way" for their members was "wholly to refrain from the agitating subject which is now convulsing the country." The decision, which led Garrison to denounce the conference as "a cage of unclean birds, and a synagogue of Satan," eventually provoked a number of desertions that culminated in the great secession of 1845. The Baptist Church suffered from similar desertions as the majority of their clergy showed little inclination to lead their congregations against slavery. Conservative forces and sectional pressures were beginning to crack the façade of Protestantism.

Garrison saw only the Christian logic of the situation. He had grown up with the evangelical beliefs that everything lay within the province of Christianity and that churches were God's agents for purifying society. Since evil was one, and all sins were related, the Christian solution meant applying Christian principles to daily life. It was as simple as that. As voluntary associations of true Christians the churches ought to lead the way in reforming society. Instead they were ignoring their responsibilities and neglecting all the "great subjects" of the age. "Oh the rottenness of Christendom," he wrote to May. "Judaism and Romanism are the leading features of Protestantism. I am forced to believe that, as it respects the greater portion of professing Christians in this country, Christ has died in vain. In their traditions, their forms, their vain janglings, their self-righteousness, their will-worship, their sectarian zeal and devotion, their infallibility and exclusiveness, they are Pharisees and Saducees, they are Papists and Jews."[17] Far from encouraging good works and personal holiness, the churches were erecting defenses against it by isolating their congregations from the world of sin and substituting worship for good works. The message of Christ was being buried beneath the rubble of ritualism. "We shall not be able to exclaim, 'O death, where is thy sting? O grave, where is thy victory?' until we have died first unto sin — crucified the old man with his lusts — put on the new man who is after Christ — and risen in spirit with Him who is able to save all who believe in Him. He in whom the Saviour dwells can never be surprised by calamity or death — he has entered into rest, even while in the flesh."[18]

"Putting on Christ," "dying unto sin," "entering into rest" — these were the concepts of perfectionism, the vocabulary of the preachers of human perfectibility. They were also the words of the Vermont visionary John Humphrey Noyes, who visited Garrison in the spring of 1837 and by converting him to perfectionism helped change the course of his anti-slavery crusade.

Christian perfectionism, the doctrine of personal holiness, taught that by accepting Christ men could become literally perfect. When men leave off sinning and accept Christ, so the perfectionists believed, henceforth it is Christ who acts in them and thus sin becomes an impossibility. In the routine of their daily lives they can achieve this sinlessness if they only want to, save their souls and at the same time regenerate society. Perfectionism erected a whole social ethic on the simple command, "Be ye perfect even as your heavenly Father is perfect," and with it proposed to make heaven on earth.

Perfectionist doctrine appeared in many guises in the United States after 1830: in the preaching of Finney and his Oberlin followers; in the spiritual communings of zealots in New York's Burned-Over District; and, in its most complete form, in the teachings of John Humphrey Noyes. Although it seemed to reflect Jacksonian beliefs in progress and the mission of America, in reality perfectionism received its inspiration from the gospel of love and the Second Great Awakening. Its origins lay in the New Theology of Finney and the New Haven School and in the conviction that "obligation and ability are commensurate." Its initial premise was the total freedom of man to follow Christ. Unlike Jacksonian Democracy with its laissez-faire principles, perfectionism was essentially exclusive, severe, and, in its final appeal, authoritarian. The perfectionists caught the vision of a holy life in the sermons of the Great Revival and, by focusing sharply on the experience of conversion, distorted the dream into a millenarian fantasy. As originally propounded by Finney, perfectionism meant simply a striving for holiness. Finney defined the true Christian as one who preferred the glory of God to his own selfish interests, and sanctification as "the strength, firmness and perpetuity of this preference." By this he did not mean a state of absolute freedom from sin but only what he called an "assurance of faith" when men "habitually live without sin and fall into sin at intervals so few and far between that, in strong language, it may be said in truth they do not sin." Thus perfection became for Finney an approximable goal rather than a final achievement — an ideal to be pursued but never completely attained. In this same spirit his followers at Oberlin preached perfectionism as a prolonged act of dedication and denounced as "misguided fanatics" those who "having begun in the spirit . . . try to become perfect in the flesh." Such parading of one's purity seemed to them to savor more of carnal will than divine grace and a second blessing.

John Humphrey Noyes was perplexed by the halfway doctrines of Finney and the hesitant affirmations of the New Haven School. As a student at Yale he imbibed a draught of free will that sent his literalist mind spinning. If Christ is perfect and men are wholly free to follow his example, he reasoned, then they may become *perfect* not in a metaphorical sense of the word but in becoming actual partakers of the divine nature and sharing in Christ's victory over sin and death. "Faith identifies the soul with Christ," he explained, "so that by His death and resurrection the believer dies and rises again, not literally, nor yet figuratively, but spiritually; and thus, so far as sin is concerned, is placed beyond the grave, in heavenly places with Christ." Noyes had received his second blessing in a Leonard Street boardinghouse in New York where, in a fevered state and near insanity, he experienced a "spiritual crucifixion" not as spectator but as victim. "And at last the Lord met me with the same promise that gave peace to my soul when I first came out of Egypt: 'if thou wilt confess with thy mouth the Lord Jesus and shalt believe in thine heart that God hath raised him from the dead, thou shalt be saved.' By faith I took the proffered boon of eternal life. God's spirit sealed the act, and the blood of Christ cleansed me from sin." Soon word spread through New Haven that "Noyes says he's perfect."[19] This indeed was the gist of the message which he came to Boston to tell Garrison.

At the time of his meeting with Garrison in 1837 Noyes was still working out the initial premises of his system. Communal living, common property, complex marriage were only hazy outlines on a shore dimly seen. What was already clear to Noyes, however, was the new relationship of the perfectionist to the society and the government of the United States, and this he proceeded to explain to Garrison, Whittier and Stanton. A week after the visit he sat down and put his views on paper for Garrison's benefit. Presuming on "a fellowship of views and feelings" which he had sensed at the interview, he went on to expound the question of the kingdom of God and its relation to the kingdom of this world. "I am willing that all men should know that I have subscribed my name to an instrument similar to the Declaration of '76, renouncing all allegiance to the government of the United States, and asserting the title of Jesus Christ to the throne of the world."[20] This was no metaphysical abstraction or dramatic gesture, he assured Garrison, but a flat statement of belief and a program for action. The United States government acted the bully swaggering about and trampling underfoot both the Constitution and the Bible, whipping slaves at the liberty-pole and blaspheming in holy places by proclaiming slavery a law of God. What then could the Christian do? Escape? "But every other country is under the same reprobate authority." The only solution lay in "coming out" from an evil society, fleeing the country in spirit, and refusing to be either a hypocrite or a tyrant. "Every person who is, in the usual sense of the expression, a citizen of the United States, *i.e.*, a voter, politician, etc., is at once a slave and a slave-holder — in other words a subject and a ruler." God would justify him in the character of subject but not of ruler, Noyes explained, and only by renouncing all cooperation with the authorities of a sinful government could he finally cease to do evil and learn to do well. Reform was merely an illusion, since reprobation and reproof, as the history of the abolition movement showed, only aggravated the sins of the people.

The sole choice left to the son of God was to declare war on the government of the United States and to wage it with the weapons of Christ — renunciation and repudiation.

In place of the erroneous axioms of American government Noyes offered Garrison some self-evident principles of his own. First, that the territory of the United States belongs to God, and the American people are guilty of infidelity in trying to perpetuate an existence outside the kingdom of Christ. Second, that all nations will be dashed to pieces before the arrival of the kingdom of God, and all governments therefore are merely "as shadows of good things to come. . . . The Son of God has manifestly, to me, chosen this country for the theater of such an assault. . . . *My hope of the millennium begins where Dr. Beecher's expires* — viz., AT THE TOTAL OVERTHROW OF THIS NATION." The United States will fall before a revolution, "a convulsion like that of France," out of which will come instead of a sanguinary Napoleon the Prince of Peace. "The convulsion which is coming will be, not the struggle of death, but the travail of childbirth — the birth of a ransomed world." To prepare for the glorious day Noyes advised Garrison to give up his "fencing-school" skirmish against slavery and join the "general engagement" by occupying the ground of universal emancipation from sin. "I counsel you, and the people that are with you, if you love the post of honor — the forefront of the hottest battle of righteousness — to set your face toward *perfect* holiness. Your station is one that gives you power over the nations. Your city is on a high hill. . . . I judge from my own experience that you will be deserted as Jonah was by the whale — the world, in vomiting you up, will heave you upon the dry land."

Garrison succumbed to this Messianic appeal with its devastatingly simple logic. Noyes made expediency and compromise cardinal sins by erecting an absolute standard of conduct

with which to measure the slightest deviation from righteousness. The simplicity of perfectionism masked its authoritarian
character, its oracular demand for total commitment to "practical holiness." It was as though Noyes had explained and
simplified all of Garrison's longings and desires. Perfectionism
satisfied his need for order at the same time it released his
tremendous energy. It offered the security of a seemingly
consistent system free from confusing exceptions and apparent
contradictions. It replaced reform with revolution complete
with apocalyptic vision and millenarian myth. But there was
an inherent paradox in perfectionism which Garrison failed
to see. It defined goals and at the same time denied the authority of institutions through which these goals might be
attained. It pointed out the good society and then refused
permission to advance toward it. Agreeing on the nature of
evil, the perfectionists were unwilling to employ the political
power needed to wipe it out. As to both means and ends
perfectionism postulated anarchy by reducing social wrongs
to a question of personal sin and appealing not to community
interest but to individual anxieties. Instead of rational appeals
to self-interest or national welfare, it offered the jeremiad. In
perfectionism, the revival doctrine of sanctification reached
its outermost limits in the mystical cult of personal piety.

Inspired by Noyes and determined to bring all of his various reform interests under a single head, Garrison set to work
adapting perfectionism to his own needs. Unlike Noyes, he
could not lay claim to a "second blessing," a regenerative
experience which could raise a theological concept into an
article of faith. He turned instead to the Bible which he
knew so well and pored over the gospels of Paul and John
for confirmation of Noyes's doctrines. "He that is born of
God cannot commit sin." "He that committeth sin is of the
devil." "There is therefore no condemnation to them who

are in Christ Jesus, who walk not after the flesh but after the
Spirit. For the law of the Spirit of life in Christ Jesus hath
made us free from the law of sin and death." Here was proof
in abundance. Excited, he wrote to Henry Wright to share
with him his discovery.

The remedy . . . will not be found in anything short of faith
in our Lord Jesus Christ [he assured him]. Human governments
will remain in violent existence as long as men are resolved not to
bear the cross of Christ, and to be crucified unto the world. But
in the kingdom of God's dear Son, holiness and love are the only
magistracy. It has no swords, for they are beaten into plough-
shares — no spears, for they are changed into pruning-hooks — no
military academy, for the saints cannot learn war any more — no
gibbet, for life is regarded as inviolate — no chains, for all are free.
And that kingdom is to be established upon earth, for the time is
predicted when the kingdoms of this world will become the kingdoms of the Lord and of his Christ.[21]

In preparing for the Day of Judgment unregenerate politicians and corrupt democracy will inevitably fail. "Our doom
as a nation is sealed," he wrote in the *Liberator* to explain
perfectionism to his readers. The day of probation is ended
and we are not saved. Republican government is doomed, for
the spirit of Christ has fled and left it "in a state of loathsome
decomposition."[22]

If the United States is destined to collapse, then why do the
perfectionists preach repentance? — "of what avail will it be
for any of us, in obedience to the command of heaven, to
take a bunch of hyssop, and strike the lintel and side-posts of
our dwellings with blood?" Garrison's reply was significant.
"Because the Lord is to pass through the land, to redeem the
captives and punish their oppressors; and when he seeth the
blood upon the lintels and side-posts, the Lord will pass
over the door, and will not suffer the destroyer to come into

our houses to smite us." At Judgment Day it will be every man for himself, and the righteous will be found with the angels.

Garrison's acceptance of perfectionism marked the ascendancy in his mind of personal salvation over social responsibility. Since its inception the anti-slavery movement had veered between the poles of individual purity and communal regeneration. Perfectionism destroyed the social force of abolition and left the Garrisonians grouped about the pole of sanctification like iron filings magnetized by the pull of holiness. His critics were right in complaining of the anarchical tendencies of perfectionism — the logical outgrowth of its principles was disunion and the denunciation of "the covenant with death."

Meanwhile he occupied himself with the "great subject," defining its terms in verse and trying to grasp the essentials of practical holiness. Perfection bestows eternal rest:

> . . . It is to be
> Perfect in love and holiness;
> From sin eternally made free;
> Not under law, but under grace;
> Once cleansed from guilt, forever pure;
> Once pardoned, ever reconciled;
> Once healed, to find a perfect cure;
> As JESUS blameless, undefiled;
> Once saved, no more to go astray. . . .

The political implications of perfectionism he explained in a letter to Henry Wright, who was no less enthusiastic about Christian anarchy. "Human governments pre-suppose that the government of God is essentially defective — not sufficiently broad and comprehensive to apply to every action of life between man and man, and every exigency that may arise in national concerns. . . . But human government rests on a choice between two evils, both of which the gospel is designed to destroy." Besides, human society cannot live in a state of anarchy without rapidly annihilating itself. "What then?" he asked Wright. "Shall we, *as Christians*, applaud and do homage to human government? Or shall we not rather lay the axe at the root of the tree, and attempt to destroy both cause and consequence together? Happy will it be for mankind, when He whose sole right it is to reign, shall come and reign."[23] Until that time he foresaw a long period of trial before he gained acceptance for these new truths. Unhappily, his own assignment of winning the assent of the American people seemed to require neither charity nor forbearance.

11

A Woman in the Pulpit

IN JUNE, 1837, Garrison attended the annual meeting of the American Anti-Slavery Society in New York. Between sessions he wandered into the Ladies Anti-Slavery Convention meeting a few blocks away and there met "Carolina's high-souled daughters," Sarah and Angelina Grimké. The Grimké sisters, keen abolitionists and fierce feminists both, were currently holding forth on the sins of the slaveholders before assemblies of New York ladies and had caused so much of a stir in the city that they were already contemplating an invasion of New England. Garrison must have been encouraging, for two weeks later the sisters arrived in Boston primed with lectures for New England audiences and anxious to enlist his support for the emancipation of women.

Sarah and Angelina Grimké, aged forty-four and thirty-two, were the prim, plain spinster daughters of a Charleston planter. Educated for the gaieties of Charleston society, the sisters reluctantly endured their share of fancy balls and theater parties until their brother, fresh from an indoctrination at Yale, mercifully set them free from worldly snares by converting them to Christian reform. In 1835 they moved to Philadelphia, where first Sarah and then Angelina joined the Quakers and became abolitionists. Both were outspoken and remarkably articulate if more than a trifle antiseptic. In that year Angelina published an *Appeal to the Christian Women of the South* and Sarah an *Epistle to the Clergy of the South,* high-toned pleas for the slave, both of which were promptly burned by the Charleston postmaster. The sisters deemed such rancor a sufficient deterrent to their return and henceforth confined their activities to the North.

The national society could hardly afford to ignore such promising material, and accordingly the sisters were invited to attend Weld's series of lectures to prepare for work in the field. They impressed Weld as much by their impatience as by their intelligence, for they threw themselves into anti-slavery work in New York as though it held the answer to woman's worth to American society. They visited Negro homes, addressed women's anti-slavery auxiliaries, held court for the leading abolitionists of the city, and meanwhile perfected their considerable histrionic talents. They were more than ready when Garrison beckoned them to Boston.

Sarah was a seeker who found in the anti-slavery crusade a temporary escape from the boredom and loneliness that awaited the spinster in the nineteenth century. She was tall, angular, homely beyond belief, on the threshold of middle age, unhappy with her status and determined to change it. She had experimented with Methodism and Presbyterianism before seeking an outlet for her feminist energies in the Society of Friends. Even among the Quakers she felt constrained by rules and customs that seemed to advertise the natural inferiority of her sex. Everywhere she turned she encountered the will to keep women in unholy subjection to men. "I am greatly mistaken," she once told Weld, "if most men have not a desire that women should be silly." They need be silly no longer, she declared; the great self-evident principles of human rights could be invoked in behalf of women as well as slaves. Angelina, younger and more impetuous, though

scarcely prettier than her sister, agreed that the cause of
woman's rights was bound to that of the slave. Already half
in love with Weld and determined to show him her real
worth, she easily mastered the art of lecturing and began to
use the anti-slavery platform as a sounding board for her
feminist as well as her abolitionist convictions. Her sister was
apt to stammer and mumble through her talks, but Angelina
soon perfected a delivery which, while properly reticent, was
also eloquent and moving.

Together the Grimkés took Boston by storm. In the beginning they spoke only to small groups of dedicated females,
but soon they branched out to "promiscuous assemblies" of
determined wives and their curious husbands who came to
hear the famous sisters exalt the national character of the
American woman. Angelina and Sarah warmed to Boston
immediately. "There is some elasticity in this atmosphere,"
Sarah reported to Weld. "I have been truly refreshed by
mingling with the abolitionists of Boston and vicinity. . . . I
feel as if I was helped, strengthened, invigorated, and I trust
the cause of God will be advanced."[1] The advance of abolition, however, was destined to be stalled by the whims of
these feminine perfectionists. Courageous and self-reliant as
they appeared, the sisters were in fact singularly dependent
upon the ideas and opinions of men. In New York they had
found a father and teacher in Theodore Weld; in Boston
they inevitably fell under the spell of the "noble Garrison."

Since his fateful interview with Noyes, Garrison had been
too busy attending conventions and worrying over the future
of the *Liberator* to devote himself wholly to perfectionism.
At the annual meeting of the Massachusetts Society earlier
that year he had squelched objections to his editorial thunder-
tones and won the support of the Board of Managers for his
plan for obtaining financial aid while keeping his editorial

independence. With the society supposedly behind him he began lashing out at the New England churches and their ministry, ridiculing the pastoral office and denouncing the complacency of congregations. Some of his censure was absurdly petty. "We object to the term 'house of God' as applied to any building made by man," he announced. "It has begotten much superstition, is not correct in fact, nor is it authorized by the gospel." He did not stop with mere carping, however, but proceeded to accuse the churches of fostering corruption and despotism and asked whether the advocates of truth were not obliged to come out from among them. Not satisfied with his general indictment he singled out Professor Moses Stuart of Andover and President Wilbur Fisk of Wesleyan as objects of rebuke. Fisk had asked Stuart for his views on the Biblical sanction for slavery; and Stuart, after careful study of the New Testament, gave as his opinion that the relation of master and slave was not, as a matter of course, abrogated between all Christians. When Garrison read this "piece of self-contradiction and absurdity," he dismissed it with the sneering observation that "no man — whether he be a Doctor of Divinity or a Doctor of Law, or the most learned rabbi in the land, can write or talk five minutes, either in vindication or palliation of the crime of slaveholding without uttering gross absurdity or flat blasphemy."[2] This was his mood when the Grimkés swept into New England.

He was in Brooklyn recuperating from an exhausting round of conventions when the Grimkés arrived. The sisters thus fell into the eager if not very capable hands of Henry Wright, his partner in perfectionism and an agent of the national society in New England. Garrison did not meet the formidable sisters until the end of the summer, but meanwhile he began surveying the questions of slavery and human government from the rarefied plane of Noyes's perfectionism. It was a dizzying perspective. Human government, he concluded, was better than anarchy just as a hailstorm was preferable to an earthquake or the smallpox to the Asiatic cholera. Forms of government hardly mattered, since all institutions rested on ambition and pride, selfishness and hatred.[3] The idea of any human government supposed that God's plan was radically defective. Left to their own devices men would rapidly annihilate themselves and peace would come with the rule of Christ.

Politicians and philosophers have sometimes foolishly speculated about the best forms of human government, and their relative adaptation to the conditions of mankind in the various parts of the Globe — whether, for instance, the republican form is not better than the monarchial, and the elective than the hereditary, in all cases. But this is idle. What is government but the express image of the moral character of a people? As a general rule, in the nature of things, the deeper a nation is sunken in ignorance and depravity, the more arbitrary and cruel will be the government established over it, both in a religious and political point of view.[4]

While Garrison pondered the apocalypse in his rustic surroundings, the Grimkés and Henry Wright were preparing the day of its coming. "Dear brother Wright," as Angelina called him, was the first and most durable of the Garrisonian radicals. He was a spare, rawboned man with granitic features, close-cropped iron-gray hair and glacial blue eyes — one of Garrison's yeomen who "have gloriously triumphed over the aristocracy of the city." By trade a hatmaker, he studied theology at Andover and at the age of twenty-six took a church in West Newbury just as Garrison launched the *Free Press* and, like him, was soon swallowed up in the sea of moral reform. He served as agent of the American

Sunday School Union, became a member of William Ladd's peace society, and joined the abolitionists in 1835. Garrison pronounced him "a valuable acquisition to our cause — a fearless, uncompromising and zealous Christian." He might have added that Wright was also restless, vain and querulous. One of the most remarkable aspects of a career studded with broken friendships was the deep affection which these two overbearing and ambitious men had for each other. Both were "ultras" who looked out at the sins of the world through the strong lens of moral absolutes and spied their salvation in works of practical holiness. When he first met the Grimkés and appointed himself their agent, Wright was one of Weld's Band of Seventy and the Children's Agent for New England. An uncompromising Christian he may have been, but an effective anti-slavery agent he certainly was not. His obsession with nonresistance and his willingness to drop the subject of slavery like a hot coal whenever the peace question arose made him something of a headache to the Agency Committee, who were less interested in the millennium than in freedom for the slave. A lecture tour by two ardent feminists endorsed by Garrison and managed by Wright contained all the explosive ingredients of a crisis.

With Wright as counselor the Grimkés quickly took up perfectionism in earnest. They read Noyes's paper eagerly and discussed with Wright the fine points of nonresistance, public worship, the status of women, and the failings of human government. "Sometimes I am ready to turn away from the contemplation of these subjects least [sic] my mind should not dwell sufficiently on slavery," Sarah confessed to Weld, but added that the more she reflected on the problem, the more she was convinced that "light on every subject is a blessing."[5] Angelina was even more obdurate. When the New England clergy began to object to her addressing mixed audiences, she replied that "the *time* to assert a right is *the* time when that right is denied," and that if she were to be of any use in the anti-slavery cause her right to labor in it must be firmly established. Anti-slavery conservatives, she complained, were trying hard to separate what God had joined together. For one, she did not see how different moral reforms could ever be kept entirely distinct. "The whole Church Government must come down," she informed the startled Weld. "The clergy stand right in the way of reform, and I do not know but this stumbling block too must be removed *before* Slavery can be abolished, for the system is supported by them; it could not exist without the Church as it is called."[6] Poor Weld, who loved Angelina but not her "highly analogical" mind, objected strenuously to arguments which he told her "reversed the laws of nature. . . . No moral enterprise when prosecuted with ability and any sort of energy EVER failed under heaven so long as its conductors pushed the main principles and did not strike off until they got to the summit level," he reminded the sisters sternly. On the other hand, every moral enterprise that ever foundered was capsized by a gusty side wind. Perfectionism and woman's rights, he could see, were blowing up a storm in Boston that might swamp the anti-slavery bark.[7]

In September the sisters met Garrison at long last. "Dear brother Garrison has been passing the day with us," Sarah reported from Brookline, "as iron sharpeneth iron so doth a man the counten[ance] of his friend and it has cheered my spirit to find that he unites fully with us on the subject of the rights of women."[8] He joined in deploring the failures of New England ministers and promised to keep the *Liberator* filled with editorials upholding the cause of freedom for women. The sisters suggested he abandon anti-slavery as the exclusive object of his paper and include all the "grand principles" of moral reform. "I feel somewhat at a loss," he admitted, "to know what to do — whether to go into all the principles of holy reform, and make the abolition cause subordinate, or whether still to persevere in the *one* beaten track as hitherto." Before he had time to decide, the Grimkés had touched off the controversy which was to end two years later in the disruption of the anti-slavery movement.

The trouble began, Sarah admitted, when the Lord "very unexpectedly made us the means of bringing up the discussion of the question of woman's preaching."[9] Even crusty Amos Phelps temporarily relinquished his Pauline prejudices and went to hear Angelina. Large and enthusiastic audiences led Sarah to conclude that the time was approaching when Christians would realize that there was neither male nor female but that all were one in Christ. That time, she soon discovered, was not yet. The General Association of Congregational Ministers, which met in the summer of 1837, saw in the Grimkés' indiscreet behavior a means of settling accounts with Garrison for his unseemly remarks on their churches. The ministers drew up a pastoral letter denouncing the tendency of reformers to introduce "perplexed and agitating subjects" into their congregations and deploring the loss of deference to the pastoral office which was the mark of Christian urbanity and "a uniform attendant of the full influence of religion upon the individual character." Without naming the Grimkés or Garrison the pastoral letter warned of "the dangers which at present seem to threaten the female character with widespread and permanent injury" by leading her to transcend "the modesty of her sex." Especially did they bewail the intimate acquaintance and "promiscuous conversation" of females with regard to things which ought not to be named, "by which that delicacy which is the charm of domestic life, and which constitutes the true influence of woman in society, is consumed and the way opened, as we apprehend, for degeneracy and ruin."[10] No longer would the Grimkés be permitted their oblique references to the sexual habits of slaveholders.

As a weapon against Garrison the pastoral letter was not very formidable and might best have been ignored, but before he mustered a reply a second allegation burst on the public, an Appeal of Clerical Abolitionists on Anti-Slavery Measures, signed by five clergymen from eastern Massachusetts. The dissenters found the courage publicly to disapprove Garrison's course and accuse him of "hasty, unsparing, almost ferocious denunciation" of everybody who disagreed with him. "The time is very fully in our recollection," they declared, "when *we* were not abolitionists; nor are we conscious that *we* were *then* either hypocrites or knaves."[11]

The clerical appeal, though the work of only a handful of ministers, had the merit of broadening the charges against Garrison from mere clerical pique at the invasion of women to a general indictment of his radical methods. For his part, Garrison was delighted with it since it gave him a chance to fight on the solid ground of anti-clericalism rather than on the shifting sands of woman's rights. Hurriedly he sent his reply for immediate publication in the *Liberator*. Ignoring the charges of personal malice and incompetence, he identified as the chief supporters of slavery those "latter-day Jesuits" and "rabbis" in sacerdotal robes who presumed to censure honest men. "Abolitionism brings ministers and laymen upon the same dead level of equality, and repudiates all 'clerical' assumption and spiritual supremacy. Nothing can be more offensive to it, than this attempt to enforce opinions in an oracular tone as CLERGYMEN."[12]

Meanwhile the *New England Spectator*, the organ of the clerical party, printed an attack from still another clergyman,

James T. Woodbury, who had been longing for the chance to squelch the *Liberator*. "I am an abolitionist," Woodbury wrote, "and I am so in the strictest sense of the term; but I never swallowed Wm. Lloyd Garrison, and I never tried to swallow him." Garrison, he continued, was bent on the overthrow of the Sabbath, the ministry, and the whole American church. "We are not willing for the sake of killing rats, to burn down the house with all it contains." With his "peculiar theology" Garrison had become a menace to the anti-slavery cause and must be disavowed. "No doubt, if you break with Garrison, some will say, 'You are no abolitionist,' for, with some, Garrison is the god of their idolatry. He embodies abolition. He is abolition personified and incarnate." He was nonetheless dangerous, Woodbury declared, and called on Christian reformers to save the anti-slavery cause from heresy and atheism.[13]

Woodbury's letter was a tactical error, for it shifted the ground of attack once more from Garrison's anti-clericalism to questions of personality. Garrison was quick to oblige his critic. His distaste was not an isolated case, he reminded Woodbury. "The robbers of God's poor, the supporters of lynch law, the chief priests, scribes and pharisees, have all been unable to 'swallow Wm. Lloyd Garrison.'" Yet in a sense, he pointed out, all thoroughgoing abolitionists had followed him from colonization to abolition, then from gradualism to immediatism. How else explain his "delightful association" with men of all political parties and religious denominations? Because of his uncompromising way of telling the truth he was, in fact, indispensable to the cause.[14]

The Executive Committee of the national society viewed this quarrel with growing dismay. On the scene was one of their agents, Henry B. Stanton, a sharp-eyed and hardheaded organizer with little patience for either Garrison's religious notions or the pompous pretensions of the clerical party. Stanton identified the cause of the row as Garrison's personal brand of "locofocoism" which had ignited the fuse of a conservative reaction. Unless the Executive Committee intervened, he warned, there would be a war of extermination that could spell the end of anti-slavery in New England. "I expect to see the *Liberator* containing 3 or 4 columns castigating bro. Woodbury and the Andover students," he predicted, " – and next week, in the *Liberator*, I expect to see 4 or 5 columns – in reply to the 'Protest' of bros. Fitch and Towne, and then in due time, another reply to their next 'protest,' and then their rejoinder, and his surrejoinder with their rebutter, and his surrebutter."[15] The dissidents demanded nothing less than the separation of the *Liberator* and the Massachusetts Anti-Slavery Society. Woodbury, Fitch and Company had been pushed to the wall and were resolved to stand it no longer; the Garrisonians were determined on war to the knife. "They will not yield an inch, to prevent the formation of a thousand new organizations." Unless an "umpire influence" from New York prevented it, the New England mutiny, Stanton cautioned the Executive Committee, would destroy the cause.

But what was the Executive Committee to do? Lewis Tappan thought the whole affair inflated to ridiculous proportions, a local squabble which the national society could well ignore. He wrote Garrison to this effect and added that he did not think the clerical appeal such a "monstrous subject" that it required all the abolition artillery in the nation to dispose of it. Besides, he reminded Garrison, the *Liberator* frequently gave cause for complaint. "THE SPIRIT EXHIBITED BY THE EDITOR PRO. TEM [Oliver Johnson] AND SOMETIMES BY YOURSELF, HAS NOT BEEN SUFFICIENTLY KIND AND CHRIST-LIKE."[16] James Birney, now a full-fledged abolitionist, went

HELEN BENSON GARRISON

GARRISON AT THIRTY

GARRISON AND WENDELL PHILLIPS

GARRISON AT FIFTY

GARRISON AT SEVENTY

BENJAMIN LUNDY

PRUDENCE CRANDALL,
THE QUAKER SCHOOLMISTRESS

SAMUEL JOSEPH MAY

EDMUND QUINCY

ANGELINA GRIMKÉ

SARAH GRIMKÉ

THEODORE WELD

HENRY C. WRIGHT

NATHANIEL P. ROGERS

ABBY KELLEY FOSTER

STEPHEN SYMONDS FOSTER

even further in reproaching Garrison for his lack of self-control. "If Mr. Garrison, or anyone else among us, thinks that *he* is authorized to judge and rebuke *as Christ judged and rebuked*, it becomes him to recall the instances of melting love, the meekness, the forbearance of the Master."[17] Garrison shot back the terse rejoinder that "Bro. Birney appears to have grown exceedingly fastidious and hypercritical."

It was Elizur Wright, however, who wrote to Garrison all the "objectionable things" that candor induced him to say. He had hoped that Garrison could have conducted his paper "without travelling off the ground of our true, noble, heart-stirring Declaration of Sentiments," but since he had chosen to wander from the straight path of abolition, he must not complain when other abolitionists as dedicated as himself objected to his novel views. Wright spoke of himself as typical of these men. "As you well know, I am comparatively no bigot to any creed, political or theological; yet to tell the plain truth, I look upon your notions of government and religious perfection as downright fanaticism — as harmless as they are absurd. I would not care a pin's head if they were preached to all Christendom; for it is not in the human mind (except in a peculiar and diseased state,) to believe them." How could Garrison expect to avoid the censure of all intelligent men when he insisted on making these heretical opinions the test of anti-slavery orthodoxy? Leave the question of government alone until the Negro was free, Wright warned — "then you may make your will upon it for all of me. . . . But if this cannot be done, why, come out plainly and say you have left the old track and started on a new one — or, rather, two or three new ones at once, and save us from the miserable business of making disclaimers."[18]

Wright's plain speaking only convinced Garrison that the forces of sectarianism had invaded national headquarters, where something was obviously amiss. "Our friends at New York," he replied ominously, "may rely upon it, that the course which they have resolved to pursue, respecting this matter, will very much displease the great body of abolitionists, and alienate them and their money from the Parent Society."[19] Justice clearly upheld the Garrisonians, and the Executive Committee must not mind if the Garrisonians, in turn, gave Justice a helping hand.

The scenario for the Clerical Conspiracy was pure *opéra bouffe*, but the questions it raised were — and still are — fundamental to American politics. Where does social reform begin — in the gradual improvement of society or in the conscience of the private citizen? What is the more effective instrument of reform — the political minority which accepts its role in a democratic society or the religious sect which repudiates the community and its laws? Is it better to accept half a loaf or refuse to take less than the whole? Who accomplishes more — the moderate who will bargain to get what he wants or the radical who will not? The choice between political reform and religious revolution had been implicit in the anti-slavery movement from the beginning. The abolitionist crusade in the United States was not simply an appendage to Jacksonian Democracy, the religious corollary to a new secular democratic spirit. The anti-slavery impulse was fundamentally a religious urge and the abolitionist pioneers were endowed with a lively sense of their mission. They saw their work as nothing less than the completion of the great Protestant tradition of Luther, Calvin, Knox, Edwards, and Wesley — they were preparing the climax of a three-hundred-year Reformation. They knew that their strength lay in the churches of America and the deep-rooted religious sense of the people which undercut the experience of revolution. They had their share of Jacksonian optimism, but for them Manifest Destiny carried a special and an overtly religious meaning — the destiny of a chosen people to bring divine light to the rest of the world. The importance of the American political experiment as they understood it lay in the attempt to fuse religious truths and political techniques. Most of them accepted the need for popular democracy even though they did not like all its consequences. Gradually, as the movement grew, the abolitionists began to feel the pressure of a hostile environment driving them to broaden the scope of their reform to include political aspirations and economic motives in addition to the original religious platform.

Thus the anti-slavery crusade, split by the same inner contradictions as was Christianity itself, marched under the conflicting standards of personal holiness and social obligation, following first the directives of an inner voice and then the dictates of common sense. The Anti-Slavery Society was both a *church* and a *sect* — an institution appealing to the community at large, and a gathered group of true believers. The anti-slavery formula, "immediate emancipation," reflected this ambiguity. Strictly construed it meant instant repentance and direct action; upon deliberation, it seemed to signify some kind of political engagement. These alternatives were also embodied in the personalities of the abolitionists themselves — in the shrewd and practical organizers like Weld, Birney, and Stanton, and the zealots like Henry Wright, Charles Burleigh, and Garrison.

It was Weld who explained the philosophy of adjustment to the Grimké sisters in the hope of winning them back from Garrison and perfectionism. He was in love with Angelina but disturbed at the thought of a wife who would dedicate both their lives to renovating the world at a single stroke. In a series of long and painfully reasonable letters he convinced them of the impracticality of their views. "Since the world began," he wrote, "Moral Reform has been successfully advanced only in one way, and that has been by uplifting a great *self evident central* principle before all eyes. Then after keeping the principle in full blaze till it is *admitted* and *accredited* and the surrounding mass of mind is brought over and *committed* to it, *then* the derivative principles which radiate in all directions from this main central principle have been held up in the light of it and the mind having already embraced the central principle, moves *spontaneously outward* over all its *relations*."[20] How did Luther give the Reformation its irresistible momentum but by making the sale of indulgences his "fulcrum and lever"? How explain the success of reform in England unless by the fact that slavery was discussed for years "in every corner; the whole English mind was soaked with it." Reformers had to be practical, he reminded the sisters, and practicality meant a realistic accommodation of means to ends. To demand a total change in the human spirit all at once or approach a society with a panacea was to reverse the order of nature and misread history and the human condition.

In attempting to counteract the millenarian spirit issuing from 46 Washington Street, Weld spoke for a growing number of abolitionists who were resolved to make anti-slavery respectable. Birney, Stanton, Wright and Joshua Leavitt were already thinking of organizing the political strength of anti-slavery and were agreed on the need to keep it free from heretical ideas. It seemed to them that Garrison was using his prestige to destroy the movement. Four years ago they too had believed in the sufficiency of a moral appeal based on the formulas of sin and repentance, but in 1837 there was need for a few second thoughts. In the first place, their faith in the anti-slavery tract, the petition and the lecture had been

shaken by an obvious lack of results. Without the support
of the churches anti-slavery was doomed. What was needed,
they realized, was an organized attempt to win over all of the
major denominations. For this reason they resented Garrison's
attacks on the clergy. How, they asked, could anti-slavery
make converts without relying on religious and political
institutions? Implicit in their argument was the assumption that the only practicable way of reforming the South
was by outvoting it. The logic of their argument led directly
to the anti-slavery political party built with economic and
political as well as moral planks. It meant secularizing abolition and adjusting it to the role of a political minority in a
democratic society. It meant accepting the limitations of
minority action — compromises, concessions, limited goals —
and working within the institutional framework of American
democracy, co-operating with churches, infiltrating political
parties or creating new ones, educating people by the slow
process of discussion, surrendering absolute judgments for
limited and conditional support, trading moral will for votes.
In short, it meant the Liberty Party, the Free Soil Party, and
ultimately the Republican Party.

Thus by 1837 anti-slavery had reached a crossroad. One
road led into the broad highway of American political reform. This was the road pointed out by Weld, Birney and
Stanton that connected with the continuity and conservative
tradition of American life. The other road was a highroad of
moral idealism which cut directly across the conservative
pattern of American society to revolution, secession and civil
war. This was the road Garrison chose.

To a certain extent his choice was dictated by the demands
of his authoritarian temperament. What concerned him was
not slavery as an institution but the slave as a child of God. If
his diagnosis was correct, American society was sick and

needed the kind of surgery that only a Christian radical could perform. Slavery was one of the symptoms of approaching decline, but there were others — the treatment of women, the oppression of the poor, expansionism and a war spirit. For all these ills perfectionism offered a total cure. But moral rehabilitation was too urgent a problem to be left to the whims of weak men with their corrupt institutions. How could he work with ministers who accepted slavery or with politicians who denied women their rights? How could he embrace children of darkness who reveled in sin? A true Christian was compelled to come out from among them, to renounce their evil ways and escape everlasting perdition. As he reviewed the anti-slavery record, it seemed to him that abolitionists had never really been either tolerant or democratic. They were servants of the Lord, not catchpenny politicians. They had spurned a compromise with the colonizationists, demolished Lyman Beecher's fanciful scheme of conciliation, and courted the most dangerous kind of unpopularity. Why should they balk at perfectionism? Everyone admitted the evil of slavery was its denial of Christ to the black man. Then any law, institution, or government which refused to acknowledge the enormity of that sin would have to be destroyed. The children of light, he saw now, were covenanted together for the subversion of wickedness and the establishment of freedom — the absolute freedom of the righteous who have escaped the bondage of sin.

Garrison's generation proceeded from the premise that there were no moral issues or political differences fundamental enough to paralyze the energies of free government. Forgetting its revolutionary heritage, it believed that moral questions, like political interests, were matters for adjustment, and that in exchange for their promise of good behavior minorities might receive a majority guarantee of fair play.

This assumption meant that the American democracy functioned effectively just so long as there were no absolute moral
judgments to clog the machinery. Garrison's belief was one
of these absolutes. For him the central fact of American life
was the immorality of slavery. If he ever convinced the people of the North of that fact, constitutional government
would collapse. His kind of agitation made civil war a distinct
possibility by disclosing the impotence of compromise and
good will in the face of the moral idealism of an elite.

To this perfectionist elite he addressed his prospectus for
the eighth volume of the *Liberator*, promising them that slavery would still be the "grand object" of his labors "though
not, perhaps, so exclusively as before." He offered these
"honest-hearted" and "pure-minded" faithful the dominion
of God:

. . . the control of an inward spirit, the government of love, and
. . . the obedience and liberty of Christ. As to the governments of
this world, whatever their titles or forms, we shall endeavor to
prove, that in their essential elements, and as at present adminis-
tered, they are all Anti-Christ; that they can never, by human
wisdom, be brought into conformity with the will of God; . . .
that all their penal enactments being a dead letter without an
army to carry them into effect, are virtually written in human
blood; and that the followers of Jesus should instinctively shun
their stations of 'honor, power and emolument.'[21]

For the power of democratic institutions he now substituted
his old belief in the absolute authority of the righteous man.

It was not with righteousness but with women's votes that
he finally defeated his clerical enemies at a meeting in Worcester. To insure a majority he arranged for the admission of
women delegates in the expectation that his foes would attempt a vote of censure. As he anticipated, the ministers appointed a spokesman to present their charges, but when he

tried to speak, he was shouted down by a host of female voices until Garrison in a magnificent gesture came forward to demand that his opponent be heard. The convention listened sullenly to the clerical complaints only to dismiss them and hurriedly vote its confidence in the continued leadership of William Lloyd Garrison. He had won the first trial of strength in the Massachusetts Society and women had made all the difference.

Meanwhile Sarah and Angelina Grimké returned to New York and the anxious Weld. Angelina had decided that she cared for him more than for the rights of women, and Sarah, less sure of Weld's wisdom but devoted to her sister, acquiesced in Angelina's decision. In their year with Garrison the sisters had ventured out on the sea of moral reform and plumbed its depth to find in the murky currents beneath the surface the hidden American prejudices against change. Garrison had proved a helpful guide if not an expert navigator. In their turn the Grimkés had shown him that in the emotional storms threatening his ship of reform women were valuable shipmates.

The alliance between Garrison and American women was hardly fortuitous. They knew in a way that men could not know what it meant to be a slave, to live under the control of another. This is what Angelina Grimké meant when she said that men ought to be satisfied with the dominion they had exercised for six thousand years "and that more true nobility would be manifested by endeavoring to raise the fallen and invigorate the weak than by keeping women in subjection."[22] Women needed no elaborate train of reasoning to convince them that slavery — the ownership of one person by another — was inhuman, and that God had made no distinction between men and women as moral beings any more than he had between black and white. They reasoned that whatever it was morally right for a man to do it was right for a woman to do. For this reason, many of the anti-slavery feminists like the Grimkés and the Weston sisters did not bother with proving the immorality of slavery — they felt it as a condition not far removed from their own. "What *then* can woman do for the *slave*," Angelina Grimké asked, "when she is herself under the feet of man and shamed into silence?"

For this reason too they responded to Garrison, whose indictment of slavery was personal like their own. Garrison also reacted to slavery experientially as a condition of dependence which destroyed the human personality by subjecting it to the will of another. His mother had attempted such a hold on him, and he had grown to manhood in subjection to her will. He too knew what it was to be owned. More than once he attempted a philosophic analysis of slavery but without success, for his real message remained simple and direct — slavery was inhuman because it killed the soul. This was the only argument he ever possessed. Every editorial, every speech, every word he ever wrote or spoke on the slavery question was a variation on this simple theme. It was this theme that established his *rapport* with American women and gave him the confidence he needed. Women thrilled to his descriptions of the pure evil of slavery, and he found in their response something which satisfied a deep need in himself. Women offered him power.

12

The Politics of Perfection

In November, 1837, Elijah Lovejoy was killed in Alton, Illinois, while defending his abolitionist press from a mob, and anti-slavery had its first real martyr. Garrison praised Lovejoy's bravery in defending freedom of the press with rifles, but he could not condone an act which threatened to destroy his illusion of the peaceful nature of anti-slavery. "We cannot . . . in conscience delay the expression of our regret, that our martyred coadjutor and his unfaltering friends in Alton should have allowed any provocation, or personal danger, or hope of victory, or distrust of the protection of Heaven, to drive them to take up arms in self-defense. They were not required to do so either as philanthropists or christians; and they have certainly set a dangerous precedent in the maintenance of our cause."[1] Boston held a protest meeting in Faneuil Hall which was marked by the dramatic debut of Wendell Phillips, who celebrated Lovejoy's sacrifice and likened him to the patriots in the American Revolution. The appearance of Phillips as a full-fledged Garrisonian emphasized the growing appeal of anti-slavery for Boston gentlemen and the need for a platform designed to exploit it. Garrison's mind, however, was moving in the opposite direction.

Lovejoy's death raised the problem of combining anti-slavery and nonresistance. How far were abolitionists obligated to practice pacifism? Garrison had no clear-cut answer. He assured his followers that he had no intention of confounding perfectionism and abolition or of making nonresistance a test of anti-slavery character. "If any man shall affirm that the anti-slavery cause, as such, or any anti-slavery society, is answerable for our sentiments on this subject, to him may be justly applied the apostolic declaration, 'the truth is not in him.'" Yet it did seem that reformers were too "unsettled" on the problem of peace and that it was time they declared themselves. If they refused the right of self-defense to the slave, how could they justify their own use of force? "And if they conscientiously believe that the slaves would be guiltless in shedding the blood of the merciless oppressors, let them say so unequivocally — for there is no neutral ground in this matter, and the time is near when they will be compelled to take sides."[2] That time was nearer than he thought. The "woman question," as he now called it, admitted of an easier solution, since it was not an "irrelevant question" but one which was "perfectly proper" to discuss. When he suggested admitting women to the New England Anti-Slavery Convention, however, he found that a perfectly proper question could also be a vexing one.

The New England Anti-Slavery Convention met in Boston on May 28, 1838. At Garrison's suggestion the delegates voted to invite women to become members, and over the objections of the clergy who protested the innovation as "injurious to the cause," they elected Abby Kelley, an outspoken feminist, to one of the standing committees. The next day the Garrisonians invaded the annual meeting of William Ladd's American Peace Society to save it from "belligerent commanders, generals, colonels, majors, corporals and all." The members of the Peace Society, who had been warned of Garrison's intentions, decided to strike first by asserting the

right of defensive war, but their motion was swamped by
the invaders, who proceeded to pass their own resolution calling for a new convention to overhaul the entire organization
and appointing a committee friendly to woman's rights and
nonresistance. On the following day he and his company
returned to the Marlboro' Chapel and the Anti-Slavery Convention, where they named another committee to help draft
a call to the proposed peace convention. Once again women
were invited to participate. Thus were the twin causes of
nonresistance and woman's rights united in what their opponents thought unholy matrimony.

All that summer Henry Wright held preparatory meetings
while Garrison publicized the forthcoming peace convention
in the *Liberator*. Their joint efforts resulted in a meeting at
the Marlboro' Chapel on September 18, 1838, of one hundred and sixty delegates, many of them radical abolitionists
of the Garrisonian stamp. In addition to Garrison, Henry
Wright and May, there was Wendell Phillips, an interested
spectator if hardly a pacifist, and Edmund Quincy, who also
had reservations about perfectionism but had come anyway.
At the first session Garrison moved quickly to seize control
of the convention. As the delegates began to answer the roll
call, he rose and with a dim smile suggested that each individual write *his* or *her* name on a slip of paper, "thus mooting
the vexed 'woman question' at the outset."[3] There were a few
dark looks from the clergy, but no one challenged the motion
or the subsequent election of Abby Kelley to the business
committee. When the redoubtable Abby took the first opportunity to call one of her clerical brethren on a point of order,
however, the ministers realized the gravity of their mistake,
rose to request that their names be removed from the roll,
and hurriedly withdrew.

While the convention debated capital punishment, Garrison

was busy drafting a constitution and declaration of sentiments for a Non-Resistance Society which would disavow all human government. "Never was a more 'fanatical' or 'disorganizing' instrument penned by man," he boasted, adding that after a "deep and lively sensation" among the delegates, it was adopted by a vote of five to one. He neglected to add that the original number of delegates had dwindled to less than fifty and that only twenty-five of these were willing to sign the document. "All who voted for it were abolitionists," he noted with satisfaction as though to prove the kinship of anti-slavery and peace.

The handful of "ultra" abolitionists who signed Garrison's Declaration of Sentiments of the Non-Resistance Society witnessed one of the most extraordinary documents in the history of American Adamic literature. "We cannot acknowledge allegiance to any human government," the declaration begins, "neither can we oppose any such government by a resort to physical force. We recognize but one KING and LAWGIVER, one JUDGE and RULER of mankind. We are bound by the laws of a kingdom which is not of this world, the subjects of which are forbidden to fight, in which Mercy and Truth are met together, and Righteousness and Peace have kissed each other. We register our testimony, not only against all war, but against all preparation for war." Garrison denied the right of self-defense to individuals as well as to nations. Until the day when government renounced war the society would withhold its allegiance. "As every human government is upheld by physical strength, and its laws are enforced virtually at the point of a bayonet, we cannot hold any office which imposes upon its incumbent the obligation to compel men to do right, on pain of imprisonment or death. We therefore voluntarily exclude ourselves from every legislative and judicial body, and repudiate all human politics, worldly honors, and stations of authority." Then came the gospel justification for this "no-government" theory:

The history of mankind is crowded with evidences proving that physical coercion is not adapted to moral regeneration; that the sinful dispositions of men can be subdued only by love; that evil can be exterminated from the earth only by goodness; that it is not safe to rely upon an arm of flesh, upon man whose breath is in his nostrils, to preserve us from harm; that there is great security in being gentle, harmless, long-suffering, and abundant in mercy; that it is only the meek who shall inherit the earth, for the violent who resort to the sword are destined to perish by the sword. Hence, as a measure of sound policy — of safety to property, life, and liberty — of public quietude and private enjoyment — as well as on the ground of allegiance to HIM who is KING OF LORDS, we cordially adopt the non-resistance principle; being confident that it provides for all possible consequences, will ensure all things needful to us, is armed with omnipotent power, and must ultimately triumph over every assailing force.[4]

Garrison's Biblical paraphrase, hastily composed and as quickly adopted, proved too much for the judicious Edmund Quincy, who with May insisted on the difference between "the man-killing, God-defying rights of power" and the "innocent functions of government." "I grant that the resort to force is never to be had, but the injury to be submitted to and forgiven," Quincy wrote to Garrison. "But the ordinary and innocent business of life can no more be carried on without these contrivances than it can without money."[5] In his view the cause of peace did not demand the sacrifice of common sense. Garrison airily dismissed his friend's objection and insisted that his Declaration of Sentiments repudiated nothing but the spirit of violence in thought, word, and deed. "Whatever, therefore, may be done without provoking that spirit of disinterested benevolence, is not touched or alluded to in the instrument."[6]

This was hardly what his Declaration of Sentiments said, but it reflected Garrison's real feelings about pacifism. None of his arguments bore close scrutiny, since it was the *idea* of moral commitment rather than the *plan* of effective action that concerned him. He prided himself on having "stirred up a breeze" in the world of reform and found it gratifying that "a few, obscure, moneyless unpretending men and women" could have set New England on its ear. He hailed his own achievement as possibly "the most important chapter in the annals of Christianity." What did it matter that only twenty-seven of the original one hundred and sixty members had the courage to approve his work — "the progress of Christianity through the world, since the time when only twelve persons were found willing to take up its cross . . . should teach . . . that it is of no consequence how many or how few subscribed to the principles and doctrines of the Declaration."[7]

William Ladd disowned the Non-Resistance Society as the illegitimate offspring of good intentions and poor logic. It was not simply the admission of women or the anti-Sabbatarian views of the nonresistants that troubled him, though these were bad enough, but the whole concept of perfection, that fountain of Christian heresy which had poisoned the proceedings and watered the seeds of schism. "Many important doctrines of the gospel," he warned, "may be pushed to absurdity, with considerable plausibility."[8] He could not doubt Garrison's sincerity, but there was such a thing as going beyond the millennium. He was content to stop there.

Garrison's harshest critic was Orange Scott, a Methodist minister from Vermont who pointed out that the new organization was not simply a peace society but a "no-government"

sect devoted to the principles of civil disobedience. It simply
would not do for Garrison to argue that peace and anti-slavery
were totally unrelated, and then in the next breath boast that
all thoroughgoing nonresistants were also loyal abolitionists.
Such jumbling of the facts looked like an attempt to give
character and influence to the nonresistance scheme by making it appear that the *abolitionists* favored it whereas most
of them considered civil government indispensable to their
cause. "Will you say," he asked Garrison, "but we trust in
God, and commit our all to him? As well might you trust in
God to edit and print your paper." What would have happened to him in the Boston riot if the mayor and his police
had not intervened? Besides, no one ever pretended that the
gospel of Christ contained all of the Christian message. Then
why this "new and loose theory"? "With your views, I cannot conceive by what authority you appoint *officers* in your
society. *They* may not, indeed, enforce obedience by penal-
ties — but then the idea of *office* keeps up a distinction, which
your principles are calculated to level." How did Garrison
justify voting in state and national elections? How could he
recommend the use of petitions — "if you believe the very
existence of a legislative body to be sin, how can you connive
at its existence, by asking of it legislative action?" All institutions, Scott concluded, must collapse before the perfectionist
repudiation of human government.[9]

In his reply Garrison struck back at a hostile world. Scott,
he announced, was a notoriously weak man who once had
supported the colonizationists. What right had he to speak
for anti-slavery? And what did his charge of anarchy mean?
The end of human government spelled not chaos but the
coming of a new order. When Scott objected to this "cheap
way of disposing of an argument" and withdrew from the
encounter, Garrison promptly dismissed Scott's retreat as

"tantamount to a confession, that he erred in judgment."[10]

The abolitionist reaction against perfectionism continued to spread both among the New England clergy and the Executive Committee in New York, who foresaw disaster in the abandonment of politics. Significantly, Garrison was more concerned with Scriptural arguments than with the practical objections of the Executive Committee. Reformers, he announced, mistook the divine purpose when they settled their cause on any single passage in the Bible instead of the whole of the gospel of Jesus, which taught total obedience to Christ. "The present governments of the world are the consequence of disobedience to the commands of God. But Christ came to bring men back to obedience 'by a new and living way.' When the cause is taken away, must not the effect cease? . . . We are for subverting the rotten, unequal, anti-Christian government of man, and establishing, as a substitute that which is divine."[11]

Here enveloped in the language of the Second Great Awakening stood revealed the American Dream. Garrison's perfectionism was less a theory or doctrine than a faith in beginning again, a belief in the "second chance." Dismissing the complexities of the question of evil and promising eternal goodness, it spurned the past for a perpetually renewable innocence. His dream of personal holiness was thus an interior version of the myth of the frontier. Stripped of its religious terminology, perfectionism recounted the fable of the American Adam, the new man in the new world, free not merely from Europe but from the burden of history. With its illusion of total freedom it encouraged a dangerous moral posture since it released the energies of a prophet — an Isaiah to the nation — standing beyond time in subjection to God. Thus the perfectionist myth contained the elements of personal and social tragedy: personal tragedy in that it fostered an other-worldliness that meant denying the reality of experience — it left Garrison reborn but cast up on that childhood beach of innocence, a beach of pure white but burning sands; social tragedy in that it was the source of a profound disillusionment. To regenerate the world Garrison invented the American saint and provided him with a power needed to make the holy society, while the actual materials for his new world were imperfect men who could understand moral ends but not peaceful means.

In January, 1839, came the report that the conservative wing of the Massachusetts Society was plotting to capture the Board of Managers and dislodge the Garrisonians. They planned to dispose of the "woman question" by refusing to seat women delegates, and then establish control over the *Liberator* and bring Garrison to account. Failing in this, they agreed to walk out and form an organization of their own. Quickly Garrison sounded the alarm and issued a call to all his "unflinching and trusty friends" to save the Massachusetts Society from a plot to wrest control from the founders. He identified the ringleaders, all of them ministers, directed by the formidable Amos Phelps, still a loyal abolitionist but a stanch advocate of male supremacy disturbed by the prospect of a host of feminine anarchists. The rebels, he knew, had the support of the Executive Committee in New York. According to rumors filtering into the *Liberator* office the test of strength would come over the question of establishing a new paper under the control of the society. "How mean, how ungrateful, how contemptible is conduct like this," Garrison fumed. "I should not greatly care for it if it had openly manifested itself — but everything about it has been managed as secretly as possible." To counteract the revolutionary movement he resorted to a stratagem of his own. He waited until Phelps left Boston on business and then hurriedly called a meeting of the Board of Managers where he suggested publishing a monthly periodical as the official organ of the Massachusetts Society. To give the appearance of impartiality the board appointed the absent Phelps to the committee along with Garrison and his henchman Quincy.

Garrison reported the results to George Benson. "It happened that he [Phelps] did not return in season from Haverhill to consult with us, and we accordingly made our report to the Board . . . to wit, that such a *monthly* ought to be printed, officially, to be called 'The Abolitionist,' and to be edited by a committee of three, to be elected by ballot. This report was strenuously opposed by Mr. P's friend (Ayres) on the ground that a weekly paper was called for, and would doubtless be established — that it would be better to defer the whole matter to the annual meeting. . . . The report was, however, accepted, and Wendell Phillips, Edmund Quincy and myself were elected editors."[12] He had won the first round.

Meanwhile his opponents had drafted a series of resolutions which they lofted as trial balloons at local meetings throughout the state. The first of these was aimed directly at Garrison's perfectionism: it declared it the duty of every abolitionist "not to content himself with merely refusing to vote for any man who is opposed to the emancipation of the slave, but to go to the polls and throw his vote for some man known to favor it." A second provided that where an abolitionist had no obvious choice between two candidates of opposing parties, "then he is equally bound to go to the polls, and vote for some true man in opposition to them both, and to do all he can, lawfully, to defeat their election." Both resolutions were aimed at the practice of "scattering" votes which Garrison had recommended in cases where there was not a distinct choice between candidates. A third resolution struck at the

independence of the *Liberator* without naming it: "Resolved,
That a weekly and ably conducted anti-slavery paper, which
shall take right, high, and consistent ground on this subject,
and constantly urge abolitionists, as in duty bound, to use
their political, as well as their moral and religious, power and
rights for the immediate overthrow of slavery, is now greatly
needed in Massachusetts. . . ."[13] These resolutions were
passed at meetings in Fitchburg and in Fall River, where the
Bristol County Anti-Slavery Society added a fourth resolution calling on the Board of Managers to establish an independent paper as soon as possible.

As the annual meeting approached, both sides rallied their
forces and began counting their votes. As usual, Garrison
overestimated the strength of his enemies. "My belief is," he
wrote to George Benson, "that they will manage the affair
with so much plausibility, and will have so many able and
influential speakers on their side, as to be able to carry their
point."[14] If they failed, they would surely secede; if they
triumphed, it would be a dark hour for the cause.

The annual meeting held in the Marlboro' Chapel on
January 23, 1839, was the largest and the stormiest in the
history of the society. In the chair sat Francis Jackson, the
Boston merchant, benefactor and personal friend of Garrison.
All of the members of the supposed cabal were present including Stanton, who carried the burden of the attack. Garrison had rounded up a sizable delegation of Boston's free
Negroes and an even larger collection of women. First on the
agenda came the reading of Garrison's annual report, which
was heavily freighted with criticism of his opponents; but
before the insurgents could assail it, Wendell Phillips moved
the immediate consideration of the so-called Fitchburg Resolutions. The insurgents opened the debate with a long and
involved indictment. Then Henry Stanton took the floor

and directed his attack at the "nullifying effects" of perfectionism on anti-slavery and the use of the *Liberator* to
spread this heresy. "It is not that other subjects are introduced into the *Liberator*," he protested, " – it is that *such*
other subjects are introduced – subjects so injurious to the
cause." Garrison's peace views might or might not prove
correct, but there was no doubt that they had lowered the
standard of abolition.[15]

In his reply Garrison resorted to an old trick: to every
one of Stanton's charges he opposed new questions. Why
had Stanton waited so long to break silence? Why had he
joined the "sectarian party" in the first place – to destroy
anti-slavery or merely to discredit veterans like himself? Who
could prove that the *Liberator* hurt the cause? Where was
the man who could deny his devotion to the slave? When
Stanton tried to interrupt, his complaints were drowned out
by roars and cheers which, Garrison boasted, "spoke more
eloquently and sincerely than the tongue of men ever did."
But Stanton was not one to give up easily. "Let me ask him
a question," he demanded of the audience. "Mr. Garrison,
do you or do you not believe it a sin to go to the polls?" After
some hesitation Garrison answered, "Sin for *me!*" Stanton
repeated the question and again came the same answer –
it was a sin for all nonresistance men to vote and thereby
recognize the claims of "carnal" government. Beyond this
point Garrison would not go. Stanton could not get him to
commit himself on the duty of other abolitionists or to admit
that there was a conflict between nonresistance and abolition.

In fact, Garrison did not need to bother with arguments.
He had the votes and soon put them to work. Stanton offered
a resolution which had technically been under consideration
from the outset – "That every member of an anti-slavery society who refuses, under any pretext, thus to act morally or

politically, or counsels others to such a course, is guilty of gross inconsistency, and widely departs from the original and fundamental principles of the anti-slavery enterprise." This resolution, along with the other Fitchburg proposals, was indefinitely postponed by an overwhelming vote. When Charles Torrey and Alanson St. Clair questioned the legality of a vote which included "female members," Francis Jackson rescued the Garrisonians by ruling without appeal that it was in order for women to vote. Stanton's terse account of the episode in a letter to Birney told the story of the first day's combat. "Garrison found himself pushed to the wall on the non-government question, and with his train bands, he made a desperate push to sway the Society over to his nonresistance views. He succeeded."[16]

The climax came on the afternoon of the next day when one of the ministers managed to make himself heard long enough to introduce a milder version of Stanton's original resolution, simply declaring it the imperious duty of every abolitionist who could conscientiously do so to go to the polls. In the course of an angry quarrel that followed Stanton reminded Garrison that in 1834 he had supported Amasa Walker for Congress and had lectured some of his colored supporters now present on the need to vote. "It is false!" Garrison shouted. Stanton, not to be caught unawares, pulled out a sheaf of quotations from the *Liberator* and requested the right to read them. By now Garrison knew he was trapped, and so did his followers, for they refused to allow Stanton to proceed. The next moment they accepted Garrison's counterresolution providing that "those abolitionists who feel themselves called upon, by a sense of duty, to go to the polls, and yet purposely absent themselves from the polls whenever an opportunity is presented to vote for a friend of the slave — or who, when there, follow their party predilections to the abandonment of their abolition principles — are recreant to their high professions, and unworthy of the name they bear." Then the convention voted, 180 to 24, to accept Garrison's annual report, which advocated woman's rights, censured the clerical party in Massachusetts, recommended nonresistance, and criticized political action.

"The Board deny that it is competent for any anti-slavery society by its votes or through its organs, to arraign either the political or religious views of its members." Such was the conclusion to Garrison's annual report. "It may with no more propriety decide that one man is morally bound to cast a vote at the polls, than that another man is morally bound to unite himself to a church." On the subject of political action, he declared, there were many conflicting opinions; all that any society might rightfully do, therefore, was to *entreat* its members to abide by their principles. No organization possessed coercive power over its membership. With this provision Garrison fastened to abolition a new orthodoxy while posing as the defender of minority rights. The Massachusetts Society was now his, but in winning control of it he had stripped it of effective power. "But the point is," Stanton remarked dolefully to Birney, "the Society hauled down its flag and run [*sic*] up the crazy banner of the non-government heresy, and we had to rally around or be ostracized." Yet even he had to admire the ease with which Garrison had crushed the revolt though he admitted that "the split is wide and can never be closed up."

Defeated in Boston, the insurgents appealed to the Executive Committee in New York, which was busy with its own problems. The split in the Massachusetts Society was only part of the gradual deterioration of the fabric of American anti-slavery in the year 1839. There were a number of causes for the loss of power and prestige of the national organization. First of all, revivals and the spirit of Christian reform were on the wane. When the national society was founded, revivalism had been at its peak; in 1839, following a depression and a conservative reaction against perfectionist theology, the churches were withdrawing their support from reform enterprises and interdenominational cooperation was disappearing. Then, too, sectional politics and the civil liberties issue publicized the work of the society but at the cost of a national program with national goals. By 1839 the American Anti-Slavery Society was only a name. Still another reason for the decline of the national society was the petition strategy which called for decentralizing control and dispersing functions to local societies. The money to run these societies was being kept at home. As the competition for funds grew sharper, the national society gradually lost control of money-raising within the states until by 1838 every state auxiliary had closed its territory to the society's agents. In Massachusetts, where Garrison's heresies aggravated the financial difficulty, the state society forced the Executive Committee to accept a system of voluntary pledges and then neglected to fill its own quota. It was obvious that the Garrisonians, hostile to political action and displeased with interference from New York, had no intention of meeting their obligations until they could control the national society. Accordingly, in February, 1839, the committee decided to force the issue by notifying the Massachusetts Board of Managers of its intention to drop the quota system and send its own agents back into the state. Straightway Garrison sensed a challenge to his independence and dispatched Wendell Phillips to New York to kill the project. "You will see by the last *Liberator*," he wrote, "that a collision has taken place between the New York Executive Committee and our Board. How it will terminate I know not. This is a sad spectacle to present to the enemies of our holy cause; but be the responsibility upon the heads of those who are attempting to lord it over the consciences of the nonresisting abolitionists."[17]

He quickly dropped the posture of self-defense when the Executive Committee sent Stanton and Lewis Tappan to argue its case before the quarterly meeting of the Massachusetts Society in March. Once again he laid his plans carefully, assembling his partisans from all over the state and assuring them that the meeting would decide "whether our sacred enterprise shall continue under the management of its old friends, or be given up to the control of politicians and sectaries."[18]

Tappan and Stanton came prepared to discuss more than finances. In February a prospectus had circulated in Massachusetts which announced that a new abolitionist newspaper was "imperiously demanded." The members of the Executive Committee now hoped to bring Garrison to terms by threatening to support the project. Their hopes were short-lived. Garrison and his lieutenants had done their work so well that on the test vote over the proposal to ignore the new ruling of the Executive Committee the New Yorkers were soundly beaten, 142 to 23. The Executive Committee now knew what it had long suspected, that Garrison could not be beaten in Massachusetts and that their only hope was a new state society. This was precisely the conclusion already reached by Garrison's conservative opponents in Massachusetts, all of whom were ready for a "new organization," as they called it. Henry Stanton and Elizur Wright stood ready to help them reorganize abolition there on a political basis. Cheered by these reports of dissatisfaction with Garrison, the members of the Executive Committee looked forward to a new order in Massachusetts which would help sustain the old cause. Before their hopes were realized Garrison and his forces raided their New York headquarters and almost seized command of their society.

Of the one hundred and eighteen Massachusetts delegates to the annual meeting of the American Anti-Slavery Society in May, Garrison controlled nearly three-fourths. He brought with him all his lieutenants — Phillips, Loring, Oliver Johnson, Henry Wright, Samuel Philbrick, Edmund Quincy, and a newcomer named John A. Collins, together with three women, Abby Kelley, Thankful Southwick and Anne Warren Weston. These he counted on to keep the faithful in line. Ten additional votes from Rhode Island and a sprinkling from Vermont gave him nearly a hundred votes in New England alone. This number, added to his strength among the Pennsylvania Quakers and upstate New York delegates, could conceivably give him a majority in the convention, especially if his women supporters were allowed to vote. It was not surprising, then, that the very first issue confronting the four hundred and thirty-five delegates was the motion put by the opponents of woman's rights that "our roll call be made up, according to former usage, and *men*, duly appointed, shall constitute the roll." Not until the afternoon of the next day, after twelve hours of bickering, did the crucial vote come on the following proposition: "Resolved that the roll of this meeting be made by placing thereon the names of all persons, male and female, who are delegates from any auxiliary society." With roughly one-quarter of the delegates' votes not recorded, the resolution was adopted by a vote of 180 to 140. A breakdown of the voting (*see top of next page*) showed where Garrison's strength lay.

Garrison promptly set his delegation to work. At his suggestion they appointed a special committee to make recommendations to the Executive Committee. The special committee quickly urged reconsideration of all the passages in

	Ayes	*Nays*
Maine	1	6
New Hampshire	1	5
Vermont	5	4
Massachusetts	72	25
Rhode Island	10	1
Connecticut	14	11
New York	45	76
New Jersey	9	2
Pennsylvania	21	7
Delaware	—	1
Ohio	2	—
Illinois	—	2
TOTAL	180	140[19]

the annual report dealing unfavorably with political action. Then he presented a resolution to the general meeting which declared that "in the original formation of this society, it was not contemplated, nor is it now desired to exclude from its membership any persons, on account of their being prevented by conscientious scruples, from participating in all the measures which the mass of the society either originally or subsequently, may have contemplated for the advancement of the Anti-Slavery cause."[20]

The leadership of the political abolitionists in the society had fallen to the taciturn, hard-driving James Birney, now its secretary and chief polemicist. For some time Birney had contemplated shifting the anti-slavery cause from religious to political grounds, and now he rallied his supporters to meet the perfectionist challenge. Garrison's calculated piece of circulocution somehow survived the attacks of Birney, but he was unable to defeat his rival's counterproposal making it the duty of every abolitionist to vote. Birney's resolution was passed by a vote of 84 to 77 only after many of the Garrisonians, worn out by the four-day wrangle, had returned to Boston. He was still strong enough, however, to defeat a proposal for sending a money-raising expedition to England. His motives were made clear later in the spring when the New England Convention voted to send Wendell Phillips on a similar mission. The real victory, however, lay in the admission of women. He still lacked the votes to manage a repudiation of politics, but if he returned next year with enough women delegates, the story might well be different.

The final act of the drama opened two weeks later at the New England Convention, where a handful of conservative diehards made one last attempt to settle with him. Once more the woman question was introduced by Phelps and quickly disposed of by the Garrisonians. Weary from months of fruitless campaigning, Phelps and Company withdrew to form their own organization, the Massachusetts Abolition Society, whose unofficial motto read "For Men Only." After they left, the Garrisonians pronounced the formation of the new society "inexpedient" and "hostile to the genius of abolition"; declared that the constitution of the national society, contrary to Birney's elaborate demonstration, did *not* enjoin voting; and closed their session after refusing a peace conference with the secessionists.[21]

The Massachusetts Abolition Society was formed for the ostensible purpose of freeing anti-slavery from its encumbrances — perfectionism, nonresistance, and woman's rights — but it was only the last of these heresies on which the new society could agree. The politically minded members of the Executive Committee in New York waited for a sign of life in the new organization only to find that the society was first and last an anti-Garrison society. However notorious

their former leader had become by 1839, he still embodied
the spirit of abolition in New England and could marshal
the supporters to prove it. Eventually any group opposed to
him would have to stand on a political platform. Such was the
conclusion already reached by Birney and his friends, who
now sought to instruct the Massachusetts Abolition Society
in the duties of voting. In an all-out attack on the "no-
government" heretics Birney leveled his sights on the vote.
How could abolitionists influence politics except by voting?
What was the sense in petitioning Congress to abolish slavery
and then refusing to elect men who would begin the work?
How could Garrison oppose political action and still claim
to be an abolitionist? Better that he withdraw from the society
and seek the destruction of law and order elsewhere.[22]

Garrison professed himself shocked with Birney's "truth-
less, slanderous, cruel" accusations — "caricatures of the
pacific precepts of the Gospel — phantasms of a distorted imagination." He particularly objected to the phrase "no-government" because the nonresistants, he asserted, held religiously
to a government of heaven if not of men. He proceeded to
make the dubious distinction between petitions and the vote
on the grounds that petitions involved *influencing* a legislative
body already in existence, while voting meant *creating* that
body. Nonresistants could uphold the right of petition, therefore, and still refuse to vote. The founders of the American
Society, he asserted, at no time intended to make voting a
duty, and Birney's remark that he himself had voted for
Amasa Walker not five years ago was entirely beside the
point. "I humbly conceive that it concerns no man, or body
of men, to know how many or how few times I have voted
since the adoption of the A.S. Constitution, or whether I
have, or have not, changed my views of politics within a
few years." Birney would do better to prove his own case

first. Suddenly, in a bewildering contradiction, he said that he expected to see political action strengthened and purified "in exact proportion to the prevalence of the great conservative doctrines of nonresistance." Perfectionism would work to pour new lifeblood into the veins of abolition — "to give it extraordinary vigor — to clothe it with new beauty — to inspire it with holier feelings — to preserve it from corruption — though not necessarily connected with it." If Birney failed to fathom his reasoning let him be silent until he could!

At this point William Goodell, now the editor of the *Friend of Man*, joined the debate. Like Birney, he failed to see how Garrison's nonresistance could free the slave. On the contrary, he was convinced that perfectionism unwittingly played into the hands of its enemies. By refusing to vote, the Garrisonians only strengthened the hold of the Whig and Democratic parties. In their leader's nonsensical doctrines radical and reactionary extremes joined to thwart the attempt of intelligent abolitionists to wipe out slavery with the vote.

To counter Goodell's charge Garrison was forced to resort to the doctrine of minority rights. There never would have been any trouble, he explained, if the political abolitionists had not tried to proscribe the nonresistants. He cared very little for the resolutions which conflicted with his own view of politics; but he would never fail to protest against any and every attempt to make the anti-slavery movement an "engine of despotism" subservient to the commands of clerical politicians and sectarian bigots. Far from encouraging corrupt politics, the nonresistants were greatly pleased to see that men who had hitherto been spellbound by the sorcery of political formulas were finally casting independent votes. "We feel a high respect for such men: such conduct leads us to hope for still better fruits." After all, the difference between abolitionists and nonresistants was only one of degree: the abolitionists aimed at freeing the Negro, nonresistants at delivering the whole world. Let nonresistance prevail and instead of having to go through a long and slow process of electioneering to find the right men to free the slaves — "instead of having to wait weeks and months until the question of repeal has been discussed" — judges, legislators and all the people would immediately "show their deeds" and confess, "and bring all the statute books together, and burn them before all men."[23] The old vision of a righteous but jealous God still haunted him, a God who needed not man with his petty contrivances. As once with the house of Israel, the Lord would covenant with the American people and inscribe His laws in their minds, His commands in their hearts.

In the summer of 1839 the reaction against Garrison deepened. The Massachusetts Abolition Society began to send its agents to local and county conventions, and several times Garrison had to dispatch a contingent of Bostonians to deal with the invaders. At a National Abolition Convention held in Albany in July he was outvoted both on nonresistance and woman's rights and presented with the title "prince of disorganizers." Then the Executive Committee in New York pronounced its sentence of excommunication. In a circular sent to its agents and auxiliaries the committee announced that their society, "recognizing the rightful power and binding obligation of the government to interpose its arm for the delivery of the slave based its plans of operation upon the *lawfulness* of political action. . . . But, within a few months past, a sentiment has been promulgated in our ranks, maintained too, by some who have been among our earliest and most efficient friends, denying the rightfulness of all human government, and consequently denying it to be a

duty to vote for men to be rulers who will employ the
prerogatives of government for the abolition of slavery. The
Anti-Slavery Society can afford no countenance to such
doctrines."[24]

While Garrison was busy fending off his critics, a group
of abolitionists under the leadership of Myron Holley, the
anti-slavery editor of the *Rochester Freeman*, met in Cleveland to consider his proposition to nominate a third ticket
for the next Presidential election. When his proposal was
defeated, Holley returned to New York to call a local convention at Warsaw, where he won over enough advocates of
political action to nominate Birney and Dr. Julius LeMoyne
on an anti-slavery ticket. The third party movement was
under way.

The Executive Committee was badly split on the question
of political action. On the one hand, Elizur Wright and
Joshua Leavitt wholeheartedly favored the idea of an abolitionist political party. Stanton and Birney, while they were
committed to the vote, doubted that a third party could
succeed. On their side, Lewis Tappan, Weld, and Gamaliel
Bailey, the editor of the *Philanthropist*, vehemently opposed
the idea of a third party devoted entirely to abolition. Thus
Garrison was not alone in assailing the third party movement in the autumn of 1839, and much of his ammunition
was supplied by Western abolitionists who still thought as
he did.

Immediate help from the West came from a different
source. In November he received a letter written from
Holley's Cleveland convention which referred to a "con-
fidential" communication from Elizur Wright to Henry
Stanton. The unknown spy quoted excerpts from the pur-
loined letter in which Wright complained of the wretched
mismanagement of the Massachusetts Abolition Society.

Wright had come to Massachusetts to edit the new society's paper, the *Abolitionist*, and already was proving more than an editorial match for Garrison. But Wright was discouraged by the apathy of the Massachusetts Abolition Society, which was so concerned with Garrison's heresies that it was neglecting the slavery question. In his letter to Stanton in Cleveland he said he hoped the convention would take "a decided step towards Presidential candidates." "Our labor will be more than half lost without them," he continued. "The South can outbid us, and hence she will buy up both political parties, as to national politics, *ad infinitum*." If the abolitionist candidates were of "good stuff," the whole cause would gain regardless of the number of votes they won. Then Wright turned to the situation in Massachusetts. "One thing *I know*. Unless you do take such a step, OUR NEW ORGANIZATION HERE IS A GONE CASE. It has been, *inter nos*, SHOCKINGLY MISMANAGED. Everything has been made to turn upon the *woman question*. The political has been left to fall out of sight." It would not do for Massachusetts, under the circumstances, to make the first move, which would have to come from the national society, and very soon. "You certainly see this," Wright reminded Stanton in conclusion. "Take my solemn assurance that IT IS LIFE AND DEATH WITH US."[25]

Garrison saw the value of the "pilfered letter," as Wright called it, in discrediting the new state society. He demanded that Wright divulge its contents, and when Wright did so in the pages of the *Abolitionist*, he copied it for his own readers. "Ordinarily," he explained in his remarks, "private correspondence should be considered sacred; but not when . . . it is found to relate not to particular persons, but to a great public enterprise, involving the rights and liberties of millions of the human race." Wright, he lamented, was sadly altered and his newspaper lost to all principle. To follow him and the Massachusetts Abolition Society would be to descend to the depths of debased and venal bargainings. "The pseudo-Abolition Society must go down 'to vile dust from whence it sprang, Unwept, unhonored, and unsung.' "[26] His editorial was both judgment and prophecy: without needed support from the politicians, the Massachusetts Abolition Society died quietly while the *Liberator*, with a thousand new subscriptions, continued to play the politics of no-government.

13

Triumph of the Saints

THE YEAR 1840 brought disillusion to the abolitionists and disaster to their organization. Garrison's decision to capture the national society split the anti-slavery coalition into two warring factions, neither of which was able to muster the manpower or find the funds to keep the militant anti-slavery spirit of the Thirties alive. His enemies, embittered by the *coup d'état*, abandoned the society to discover in the light of reappraisal that their objective lay in politics and the vote. When the smoke of battle lifted over the annual meeting of 1840, Garrison found himself in control of an organization that had lost half its personnel and all its power, an instrument useful now only as a sounding board for his dissonant prophecies of Armageddon.

Disorder also ruled the domestic scene as Garrison's debts kept pace with his growing family. His second son, William, was born in 1838, and another son, Wendell, two years later. In September, 1839, he rented a house in Cambridgeport, "very neat in its appearance," though hardly more spacious than the Boston quarters. Yet it was cheap — two hundred and fifty dollars a year — a factor that weighed heavily with him. His ever-faithful man Friday, Oliver Johnson, concerned as always for the welfare of his chief, promised to board with them and help repair the family budget; but the pile of unpaid bills kept reminding Garrison of the chaotic state of his finances. "At present, I am greatly embarrassed for want of money," he confessed to George Benson. One hundred and fifty dollars of his salary was still owing, and the Massachusetts Society had yet to pay him his expenses for the current year. The cost of moving and furnishing the new house had drained the last of his resources. To meet immediate expenses he borrowed a hundred dollars from Francis Jackson and another hundred from Samuel Philbrick, the retired Quaker merchant and abolitionist. "They will expect me to fulfill my word," he explained to Benson. "My object in writing to you is to know whether you can borrow that amount for me, so as to give me more time to 'turn myself.' "[1] He never doubted that the Lord would provide, but it seemed sometimes that He was an unconscionably long time getting around to it.

Part of the borrowed money went to care for his brother. After twenty years at sea James had suddenly appeared in the Boston Navy Yard, still an alcoholic and now mortally ill with cancer of the spine. Garrison secured a leave of absence for him and set about getting him discharged from the Navy, an unpleasant job that involved asking favors of Congressman Caleb Cushing. Cushing proved helpful, however, and "poor James" was released and came home to Cambridgeport. At Lloyd's suggestion he began writing his memoirs, a nightmarish account of his boyhood fall from grace and his years aboard ships of the line in the United States Navy. His descriptions of the inhumanity aboard ship and on the beach — of tyrannical officers and drunken fights, floggings and depravity — present a remarkable picture of life in the nineteenth-century American Navy. Also at his brother's urging, James filled his confession with a bitter reflection on the "Fatal Poison." "That I am a doomed man is certain, and can not avoid Fate," he admitted, adding perhaps for Lloyd's benefit, "and none but God, and my self, can tell what I have suffered in body and in mind for my rashness."

Life with his virtuous brother must have been hard for James, who found the abolitionists' unctuous manners and "stentorian lungs" too much for his liking. Lloyd expected gratitude, and James tried hard to be grateful for the oppressive kindliness and the sermonizing. Helen he came to love deeply before he died, and perhaps it was she who reconciled him to the misery of his last two years. Lloyd, his memories of boyhood already dim, saw only a pathetic example of the evils of liquor in his wasted brother. "Earnest is my prayer to God, that he may be led to review his past life," he wrote to his wife, "and to perceive how widely he has departed from the path of rectitude, to the ruin of his immortal soul."[2] Repentance and reconciliation — the old prescription for salvation. James, in his turn, might have prescribed humility for his brother.

The financial troubles of the *Liberator* were solved temporarily by terminating Knapp's contract as printer. Knapp was inefficient and had lately taken to drink, but he was also an original partner who had helped sustain the paper through seven lean years. Over his protests the Board of Managers appointed a committee consisting of Francis Jackson, Ellis Gray Loring, Edmund Quincy, and Samuel Philbrick to come to terms with him and henceforth manage the finances. After a consultation with Garrison the committee decided to pay Knapp one hundred and fifty dollars. Knapp not unnaturally made his grievances known to the whole abolitionist community, for he reasoned that Garrison was abandoning a friend to save his paper. Garrison suffered few qualms of conscience. "To say that I separated from my friend Knapp with great reluctance and pain of mind — that I exerted myself to the utmost to retain him as printer of the *Liberator* — that I greatly compassionated his forlorn condition, and did everything in his behalf that friendship and sympathy could suggest — is simply to assert the truth, which all my friends in this quarter know full well."[3] For those who preferred it, Knapp's version was available for the asking.

The year 1840 opened on a "political gulf that yawns to devour."[4] In western New York the political abolitionists were driving toward the formation of a third party. In New York City the Executive Committee was preparing to close up shop and turn the direction of the movement over to its auxiliaries. Some of the New York group, Leavitt, Stanton, and Birney, were ready to join forces with the third party men upstate. It seemed to Garrison that only the Massachusetts Society remained loyal to the old cause of moral suasion.

His friend and chief adviser Henry Wright, who was scouting abolitionist activities in western New York with one eye on the millennium and the other on scheming politicians, warned of the coming "desperate struggle for political power" at the spring meeting of the national society and advised him "to exert all your influence in Connecticut and Rhode Island to get delegates to New York in May."[5] Garrison took his advice and spent the early spring making the circuit of local and county conventions, submitting resolutions that bristled with hostility to church and state. At a meeting in Lynn in March he gave an indication of how far he was prepared to go by submitting two resolutions which were passed without dissent.

Resolved, That Freedom and Slavery are natural and irreconcilable enemies; that it is morally impossible for them to endure together in the same nation; and that the existence of the one can only be secured by the destruction of the other.

Resolved, That slavery has exercised a pernicious and most dangerous influence in the affairs of this Union from its foundation to the present time; that this influence has increased, is increasing, and cannot be destroyed, except by the destruction of slavery or the Union.[6]

Meanwhile the advocates of a third party were completing their plans for independent nominations. At Albany on the first day of April a convention called by Myron Holley and Gerrit Smith agreed on the Presidential ticket of Birney and Thomas Earle, the Pennsylvania Quaker. It was a small beginning: the Albany Convention numbered only one hundred and twenty delegates, of whom one hundred and four were from western New York. Even then, the vote to nominate a ticket had been surprisingly close — 44 to 33. Nevertheless, the call to "unite patriots, philanthropists and Christians, to put down the slavery of all parties, and put up the principles of the Declaration of Independence, at the ballot box" was a challenge Garrison had to meet.[7]

Reviewing the rise of the third party movement, he was sure he discerned a pattern. The trouble began when Stanton and Birney decided to build a party engine for their own selfish purposes. They had worked their mischief in Massachusetts until his loyal abolitionists rallied to rout them. Defeated there, they retired to the West, where they inveigled Holley into calling the Albany Convention. The final step would be a desperate push at the annual meeting in New York to convert the parent society into a political party. This he had to prevent at all costs.

He began by examining the philosophy of the third party movement. Gerrit Smith, one of its leaders, argued that since neither the Whig nor the Democratic Party could be purged of its pro-slavery elements, abolitionists were forced to create one of their own. Garrison replied with a curious analogy. There was no more reason, he said, for "a war of extermination" against the two existing parties than for one against Methodism or Unitarianism. "If we must have a new political party to abolish slavery, must we not also have a new religious sect for the same purpose? . . ." American politics needed new men, not new labels; Christian voters, not party hacks. In voting for an enlightened abolitionist without regard to party labels the anti-slavery contingent did all that was required. Just how abolitionists could secure nominations in parties openly hostile to them he did not say.

The work of explaining nonresistant perfectionism was made doubly difficult by his inability to think through to logical conclusions. In the first place, he was not a thorough-going nonresistant, as two recent examples clearly showed. The Massachusetts Militia Law exempted only Quakers and provided a fine for anyone else who failed to train at the annual muster. When his friends asked his opinion on the propriety of paying the fine, he said that he saw no reason "why a military fine may not be paid, as well as any other exacted by a government based on force." "If I refuse to bear arms — if I will not procure a substitute — if I bear an open and uncompromising testimony against the military system — I do all, in my opinion, that is required by Christianity."[8] Principle need not prevent a sensible accommodation. Then when the legislature opened up the liquor traffic by repealing the Massachusetts License Law, he fought the repeal and even proposed a new and more stringent regulation. Civil law had its uses even for a millenarian.

As the third party movement gathered momentum in the spring of 1840, criticism of Garrison increased. Some of the political abolitionists accused him of secretly favoring Harrison. Others hurled gibes at "that fellow," as Gamaliel Bailey called him, "with his troop of males and females." William Goodell, now thoroughly convinced of his old friend's ruthless will to power, composed a satire entitled *How to Make a Pope.* Take an ardent and strong-minded leader, Goodell said, surround him with unquestioning friends, and soon the belief will spread that he is infallible. So it had been with the bishops of Rome and so it was now with William Lloyd Garrison.

Garrison's reply was *An Address to the Abolitionists of the United States,* commissioned by the Massachusetts Society and circulated as a warning to tried-and-true abolitionists to disregard the Albany Convention. "The call is presumptuous, comes from no authority, and should receive general condemnation." It was evident, he continued, that there was a "small but talented" body of restless men in western New York who were determined to form a third party with the hope of being lifted by it into office. Whether theirs was a desire for political spoils or simply an error in judgment, the damage to the anti-slavery cause was the same. "Let us not sanction a precedent, which shall encourage, nay authorize a few irresponsible individuals at any time to appoint a national gathering of abolitionists, as it may suit their caprice or ambition, in order to promote some selfish or local purpose."[9] Elizur Wright quickly retaliated with a blast at the Board of Managers of the Massachusetts Society for hiding behind their roaring giant. Garrison countered by impeaching Wright as a trimmer and dismissing his paper as a travesty. On and on raged the battle of epithets.

Already there were signs of disaffection in New England. In Maine the state society came out for political action; and in western Massachusetts, where the Whigs were traditionally strong, anti-slavery men began to look to the party for leadership. Garrison lashed out at the politicians. Moral suasion, he cried, had always worked in the past — why abandon it now? "Yes, blessed be God, it can be done, in His name, and by the power of his truth!"[10] He was preaching to the converted: not many abolitionists outside his own bailiwick could be convinced of the "depravity" of political abolition or the "Machiavellism" of its leaders. As though he realized the weakness of his case against a third party, he dwelt on the futility of political plans and advised his followers not to concern themselves with the forthcoming election. It was possible, he admitted, but not likely that a change in administration would prove helpful, and anyway, the abolitionists were powerless to decide the matter. "Their great and only concern should be, to revolutionize the public sentiment of the land by truth and light; and having done this, they will have accomplished the overthrow of slavery."[11] The task of actually freeing the slaves he would leave to others, but not to those "unprincipled" abolitionists who needed the franchise in order to keep from walking crookedly, nor to ambitious schemers who wanted to be elected to office. Such men lacked faith in God and the simple instrumentalities which He had adopted for the suppression of evil in the world. If moral suasion had multiplied ten thousand efficient societies in eight years, who knew what the future held? "A little *can* and will leaven the whole lump."[12]

But what then? How were the people to show their disapproval of slavery except by voting it down? Just what did he want the American people to do? His silence suggested that he opposed the third party movement because he knew he could not control it, because he saw a day coming when abolitionists would cease to listen to him. This fear, his critics reasoned, lay behind his decision to take over the American Anti-Slavery Society.

The society Garrison set out to capture in May, 1840, was already moribund. All hope of an effective program died the previous December with the refusal of the Massachusetts Society to provide any money whatever. The Executive Committee made one last desperate appeal at a special meeting in January, but no funds were forthcoming from delegates who knew all too well just how weak the society had grown. Instead, a committee was appointed and given the power to decide the future of the organization and plans were made for the transference of the *Emancipator* to the New York City Anti-Slavery Society. The committee issued its report recommending that the national organization either be allowed to operate where it pleased or be disbanded. On the assumption that the old privilege would never be restored, the Executive Committee looked forward to dissolving the society in May, disposing of its stock of tracts and pamphlets, and completing the sale of the *Emancipator*. In the meantime they pondered Leavitt's suggestion that they continue to operate *ex officio* as a clearinghouse.

When news of the Executive Committee's plans reached Boston, Garrison issued his countermanifesto. "That society must and will be sustained, under the guidance of a trustworthy committee, let who will plot to destroy it, whether treacherous friend, or open foe."[13] He called for a strong delegation of "unswerving, uncorruptible friends of the cause" to go to New York and save it. The same power which had sought the life of the Massachusetts Society, he told them, now threatened the whole movement. "It has thrown its mask aside, and unblushingly declares that our sacred cause cannot be safely trusted in the hands of 'the common people' — the farmers, mechanics, and workingmen — but must be placed under the control of a select body of men in order to give it respectability and success!" To accomplish their ends the traitors would come to the annual meeting ready to demand the repeal of the rule allowing women to vote. Then they would try to rush through the convention a resolution making voting mandatory for members of the society and outlawing the nonresistant abolitionists. It would require great vigilance on the part of the real friends of the slave to defeat this scheme. "In whatever part of the country you reside, we call you to rally at the meeting as one man."[14]

Unwilling to leave it to chance or the uncertain consciences of men to provide him with a majority, he decided to pack the annual meeting, a fairly simple maneuver since there was no rule limiting the number of delegates from any one state. This meant, in effect, that the society would fall to anyone with enough votes. His votes would have to come from Abby Kelley's feminine anti-slavery contingent whose headquarters was the Essex County Society in Lynn. The problem of transporting the ladies along with an unusually large delegation of men was solved by the general agent, John Collins, who suggested chartering a special train to Providence and from there a steamboat to New York. The fare was cheap, and arrangements could be made for boarding the delegates in the homes of colored friends in the city for twenty-five cents a day. The results of Collins's work were described by Garrison himself. "A few came from the land of 'down east' and the thick-ribbed hills of the Granite State; but especially from the counties of old Essex and Middlesex, and Norfolk, and Plymouth, and Suffolk, in Massachusetts, they came promptly and numerously at the summons of HUMANITY, in spite of 'hard times' and the busy season of the year, to save our heaven-approved association from dissolution, and our broad platform from being destroyed."[15]

From the railing of the steamship *Rhode Island* Garrison

watched "a heart-stirring and rare spectacle" as hundreds of his delegates marched up the gangplank while Collins checked them off. "There never has been such a mass of *'ultraism'* afloat," he wrote, "since the first victim was stolen from the fire-smitten and blood-red soil of Africa." A three-day nor'easter cleared just as the *Rhode Island* put down Narragansett Bay, a sign, some thought, of God's pleasure with His annointed. A glorious sunset and full moon put the passengers in the proper spirit for a night of anti-slavery lectures — seven in all — and when the ship docked in New York it was dawn. Four hundred and fifty delegates from New England descended on the city ready to rescue the American Anti-Slavery Society from oblivion. Four hundred of them came from seaboard counties in Massachusetts; one hundred and fifty were women; twenty-seven only were nonresistants. "They were, indeed, the moral and religious *elite* of New England abolitionism, who have buckled on the anti-slavery armor to wear to the end of the conflict, or to the close of life."

The annual meeting was held in the Tappans' Fourth Free Church on the corner of Madison and Catherine Streets. Arthur Tappan, the president of the society, hearing of the impending crisis, chose not to attend, a tactical error that allowed Francis Jackson to preside. The Executive Committee had known that the Garrisonians were beating the bushes for delegates and had hurried to follow their example. Over a thousand delegates crowded the first session and sat restlessly through the interminable opening ceremonies which could not hide the rising tension. Then came hours of debate filled with pious hypocrisy and mutual recrimination; but when a vote was finally taken on the admission of women, Garrison's party won 557 to 451.[16] He had used his "Lynn majority" to good advantage. Lewis Tappan promptly re-

signed from the Business Committee and soon thereafter led
the exodus of anti-Garrisonians from the hall. Over four
hundred left the meeting for a conference room in the
church basement, where they drew up plans for a new
society. Upstairs the Garrisonians rejoiced. "It was our anti-
slavery boatload that saved our society from falling into the
hands of the new organizers, or more correctly, disorganizers," Garrison boasted, not without truth.

While the secessionists launched their new American and
Foreign Anti-Slavery Society, the Garrisonians, or the "old
organization," as they now called themselves, made quick
work of refashioning their institution. First they elected
Lucretia Mott, Maria Weston Chapman, and Lydia Child
to the new Executive Committee and then passed resolutions
censuring the secessionists and denouncing both the American church and the third party movement. "We have made
clean work of everything," Garrison chortled, " — adopted
the most thorough-going resolutions, and taken the strongest
ground, with *crashing* unanimity."[17]

The old organization — now "our society" — hardly seemed
worth the fight. The treasury was empty, its stock of literature gone, the allegiance of most of the state organizations
lost. From now on, the American Anti-Slavery Society functioned chiefly as an auxiliary of the Massachusetts Society.
The secessionists had taken the *Emancipator* with them, and
there were almost no funds available for a new paper. Un-
perturbed, Garrison set up headquarters in Nassau Street
as a temporary clearinghouse for the little business which
now befell the organization. Mrs. Child agreed to try editing
the *National Anti-Slavery Standard*, the new paper, and
delegates were appointed to the World Anti-Slavery Convention to be held in June in London. Garrison was well
pleased with his work. "Our campaign has just closed and a

severe siege we have had of it, and a glorious triumph we
have achieved." What the fruits of victory would be no one
knew.

Garrison always represented the schism of 1840 as the
victory of progressive reform over the reactionary forces of
sectarianism and political double-dealing. The real issues
were somewhat different. In the first place, the division was
not solely the result of woman's rights: The participation of
women was only the immediate cause. The Executive
Committee and its allies knew that Garrison planned to use
his women delegates to defeat political anti-slavery and introduce the principles of no-government. Lewis Tappan had
seen the issue clearly from the beginning. The national
society broke apart, he told Weld, "chiefly because Garrison
and his party . . . foisted upon the Amer. Anti S. Soc. the
woman question, no government question, etc., and the bad
spirit shown by the Liberator, etc." Garrison had been the
aggressor from the beginning. "W.L.G. introduced the question into the Anti S. Soc. to make an experiment upon the
public. He had avowed before that there were subjects
paramount to the Anti S. cause. And he was using the Society
as an instrument to establish these notions. Since he introduced this question the slave has been lost sight of mainly."[18]
The capture of the national society marked the height of
Garrison's anti-slavery career and ironically the beginning of
its decline. Having rejected politics and turned his back on the
church, he could lead his "old society" in just one direction
— toward the principle of "No Union with Slaveholders" and
the doctrine of secession.

Leaving the affairs of the society in a muddle, he hurried
off to London in hope of arriving in time for the first session
of the World Convention. The World Anti-Slavery Convention had been called by the British abolitionists at the sug-

gestion of the New York Committee to discuss the progress
of West Indian emancipation and accelerate the work in
America. The first call was issued to all "friends of the
slave," but when the English learned that the Massachusetts
abolitionists planned to demonstrate for the rights of women
by appointing female delegates, they sent a second invitation
reminding the Americans that "gentlemen only were expected to attend." These careful reminders went unheeded
in Massachusetts, where Maria Chapman and Harriet Martineau, an honorary member of the Massachusetts Society,
had already been appointed delegates.

After the secession, the "old organization" appointed Garrison, Charles Remond, William Adams and Nathaniel P.
Rogers as its accredited delegates. Remond, a free Negro of
intelligence and ability, was one of the most effective
lecturers in Garrison's collection. Just thirty years old and
wholly self-educated, he had joined the Garrisonians three
years before and served as agent of the Massachusetts Society.
He was a proud man with a quick temper and a savage wit,
and as a campaigner did more than anyone except Frederick A. Douglass to acquaint audiences in the Northeast with
the intellectual potential of the Negro. William Adams was
a Quaker from Rhode Island, a loyal Garrisonian and a man
of unexceptionable parts. Nathaniel P. Rogers, the fourth
member of the delegation, had only recently taken up the
anti-slavery cause and was destined to become a particularly
painful thorn in Garrison's side. Rogers once boasted that
he could "out-Garrison Garrison," and so he could. Ten years
older than his chief, secretary of the New Hampshire Society
and nonresistant editor of the *Herald of Freedom*, he had
emerged suddenly in the stormy days of 1839 as a valuable
ally and was being groomed for the new post at the *Anti-
Slavery Standard* in case Mrs. Child refused. "The more I

see of Rogers, I love him," Garrison wrote to Helen from New York, "and his friendship for me is ardent and sincere."[19] It would remain so for three years.

The "new organization" also sent delegates to the World Convention, among them Birney and Stanton, who were resolved on preventing Garrison from bamboozling the British abolitionists as he had the Americans. Joshua Leavitt spoke for all of the secessionists when he expressed the hope that the winds would prove "over-organized and delay their champion." Leavitt's wish was granted — the *Columbus* with its radical cargo took twenty-five days to reach Liverpool. Garrison improved his time by remonstrating with the captain for putting Remond in steerage, and studying the condition of the sailors in the merchant marine. When things grew dull, he chided the passengers for their drinking habits and loose morals. He was glad to part company with such "immoral creatures" when on June 16 the *Columbus* docked in Liverpool. By then the World Convention had been in session for three days.

He arrived at Freemasons' Hall in Great Queen Street to find the fight for admission of women already lost. In the balcony sat Lucretia Mott, Ann Phillips, Elizabeth Cady Stanton and the rest of the women delegates surrounded by attentive gentlemen from the floor but denied the right to participate. Wendell Phillips, heeding his wife's instructions not to "shilly-shally," had done his best to crack English reserve. At the opening session he moved that all *persons* accredited by any anti-slavery society be admitted to the convention, but immediately the defenders of male order protested, English clergyman vying with American to explain why the ladies, amiable as they were, had no right to be there. Phillips's motion was struck down, his protest tabled, and his female admirers escorted to the balcony, where Garrison found them.[20]

Apprised of the situation, Garrison agreed not to disturb the convention "by renewing the agitation of the subject already decided," but he was determined to add his protest by joining the ladies. Lucretia Mott thought it a foolish gesture and said so, though Rogers was sure their silent protest shocked the English. "Haman never looked more blank on seeing Mordecai sitting in the king's gate with his hat on, than did this 'Committee in Conference' on seeing us take the position we did."[21] The Garrisonians stayed with the women for the rest of the convention, deaf to the entreaties from the floor to come down. Daniel O'Connell objected to the exclusion of women, as did John Stuart Mill's friend John Bowring, but the majority of the delegates were well satisfied with the location of the ladies and their champion. Garrison had the bad grace to suggest to friends that Phillips had mismanaged the affair, and wrote to his wife that "had we arrived a few days before the opening of the Convention, we could have carried our point triumphantly."[22] His unfair remark told only of his dissatisfaction with the results of the convention.

He was dissatisfied with his whole visit, which contrasted sharply with his reception seven years earlier. Thanks to Birney and Stanton the English abolitionists knew all about his "steal." There were the usual elaborate dinner parties at Samuel Gurney's and William Ball's and luncheons with Fowell Buxton and Lord Morpeth. The Duchess of Sutherland and Lady Byron lavished attention on Remond and Rogers, while Mrs. Opie and Elizabeth Fry saw to it that Garrison did not lack for edifying entertainment. But he was not asked to speak at the anniversary meeting of the British and Foreign Anti-Slavery Society, though Birney and Stanton were. He did manage an impromptu talk at a soirée following the meeting, where he aired his "singular views," as Birney called them. "He has gained, I think, but few adherents to them," Birney observed with some satisfaction.[23] One evening he surprised his hosts by contending for a universal reform of language; at another dinner party he astonished the well-fed guests with a lengthy discourse on perfectionism. "I let out all my heresies, in my intercourse with those who invite us, and have made no little stir in consequence," he reported proudly to his wife.[24] Birney thought his performances laughable, and Elizabeth Stanton, Henry's outspoken bride, remarked that every time he opened his mouth out came folly. At still another soirée he proceeded to bear "faithful testimony" against Drs. James Hoby and Francis A. Cox, revered figures in the English religious community, because they had not condemned all aspects of Southern life. Perhaps it was the general expression of disappointment among his hosts or simply his own at being elbowed aside for the representatives of the "new organization." At any rate, he was content to be hurried off to Scotland by Thompson for a series of meetings at Edinburgh and Glasgow. "Though I like England much, on many accounts," he told Helen, "I can truly say that I like Scotland better."[25]

In Glasgow he encountered opposition of a new kind. Outside the Emancipation Chapel where he was to speak he found Chartist pickets distributing handbills captioned *Have We No White Slaves?* and exposing the working conditions in the mills and mines. He took one and read it to the assembly inside. Were there white slaves as well as black? "NO," he replied. " — broad as is the empire, and extensive as are the possessions of Great Britain, not a single *white* slave can be found in them all." There was a difference between chattel slaves and "those who are only suffering from certain forms of political injustice or governmental oppression." Admittedly, there were poor people dying of starvation and little children working long hours in mills, and there were also hundreds of thousands of laborers deprived of their political rights. But British abolitionists were not blind to "suffering humanity" at home; they were friends of the poor and lowly. "Are they not so?" he asked. "No! No!" called out several voices. "Then," he stammered, "I am very sorry to hear it." After he sat down a Chartist attempted to answer him only to be shouted down. "I, for one, should have had no objections to his being heard," Garrison later explained, "yet he was clearly out of order, and had no just cause to complain of the meeting."[26] This kind of agitator with his "rude behavior" and "criminal conduct" upset him. Where were the appeals to reason, justice and the law of God — where the unwavering reliance upon Christian truth? It was clear that England and Scotland were no longer as he had remembered them.

In London, Garrison talked with Robert Owen but found the old man's ideas "absurd and demoralizing," wild dreams that would "make shipwreck of any scheme under its guidance, in due season."[27] Perhaps a man's environment did affect his development, and there was no doubt that a drastic reorganization of society was needed, but an inner rather than an outward reordering, a change of heart, not socialism.

Garrison's conservatism had deep roots. As a moralist first and last he believed that any permanent change in the social structure would have to be preceded by a general renovation of the human heart. Thus his views tended to uphold the political *status quo* and to defend *laissez-faire* capitalism by redirecting the current of reform into channels remote from the economic and social evils of his day. In the first issue of the *Liberator* he had denounced attempts "to inflame the

minds of our working classes against the more opulent. . . .
That public grievances exist, is undoubtedly true, but they
are not confined to any one class of society." Ten years had
not altered this view. He noted the glaring contrasts in English society, the "suffering and want staring me in the face
on the one hand" and the "opulence and splendor dazzling
my vision on the other,"[28] yet no solution occurred to him
except that of "going about doing good." Here was the
paradox of his moral suasion: just as the doctrine of immediate
emancipation logically implied a social revolution of epic
proportions, so his condemnation of the evils of an irresponsible industrial system called for a profound economic change.
In neither instance was he willing to face the consequences
of his moral vision.

In August he was back in Boston for a reception at Marlboro' Chapel where he struck a new patriotic note which
must have startled his audience. "I thank God that I was
born in the United States," he told them, "that my field of
labor lies in the United States." He saw now that the English
abolitionists — those once worthy members of the British
and Foreign Anti-Slavery Society — had been remiss in their
duty toward their own people. British anti-slavery had never
been tried in the fiery furnace; it shunned the company of the
real American abolitionists "with pro-slavery and delicacy
of feeling." At last the truth! He had been rejected and his
followers ignored. The Atlantic community of feeling had
dissolved, and henceforth Americans could look only to their
own resources.

These resources seemed meager indeed in the autumn of
1840. Shorn of most of its auxiliaries, the old organization
was on the verge of collapse. Each number of the *Anti-
Slavery Standard* promised to be the last; rent was owing on
the Nassau Street headquarters. Ignoring the advice of Quincy

and Phillips, who foresaw bankruptcy, he decided to send an agent to England to solicit funds among the few English abolitionists still loyal to him. The mission was a "dernier ressort," undertaken with great reluctance, but the critical condition of the society made an appeal for funds imperative. Without aid from abroad, he admitted, "I am apprehensive that the American Anti-Slavery Society, with the *National Standard*, Rogers and all, must sink."[29] He did not exaggerate — the situation was desperate.

The financial troubles of the old organization were compounded by numerous defections from nonresistance as the Presidential election approached. Collins, who was struggling to hold the loyalty of anti-slavery men in western Massachusetts, advised Garrison again and again to adapt his program to withstand a "whirlwind of Political enthusiasm. . . . I really wish you understood perfectly the exact position the friends of the old organization hold to the two great political parties. . . . They are politically intoxicated. The enthusiasm of Bank and Sub-Treasury, Harrison and Reform, has taken entire possession of them."[30] Typical of this new attitude was the case of George Bradburn, a minister from Attleboro, a loyal Garrisonian and friend of the *Liberator*. Bradburn had suddenly made up his mind to vote Whig because the party, at least in Massachusetts, was more friendly to the abolitionists than the Democratic Party. Garrison dismissed such explanations as conniving at robbery. "Let no whig or democrat abolitionist," he implored, "sacrifice his anti-slavery principles, or go with his party, at the coming election, on the grounds that he thinks or knows that someone else will prove recreant."[31] Yet this was precisely what was happening everywhere. "The fact is," he admitted ruefully, "and we cannot and ought not to hide it, a large proportion of the abolitionists in this State and elsewhere, are

determined to go with their party at the approaching election; and they will not attend our meetings until after the
election, even if at all. This is not less humiliating than true."[32]

To recall Massachusetts abolitionists to their duty he held
two conventions in October. The first at Worcester proved
"very interesting, but the number of delegates not large,"
and the second at Springfield came "very near being a total
failure." Each week the *Liberator* censured the "arbitrary
and proscriptive" spirit of political parties, and its editor reminded readers that the organization of a party "was never
dreamed of by abolitionists in the days of their purity and
simple reliance on truth." He even went so far as to identify
the third party with the new organization "full of self-seeking,
and swayed by sectarian motives." It was with obvious relief
that he announced the end of the Presidential campaign. It had
been all of the devil, nothing of God. The American people
were obviously losing their self-respect. Log cabins, hard
cider, parades and triumphal arches — what were these but
conclusive proof of the "besotted state" of the public mind?[33]
With regret he turned from the unenlightening spectacle of
democratic politics to the question of universal reform and
attended the Chardon Street Convention, that singular conference of reformers and cranks which met for three days in
November without reaching any conclusions or passing a
single resolution.

Emerson has left the best account of the Chardon Street
Convention. "Madmen, madwomen, men with beards, Dunk-
ers, Muggletonians, Come-outers, Groaners, Agrarians,
Seventh-day Baptists, Quakers, Abolitionists, Calvinists, Unitarians and Philosophers — all came successively to the top,
and seized their moment, if not their hour, wherein to chide,
or pray, or preach, or protest."[34] The truculent prophet
Joseph Palmer was there striding through the assembly with

his holy beard and defying any man to cut it off. So was "that flea of conventions" Abby Folsom, primed with her interminable harangue in defense of freedom of speech. Also Dr. George W. F. Mellen, another cracked vessel of the Lord who frequently interrupted the proceedings. But there were also Theodore Parker and George Ripley, Bronson Alcott, Emerson himself, William Ellery Channing and his nephew William Henry Channing, the ubiquitous Henry Wright, Abby Kelley, the recluse poet Jones Very, Father Taylor, the sailor-preacher, and Maria Chapman — all met for a sharing of views, bound together by their search for something "better and more satisfying than a vote or a definition."

The convention had been called by the Friends of Universal Reform for the purpose of examining "the validity of the views which generally prevail in this country as to the divine appointment of the first day of the week as the Christian Sabbath, and to inquire into the origin, nature, and authority of the Ministry and the Church, as now existing."[35] Garrison had not signed the original call — he believed the convention "premature" — but that fact did not prevent the press generally from ascribing to him the whole notion of an "infidel convention." Once he learned of the "mighty stir" the meeting would make in Boston, however, he joined in doing "with our might what our hands find to do."[36]

The Chardon Street Convention was one of the few meetings in a lifetime of conferences and convocations in which Garrison found himself on the Right with the conservatives. It opened with a lively skirmish over the question introduced by the Come-Outers of abolishing parliamentary procedure altogether and proceeding without chairman and without restraint. Though the motion was defeated, parliamentary order was not forthcoming. Joshua Himes demanded that the convention accept only the Old and New Testaments as proof for all arguments. When a storm of protest descended on Himes and his fellow ministers, Garrison came to their aid by requesting that all those who rejected divine authority be barred from participating. "I expressly declared that I stood upon the Bible, and the Bible alone, in regard to my views . . . and that I felt that if I could not stand triumphantly on that foundation, I could stand nowhere in the universe."[37] The convention would be bound by no such niggling rule as this. When John Pierpont introduced the proposition "That the first day of the week is ordained by divine authority as the Christian Sabbath," Scriptural proof was tossed to the winds. Accompanied by cries of "Infidel!" and "Atheist!" or "Priest!" and "Bigot!" the speakers, often two or three at once, clamored to be heard. Periodically Abby Folsom or the unfortunate Dr. Mellen conducted a foray on the rostrum only to be turned back by saner minds intent on hearing the ponderous arguments of Amos Phelps and Dr. Samuel Osgood. Father Taylor spoke fervently and frequently. Emerson, who confessed to watching the clock at philanthropic conventions, said nothing, preferring to leave it to the genius of Bronson Alcott to summarize the sense of the meeting in orphic sayings.

It was all delightfully zany — no minutes, no resolutions, no reports, no results — simply "the elucidation of truth through free discussion."[38] The truth which these men were seeking lay outside the Jacksonian compass, beyond all projects, plans, blueprints, all "small, sour, and fierce schemes." The Chardon Street Convention was a strange collection of reformers in whom the social sentiment was weak and the dictates of what Emerson called "the great inward Commander" were particularly strong. The very principle the members admitted seeking they had already found, for they came to the Chardon Street Chapel believing that the individual was the world. They were philosophical anarchists who were perfectly willing to be dismissed as "the sentimental class" by the so-called realists of American politics because it was just the "reality" of Manifest Destiny and the margin of profit they questioned.

Although he was fairly overwhelmed by his colleagues, Garrison sensed that they were the prophets of a new age, critical of their society but strong in their belief that they could redeem it. Some of them saw the cure in the regeneration of the individual; others dreamed of a new life in a Fourierist phalanstery or a New Harmony. All were agreed that there was much that was wrong with America. Garrison still believed that slavery was the evil and Christ the cure; but whether the millennium would be built by men or come by divine dispensation he no longer knew.

14

"No Union with Slaveholders"

O N AN AUGUST DAY in 1841 two carriages rolled slowly through Franconia Notch in the White Mountains. In the first chaise rode two New Hampshire abolitionists, Thomas Beach and Ezekiel Rogers, deep in conversation, and behind them came Garrison and Nathaniel Rogers, his new friend and headstrong colleague, singing hymns at the top of their voices. All four were on their way to an anti-slavery meeting. Suddenly Garrison noticed a cloud of smoke coming from the carriage ahead — it seemed to be rising from beneath friend Ezekiel's beaver hat. He stared. Could it be tobacco smoke? Had Ezekiel become a chimney flue? He called to him and remarked the incongruity of an abolitionist's profaning his mouth with the stupefying weed. Might as well make it a rum-duct! "We had halted at the Iron Works tavern to refresh our horses," Nathaniel remembered, "and while they were eating, walked to view the Furnace. As we crossed the little bridge, friend Rogers took out another cigar, as if to light it when we should reach the fire. 'Is it any malady you have got, brother Rogers,' said we to him, 'that you smoke that thing, or is it habit and indulgence merely?' 'It is nothing but habit,' said he gravely; 'or, I would say it *was* nothing else,' and he significantly cast the little roll over the railing into the Ammonoosuck. 'A revolution!'

exclaimed Garrison, 'a glorious revolution without noise or smoke,' and he swung his hat cheerily about his head."[1]

The schism of 1840, another revolution without casualties, opened a decade of confused politics both within the anti-slavery movement and in the country at large. The annexation of Texas planted the slavery issue in Congress, where it grew like a virus for fifteen years, draining off the energies of legislators and paralyzing the business of government. With the enormous new area seized from Mexico, the United States acquired the problem — abstract and hypothetical as it may have seemed at first — of the status of slavery there. The dragons' teeth of a future civil war were strewn over the rocky plateaus of Mexico by Winfield Scott and Zachary Taylor, each too busy countering the political ambitions of the other to foresee the results of their conquest.

The decade opened at home with the death of the new President and the strange sight of a Virginian of only nominal Whig loyalties in the White House. Four years later the Whigs again looked on in dismay as Birney's Liberty Party stole enough of Clay's New York votes to throw the state and the election to Polk. Then it was the turn of the Democrats when David Wilmot drove a sectional wedge into the party by attempting to ban slavery from the new territory. In 1848 political disorder reached its climax, and the country witnessed the spectacle of Conscience against Cotton, Hunker against Barnburner, Free Soil against Manifest Destiny. It was a period of broken alliances as parties scrambled to adjust to the reality of the slavery question and new men began following new sectional directives. No matter where they began — in Charleston or Boston, in cotton plantation or cotton mill — these sectional lines of force led straight to Washington, the new center of agitation over slavery.

It was also a period of reorganization and retrenchment

for abolitionists, who belatedly recognized the institutional breakdown which the schism had caused. Once a year, until they tired of the farce, Garrison and his followers made the trek to New York for the annual meeting of the American Anti-Slavery Society, listened to three days of speeches, each more radical than the last, and returned to Boston. Nor was the secessionist American and Foreign Anti-Slavery Society — the "soulless new organization," as the Garrisonians continued to call it — any more representative of abolitionist sentiment in the North. Weld disowned it, and despite the exertions of Lewis Tappan, many of its supporters soon drifted into the Liberty Party camp. Yet the Liberty Party vote in 1844 totaled only sixty-two thousand, a gain of eight hundred per cent over four years but hardly an index of Northern views on the expansion of slavery. Three conclusions appeared inescapable: the national organization was dead, the careers of many of the pioneers were at an end, and the anti-slavery impulse had broadened. In 1846, at the outbreak of the war with Mexico, abolitionists were amazed to discover that the North, and particularly New England, had developed an anti-slavery conscience. No one could quite explain the phenomenon.

Confusion reigned in the Garrison household, as though completing its mastery over moral reform by disrupting the affairs of its leader. Babies arrived regularly — Charles Follen Garrison in 1842; Fanny, her father's favorite, named for his mother, in 1844; Elizabeth Pease two years later; and Francis Jackson in 1848 — five boys and two girls. The baby Elizabeth lived only two years, and Charles died at the age of seven, scalded by a steam bath, a victim of his father's faith in medical quackery. His children found him a happy and surprisingly indulgent parent, given to pranks, boisterous games, and family outings. He worried a good deal about his

health and suffered from all manner of ailments, real or
imaginary, aching joints, gastric complications, heart palpita-
tions, recurrent headaches. Not a year passed that he did not
add to this list of infirmities, as though his body protested
his puritanical principles. He bore cheerfully his friends'
jokes at his hypochondria while waiting patiently for another
doctor to consult and another diagnosis to consider. Once
Phillips and Quincy prevailed upon him to see Dr. John Warren about a swelling in his chest (he called it his "devil"), but
Warren found nothing wrong with him. Mostly he preferred
the various services of itinerant quacks, country bone-setters,
faith-healers and animal magnetists, homeopaths and hydro-
paths. Nothing pleased him more than a disagreement in
diagnosis. "Who shall decide," he chuckled, "when doctors
disagree?" When Warren and then Bowditch pronounced
him sound, he started the rounds of "clairvoyants," as Quincy
irreverently called them, "who examined his internals with
the back of their heads." "The ocular, or *occipital*, evidence
of these last worthies," Quincy added dryly, "is the most
satisfactory to his mind. To most men, the circumstance
that they gave diametrically opposite accounts of the case
would be startling, but then G. believes them both equally,
which arranges the affair satisfactorily."[2] The family medicine
shelf held everything from Buchan's Hungarian Balsam of
Life to Dr. Church's Pectoral Pills. Once Garrison took a
dose of the same Dr. Church's Anti-Scrofulous Panacea and
exclaimed that he felt it permeating the whole system. "Permeating the system!" Dr. Weston snorted. "Why, it was
the first time he had taken a glass of grog, and he didn't know
how good it was."

For years the family drifted from one home to another.
Wherever they were, their home was an anti-slavery hotel
with a housekeeper, an occasional neighbor, and two or

three visiting friends of universal reform who had heard of
Garrison's love of conversation and his wife's table. The
Boston clique saw to it that he did not lack for necessities.
"I see you have a houseful of people," Charles Hovey wrote
to Helen in sending her a barrel of flour. "Your husband's
position brings him many guests and expenses which do not
belong to him." God continued to provide but in small
amounts. "I am never so far in funds as to have a spare dollar
by me, using what economy I can," Garrison complained. His
financial dependence on well-to-do friends, however, entailed
no loss of self-esteem.

In 1842 James Garrison died. Lloyd improved the occasion
of the funeral by delivering a lecture on the evils of war and
alcohol. Though he spoke of his brother's fortitude and
resignation, he scarcely understood the tragedy of James's
struggle. James had escaped his mother's domination by running away and turning to drink; Lloyd, while he never had to
escape, had transferred his resistance to maternal authority
into a hatred of society and a compulsion to tear it down.
Before he died James might have seen that his brother's
search for sainthood and obsession with purity, his anxiety
and hostility, were somehow related to the image of the
mother they both professed to have cherished. But Lloyd
was bent on saving him and had convinced him of his "evil
qualities." His death brought Garrison no closer to a self-
confrontation than questioning whether James died "reconciled to God."

Garrison was away from home more than ever now that
he had joined the anti-slavery lecturers in the field. One result of the schism of 1840 and the rise of the Liberty Party
was the need for fence-mending in New England and western
New York. Leaving his paper in the hands of Johnson and
Quincy, he took to the circuit with Phillips, Remond and

Frederick Douglass, younger and hardier lecturers whose hectic pace wore him down. Douglass he discovered at a New Bedford meeting and developed him into one of his most successful lecturers until the young man proved too headstrong to be harnessed. Douglass's strength on the platform lay in his dignity and lofty tone. Remond was witty and quick with repartee, high-spirited and fractious. Phillips possessed the power of improvisation, a theatrical suppleness and urbanity that made him the greatest of the anti-slavery orators. Garrison lacked all of these qualities. His forte was earnestness, and his best audiences were usually Quakers. "Garrison just suited them," Sydney Gay remarked to Edmund Quincy of one of Garrison's appearances in Philadelphia. "His soberness, his solemnity, his earnestness — his evident deep religious feeling — his simplicity — all these were just what the Quakers love, & they gathered about him as their fathers did about Fox, & said yea! verily! he is a prophet!"[3]

He was known now as one of the "old men" in the movement, though only in his late thirties, and was in constant demand as a speaker. He spent most of the year 1841 traveling in New England and attending local conventions in the attempt to strike the spark of organization again. In the fall of 1842, together with Douglass, Abby Kelley and Charles Remond, he toured western New York with the hope of bringing some of the wayward politicians back into the fold. Though the invasion failed and there were almost no converts, his "menagerie" performed well under adverse conditions. His greatest difficulty was persuading Douglass and Remond, neither of them particularly concerned with the rigors of a schedule, to keep their appointments. At Syracuse, Garrison reported, "the tumult was tremendous" following an ill-chosen comparison of the Methodist Episcopal Church to a New York brothel. "Rotten eggs were now thrown, one of which was sent as a special present to me, and struck the wall over my head, scattering its contents on me and others."[4] Benches were hurled and windows smashed to the tune of hisses and curses before the meeting was hastily adjourned. He told his wife he still believed that "genuine anti-slavery" would gain a foothold there, but his opinion was not shared by his colleagues who realized that, adapted to the rocky soil of New England, Garrisonism was not destined to flourish on the banks of the Genesee.

While its editor canvassed the countryside the *Liberator* languished. Lydia and David Child's *National Anti-Slavery Standard*, though Garrison disapproved its Whig bias, was ably conducted and for the moment self-sustaining, while his own paper stood in need of editorial as well as financial repair. The truth was that it was badly edited and frequently uninteresting. In the first place, the layout was eccentric. Articles were thrown in "higgledy-piggledy," readers complained. No single issue was complete, matters were too often left at loose ends with the promise of "more anon" or "more next week" when "next week" never came. Then there were not enough carefully written editorials, too many off-the-cuff commentaries and too few well-chosen articles. In an election week why was there no comment on the political situation? Why the time-lag between news stories on page one and editorials on page three? Quincy remonstrated with him and warned that unless he corrected his careless habits the *Liberator* would have to be discontinued. "Now we know that you have talent enough and to spare to write editorials, such as no other editor can; that you have the most ample materials for the best of selections, and eminent tact and sagacity for judging what is timely; and, moreover, that you have abundance of time for doing all this, if you would but have a little *method* in your madness." All that was lacking, Quincy explained, was industry and application.[5] Quincy asked the impossible: as the years went by, the *Liberator* grew more and more personal, disorganized, and erratic as its editor lost the fiery zeal of his youth.

The disruptive forces within the anti-slavery movement after 1840 were several, but most important, perhaps, was a sudden awareness among abolitionists of the complexity of social evils and their growing reluctance to isolate slavery as the universal wrong. They saw that poverty and suffering were not heaven-directed but man-made, and they began to consider solutions that fell short of a regeneration of the human race. In short, they discovered social planning. A dramatic example of the discovery of utopian planning was the career of John A. Collins, General Agent of the Massachusetts Society and Garrisonian knight-errant. Collins joined the anti-slavery movement as a young theological student at Andover, where he proved his usefulness by uncovering the "clerical plot" against Garrison. His rise thereafter was meteoric, and in 1840 he was selected to undertake the delicate mission to England for funds to bail out the American Anti-Slavery Society. His expedition, perhaps the most inglorious of all abolitionist appeals to British philanthropy, ended in failure, and he had to borrow the passage money back to Boston. But his visit was the beginning of his education in the problems of industrial civilization. The horrors of Liverpool slums and brutal working conditions in the Midlands convinced him that the English suffered from "the same prejudice against poverty, that we do against color."[6] The English themselves were guilty of "a vast and complicated system" of slavery, a form as dangerous as it was subtle, which gave to the poor subject the appearance of freedom the more successfully to grind him to powder. *Laissezfaire*, he concluded, had created a nation of drones virtually slaves though technically free. Neither Corn Law nor Chartism held the answer to the dislocations caused by industrialism; nothing would suffice "until the entire social structure, from which the state is but an emanation, is completely changed."

Collins left England a convert of Robert Owen, and although he took up his abolitionist duty on his return, his heart was no longer in it. It seemed to him now that slavery was only a small part of the vast question of social reorganization. In 1843 he formed the Society of Universal Inquiry and Reform on the premise that competition was a failure and that the future of America lay in self-sustaining communities of three hundred families happily free from the curse of acquisitiveness. Soon thereafter his society bought three hundred acres outside Skaneateles, New York, and began working the land on the principle of "Unity in Love." Garrison, though interested in the scheme, was sure that Collins's underlying moral philosophy had been disproved by "myriads of facts, drawn from a world lying in iniquity," and predicted that the experiment would prove "the baseless fabric of a benevolent dream."[7] He admitted that Collins was both earnest and dedicated, but rejected his ideas as "deceitful."

Another experiment, more interesting and closer to home, was Hopedale, founded at Milford, Massachusetts, by a fellow abolitionist and nonresistant Adin Ballou. Ballou was descended from a long line of nonconformists, and he had already been ousted from his Universalist pulpit for heresy when he transformed the Jones Farm in Milford into Fraternal Order Number One. At Hopedale each member agreed to work eight hours a day for fifty cents and to give the community one dollar a week for room and board. This arrangement, Ballou explained, was "to facilitate the honest

acquisition of individual property for laudable purposes."
Thus, though it aimed at restoring pure Christianity, Hopedale was not communist. Like Garrison, Ballou was interested in every reform of his age — peace, woman's rights,
temperance, and anti-slavery. He built a Thompsonian water
spa on the premises where ailing members could try cures of
hot herbs and vapor baths. The community presented lectures
on phrenology and mesmerism and séances with spiritualists.
Liquor and tobacco were forbidden at Hopedale, tea and
coffee discouraged, and the dietary schemes of Sylvester
Graham and Catherine Beecher much applauded. Ballou's
newspaper, the *Practical Christian* (a title borrowed from
Garrison), kept the gentile world abreast of activities in the
community. Its motto — "Absolute Truth, Essential Righteousness, Individual Responsibility, Social Reorganization,
Human Progress, Ultimate Perfection" — offered something
for everybody.[8] Members of Hopedale may have been reaching for the millennium, but they were also, in Ballou's estima-
tion, "plain practical people . . . very much like the middle
class of New Englanders generally," conscientious, earnest,
imperfect. Not so imperfect, however, as to be incapable of
substituting "Religious Consecration" for "Fragmentary,
Spasmodic Piety."

It was just Ballou's promise of practical righteousness which
Garrison doubted the power of any cooperative scheme to
achieve. That there were evils in society "too dreadful to be
contemplated by any human heart" he would not deny; but
that they sprang from external causes rather than "the evil
propensities of mankind" he could not agree. Ultimately the
regeneration of society reduced itself to a question of the individual and his God. "Outward circumstances do indeed frequently and extensively exert a disastrous influence on the
feelings and actions of the people; but the creator or cause

of these circumstances have not been either Nature or a beneficial Creator, but 'an evil heart of unbelief' in man — an unwillingness to perform right actions — an almost universal
disposition to reject 'the golden rule' as an unsafe rule of
action — a disregard of the laws of being — a contempt for the
commands, and a distrust in the promises of God."⁹ Bad laws,
hunger, poverty, and destitution, he knew, were the evil
fruits of the corrupt tree of man.

Then his brother-in-law George Benson decided to lay his
axe to the roots of the tree. In 1841 he sold the family farm
in Brooklyn and began a study of "the great subject of social
organization." "Where do you settle?" Garrison joked.
"What say you to a little community among ourselves?"¹⁰
Benson replied by founding within the year the Northampton
Association of Education and Industry. The Association was
divided into two separate enterprises — an industrial community of one hundred and twenty-five members and a stock
company of investors. Members of the community received
eighty cents a week for board, fuel, light and rent, and twenty
dollars a year for clothing. If their expenses exceeded this
amount, they were deducted from their share in the profits
from the brick factory and shingle mill. Benson's community
lasted four years, slightly longer than the Skaneateles experiment.

Garrison spoke with pride of his brother-in-law and his
friends as "among the freest and best spirits of the age," and
he was a frequent visitor at the community. Yet he clung
to the belief that permanent changes in society originate
"within the individual and work outwards." It was Christ's
example that made better citizens. The trouble with community schemes — Bronson Alcott's as well as Robert Owen's
— was that they ignored this simple truth. "The chief ob-
stacles to the success of these communities or associations will

lie in the breasts of their members, and not in the present
state of society."[11] His old Federalist conservatism led him to
reject as "radically defective" any plan involving new property relationships. Inequality of wealth he dismissed as simply
an "outward symptom" of an "inward disease," and he insisted only religion could bring down the lofty and exalt the
depressed. "Every axiom of political economy that is not
based upon a law of God is, at best, but a cunning falsehood
or a plausible artifice. To attempt, therefore, to secure property to a nation in any other manner than by seeking the
intellectual and moral improvement of the people — in one
word, by *christianizing* them, is something worse than a
blunder. It is to suspend the laws of the material world, and
expect that grapes may be gathered from thorns, and figs
from thistles. It is to unhinge the moral government of the
universe, and suppose that a great improvement can be made
upon the original plan."[12] Peace to the ghost of Federalism
and a sigh for the days when saving religion and sound politics linked arms!

Garrison had even less sympathy with the religious mania
sweeping New England after 1840 — the millenarian fantasy
of Father Miller. Miller's pre-millennial advent, first scheduled
for 1843 and then for October 22, 1844, won a number of
converts in Boston, notably Joshua Himes, pastor of the
Chardon Street Chapel, and Charles Fitch, once a member of
the "clerical conspiracy." In Himes, Miller found a revival
promoter without peer who helped spread his doctrines
throughout New England and western New York. Miller's
notions, like the Christian communism of the utopians, were
implicit in perfectionism; but instead of making their heaven
on earth the Millerites were content to accept it from the
hand of God. Agreeing that Miller and Himes were "good
men" favorably inclined toward reform, Garrison neverthe-

less dismissed their ideas as absurd. "As the French Revolution was the legitimate product of the false religion of France, to whom all its excesses and horrors are to be attributed, so is the present 'Miller mania' to be traced to the false teachings of a dumb and blind priesthood, and an apostate church, for centuries."[13] The fallacy in Miller's reasoning, Garrison held, was not his doctrine of a second coming but his unwarranted assumption that it lay in the future. As a disciple of John Humphrey Noyes, Garrison believed that Christ had returned eighteen hundred years ago. Jesus had told Paul that "this generation shall not pass until these things are fulfilled," and had returned about the year 60 A.D. after the apostles had prepared for His coming. His return spelled the end of the apostolic ministry with its church, and His new dispensation set men wholly free to follow Him. This was the "correct" view of the advent against which Miller set his "novel and preposterous" explanation.[14] Man's salvation thus lay in a return to the simple Christianity of the disciples. Here in the dim recesses of the first century the mistake had been made, the sin of disobedience committed. To make a better world, to free the slave, abolish inequality, banish suffering, people would have to recognize their errors and return to the point where they went wrong. Innocence had somehow been lost, but not forever — by destroying wicked institutions and corrupt laws men could recapture it. Their future lay buried deep in their past, their salvation in an eternal return. The way to Garrison's utopia led through the doors of time and memory and down the path of the original garden.

His views on the Bible were changing more rapidly than he admitted. His critics still called him an "unbeliever" and "a total stranger to the spirit of Christ," but he insisted that the Scriptures were his "text-book" and worth all the other books in the world. The text required no analysis, however, for he

was convinced that Christianity was neither argumentative
nor metaphysical but dealt with self-evident truths and spoke
an authoritative language. Theologians and preachers were
too concerned with metaphysics and legal niceties, and neglected the plain, simple, soul-stirring message of the gospel.
Besides, the art of Scriptural quotation was known to the
devil. A hireling clergy quoted Paul who advised servants
to obey their masters, ordered women to keep silence in the
churches, and recommended a little wine for thy stomach's
sake. Garrison made a note to avoid Scriptural arguments
from now on, to teach "vital godliness" in place of "sectarian
theology." He would show an unbelieving world that the
true church was simply the fellowship of believers and that
ecclesiastical bodies were only cages of unclean birds and
stables of pollution. "Has God made it obligatory upon us,
(and we believe he has,) to have no fellowship with iniquity,
and yet at the same time does he require us to sustain that
which is in fellowship with all iniquity?"[15] Clearly not! The
true Christian had no choice but to denounce evildoers and to
come out from among them.

Like all of the religious persuasions of the day, Garrison's
definition went by a name. "Come-Outerism," so called because its believers preached "coming out" of corrupt churches,
was as old as Christianity. The idea of secession in the name
of a rigorous piety had governed the Donatists in the fourth
century, the Albigensians in the eleventh, the Anabaptists in
the sixteenth, and the New-Lights in the eighteenth. Logically, the command to come out from iniquity was a part of
perfectionism — it completed it. A man who has achieved
perfection in this world risks losing it if he continues to hold
communion with the unsanctified. He must leave the unenlightened and their church or give up his status as a saint.
There were two main types of Come-Outers in America be-

fore the Civil War: those who simply tested the churches by anti-slavery standards and, finding them wanting, departed; and the "genuine infidels," as Garrison called them, who rejected the whole institution of church and clergy. The difference between the two types was only one of degree, since most of the more radical Come-Outers were violently anti-slavery. New England Come-Outerism seems to have originated among pietists on Cape Cod, but with the Second Great Awakening it spread rapidly. The Come-Outers were Christian anarchists who were often unable to agree on anything besides their duty to leave a particular church. Perfectionists on the march, they strode out of their churches on to the farthest reaches of Christian piety and, in the case of Garrison's friends, to the brink of insanity.

Garrison saw the Come-Outers as the harbingers of a second Reformation, prophets destined to do for Protestantism what Luther did to the Catholic Church. He particularly admired them for their self-reliance. They recognized no man as apostle, prophet, presbyter, elder or deacon; they observed no church form and were amenable to no tribunal; they were bound by no creed, and they recorded their testimony against all existing religions as destitute of the primitive gifts and guilty of imposture. Surely the future of Christianity lay with such free spirits as these who sought to atone for sinful men by defying them. In the years after 1840 Come-Outerism infiltrated his anti-slavery movement and transformed it into a secessionist crusade.

The chief prophet of Come-Outerism was Garrison's new friend Nathaniel Rogers. "We have a very humble but very faithful little squad of abolitionists in this place & in our state," Rogers wrote to a friend in 1842. "They are at this moment a little more radical, than the leading influences that surround Garrison."[16] As editor of the militant *Herald of Freedom* and

the leader of ultraism in New Hampshire, Rogers was in a
position to know. A graduate of Dartmouth and a successful
lawyer, he had abandoned a lucrative practice to organize
anti-slavery in the state. After witnessing the affair of the
"clerical appeal" he became convinced of the guilt of the
clergy and accepted perfectionism without reservation. His
obsession with consistency disturbed the Boston clique, whose
urbanity and sophistication he distrusted. "I wish we could
let politics entirely alone," he told those friends who thought
his views too severe. "Parties cant seem to handle principles.
They dont know how." Rogers felt that organizations of any
kind inevitably abused power, that even small groups simply
found it impossible to do right. He reasoned that only by
rejecting power and refusing even to recognize its symbols
could the righteous man escape its demonic clutches. Accordingly, he urged that anti-slavery meetings be conducted without officers, notes, rules of order, or parliamentary procedure.
He favored a return to the Quaker idea of "the sense of the
meeting," and chided Garrison for his failure to avoid all the
pitfalls of politics. "Garrison holds politics a mortal sin — yet
he fills his paper with the doings of politicians, & censures
them for not turning their politics to better account. And he
holds to embodying the anti-slavery movement in real political form — with all the formalities of parliament or Congress." For Rogers, moral suasion meant "mere speech." "Tell
the truth. Let everybody tell it — & in their own way. And
if they transcend propriety — *tell them so* & if they wont
conform, let them go unconformed. That's my sort of moral
suasion. Any thing short of it is *war*." Rogers reached the
peak of disorganization when he discovered the immorality of
treasuries and budgets and suggested that henceforth anti-
slavery lecturers support themselves like Buddhist monks with
begging bowl.

In Stephen Symonds Foster and Parker Pillsbury, Rogers found two disciples worthy of his mettle. Foster was undoubtedly the most aggressive and humorless reformer ever to grace the anti-slavery stage. He was born in New Hampshire in 1809, the ninth of thirteen children of a dirt-poor farmer. He put himself through Dartmouth, and as a student there was jailed for refusing to perform militia service. Hauled off to the town lock-up, he sat down and wrote a blistering letter to the authorities complaining of the vermin and the filth and was rewarded by seeing the warden dismissed. This was the approach to reform which he employed with varying success for the next twenty years. After finishing his course at Union Seminary in New York, he held a Congregational pulpit until 1839, when he left the church in disgust and joined the Garrisonians. He was a born trouble-shooter, a crank, and a monomaniac on the subject of free speech. "I could wish that bro. Foster would exercise more judgment and discretion in the presentation of his views," Garrison complained after Foster's epithets had touched off a near riot in Syracuse, "but it is useless to reason with him, with any hope of altering his course, as he is firmly persuaded that he is pursuing the very best course."[17] The best course for Foster was the course of greatest resistance. His favorite mode of operation was to stride into a church on a Sunday morning and plant himself in the front pew. He would wait until time for the sermon and then rise and ask in a resonant tone to be heard in the name of three millions of suffering humanity. Usually he was tossed out. Once in Portland, Maine, he landed in the street and broke his collarbone. In Concord he was kicked down the aisle out into the street and beaten. The next day he appeared in court, bandaged but unrepentant, to refuse to answer to charges of disturbing the peace. He did admit to disturbing the uneasy peace of the American church, however, and believed that the ends justified any means. Suppose a church were on fire, he asked, would he then be right in interrupting the service to tell the congregation? What then if the whole nation were on fire? . . . At this point his lecture frequently ended in violence. If not, then he proceeded to single out the minister for comparison with a recently executed criminal or liken his congregation to the patrons of the local house of ill fame. In 1843 he collected some of these pungent observations in a seventy-two-page pamphlet entitled *The Brotherhood of Thieves: or, a True Picture of the American Church and Clergy*. The title was the least offensive statement in the book.

Foster finally discovered a kindred spirit in Abby Kelley and married her in 1845. Until then his partner in disorder was Parker Pillsbury, another master of the art of conversion by attrition. Pillsbury was a native of Massachusetts who had left the Congregational Church and gravitated into Rogers's orbit in New Hampshire. He was gentler and more intelligent than his traveling companion, but he too delighted in setting the pulpit "into a pretty considerable kind of a fix." Together Pillsbury and Foster took the new gospel of Come-Outer abolitionism into every roadside village in New Hampshire and then ventured farther afield into Massachusetts and Connecticut. "Our influence is fast becoming a source of terror to the pro-slavery pulpit if not to the pro-slavery parties," they reported gleefully to Garrison, "and no pains are spared by men in high places to brand our most active and devoted friends as 'heretics,' 'infidels,' and 'dishonest men.' "[18]

No one in the Boston circle thought Foster and Pillsbury worse than mountebanks. Ellis Gray Loring, before he left the Garrisonians in despair, wanted it clearly understood that he did not discuss anti-slavery in Foster's language. Phillips, who could employ the barbed word to advantage, thought both were needlessly aggressive. So did Quincy and Francis Jackson. Even Garrison agreed that Foster, at least, was "morbidly combative." The Come-Outers made common cause with the older radicals like Henry Wright and Abby Kelley, and forming a nucleus of radical pacificism, they began to challenge the hegemony of the Bostonians. At the New England Convention in 1841 they fought Garrison's resolution, which simply spoke of the clergy as "wickedly preeminent," and substituted one of their own, calling it a "BROTHERHOOD OF THIEVES." Later that same year they recommended that abolitionists defeat Jim Crow regulations on the railroads by taking seats reserved for Negroes. This resolution, introduced at a quarterly meeting, was finally defeated through the efforts of the Boston clique, but for a while feelings ran high. Garrison himself warned of the danger of abolitionists becoming "invidious and censorious toward each other, in consequence of making constitutional peculiarities virtuous or vicious traits."[19] Word spread among the Come-Outers that Garrison was growing "cautious" and "conservative." For fifteen years there had been no enemies to the Left, but now his comfortable position on the lunatic fringe of American politics was threatened by a handful of fanatics chasing the illusion of purity.

It was not true that Garrison had grown cautious or modified his demand of the South. The years just before the Mexican War saw the rise within his organization of a new radicalism powered by the secessionist energy of Come-Outerism. Like many men with neither great intelligence nor deep feelings, Garrison was extraordinarily sensitive to the opinions of others. He realized that the New Hampshire triumvirate was simply putting his perfectionism into practice and that Come-Outerism was symptomatic of the gradual dispersion

of abolitionist strength. Institutional anti-slavery was breaking up, a process which Phillips identified when he pointed
out that "the *organization* may have met with some check —
but the *enterprise* is taking stronger & stronger hold of the
public."[20] From now on Garrison concerned himself with the
anti-slavery enterprise. The best way of spreading the gospel
now appeared to be the spontaneous local meeting where
itinerant anti-slavery lecturers like Foster and Pillsbury performed in their best Old Testament manner. These meetings
were inexpensive and easily arranged; the agents were generally satisfied with their meager earnings and content that they
should be "thoroughly understood," as Foster explained, "by
the *people* to whom alone we now look for support." This
meant going to the people with a moral argument, democra-
tizing anti-slavery and simplifying it even to the point of
distortion. The other alternative after 1840 was political
action which carried the risk of all movements dependent
on votes. Political action meant the Liberty Party, and Garrison expressed his opinion of that when he asked how many
votes Jesus of Nazareth cast into the ballot box. The logic
was shocking but his point was unmistakable.

Much of his opposition to the Liberty Party was the product of his smoldering hatred for Birney, Leavitt and the other
"apostates" who had walked out of the old society in 1840
taking the *Emancipator* with them. He never forgave them
this "swindle." When Birney agreed to head the Liberty
Party, Garrison continued to plague him with charges of
being Leavitt's "dupe," a man without "mercenary motives,"
but obviously "not to be relied on in cases of strong temptation." He accused Birney's followers of being "vandal enemies" who had abandoned true abolition out of "miserable
jealousy" of its leaders. The object of the Liberty Party, he
implied more than once, was not the abolition of slavery but

the overthrow of William Lloyd Garrison. It was an organization "conceived in sin," "utterly unprincipled," and therefore "the most dangerous foe with which genuine anti-slavery
has to contend." Periodically he ran down the list of "defectors" in an editorial, asking the whereabouts of each of them.
Where was James Birney? "In Western 'retiracy,' waiting
to be elected President of the United States, that he may have
the opportunity to do something for the abolition of slavery!"
What was Henry Stanton doing now? "Studying law (which
crushes humanity and is hostile to the gospel of Christ)."
What about Elizur Wright? Where was he? Selling a translation of French fables he had made. And Whittier and his
friends — all lost to the cause, all bewitched by the sorcery
of political action.[21]

Lamentations like these were pure hokum and the Liberty
Party men did not hesitate to brand them as such and to
make a few accusations of their own. Garrison, they retorted,
had arrived at a "sublime abstractionism" and was so busy
with keeping his own skirts clear that he ignored the slave.
Suppose all the opponents of slavery were William Lloyd
Garrisons — who would stop the slavocrats from exercising
complete dominion over the whole country?[22] More abolitionists each year were apparently reaching similar conclusions, for each year the Liberty Party won more votes until,
in 1844, Birney received over sixty-two thousand. In the
Massachusetts gubernatorial election of the previous year
Samuel Sewall, Garrison's old friend but now a "defector" to
the Liberty Party, received sixty-five hundred votes, while
only one hundred and eight abolitionists followed Garrison's
instructions to "scatter" their votes. At times like these Garrison changed his tone and openly admitted that there was a
"considerable increase" in Libery Party strength. "We have
never opposed the formation of a third party as a measure

inherently wrong," he wrote as though to put a new face on his opposition, "but have always contended that the abolitionists have as clear and indisputable right to band themselves together as those who call themselves whigs or democrats."[23] It was simply that political action was inexpedient at this time; an anti-slavery party was premature; there was still too much "preliminary toil" to be performed.[24] Such statements fooled no one, least of all the Liberty Party.

He came closer to his real objection to the Liberty Party when he referred to the "partial nature" of its goals and its concern with the economic and political rather than the moral aspects of slavery. "Its impolicy in a pecuniary point of view is dwelt upon far more glowingly than its impiety and immorality." Appeals were made to the pocketbook, not to the conscience, "to the love of political preferment, rather than the duty of Christian reformation."[25] Defenders of the Liberty Party found this reasoning incomprehensible. What use was moral suasion, they asked, without good works? "Without these, we may talk fluently and loudly, may argue and conclude, may exhort, entreat, rebuke; but nothing of moral suasion can we employ."[26] Principles without the votes to make them stick seemed to the Liberty men of no use whatever.

Not votes but "vindicating the principles of eternal justice" interested Garrison. He was sure that abolitionists could never improve on the "apostolic mode" of changing corrupt institutions, that is, by "the foolishness of preaching." "*How shall the people be brought to repentance?*" — this was the question, and the answer — "Moral suasion . . . is the mode appointed by God to conquer error, and destroy the works of darkness."[27] His language betrayed his old concern with purity. It was not a matter of laws to be passed or steps to be taken, but of *error* to be rooted out and *repentance* to be exacted. Again, it was not simply the freedom of the Negro he sought. He wanted to bring America to its knees, penitent in sackcloth and ashes, to help it escape sin and death by destroying evil.

This dream of escape was the source of his interest in all the other reforms and fads of the Forties — utopianism, perfectionism, phrenology, Graham bread, water cures, and spiritualism. All of these movements offered a form of escape: utopianism from the injustices of a competitive economy; perfectionism from the domination of the Church; Grahamism from ill-health and neuroses; phrenology and mesmerism from individual responsibility; spiritualism from the finality of death. Garrison was involved with all of these movements in the course of his life but with none more completely than abolitionism. He was possessed by the image of the shackled slave because it cried out for Armageddon. An endless fascination with upheaval was the one constant of his life, the polestar in the murky rhetoric of his editorials. It explained the vocabulary of violence, the endless references to "revolution," "chaos," "blood," and "overthrow." His hatred of institutions lay deeper than his evangelical bias, deeper even than his aversion to slavery. For him hostility to the established order and the authority it wielded was a fundamental need. It was of no consequence, he reasoned, that the anti-slavery pioneers had not envisioned an assault on existing institutions. They never knew the power of entrenched wickedness. On the other hand, he had decided to examine anti-slavery hostility in every institution in the country — "and if it can be shown that this hostility springs naturally from the despotic assumptions of such institutions, I do not see why abolitionists may not assault the institution itself, as well as its pro-slavery influence — lay the axe at the root of the tree, as well as cry out against its fruit."[28] The institution he now marked for destruction was the American Union.

It was the radicals who first explained to Garrison the connection between Come-Outerism and anti-slavery. "One of two things must be done," Abby Kelley wrote to him in 1843, " — either the American Society and the Mass. Society must stand on the 'come-outer' ground or I must, as an individual, detach myself from them — I must clean my hands from the blood of the slave that is spilt by support of slavery in church and in state."[29] By 1843 Garrison was well down the road to disunion himself, having seen and accepted the duty which Come-Outerism placed on him. As early as November, 1841, at the height of the petition debate in Congress, he addressed an open letter to the "desperadoes" of the South informing them that they might leave the Union whenever they chose. "They ought not to be allowed seats in Congress," he decided. "No political, no religious co-partnership should be had with them. . . . So far as we are concerned, we 'dissolved the Union' with them, as slaveholders, the first blow we aimed at their nefarious slave system. We do not acknowledge them to be within the pale of Christianity, of republicanism, of humanity."[30] Privately he told friends that disunion was only a question of time and that the bloody-minded South could only be brought to terms through terrible retribution.

On January 12, 1842, John Quincy Adams presented to the House a petition signed by Benjamin Emerson and forty-five citizens of Haverhill, Massachusetts — all Democrats with Locofoco principles — praying that the Union might be speedily dissolved. The petition was not the first of its kind to reach the House: Adams reminded Robert Barnwell Rhett of South Carolina that not long ago he had offered a similar appeal. This fact did not deter the Southern bloc from threat-

ening a vote of censure, but Adams squelched their plans by
recalling that at the trial of Warren Hastings, Burke spoke
for a month. Two weeks after Adams's skirmish Garrison
and his Massachusetts Society held a rally in Faneuil Hall to
unroll the Irish Petition signed by famed Daniel O'Connell
and seventy thousand Irishmen urging their American brethren to support the abolitionists. In the course of the meeting
Garrison offered three incendiary resolutions. The first provided that Massachusetts Senators and Representatives who,
like Adams, were denied their rights in Congress, "ought at
once to withdraw to their homes." His second resolution proclaimed the Union "a hollow mockery," and a third announced the time approaching "when the American Union
will be dissolved in form as it is now in fact."[31] To George
Benson he wrote that he was both

an Irish Repealer and an American Repealer. I go for the repeal
of the Union between England and Ireland, and for the repeal of
the Union between North and South. We must dissolve all con-
nexion with those murderers of fathers, and murderers of
mothers, and murderers of liberty and traffickers in human flesh,
and blasphemers against the Almighty, at the South. What have
we in common with them? What have we gained, what have we
not lost, by our alliance with them? Are not their principles,
their pursuits, their policies, their interests, their designs, their
feelings, utterly diverse from ours? Why, then, be subject to their
dominion? Why not have the Union dissolved in form, as it is
in fact — especially if the form gives ample protection to the
slave system by securing for it all the physical force of the North?
It is not treason against the cause of liberty to cry 'Down with
every slaveholding Union!' And, O, that I had a voice louder
than a thousand thunders, that it might shake the land and elec-
trify the dead — the dead in sin, I mean — those slain by the hand
of slavery.[32]

The more he studied it the more compelling the idea of Northern secession became. In an editorial in April, 1842, he reverted to the haunting childhood nightmare of the shipwreck. "It is now settled beyond all controversy," he wrote, "that this nation is out on a storm-tossed sea, without compass, or chart, or rudder, and with the breakers of destruction roaring all around her. . . . They who would be saved must gird themselves with life-preservers, and be prepared to fill the life-boat without delay." Escape to Eden while there is still time, he seemed to be saying, make the repeal of the Union your salvation! Then suddenly he placed a new motto on the masthead of the editorial column: A REPEAL OF THE UNION BETWEEN NORTHERN LIBERTY AND SOUTHERN SLAVERY IS ESSENTIAL TO THE ABOLITION OF THE ONE AND THE PRESERVATION OF THE OTHER.

Garrison took his disunion text from the twenty-eighth chapter of Isaiah: "We have made a covenant with death, and with hell are we in agreement." The covenant was the United States Constitution which a whole new group of Liberty Party theoreticians was expounding as anti-slavery. As long as he had believed in the possibility of governmental action in behalf of the slave, Garrison held to the view that the Founding Fathers had intended to contain and eventually to abolish slavery. Now that a political party sought to elaborate the anti-slavery content of the document, he reversed his position and denounced the Constitution as a corrupt bargain. For once, he went to the sources. In the *Federalist Papers* he found nothing but exhibitions of profligacy, selfishness, and "a shocking violation of heaven-attested principles." Ignoring the Northwest Ordinance, he identified the key to the Constitution as the three-fifths clause, which proved that the United States was "conceived in sin, and brought forth in iniquity." No man could innocently support it and no party could act under it. "The political ballot-box is of Satanic origin, and inherently wicked and murderous," he concluded with regard to the constitutional provisions for voting. "We must cease to sanction it, or give up our profession of Christianity."[33] If Birney and Liberty Party men felt otherwise, they were either fools or hypocrites.

Disunion was a good deal further than most abolitionists, even loyal Garrisonians, were prepared to go. Lydia and David Child, who had reluctantly assumed joint editorship of the *Standard* on the understanding that Garrison would leave them alone, complained that he was foisting his own private views on the national society. Following their lead, that society at its annual meeting in 1842 refused to consider the question of disunion as a topic for the usual resolutions. But the next year Garrison collected enough votes in the Massachusetts Society to pass his resolution calling for an end to the Union. "We dissolved the Union by a handsome vote, after a warm debate," Quincy reported to Webb. The disunion question, "wrapped up by Garrison in some of his favorite Old Testament Hebraisms by way of a vehicle," slid neatly through the assembly.[34]

The same motion did not fare so well at the annual meeting of the American Society in New York that year. The chief order of business in 1843 concerned the fate of the society itself. Some of the members favored disbanding it on the spot; others were for moving it to Boston for the reason, as Quincy explained, "that there was literally nobody in New York but James S. Gibbons who either would or could act as a member of the Executive Committee." When the exchanges of opinions grew sharp, someone suggested in the interests of morale that the matter be turned over to a committee of twenty-five empowered to decide the question once and for all. In the committee Garrison, Collins, Foster, and Abby Kelley led the faction favoring removal of the society to Boston. Quincy, Phillips, and Caroline Weston of the Boston clique vehemently opposed the move on the grounds that it was tantamount to disbanding the national society. There was a noticeable chill when Quincy stiffly suggested that if the move were voted, certain of the "Boston friends," by which he meant Phillips and himself, might not continue to support the society. "Garrison dilated his nostrils like a war-horse, and snuffed at us," Quincy recalled. He said that of course, if the "Boston friends" were unwilling to take trouble and responsibility, then there was nothing to do but get along in the old way. A compromise was worked out, however, which gave a quorum in the Executive Committee to Boston so that business meetings might be held there while nominal headquarters were continued in New York. Garrison was forthwith elected president of the American Anti-Slavery Society. He "*nolo episcopari'd*" a bit, Quincy noted maliciously, but ended by accepting the honor gratefully.[35] It was the opinion of the society that he made an excellent presiding officer at public meetings where he was limited to introducing speakers, but that in debates he did not answer so well since he was very apt to do all the talking himself. With Garrison in the president's chair it was only a question of time before the American Society, like the Massachusetts organization, should bow before his secessionist will.

The defeat of the friends of the Union within the national organization came the following year, in 1844. Backed by his host of New England radicals and upheld by the honors of his office, Garrison celebrated the tenth anniversary of the society by completely rewriting the Declaration of Sentiments. Henceforth members were pledged to the rallying cry "No Union with Slaveholders," as well as to renouncing the Constitution as a covenant with death and an agreement with hell. The society was further committed to opposing all political parties and spreading the doctrine that "the strongest political influence which they can wield for the overthrow of slavery is, to cease sustaining the existing compact by withdrawing from the polls, and calmly waiting for a time when a righteous government shall supersede the institutions of tyranny."

Garrison's resolutions and new Declaration of Principles were accepted by the society only after a minority bitterly opposed to them had been silenced. Ellis Gray Loring and David Lee Child, both loyal Whigs, might have been expected to balk at disunion and so perhaps might the Quakers. But there were other veterans in the cause, dedicated but prudent men, who doubted the wisdom of disunion and objected strongly to the speciousness of the prophet's words. He answered their objections with another quotation from Isaiah — "For the Lord spake thus to me with a strong hand, and instructed me that I should not walk in the way of this people. . . ."

Removed from their political setting, Garrison's statements stand out in hallucinatory starkness. Yet this kind of moral absolute was commonplace in the charged atmosphere of the election year 1844, when voters realized that the admission of Texas hung in the balance. Thomas Walker Gilmer, Virginia's favorite son, declared that annexation was absolutely essential to American security, that only hasty approval could prevent Great Britain's seizing Texas and abolishing slavery there. Other Southern spokesmen, holding that any check on the expansion of slavery would split the Union, argued at the same time for Senator Robert John Walker's "diffusion theory" by which annexation was to hasten the end of slavery by "diffusing" the institution throughout the new territory. Fantasy was in the air and threats of secession abounded.

At the close of the session in 1843 Adams and twelve other anti-slavery members of the House issued a circular summarizing the history of the Texas negotiations and warning that annexation would be identical with dissolution of the Union. Following their lead, the Whig legislature of Massachusetts passed a resolution (killed by Democratic Governor Marcus Morton) declaring that annexation could only be regarded by the people of the Commonwealth as "dangerous to its continuance in peace, in prosperity, and in enjoyment of those blessings which it is the object of free government to secure."[36] The gap between the abolitionists and the people of the North was beginning to close.

On April 12, 1844, Calhoun, now Secretary of State, signed the annexation treaty and sent it to the Senate with the explanation that hurried approval was needed to forestall British interference with slavery in Texas. What was called slavery, Calhoun added, was in reality a political institution essential to the peace, safety, and prosperity of those states in the Union in which it existed. American slaves were better off than many British or American workmen; and until abolitionists on both sides of the Atlantic learned this, they would do well not to meddle. Calhoun's remarks opened a new phase of the slavery controversy, the beginning of a close cooperation of Southern politicians and intellectuals in defense of the "peculiar institution," and in the North a new liaison between moderate abolitionists and insurgent Whigs. Southern plans for a quick ratification misfired when Calhoun's rival, Thomas Hart Benton, in a bid for Senate leadership, detached enough Southern votes from the annexationist party to defeat the treaty (June 9, 1844). Polk's election, however, was correctly interpreted by the South as a mandate for annexation, and on February 27, 1845, the joint resolution adding the new territory to the Union was accepted by both Houses.

Three days before he left office President Tyler signed it.

Annexation caught the Massachusetts General Court still in a refractory mood. It passed resolutions declaring first of all that there was no precedent for the admission of new territory by legislative act, and secondly, that in ratifying the Constitution Massachusetts had never delegated this power to the federal government. Next it asserted that the joint resolution violated the Constitution by perpetuating slavery and extending the unequal ratio of representation over the new territory. Finally, the legislature announced its readiness to cooperate with other states in refusing to recognize annexation, and "by every lawful and constitutional measure, to annul its conditions and defeat its accomplishment."[37] If the General Court's invitation to disobedience did not measure up to Garrison's standards, it was as close as a group of politicians could come in the year 1845.

Some of these same men crowded into Faneuil Hall one evening in January, 1845, to attend an Anti-Texas Convention. Among the delegates was Charles Francis Adams, the able if antiseptic son of Old Man Eloquent and an articulate opponent of slavery in his own right. At the moment he was editor of the *Boston Whig*, the organ of the younger members of the party with strong anti-slavery tendencies. Charles Sumner, massive and pompous, was there along with the quieter but equally tenacious Henry Wilson. Also Horace Mann, a reformer turned politician, and John G. Palfrey, Harvard professor and editor of the *North American Review*, Stephen Phillips, the Salem merchant, and George Hillard. These men were already growing restive under the leadership of the "Cotton" conservatives in the Whig Party, and it would not be long before they bolted and took their "Conscience" platform into the Free Soil Party. This evening, however, they had met simply to protest the annexation of

Texas and listen to speeches. One of the speakers, it was said, would be Garrison himself.

Waiting his turn on the rostrum, Garrison turned his mind from these new faces to the other friends he had made in his fifteen years of agitation. Many of them were gone, their affection chilled by his wintry righteousness and domineering manner. The roll call of discarded friends grew each year — Lundy, now dead, the Tappan brothers, Goodell, Leavitt, Elizur Wright, the Grimkés and Theodore Weld, Amos Phelps and John Whittier. More recently, George Bradburn, gone over to the Whigs, and the Childs — David and Lydia — no longer able to bear his dictatorial manner. The list of the rejected and damned would continue to grow — Nathaniel Rogers, Frederick Douglass, Ellis Gray Loring, finally even Phillips himself. These new recruits before him this evening could not make up the loss of tried anti-slavery comrades. They spoke with respect of his services in the cause and deferred politely to his religious opinions, but they did not agree with him. He suddenly realized that at the age of forty he had become the veteran of the anti-slavery movement, almost the lone figure of virtue and strength he had always wanted to be.

These disturbing thoughts were drowned in the applause that welled up and engulfed him as he rose to speak. Not many in the audience could accept his ideas, but all were visibly moved by his manner — the ponderous rolling periods, the mournful pauses, and the flat hard voice rising again to new charges. His words fell like "fiery rain," Sumner remembered. "We deem it our duty . . . no binding force whatever . . . the Constitution has been overthrown . . . the Union has ceased to exist . . . treat the General Government as a nullity . . . assemble in convention without delay . . ." The ovation at the end of his speech was a signal not of approbation but of respect. His audience seemed to realize that though they could never come to like this inflexibly righteous man, they could not help but respond to his force. He might well be fanatical — no doubt he exaggerated — but some of the things he said about the Southern plot to extend slavery to the Pacific made sense. In the half-light of Faneuil Hall and the dimness of their growing doubts they sat wondering.

Later that year, in October, after the Texas protests had begun to subside, the *Liberator* paid its editor's last respects to the nonresistance cause which was slowly expiring. Nonresistance and the redemption of the world, Garrison wrote, were clearly synonymous. "Where it prevails, there can be no shedding of human blood, no violence, no lawless conduct." The cause of peace might have lost its appeal temporarily but it would never die. In the next column there was an account of his speech to the Middlesex Anti-Slavery Society. "Give us but five years to agitate the question of dissolution," he had said, "and at the end of that brief period, see whether we have made any progress in changing public sentiment. . . . We believe that the dissolution of the Union must give the death-blow to the entire slave system."[38] Already he foresaw a revolution which would come complete with noise and the smoke of guns.

15

Compromise

IN MAY, 1846, the United States declared war on Mexico. Zachary Taylor spent the Fourth of July that year in the captured village of Matamoros awaiting reinforcements and treating his weary soldiers to Mexican cooking and patriotic speeches. Two thousand miles to the northeast the "beautifully small" troop of loyal Garrisonians gathered in Dedham Grove to hear their leader's last indictment of the war before sailing to England. Two weeks later he boarded the *Britannia* in Boston Harbor and arrived in Liverpool on July 31 for a reunion with his English friends.

His Boston friends were decidedly unenthusiastic about the visit, his last before the Civil War. At an Executive Committee meeting in June they sat by while he quarreled with young Sydney Gay over the management of the *Standard*. The Childs could have told Gay that Garrison would tolerate no one who showed the least editorial independence. Lydia said that Garrison's idea of a proper editorial was a preamble and a dozen resolutions, and that when he went to heaven he would present Saint Peter with resolutions that protested being admitted by a traitor who had betrayed his master, a bloodthirsty villain who cut off the high priest's ears, and a miscreant who had been warned thrice by the beast.

His spat with Gay arose over the question of whether

contributors to the *Standard* should sign their editorials. He
accused Gay of trying to get credit for editorials he had not
written and of plotting to seize control of the paper. While
he and Gay thrashed out the question of signatures, the rest
of the committee grew more and more glum and did not
brighten when he broached the subject of another pilgrimage
to England. "The poor thing wanted to be stood by and put
through with warmth & energy," Caroline Weston wrote to
her sisters, "but if the board were cataleptic about Sydney,
they were equally so about him."[1] Finally Phillips and Quincy
gave in; James Russell Lowell, who had recently joined the
group, withdrew his objections; and Francis Jackson promised
to underwrite the trip. All that was needed was a reason for
going. This he manufactured out of the transgressions of the
Free Church of Scotland which had accepted funds from a
slaveholding Presbyterian congregation in South Carolina. He
left the country in the midst of its first anti-slavery crisis in
order to protest the "foul deed" of the Free Church and
demand that they "Send Back the Money."

Enlightening the Free Church of Scotland, he protested,
required "great exertions." English and Scotch abolitionists,
however, were of the opinion that his services to anti-slavery
would be greater if he confined himself to it instead of letting
fly at the church, the Bible, or any other "great object" that
stood in the way of universal liberty. In London he visited
Thompson and was disturbed to find that he had taken to
using tobacco. "If I can induce him to give up this habit, and
sign the tee-total pledge in regard to snuff," he told his wife,
"I shall feel it worth the expense of coming to London." The
city, which teemed with pubs and prostitutes, shocked him.
Standing in front of the Lord Mayor's house one night, he
was accosted by a handsomely dressed lady of the evening
who gave him "the most earnest glances in a manner revealing

her desire. . . . After advancing a few steps she turned round, and in the most insinuating manner acted as though she expected me to go with her. . . . My heart sank within me to think of the horrid fate of that unfortunate creature."[2] He was glad that he was a Bostonian.

Frederick Douglass, already on a mission in Scotland, appeared with him at most of his lectures. Together they toured from London to Edinburgh, Bristol to Belfast, holding "real old fashioned old-organized meetings" at which they declared "the whole counsel of God" and handled their subjects "without mittens."[3] Garrison spoke to William Lovett's moral suasion Chartists and interviewed Mazzini, whose mystical Christian nationalism and romantic temperament fascinated him. In Glasgow his admirers presented him with a silver tea service. Except for the formation of an Anti-Slavery League to oppose the conservative Evangelical Alliance, however, he accomplished little for American reform. Douglass, on the other hand, received seven hundred dollars from English abolitionists to purchase his freedom. Garrison contributed his "mite," only to be severely criticized by his followers back home for recognizing the slave traffic. Such was not the case, he explained. "Never have I entertained the opinion, for a moment, that it was wrong to ransom one held in cruel captivity, though I have always maintained, in the case of the slave, that the demand of the slaveholder for compensation was unjust."[4] He saw no contradiction in denouncing a claim as unfair while submitting to it in order to save an individual slave.

It was on occasions like these that his humanitarian feelings broke the restraints of dogma and sent his principles flying. In Drogheda on the way to Belfast he was appalled by the sight of starving Irish children begging by the roadside, and grew indignant with the Dublin abolitionists who refused donations from American slaveholders. "I really think there is a broad line of demarcation to be drawn between a case in which money is obtained from the slaveholders solely because they are first recognized as 'members of the household of faith,' and that in which it is given voluntarily (as in the Irish case) without any sanction of slaveholding being either required, volunteered, or understood."[5] Righteous as he seemed, he was not willing to weigh a moral principle against the life of a child.

In November he came home bringing with him the silver tea set on which there was a sixty-dollar duty. The excise was finally paid by his women friends, but it was enough to make him a confirmed free-trader who denied the right of any country "to erect geographical or natural barriers in opposition to these natural, essential and sacred rights."[6] He would have been surprised to learn that his language as well as his ideas were those of the South Carolina Exposition.

He returned to a political situation in Massachusetts already tense with anti-slavery strain. The trouble began in Washington one evening the previous August when David Wilmot, a portly young Democrat from Pennsylvania, offered to an appropriations bill an amendment which closed to slavery all the territory acquired in the war with Mexico. Passed by the House, the Wilmot Proviso died in the Senate but not before it had raised the issue which would dominate American politics for the next fifteen years. Southern legislatures denounced it, Northern reformers hailed it as a sign of moral awakening. In the South there was talk of secession; in the North, of free men and free soil. The Whig Party could not long withstand these sectional pressures, and nowhere was its plight more obvious than in Massachusetts, where the "Young Whigs" — Charles Sumner, Henry Wilson, John Gorham Palfrey, Rockwood Hoar, George S. Hillard, Stephen Phillips and Charles Allen — were rallying around Charles Francis Adams's free soil *Daily Whig*. Ever since the declaration of war Wilson had tried unsuccessfully to put the legislature on record as opposing the extension of slavery. In the course of one of the debates his colleague Hoar declared that it was "as much the duty of Massachusetts to pass resolutions in favor of the rights of man as in the interests of cotton." Hoar's quip stuck, and from then on the dispute was one between Cotton and Conscience. At the state convention of the party in September, 1847, the Conscience faction submitted resolutions opposing slavery "wherever it exists" and pledging Whigs to "continue in all constitutional measures that can promote its abolition." When Robert Winthrop's Cotton faction defeated their bid for an anti-slavery platform, the Young Whigs retired to await the coming of a Presidential year.

Garrison was excited by the sudden appearance of an anti-slavery Whig bloc as well as by the Wilmot Proviso, which he immediately claimed as an abolitionist triumph. It was true that Wilmot's majority had dwindled away when the appropriations bill was finally passed and that the war went on despite the opposition of New England. Yet every day more people in the North were becoming convinced of what James Russell Lowell's crusty Hosea Biglow called "the over-reachin' o' them nigger-drivin' states." When the discouraged Wilmot asked if the North would ever find its courage and its voice, the answer came from his own colleagues. Robert McClelland of Michigan warned that slavery would expand "wherever man, in his cupidity and lust for power can carry it." David Brinkerhoff of Ohio asked whether the extension of slavery "at which posterity will blush, which Christianity must abhor," ought to be the work of representatives of free men. A Representative from Alabama deplored these "ill-starred agitations" which were disrupting the normal business of the House but he could not stop them. Garrison applauded the new freedom of debate in Congress. Now any Northerner could speak out against slavery and be heard.

His opposition to the war mounted as the months passed: he prayed for "success to the injured Mexicans and overwhelming defeat to the United States."[7] He went further and outlined a defeatist program for the Garrisonians "now boldly and continually to denounce the war, under such circumstances, as bloody and iniquitous — to impeach the government and the administration — to wish success to the Mexicans as the injured party, who are contending for their firesides and their country against enslaving and remorseless invaders."[8] Let the abolitionists' testimony burn as never before into the national conscience. It no longer mattered that his organization lay in shambles and his admirers grew fewer each year, for he was convinced that his little remnant was slowly gaining ascendancy over the public mind. Whigs and Democrats still feared disunion like the plague, but they would come to it soon enough. Meanwhile he could afford to wait.

Control of the national organization as well as the Massachusetts Society now rested with the Boston clique, who were beginning to exert a new influence over their leader. Gone was the fiery zeal of the Come-Outers. Rogers had died worn out by a factional dispute with the Bostonians and disillusioned by Garrison's unwillingness to accept all the implications of Christian anarchy. Henry Wright had virtually abandoned anti-slavery for anti-Sabbatarianism. Stephen Symonds Foster was losing his martyr complex in marriage, and Parker Pillsbury had settled on a less hazardous manner of spreading the gospel. The backfires of religious radicalism were smoldering out, and the decisions were now made *in camera* around

the polished grates in Essex Street drawing rooms according
to Phillips's advice "to have only a few."[9]

By 1847 the Liberty Party was foundering. If abolition
embarrassed the politicians, politics was proving the undoing
of abolitionists. In the previous year the state of New York
called a convention to write a new constitution. Some of the
Liberty Party men, who hoped to win broader suffrage for
Negroes, decided to advocate alliances with Whigs and Democrats in return for the promise of support for an extended
franchise. Birney refused to have anything to do with the
scheme and warned his followers of the danger of entangling
alliances. The new state constitution bore out his warnings:
by its terms Negroes were not considered in the apportion-
ment of representation, and a property qualification was established large enough to disqualify almost every Negro in the
state.

The New York constitutional convention merely under-
scored a problem which had troubled the political abolitionists
from the beginning, the question of a platform. They knew
that they could never build a successful party merely by
pledging members not to vote for pro-slavery candidates. But
to pile the anti-slavery platform with a stack of new planks —
anti-bank, anti-tariff, anti-Masonry — was to risk toppling the
whole structure. Many of the Liberty Party men, however,
shared the business ethic of the small entrepreneur; and to
them the advantages of combining anti-slavery and a small
businessman's credo seemed obvious. A group of schismatics
under the leadership of William Goodell formed the Liberty
League in June, 1847, and proceeded to write a platform that
included land reform, free trade, abolition of monopolies,
direct taxation, and prohibition of secret societies along with
the usual anti-slavery plank. The Liberty League promptly
nominated Gerrit Smith for President of the United States.

It was a measure of the confusion besetting political abolitionists in 1847 that Smith, who less than a year before had vehemently opposed broadening the platform, accepted the nomination while continuing to work with the old Liberty Party. He paid for his indecision when the Liberty Party Convention in the fall of 1847 defeated his attempt to introduce some of the League's ideas and gave the Presidential nomination to John P. Hale of New Hampshire. From both Smith's point of view and that of the Liberty Party itself it looked as though political abolitionists would never succeed in uniting on an anti-slavery program.

Garrison was delighted with the dissension in the Liberty Party. He decided to help kill the political dragon and then display the carcass on a tour throughout the Mississippi Valley. Before leaving Boston he prepared for his mission by attacking the Liberty League in a series of editorials as a hopelessly unrealistic venture. Its nominees, he noted maliciously, might as well conclude at the outset that a private station was a post of honor. The Liberty Party with its doctrine of the unconstitutionality of slavery, however, was a more serious matter. He pointed out that Birney, Smith, and Goodell had originally denied the power of Congress to interfere with slavery but now unaccountably were reversing their position. "And should that party succeed at any time in electing to Congress a majority of Senators and Representatives, does it mean to pass a law, and of course to enforce the law, declaring slavery to be unlawful on any portion of American soil?"[10] This would mean disunion, yet anything short of it was abject surrender to the slavocracy. Why not go the whole way by accepting the logic of Northern secession?

To find this answer, he started west in August, 1847, taking with him Frederick Douglass, who had reasons of his own for going. English abolitionists had suggested the advantages of an American anti-slavery newspaper edited by a Negro; and Douglass, realizing that the seaboard was oversupplied with competing abolitionist journals, wanted to investigate Cleveland as a site for his paper. Garrison received the project coldly, for he wanted no new rival either in Massachusetts or Ohio. He tried to convince Douglass that his talent lay in lecturing, but the headstrong Douglass immediately suspected his motives. The tour put a severe strain on their friendship.

They stopped first in Norristown for the tenth anniversary meeting of the Eastern Pennsylvania Anti-Slavery Society, one of the last of the Garrisonian redoubts. Although Garrison and Lucretia Mott spoke long and forcibly, Douglass was the star attraction. He gave a sharp and pungent exposition of secessionist doctrine, not even pausing when a gang of rowdies began to smash the windows of the meetinghouse. On the trip from Philadelphia to Harrisburg they got another taste of racial prejudice which made them realize how tolerant New England really was. Douglass had taken a place in the rear of the railroad car instead of the customary spot near the door. Suddenly, he was dragged from his seat and tossed into the aisle by a drunken lawyer who threatened to knock his teeth down his throat. He got slowly to his feet and methodically dusted himself off. Then, staring contemptuously at his assailant, he told him that only the obvious fact that he was no gentleman saved him from a duel with any weapons he might choose. The nonresistant Garrison suffered an uneasy moment before the lawyer mumbled another insult and returned to his seat.

Harrisburg lived up to its reputation as a pro-slavery town. Garrison was allowed to finish his lecture, but the minute the "nigger" rose to speak, the hostile audience sprang to life. It was the most violent demonstration Garrison had seen since the Boston riot. "They came equipped with rotten eggs and brickbats, firecrackers and other missiles, and made use of them somewhat freely," he wrote to Helen, " — breaking panes of glass, and soiling the clothes of some who were struck by the eggs. One of these bespattered my head and back somewhat freely."[11] Douglass was struck with a brickbat; Garrison escaped with only a moist head.

A happier reception awaited them in Pittsburgh, where there was a sizable colony of free Negroes. A twenty-piece band waited until three o'clock in the morning to serenade Douglass on his arrival, and he had to speak five times in three days. His strong baritone voice began to give out; by the end of the tour he could hardly croak. Garrison also drove himself hard, speaking several times a day and then conversing endlessly with his hosts after his performances. Following an unsatisfactory meeting in New Brighton, Pennsylvania, the two jaded lecturers were joined by Stephen Foster, fresh from the East, and the threesome moved on to New Lyme, Ohio, for a three-day meeting with the Western Anti-Slavery Society. The Western Society was the lone outpost of Garrisonism in Ohio. Its members had decided to pit their leader and his secessionist ideas against the political anti-slavery of Joshua Giddings. Giddings had been a young country lawyer when Weld converted him to abolition and, once elected to Congress, he joined John Quincy Adams in fighting for the right of petition. He was a durable contestant, not brilliant, but stubborn and opinionated. At the time of the Creole affair he showed his contempt for a threatened Whig vote of censure by resigning his seat, standing for re-election, and triumphantly returning to the House. Giddings was neither a profound anti-slavery theoretician nor an especially acute parliamentarian, but his rough-and-ready style of debate and his devotion to free soil principles made him just the man to force Garrison to define and defend disunion.

As he first explained it, Garrison's doctrine of disunion was a pure moral abstraction devoid of practical considerations. "Friends of liberty and humanity must immediately withdraw from the compact of bloody and deceitful men, to cease striking hands with adulterers." Nothing more. Given as an ultimatum from God, disunion was as empty of specifics as a Cartesian proposition. Though he insisted that his doctrine was one of "order and obedience," he had, in fact, not a formula but a letter of marque from God. Faith in God obviated the need for a plan. "The form of government that shall succeed the present government of the United States," he wrote in 1844, "let time determine."[12] It would be a waste of effort to argue the question until all the people were regenerated and turned from their iniquity. Meanwhile the value of secessionist agitation lay in arousing the North, and convulsing the South by showing it the enormity of its sin.

The Mexican War put secession in a new light, and gradually he began to think of it as a practical solution to the slavery problem. "We do not think any one state will go out of the Union alone," he wrote in May, 1847. "The movement will be simultaneous throughout New England, and probably throughout all the non-slaveholding states." First a line would be drawn separating slave from free states. The Southern states would have to combine into a confederacy, "for, aside from the appalling fact that she would have three millions of enemies in her midst, smarting from numberless wrongs and outrages, how would she be able to prevent the escape of any indefinite number of her slaves to the new republic?" Even a Southern confederacy could not hold its slaves, who would "leap in the twinkling of an eye, and be beyond the reach of danger." What state would then be willing to be a border state? "Each would inevitably be compelled to emancipate all the slaves on its soil; and then the same necessity would be imposed upon the States next in geographical position; and this would lead to a general and peaceful abolition throughout the entire South."[13] So he argued now to the dismay of Joshua Giddings and his Ohio farmers. Giddings proved kind and generous, but Garrison thought his arguments specious and reported to Helen that he had with him "the understanding and conscience" of the overwhelming majority.

At Oberlin, where he stopped for a few days, he examined the wilderness college and met the famous Dr. Finney. He was pleased to see the evangelistic enterprise flourishing but objected to Oberlin's ecclesiastical leanings which tended to "impair the strength of its testimony, and diminish the power of its example." Finney surprised him, however, by telling the graduating class that they must be "anti-devil all over" and join all the reforms of their age. Garrison debated disunion again, this time with crusty Asa Mahan, whose opinions he found "perfectly respectable" but "neither vigorous nor profound."[14] He left for Cleveland satisfied with the effect of peaceable secession on the college.

The feverish pace and the intense heat of the Midwestern summer were taking their toll. Garrison's agents had arranged three and sometimes four lectures a day, often twenty miles apart. He spoke in steaming lecture halls and damp pine groves, wherever he could collect an audience, and when Douglass's voice gave out, he substituted for him. "My labors, for the last four weeks, had been excessive — in severity far exceeding anything in my experience. Too much work was laid out for both Douglass and myself, to be completed in so short a time; yet it was natural that our Ohio friends should wish to 'make the most of us' whilst we were in their hands."[15]

He was to remain in their hands for two more months: in Cleveland he fell desperately ill with what a homeopathic surgeon called an "intermittent fever with a tendency towards typhoid." For nearly six weeks he lay in the house of his Cleveland friends too weak to move. Meanwhile Douglass left for Syracuse and Rochester to scout out a site for his newspaper. When Garrison recovered and found that he had been abandoned in his illness for a project of which he strongly disapproved, he was furious with Douglass and complained bitterly of his "impulsive, inconsiderate and highly inconsistent" behavior.[16] In November he was enough better to come home to Boston, but once arrived suffered a relapse and remained invalided until the first of the year.

Once he recovered from his Western tour he plunged into still another conference, this one an Anti-Sabbath Convention at Theodore Parker's Melodeon to help protest what Parker called the fierce "this-worldliness" of New England. Garrison and Parker, despite the great intellectual gulf between them, were kindred souls. Parker had been converted to abolition largely by the example of Garrison and his followers and had also succumbed to the pull of universal reform. He had attended the Chardon Street Convention and now heartily approved of another such meeting to destroy the superstition and cant which kept the masses "in their present low state."[17] He had no fear of revolutions, he told Garrison; Americans had conservative principles enough.

Most of the Garrisonians rallied to the call. Phillips refused to attend, and Quincy was annoyed with Garrison for chasing the will-o'-the-wisp of theological problems instead of concentrating on slavery. "It really seems as if the Devil always would put his foot in it," he complained, "whenever the antislavery cause has got into a tolerable position, so as to keep it in hot water."[18] He signed the call anyway, protesting all the while against Garrison's private idiosyncrasies.

For Garrison the very existence of Massachusetts blue laws was challenge enough. His call to "The Friends of Civil and Religious Liberty" presented still another preamble and a long list of resolutions attacking a "Sabbatizing clergy" and its "merely ceremonial religion." The convention debated his propositions with imagination and gusto, although the members could agree on nothing more than a general disapproval of Sunday laws. The accounts in the *Liberator*, however, and its editor's vendetta against an "arrogant priesthood" suggested nothing less than a theological revolution.

He was discovering that the right of private judgment in theological matters led straight to rationalism. The problem of the age as he saw it was that of winnowing the chaff of superstitition from the grain of Christian ethics. In the case of dogma this seemed simple enough. He rejected the phrase "Mother of God" as absurd and blasphemous. "If Mary was the *mother* of God, who was the father of God?" He also objected to the verse in Wesley's hymn which began "O love divine! what hast thou done?/The immortal God hath died for me!" as a contradiction in terms. The question of Christian ethics, he admitted, posed greater difficulty. He insisted that the "wine" mentioned in the Bible was unfermented grape juice, but argued that "the expediency, the morality of wine-drinking is not to be settled by an appeal to any book." His case for abstinence rested on "chemical analysis" and the moral consequences of imbibing. The same was true of all the obligations of men to their fellow men, which were "in no degree affected by the question whether miracles were wrought in Judea or not, with whatever interest that question may be invested."[19]

It was probably Theodore Parker who first led Garrison

to re-examine the doctrine of plenary inspiration. Parker's was a mind tougher and better trained than any he had found yet, and his "applied Christianity" struck an immediate chord of response. Parker believed that there had been three ages in the world, the age of sentiment, the age of ideas, and the age of action. In failing to socialize Christianity the church lagged behind the growth of modern institutions. The first task for Christians in the new age, he believed, was to disabuse themselves of superstition. Garrison was greatly impressed with the "Christ-like" arguments of Parker. In an editorial attacking plenary inspiration he spoke of the Bible for the first time as the product of many minds. "To say that everything contained within the lids of the Bible is divinely inspired, and to insist upon the dogma as fundamentally important, is to give utterance to a bold fiction, and to require the suspension of the reasoning faculties. To say that everything in the Bible is to be believed, simply because it is found in that volume, is equally absurd and pernicious."[20] It was for the reason to search the Scriptures and decide what was true or false.

If Garrison's ideas seemed saturated with the musty air of eighteenth-century deism, it was because he took them from Tom Paine, whom he had always believed "a monster of iniquity." Reading Paine proved a stimulating experience for one recently delivered from "the thralldom of tradition and authority." Paine taught him to apply the "test of just criticism," to measure the Bible by the standards of reason and utility, the facts of science, historical confirmation, and "the intuition of the spirit." When Garrison accepted Professor Benjamin Silliman's findings as proof that the Mosaic cosmogony was untenable, he stood in the best deist tradition. Like Paine, he accepted the Enlightenment fiction derived from Newton that the physical and social worlds were governed by identical laws. The Bible, he now believed, must reinforce the findings of "human experience." By "human experience," however, he meant no such rigid intellectualism as Paine envisioned, but a "felt experience," a testimony of the heart, an intuition wholly compatible with his orthodox upbringing. His was the kind of pseudo-rationalism that allowed for no real doubts as to the superiority of Christianity but only objected to the manner in which its truths were received. His hatred of institutions and authority blinded him to the real conflict between faith and reason and limited his revolt to a petty war against a weakened church and outworn doctrine. Had he been able to advance beyond this point and see the forces of historicism at work, he might have achieved a serviceable rationalist critique based on associational and environmental psychology. Clearly this was too much for a mind which drew its strength not from intellect but from will.

Insofar as he thought about philosophy at all Garrison intuitively held that there were fundamental laws of human nature instinctively grasped that told men what was right. Thus all the people really needed was conscience. Paine's deism, superficial as it might have been, had the merit of being militantly anti-clerical and frankly revolutionary. When Paine joined the French Revolution to fight for the rights of man, he was following his premises to their logical conclusion. He identified religious superstition with corrupt European monarchy, and reason with New World democracy. Paine's easy assumptions were no longer valid at a time when the separation of religion and politics in America was almost complete. It was just this separation of religious protest from political radicalism, of free thought from class conflict, that gutted Garrisonism of its revolutionary content. In Europe after the French Revolution anti-clericalism joined the social revolution; in America free thought grew up a peaceable citizen. Garrison typified this American penchant for combining reason and religion into a belief no more revolutionary than social gospelism. He personified the dilemma of the religious radical in America, the avowed nonrevolutionary who, despite himself, made a revolution.

The year 1848 opened on a note of hope everywhere — in Paris, where the monarchy was broken on the barricades, in Berlin, London and Vienna. To most Americans it seemed as though they had finally succeeded in exporting their own revolutionary example, that Europe had finally accepted the blessings of democracy. Garrison shared their conviction. "The republican form of government is triumphantly established in France," he announced after the February Days. "It is, however, but the beginning of the end — and that end is the downfall of every throne in existence within a score of years."[21] When the June Days brought the inevitable disillusionment, he was too busy studying the revolution in the American party system to notice the failure of liberalism in Europe. The Free Soil revolt, though it too proved abortive, planted the slavery issue in the center of American politics, where it remained until the Civil War.

Both Whigs and Democrats faced the election of 1848 with dissension in their ranks. Democratic unrest centered in up-state New York, where the party was divided into two warring factions — Hunkers and Barnburners. The Barnburners were a curious combination of idealists and opportunists. Some of them were simply disgruntled politicians nursing hopes of regaining lost patronage; but there were others like Preston King, David Dudley Field and William Cullen Bryant, the able editor of the New York Evening Post, who were moderate abolitionists ready to oppose the Hunkers on the question of extending slavery. In Pennsylvania, the Democrats faced incipient rebellion from Wilmot and his friends, and in Ohio, Salmon P. Chase threatened party regulars with revolt.

When the Democratic Convention met in May and nominated the expansionist Cass, the Barnburners walked out. Led by the wily "Prince John" Van Buren and harboring a number of patronage-minded party hacks, the dissident wing of the Democracy nevertheless formed the center of anti-slavery feeling that soon produced the Free Soil Party.

The other two sources of the Free Soil movement were two pockets of Whig discontent, one in Massachusetts and the other in Ohio. Horace Greeley warned his fellow Whigs at the beginning of the year that if they nominated Taylor, they would elect him but destroy the Whig Party. Greeley was right. Beaten by the regulars at the nominating convention, the "Young Whigs" bolted and held their own convention at Worcester. Insurgent Whigs in Ohio held a similar meeting, where they called for a national convention at Buffalo. The Free Soil roster was completed when the remnants of the Liberty Party gave up their candidates and a strong anti-slavery plank to join the insurgent Whigs and Democrats.

Like all American third party movements, the Free Soil Party was an amalgam of high-mindedness and chicanery. Its platform was clear enough: slavery was declared a state rather than a national institution and as such must be excluded from the territories. In their selection of a candidate, however, the old campaigners showed their mastery of the art of political jugglery. The Liberty Party men were reluctant to give up their candidate Hale, but the Conscience Whigs, who held the balance of power and were hungry for votes, swung the nomination to Van Buren. Before ten thousand spectators in Buffalo's City Park the Free Soilers tied their political fortunes to "free soil, free speech, free labor, free men," and the slightly shopworn reputation of "Little Van."

Garrison was vacationing at Northampton with his brother-in-law when the Free Soilers launched their series of rallies in Massachusetts. He went to one of them and was surprised to find many of his old colleagues there. The North, he told them, had missed its best chance to abolish slavery when Texas was annexed. The Free Soil platform was weaker than a spider's web — "a single breath of the Slave Power will blow it away." Yet if Free Soil fell far short of disunion, it was still a step toward it and perhaps the beginning of the end. His problem, therefore, was how to give the Free Soilers due credit without sanctioning their principles. The danger lay in the temptation they offered to loyal abolitionists to bow down just this once in the house of Rimmon and vote. "Calm yet earnest appeals," he announced, "must be made to our friends to preserve their integrity, and not lose sight of the true issue."[22]

Whatever the issues, the results of the election of 1848 were never in doubt. When the Northern Whig leaders reluctantly swung their support behind Taylor, his victory was assured. He and Cass each carried fifteen states, but Taylor won Massachusetts, New York, Pennsylvania and 140,000 more votes than his opponent. The Free Soil Party received 300,000 votes and nine seats in Congress, and in Massachusetts it ran ahead of the Democratic ticket. Garrison misjudged its strength but not its significance. Free Soil brought an end to the uneasy truce between North and South.

There was another leader worried about the behavior of his followers in the election year of 1848. John C. Calhoun took the occasion of his visit to Charleston in the summer to apprise his constituents of a Northern plot to exclude slavery from all of the territories. How could South Carolina decide between a Michigan Democrat and an uncommitted Whig? Let the state ignore the Presidential canvass and await the course of events. If the North was not to be deterred from the path of aggression, the South would unite under the leadership of South Carolina into a great Southern republican party based on slavery. Calhoun's advice was not lost on the New England press. The *Boston Recorder*, noting the similarity of Garrison's and Calhoun's solutions, remarked that "the Garrison faction ought to admire Mr. Calhoun for he is aiming at the same object with them, though with a thousand times more energy and likelihood of effecting their wishes." Calhoun had forty Congressmen to do his bidding, and Garrison not one.[23]

Calhoun's Congressmen were deployed soon after the sitting of the new Congress to meet the attack of the Free Soilers. On December 11, 1848, the Free Soilers in the House introduced a resolution instructing the proper committee to bring in a bill prohibiting the slave trade in the District of Columbia. This move sent the Southern Congressmen scurrying into caucus, from which they emerged with Calhoun's "Address of the Southern Delegates to Congress to their Constituents" calling for a Southern convention. As propaganda Calhoun's "Southern Address" was a masterpiece; as prophecy it showed the clear but tragic vision of a dying man. The South, he predicted, would never give up slavery voluntarily. When emancipation came, it would be forced on the South by a federal government dominated by Northerners. "It can then only be effected by the prostration of the white race; and that would necessarily engender the bitterest feelings of hostility between them and the North." Garrison's prediction had not changed, but for once his certainty allowed him to be brief. "Our Disunion ground is invulnerable, and to it all parties at the North must come ere long."[24]

In the aftermath of the Mexican War it seemed that Garrison and Calhoun spoke the mood of the nation as it approached the problems of administering the new territory. The proposals for its disposition were various, but the language in which they were discussed was surprisingly similar. Robert Toombs of Georgia, hitherto considered a moderate, lashed out at the Free Soilers who refused to abandon the Wilmot Proviso. "I do not hesitate to avow before this House and the country, and in the presence of a living God, that if by your legislation you seek to drive us from the Territories and to abolish slavery in the District, I am for disunion; and if my physical courage be equal to the maintenance of my convictions of right and duty, I will devote all I am and all I have to its consummation." When Edward D. Baker of Illinois denied the possibility of peaceful secession, Alexander Stephens countered with an ultimatum. "I tell that gentleman, whether he believes it or not, that the day in which aggression is consummated on any portion of the country, this Union is dissolved." Salmon Chase replied for the Free Soilers by reminding Southerners that "no menace, no resolves tending to disunion, no intimations of the probability of disunion, in any form, will move us from the path which, in our judgment, it is due to ourselves and the people we represent to pursue." Edward Everett, hardly an abolitionist, wrote to his friend Nathan Appleton that peaceful separation held the only answer to the slavery question.

Public opinion in both sections of the country rushed ahead of Congressional threats. The *Sumter* (South Carolina) *Banner* called for "SECESSION OF THE SLAVEHOLDING STATES IN A BODY FROM THE UNION AND THEIR FORMATION INTO A SEPARATE REPUBLIC." The editor of the *Cleveland Plain Dealer* declared that rather than see slavery extended a single inch "we would see this Union rent asunder." "The North," reported another Ohio paper, "is determined that slavery shall not pollute the soil of lands now free . . . even if it should come to a dissolution of the Union." Thus, at a time when his apparently irresponsible doctrine of disunion and a suicidal policy of proscription had reduced his society to a mere skeleton, Garrison's secessionist ideas were reflected in and beginning to color the national mood. If a majority of Americans in the North and the South refused to accept disunion and tried to ignore the abolitionists and the fire-eaters, it was because the slavery issue remained an abstraction, not unreal but remote. For most Northerners in 1850 slavery was already a moral issue, but one to be met obliquely by a policy of containment rather than head-on by immediate emancipation.

This was the cautious attitude which Clay and Douglas brought to the Thirty-first Congress and the drafting of a compromise. Clay's ill-starred Omnibus Bill, the basis of the Compromise of 1850, was an attempt to meet both Free Soil objectives and Southern expansionist aims. As finally passed piecemeal by Congress it favored the South. The final compromise provided for the admission of a free California and established governments in the rest of the territory; it assumed the public debt of Texas and redrew its western boundary so as to exclude New Mexico. As a concession to the North the compromise prohibited the slave trade in the District of Columbia but stipulated that slavery should never be abolished there without the consent of its residents or without compensation. It further declared that Congress had no power to interfere with the interstate slave trade. Finally and most significantly, it included a new and stringent Fugitive Slave Act. Fugitive slaves were denied trial by jury and could not testify on their own behalf. The power of enforcement was given to federal commissioners who received a fee of ten dollars in case of conviction, only five if the fugitive was freed. This provision, Wendell Phillips said, fixed the price of a South Carolina Negro at a thousand dollars and that of a Yankee's soul at five. Any citizen attempting to prevent the arrest of a fugitive was liable to a fine of a thousand dollars, six months' imprisonment, and damages up to another thousand dollars. The Fugitive Slave Act destroyed any hope for a satisfactory solution to the slavery problem. Without it the South would have refused the compromise; with it the compromise was worthless.

The Compromise of 1850 was the work of elder statesmen born in another century for whom the Union was a sacred concept and a mystical reality. In his defense of the compromise Webster ridiculed the idea of disunion. "Secession! Peaceable secession! Sir [addressing Calhoun and, by implication, Garrison], your eyes and mine are never destined to see that miracle." Clay asked his colleagues to weigh the issues carefully. "In the one scale, we behold sentiment, sentiment, sentiment alone; in the other, property, the social fabric, life, all that makes life desirable and happy."[25] For Clay "sentiment" meant fanatical belief in abstract principles, and he and Webster feared the destructive power of these abstractions. They knew the difference between the disruptive principles of the Declaration of Independence and the chastened realism of the Founding Fathers, and they preferred the latter. Both men were to die within two years, carrying with them to the grave the hope for a pragmatic solution to the slavery problem.

This indictment of Garrison was not wholly unjust. Garrison knew little of slavery as an institution and cared less. He *was* an abstractionist, but so was the new generation of American politicians — the William Lowndes Yanceys, Robert Barnwell Rhetts, James Hammonds, the Chases, Sewards and Stevenses, Wilsons, and Sumners. So too were the American people they represented. Americans in the year 1850 were of two minds about themselves and their destiny — on the one hand, they were seeming materialists concerned with wealth, power and progress; on the other, idealists perpetually dissatisfied with their limited achievements which they viewed as steppingstones toward a final spiritual goal. This goal was indicated however indistinctly in the Declaration of Independence. Rufus Choate might dismiss the Declaration as a collection of "sounding generalities," but for most Americans it embodied their ideal of the good society. The gross contradiction of slavery in a nation which purported to believe in the equality of men was a fact with which they knew they must reckon eventually. Try as they might to hide it in Manifest Destiny and an expanding frontier, Americans returned to the slavery problem, first as a question of what Clay called "sentiment," but then, as the decade progressed, in the drama of the Kansas–Nebraska Act and John Brown's raid. By then abolitionist "sentiment" had become reality.

For the moment, however, cries of "The Union is saved!" rang through Washington and echoed in New York, Baltimore, New Orleans, and St. Louis. Bonfires and cannon salutes welcomed Clay on his triumphal journey north to the Newport beaches while Douglas was left to do the real work of patching together the remnants of this Omnibus Bill. In Boston a thousand merchants publicly thanked Webster for recalling them to their duties under the Constitution. Douglas promised never to give another speech on slavery and urged his colleagues to forget the subject. Horace Mann looked around at the remnants of the Free Soil contingent in Congress and sighed. Webster was damned by the abolitionists as a traitor and a turncoat, "the saddest sight in all the Western world." Fallen though he was, he was still powerful enough to read out of the party those Free Soil Whigs who were "hostile to the just and constitutional rights of the South." In the South the Nashville Convention, called to protect Southern rights, failed to keep the spirit of secession alive. Supporters of the compromise closed ranks, and the Rhetts, McDonalds, Yanceys, and Quitmans were left to await another crisis. In Mississippi the radical Jefferson Davis was defeated for governor by the moderate Henry S. Foote; and the state convention declared that the right of secession was "utterly unsanctioned by the Federal Constitution." In South Carolina Yancey formed his Southern Rights Association without the help of the planters, who were no longer in the mood to feed the hunger of the fire-eaters. Thirteen cents a pound for cotton did not make for revolution.

In New York, where Garrison held the annual meeting of the American Anti-Slavery Society in May, 1850, merchants had organized a Union Safety Committee to put down abolitionism and use their commercial ties to draw the Union back together. On his arrival Garrison found public opinion strongly against him. For weeks Bennett's *Herald* had accused him of bringing the country to the brink of dissolution. On May 7 the *Herald* appealed to the "regulators" of New York opinion to see to it that Garrison did not misrepresent the views of the city. "The Union expects every man to do his duty," ran the editorial, "and duty to the Union, in the present crisis, points out to us that we should allow no more fuel to be placed upon the fire of abolitionism in our midst, when we can prevent it by sound reasoning and calm remonstrance." The *Herald* sounded a different note when on the day of the meeting it called Garrison the American Robespierre whose only object was to destroy, and called upon New Yorkers to destroy him first.[26]

The task of harassing the Garrisonians at the annual meeting fell to Captain Isaiah Rynders, a forty-six-year-old Tammany ward-heeler, riverboat tramp, and weigher in the New York Customs House. The year before, Rynders had proved his talent at rabble-rousing by engineering the Astor Place riot against the English actor Macready. Later he had been arrested for the brutal beating of a vagrant in a New York hotel. He was just the man for the job Bennett had in mind.

On the opening day of the meeting at the Broadway Tabernacle, Rynders planted his henchmen in the balcony to await his signal. Anticipating trouble, Garrison had taken the precaution of inviting the chief of police to attend the sessions, and the chief had dispatched a precinct captain to keep order. To avoid notoriety Garrison had even exchanged his reformer's turned-down collar for a fashionable stand-up model. He opened the meeting by reading from the Scriptures a passage directed at the new Fugitive Slave Law. "Associate yourselves, O ye people, and ye shall be broken in pieces; gird yourselves, and ye shall be broken in pieces. . . . They all lie in wait for blood; they hunt every man his brother with a net. . . . Hide the outcasts, betray not him that wandereth; let mine outcasts dwell with thee; be thou a covert to them from the face of the spoiler."

Resigning the chair to Francis Jackson, he took the floor and began to deliver a cut-and-dried speech on the inconsistency of American religious faith with American practice. To illustrate his argument he singled out the Catholic Church as an example of pro-slavery feeling. At this point Rynders made his move. Were there not other churches just as guilty, he demanded? Garrison quietly admitted that there were and proceeded to name the Episcopal, Methodist, Baptist, and Presbyterian Churches. Once again Rynders bellowed from his post in the organ loft. "Are you aware that the slaves in the South have their prayer-meetings in honor of Christ?"

MR. GARRISON: — Not a slaveholding or a slave-breeding Jesus. (Sensation.) The slaves believe in a Jesus that strikes off chains. In this country, Jesus has become obsolete. A profession in him is

no longer a test. Who objects to his course in Judea? The old
Pharisees are extinct, and may safely be denounced. Jesus is the
most respectable person in the United States. (Great sensation,
and murmurs of disapprobation.) Jesus sits in the President's
chair in the United States. (A thrill of horror here seemed to run
through the assembly.) Zachary Taylor sits there, which is the
same thing, for he believes in Jesus. He believes in war, and the
Jesus that 'gave the Mexicans hell.' (Sensation, uproar, and confusion.)[27]

Instantly Rynders and his gang rushed for the stairs and
poured out on the stage. Rynders strode up to Garrison and
waved his fist in his face. "I will not allow you to assail the
President of the United States. You shan't do it." Calmly
Garrison told Rynders that he must not interrupt. "We go
upon the principle of hearing everybody. If you wish to
speak, I will keep order, and you shall be heard." The uproar grew louder.

The Hutchinson family broke into a hymn, but Rynders
and his men drowned them out with catcalls and whistles.
Violence was narrowly averted when a hotheaded young
abolitionist leaped to the platform and threatened to kill the
first man who laid a hand on Garrison. Suddenly Francis
Jackson offered Rynders the floor when Garrison had finished
speaking, whereupon Garrison sat down and with a serene
expression waited for Rynders to proceed. Rynders ranted
and gesticulated, ranging up and down the aisles followed by
his henchman "Professor Grant." In a wild and incoherent
harangue the "Professor" undertook to prove that physiognom-
ically Negroes were not men but animals. When he finished,
Frederick Douglass stepped to the front of the platform and
drew himself up to his full height for a reply. "The gentleman
who has just spoken has undertaken to prove that the blacks
are not human beings. He has examined our whole confor-

mation. I cannot follow him in his argument. I will assist him in it, however. I offer myself for your examination. Am I a man?" Still Rynders would not give in. Over the laughter he shouted, "*You* are not a black man; you are only half a *nigger*." "Then," Douglass replied with a bow, "I am half-brother to Captain Rynders."

Douglass finished by calling on the Reverend Samuel R. Ward, a Negro so black, Phillips said, that when he closed his eyes you could not see him. "Well, this is the original nigger!" Rynders jeered. Ward acknowledged the remark with a flourish. "I've heard of the magnanimity of Captain Rynders, but the half has not been told me!" He went on to develop Douglass's theme, admitting the failure of the free Negro to establish himself in the North and arguing impressively for more help from the whites. When he sat down, Rynders and his company drifted off the stage and out of the hall. The society had won the day.

The next day Rynders returned with reinforcements to finish the job while several police captains nonchalantly looked on. Neither Pillsbury nor Foster, both old hands at dealing with unruly demonstrations, were able to make themselves heard above the din. Garrison refused to capitulate. He announced that free speech was still the rule and that all those who desired should receive a full and fair hearing. Rynders, realizing how narrowly he had escaped humiliation the day before, refused the invitation and stuck to his harassing tactics. Then Charles Burleigh cantered to the rostrum, his black beard and long curls streaming in the breeze. "Shave that tall Christ and make a wig for Garrison," Rynders shouted. Finally, Rynders and his gang, who knew that no one would stop them, took over the meeting. Marching to the platform and elbowing the abolitionists aside, they noisily voted a resolution that Garrison's "humanity-mongers" con-

fine their work to the free Negroes in the North. "Thus
closed anti-slavery free discussion in New York for 1850,"
noted Greeley's *Tribune*.

"It was not an offence against the abolitionists that the
mob committed when they broke up Garrison's meeting,"
commented the *Philadelphia Ledger*, "but an offence against
the Constitution, against the Union, against the people, against
popular rights and the great cause of human freedom."[28] Nor
was it a ghostly abstraction that Garrison faced in the Broadway Tabernacle but a live issue that provoked hatred and
violence. For a brief moment he had recognized the inherent
tragedy of the slavery question when he found himself
cornered by Rynders and his bullies, who had no intention
of accepting his rules. Then, sensing the futility of free discussion, he called on the police.

16

The Great Slave Power Conspiracy

URING THE DECADE before the Civil War, Garrison's
prestige rose as his personal influence began to decline.
He achieved the respect he longed for but at the expense of
command. "The period may have been when I was of some
consequence to the anti-slavery movement," he told his
followers in 1852, "but it is not now. The cause is safe in
the hands of its friends."[1] These friends were more than
ever a comfort to him. One of them, Francis Jackson, bought
him a new house in Dix Place; another invited him to the
Town and Country Club; others induced him to publish
a volume of speeches and poems to establish himself as a
man of letters. Each year his circle of admirers widened.
At a testimonial dinner for John P. Hale he sat with Sumner,
Wilson, Horace Mann, Palfrey, and Richard Henry Dana,
and praised the politician whom five years ago he had dismissed as half an abolitionist. Suddenly he became one of the
most popular lecturers on the anti-slavery circuit. Those
who used to come to hear the "monster" now gathered to
listen to a "marvellous proper man." His friends noted with
relief the passing of the prejudice against him. "He speaks
as one having authority & office," Miller McKim wrote to
Sarah Pugh. ". . . He strikes a chord which is pure & vibrant,
the common people always hear him gladly. All classes are

drawn toward him; the bad respect & the good love him."[2]

He was acutely conscious of this new respect and worried lest, "ill-judged and unfairly estimated," he fail to exploit it. He avoided hostile audiences that in the old days he would have enjoyed baiting. Now he asked whether a town was "safe" for abolition before agreeing to speak there, not because he was afraid of a few brickbats but because he hated to risk his reputation and waste precious time. As he approached fifty he grew closer to his family and preferred the company of his children to barnstorming around the countryside with Pillsbury and Foster. Although he was in great demand as a lecturer and spoke on the average of once a week to anti-slavery audiences in the state, he could hardly wait to get back to Helen and the children. He welcomed the demands that Fanny and the boys made on him, whether it was a school lesson to be prepared or a game of hide-and-seek. Gradually he was acquiring all the comfortable habits and the outlook of middle-aged respectability.

Indeed, the whole abolitionist enterprise, while hardly popular, enjoyed a new regard now that the Boston clique had succeeded in raising its social tone. Phillips and Quincy were chiefly responsible for the atmospheric change in Boston, Phillips by recruiting new talent among the old families, and Quincy by weeding out the more unkempt of the Garrisonians. Apostles like Charles Burleigh who dramatized their devotion to Christ by lecturing in full beard and flowing robes were relegated by Quincy's edict to those parts of the state which were least civilized. Henceforth, Quincy ordered, agents should appear decently bathed and clothed; the cause of the slave was not to be advanced by apostolic dirt. "I should prefer *not* to have hair in my diocese," he instructed the General Agent.[3] In place of beards and cranks, perfectionists and millenarians, there appeared early in the Fifties a group

already sinking in the mire and filth of poverty and crime, and to prevent others being swept into the same vortex, whose condition and tendencies are hurrying them thither."[7] On the other hand, he admitted that he had no plan himself and told the American workingmen that for the present they would have to rely on the "generous impulses" of their betters. His belief that free society rested on an intelligent workingclass was undercut by his assumption that technology and unrestrained competition would automatically create one. His economic views tended to support the very doctrine of progress which his moral radicalism protested so vigorously. Somehow his dream of the destruction of American institutions stopped short of industrial capitalism.

Garrison's failure to see the inconsistencies of private-profit perfectionism did not prevent him from exposing the hollow patriotism of mid-century America in the Kossuth affair. In December, 1851, Louis Kossuth, already the toast of liberal Europe and a romantic exile *par excellence*, prepared the United States for his debut by sending ahead a manifesto which proclaimed his complete neutrality on the "domestic issue" of slavery and requested his friends to do nothing that might in any way embarrass the cause of Hungarian freedom. This announcement Garrison interpreted as a complete surrender to the slavocracy. "He means to be deaf, dumb, and blind, in regard to it! Like the recreant Father MATHEW, to subserve his own purpose, and to secure the favor of a slaveholding and slave-breeding people, he skulks — he dodges — he plays fast and loose — he refuses to see a stain on the American character, any inconsistency in pretending to adore liberty and at the same time, multiplying human beings for the auction block and the slave shambles."[8]

In exposing Kossuth's nationalist pretensions Garrison uncovered a fundamental weakness in American democratic thought. Two years earlier at the height of the reaction in Europe he had written an editorial comparing Kossuth and Jesus. Admitting that Kossuth was a "sublime specimen" of patriotism, he nevertheless questioned the scope of his vision. "He is a Hungarian, as Washington was an American. His country is bounded by a few degrees of latitude and longitude, and covers a surface of some thousands of square miles." Kossuth was strictly national, concerned solely with the independence of Hungary, for which he was willing to disregard "all the obligations of morality."[9] Garrison never read the Hungarian Declaration of Independence and was not aware that Kossuth's Magyar ideals did not extend to Croats and Slavs. The best exposé of Hungarian pretensions to American sympathy were two articles of Francis Bowen's in the *North American Review* which identified the ambiguous legacy of the American Declaration of Independence and showed how Kossuth's revolution qualified on the score of self-determination but, in denying freedom to minority groups, failed the test of civil rights.[10] Garrison only sensed what Bowen knew for a fact, that national unity and civil rights were not always compatible. In his groping way he had discovered the limits of nationalism and the difficulties of harmonizing individual liberty and national self-determination.

All of Garrison's reform interests suffered from his inability to bring to them a coherent philosophy. His concern with woman's rights was at best sporadic. He supported the Seneca Falls Convention in 1848 and attended the first woman's rights convention in Massachusetts at Worcester in 1850. His nonvoting perfectionism, however, made him something less than an enthusiastic supporter of the franchise for women. "I want the women to have the right to vote, and

I call upon them to demand it perseveringly until they possess it. When they have obtained it, it will be for them to say whether they will exercise it or not."[11] Elizabeth Cady Stanton and Susan B. Anthony might have been pardoned for believing that the advancement of women in America was a matter best left to themselves.

As he grew older he became fascinated with the claims of spiritualism and avidly followed the debate over "spiritual manifestations," hoping to find proof of their reality. One evening he attended a séance held by Leah Brown, one of the Fox Sisters, and watched while tables were overturned, chairs flung across the room, and even heard the spirit of Jesse Hutchinson rap out anti-slavery hymn tunes on the table. He was convinced that no satisfactory answer to the occult powers of mediums had been established by their critics. "If, here and there, an individual has succeeded in imitating certain sounds that are made, and imposing on the credulity of those present, it is only as genuine coin is often so ingeniously counterfeited as to make it difficult for even the money-changer himself to detect the difference; it does not touch one of a thousand cases where the parties have been above reproach and beyond suspicion."[12] Nevertheless, he was troubled by the fact that none of the messages from the distinguished inhabitants of the spirit world bore the slightest resemblance to their earthly personalities. One message from Nathaniel Rogers even asked forgiveness for quarreling with him while in the flesh!

Less confusing was the "Harmonial Philosophy" of Andrew Jackson Davis, whose "psychometric examination" of public men also drew on occult powers. By examining a lock of Garrison's hair (more would have been difficult to find) Davis was able to throw his mind into a clairvoyant state in which his subject's true character appeared clearly. He found that Garrison was possessed of a physical system "evenly balanced and well developed" and a temperament "peculiarly domestic and social. . . . His is a high order of intellect, but not the highest. It is more than usually well arranged and evenly balanced; superior in this particular to most public and literary men."[13] Some minds, Davis concluded, were mere receptacles, but here was a source.

That Garrison was a source of the myth of the Great Slave Power Conspiracy there can be no doubt. The political conflicts of the Fifties came in large part from the growing conviction in the North that slavery menaced free society. Ever since he joined Lundy, Garrison had identified antislavery with civil liberties, which he defined as "natural rights" constituting a body of "higher law." Twenty-five years of agitation had failed to endow his abstractions with the breath of life, but after 1850 events were combining to give his doctrine of secession an artificial life.

The Northern disunionists [Garrison wrote in 1852], affirm that every human being has an inalienable right to liberty; consequently, that no man can be held in slavery without guilt; and, therefore, that no truce is to be made with the slaveholder. They declare slavery to be morally and politically wrong, and its extinction essential to the general welfare; hence, that neither sanction nor toleration is to be extended to it. They are not less tenacious, not less inexorable, and certainly not less consistent, than the Southern disunionists. The issue, therefore, which these parties make, separates them as widely from each other as heaven from hell: do such 'extremes' meet? What is there extreme about it, absurdly? 'If the Lord be God, serve him; if Baal, then serve him.' Is it a case for conciliation, for 'truck and dicker,' for insisting upon a quid pro quo? To yield anything, on either side, is to yield everything.[14]

The continuing crisis after 1850 made these words ring true.

The Fugitive Slave Law raised the curtain on a moral drama that ended in civil war. Only gradually did the slavery issue emerge as its tragic theme, and even then it often wore the mask of political and economic interests. Nor can it be said that the majority of the people in the North ever confronted it squarely until they were forced to, but chose instead to view it obliquely as a territorial problem. Their consciences, as Garrison reminded them, were bounded by the 36°30' parallel. Still, the moral question was omnipresent. It arose in many different forms, only partly obscured by available issues — land policy, tariffs, territorial regulations — but giving the political conflicts of the decade their peculiar intensity. Looked at in one way, the return of a few hundred escaped slaves was not worth a war, and it may have seemed that despite the obstructionist tactics of the anti-slavery party, a solution might have been found short of violence. For those Bostonians, however, who lined the streets to watch Anthony Burns march back to slavery, or the citizens of Syracuse who rescued the Negro Jerry and then defied the authorities, the Fugitive Slave Law came as a fulfillment of abolitionist prophecy. "I respect the Anti-slavery society," Emerson wrote in the wake of the rescues. "It is the Cassandra that has foretold all that has befallen, fact for fact, years ago."

A morality play is a drama of abstractions, and it was with abstractions that Americans increasingly concerned themselves as the decade moved forward, just as in the case of the Fugitive Slave Law the North acted out of moral revulsion and the South out of righteous determination. The country was entering a labyrinth from which there was no sure avenue of escape. All this Garrison had foretold years ago.

The Compromise of 1850 brought Garrison's appeal to the

law of nature to the floor of Congress. In his reply to Webster's Seventh of March speech, Seward gave the "higher law" doctrine its classic expression. "But there is a higher law than the Constitution," he told Webster, "which regulates our authority over the domain, and devotes it to the same noble purposes." The territory of the United States was part of the common heritage of mankind, and the people residing there were stewards of God entrusted with the enforcement of higher law. The South could no more prevent the discussion of slavery than it could stop the onrush of progress. The agitation against slavery would not stop, Seward told his Southern colleagues, not even war could prevent it. "It will go on until you shall terminate it in the only way in which any State or nation ever terminated it — by yielding to it — yielding in your own time, and in your own manner, indeed, but nevertheless yielding to the progress of emancipation."

After the Compromise of 1850 it was the North which appeared to be bending to the will of the South by yielding to the Fugitive Slave Law. This law brought the civil rights issue into sharper focus than at any time since the battle over petitions. By giving the slaveholder the legal right to recover his property in any state in the Union, it seemed clear proof of Southern intention to spread slavery throughout the country by first establishing the right to recapture slaves, then the right to bring them into the free states and hold them there. It was a fact that only a relative handful of escaped slaves were ever returned under the new law. It was also true that both sections exaggerated the sins of the other, the North accusing the slaveowners of devilish designs on the free Negroes, and Southerners accusing Northern states of obstructing justice. Yet it was a poor kind of justice that could be had under a law which denied trial by jury and made the word of the master sufficient to establish title.

Boston abolitionists met the law with a new theory of nullification and a brand of civil disobedience that went far beyond Garrison's nonresistance creed. Theodore Parker told his congregation at the Melodeon that when governments perverted their functions and enacted wickedness, there was no law left but natural justice. It was the function of conscience to discover to men the moral law of God. "Having determined what is absolutely right, by the conscience of God, or at least relatively right, according to my conscience to-day, then it becomes my duty to keep it. I owe it to God to obey His law, or what I deem His law; that is my duty. . . . I owe entire allegiance to God."[15] Garrison went to hear Parker's opinions but heard instead his own arguments, polished a little and tightened, but the same old arguments for the ultimate authority of conscience. Parker did more than preach; he helped organize Boston's Vigilance Committee, elected at a protest meeting at Faneuil Hall. The purpose of the Vigilance Committee was to protect fugitives and the colored inhabitants of Boston and vicinity from any persons acting under the law. Once again the city witnessed a mob of gentlemen of property and wealth but this time on the side of anti-slavery. The directorate included Phillips, Samuel Gridley Howe, Tom Higginson, Ellis Gray Loring, Henry Bowditch, Charles Ellis, and the Negro lawyer Lewis Hayden. Garrison, whose nonresistance opinions were widely known, was purposely left off the committee.

At first the Vigilance Committee occupied itself with printing and distributing Parker's handbills which warned the Negroes of Boston against slave-hunters, but soon it had a chance to act. In 1848 William and Ellen Craft, two Georgia slaves, had escaped North by a most ingenious ruse. Ellen, who was light-skinned, bandaged her face and passed as a young man journeying to Philadelphia for medical consultation attended by a manservant. From Charleston the Crafts traveled to Richmond, from there to Baltimore, Philadelphia, and finally Boston, where the Boston abolitionists heralded the arrival of the courageous couple and publicized their daring escape. They had lived unmolested in the city for nearly two years when one evening in October, 1850, Parker came home to find Henry Bowditch waiting with the news that two slave-catchers from Georgia were in town looking for the Crafts. The committee sprang into action. They spirited William off to Lewis Hayden's house and provided him with a pistol. Parker himself drove Ellen to Ellis Gray Loring's home in Brookline, where she remained until the committee deemed it safe for her to return to the city. For another week Parker kept her at his place, writing his sermons, he said, with a brace of loaded pistols before him. Then he marched down to the United States Hotel, where the unwelcome guests were staying. While his Vigilance Committee lounged ominously in the lobby and up the staircase, Parker held a conference with the two slave-catchers. "I told them that they were not safe another night," Parker boasted. "I had stood between them and violence once, I would not promise to do it again. They were considerably frightened."[16] The agents left town on the next train.

The Vigilance Committee took a long step toward mob rule in the case of "Shadrach," a waiter at the Cornhill Coffee House. Frederic Wilkins, or Jenkins, who had acquired the name Shadrach, was seized on the morning of February 18, 1851, by the United States marshal and lodged in the Court House under special custody. As soon as the Vigilance Committee heard of the arrest, Richard Henry Dana hurried to

Chief Justice Lemuel Shaw, only to be told that the disposition of a fugitive slave was too frivolous a matter for a writ of *habeas corpus*. In the meantime Lewis Hayden was taking matters into his own hands. He rounded up twenty men from "Nigger Hill" behind the State House and marched into the Court House and straight into the courtroom with his guard. Not a soul moved to stop them as they seized Shadrach, nearly tearing his clothes off his back in the process, and rushed him down the stairs "like a black squall" into a waiting carriage that drove him to Cambridge, the first stop on the northwest road to Concord, Leominster, Vermont, and finally Canada. The rescue of Shadrach went far beyond the threat of violence. Here was open defiance of the Fugitive Slave Law. From Washington came immediate orders to prosecute Hayden and the rest of the vigilantes — three Negroes and two white men. The case ended in a mistrial when a single juror stubbornly held out for acquittal. A year or so later Dana was approached by a quiet, plain-looking man who asked if he remembered him.

"Yes," Dana replied quickly. "You were the twelfth juror in Shadrach's case."

"That's right!" came the rejoinder. "I was the twelfth juror in that case, and I was the man who drove Shadrach over the line."[17]

Garrison's nonresistance scruples did not prevent him from rejoicing over the rescue of Shadrach. "Thank God Shadrach is free! and not only free but safe under the banner of England." A quick rush on the Court House, nobody hurt, nobody wronged, simply a sudden transformation of a slave into a free man "conducted to a spot whereon he can glorify God in his body and spirit, which are his." Millard Fillmore might issue proclamations and Henry Clay propose to investigate everyone who dared peep or mutter against the law, but the "poor, hunted, entrapped fugitive slave" had been freed![18] Before Garrison could ponder the difficulties of reconciling lawbreaking and nonresistance, the Sims case broke, and this time the Vigilance Committee lost.

Thomas Sims, a boy of seventeen, was apprehended on April 3, 1851, and charged with theft of the clothes he wore and with being a fugitive slave from Georgia. His lawyers, the intrepid Dana, Samuel Sewall and the Democratic politician Robert Rantoul, were as able counsel as the city offered. They presented Judge Shaw with a writ of *habeas corpus* which he refused to honor, and then prepared to fight a delaying action. Thomas Higginson, the young firebrand from Newburyport, who had other ideas, rushed down to the city to find the Vigilance Committee assembled at the *Liberator* office discussing the merits of various rescue schemes while Garrison sat silently composing an editorial. The committee could agree on no workable plan, and the members adjourned tired and discouraged to join the small crowd of demonstrators outside the Court House. That evening Higginson concocted a harebrained plan whereby on a given signal Sims would leap out of the upper-story window and into a pile of mattresses which would be rushed out from a nearby alley; but Sims's jailers soon dashed his hopes for a rescue *á la* Dumas by putting bars on the windows overnight. At three o'clock in the morning of the thirteenth, word reached the committee that Sims was being removed to a coastal vessel in Boston Harbor. Parker, Phillips, Bowditch, Channing and the others had just time to improvise a coffin draped in black and form a death watch behind the procession of marshals escorting Sims. Garrison was there praying with the rest for the deliverance of the fugitive. But Sims was not to be delivered. Three times the marshal had tried to buy him back, and three times Sims's owner had refused.

There was a lot more than the freedom of one Negro at stake — slaveowners wanted bodily proof of their victory over the State of Garrison.

In Syracuse later that year the abolitionists had their revenge when a mob overpowered the guard, snatched the Negro "Jerry" and bustled him off to Canada. The Jerry rescue also brought indictments — eighteen in all were arraigned, among them Samuel J. May and Gerrit Smith. May's nonresistance faith had broken under the strain, and he wrote to Garrison to tell him so. "Perhaps you will think that I go too far in enjoining it upon all men to act *against* the Fugitive Slave Law as they conscientiously believe to be right, even if it be to fight for the rescue of its victims. But I know not what counsel to give them. And let me confess to you, that when I saw poor Jerry in the hands of the official kidnappers, I could not preach non-resistance very earnestly to the crowd who were clamoring for his release. And when I found that he had been rescued without serious harm to any one, I was as uproarious as any one in my joy."[19] May told Garrison that if the abolitionists did not kill the infernal law, it would kill them, and that when it came to the death-grapple, no man who believed in freedom could disarm himself. Garrison was no longer sure.

He replied tentatively to the vigilantes in a long review of Harriet Beecher Stowe's *Uncle Tom's Cabin*, a critique that betrayed both a failure of imagination and a confused view of the nonresistance question. He had nothing but praise for Mrs. Stowe's powers of characterization, which, he confessed, set his nerves trembling and made his heart "grow liquid as water." He was particularly moved by the figure of Uncle Tom, who personified the triumph of Christian nonresistance. "No insult, no outrage, no suffering, could ruffle the Christlike meekness of his spirit, or shake the steadfastness of his faith."[20] That the slaves ought to wait patiently for a peaceful deliverance and abstain from all insurrectionary movements went without saying, but what of those white men who were attempting to free them? In his mind a change in complexion did not materially alter the case. Violence and the love of Christ were still irreconcilable, and theoretically no provocation whatever could justify a resort to force. He was too skilled an agitator, however, not to recognize the possibilities of a threatened slave insurrection; and once again he reminded Southern whites that with their revolutionary heritage they could not deny the right of resistance to their slaves. If this warning weakened the fiber of Christian pacificism, so did his evasions of the question of disobeying the Fugitive Slave Act. "A great deal is said at the present time and perhaps not too much, in regard to the Fugitive Slave Law," he told an audience of Pennsylvania Quakers. "Many persons glory in their hostility to it, and upon this capital they set up an anti-slavery reputation. But opposition to that law is no proof in itself of anti-slavery fidelity. That law is merely incidental to slavery, and there is no merit in opposition which extends no further than to its provisions. Our warfare is not against slavehunting alone, but against the existence of slavery."[21] Yet sooner or later, as May had warned, he would have to face the issue of resistance to government and law, if not over the question of returning escaped slaves, then over the extension of slavery into the territories.

On May 22, 1854, the Nebraska Act was passed "against the strongest possible remonstrances," Garrison wrote, "against the laws of God and the rights of universal man — in subversion of plighted faith, in utter disregard of the scorn of the world, and for purposes as diabolical as can be conceived of or consummated here on earth."[22] The law was based on three principles: popular sovereignty, the right of appeal to the Supreme Court, and repeal of the Missouri Compromise. Stephen Douglas, the architect of the law, may have believed that geography and climate closed Kansas and Nebraska to slavery, and he might argue that it was the North, not the South, which first broke the Missouri Compromise. None of these explanations, not even his brilliant defense of the bill against the partisan attacks of Seward and Chase, convinced Northerners of his realism or his honesty. In private Douglas called slavery "a curse beyond computation to both black and white," but that was not what his bill said. His bill declared that the Missouri Compromise violated the principle of Congressional nonintervention with slavery and was therefore "inoperative and void." Douglas admitted that his philosophy was opportunistic and explained to his supporters that he must either champion the policy of his party "or forfeit forever all that I have fought for."[23] Who was he to oppose his individual judgment against the combined wisdom of a great party? Douglas's doctrine of popular sovereignty was a confession of moral bankruptcy: it gave the people in the territories the power to decide the slavery question while it denied that there were any principles needed to guide them in their choice. His Nebraska Act enshrined the sovereignty of the people at the expense of human rights. It also made more abolitionists overnight than Garrison had in twenty years.

The cost of the Nebraska Act to the Democratic Party proved considerable. Their majority of eighty-four in the House fell to a minority of seventy-five; of the forty-two Northern Democrats who had voted for the bill, only seven were re-elected. Illinois sent Lyman Trumbull, an antislavery Whig, to join Douglas in the Senate. The *National Intelligencer* estimated that the party's loss in popular votes neared 350,000. This, however, was not all gain for anti-slavery, for the most remarkable aspect of the 1854 elections was the vote polled by the American Party. In Massachusetts, Henry Wilson was forced to run on the nativist ticket, and in New York the Know-Nothings overwhelmed the abolitionists. Seward was unavailable to head a new party; Chase was available but not well enough known in the Northeast; Sumner was able, willing and unpopular; Lincoln was only a rising figure in Illinois politics. "All the Whigs expressed disapproval of the Nebraska Bill, but take no action," Dana commented sadly. "The Democrats differ and are paralyzed by the Executive. . . . We can have no effectual vent for opinion. This depresses and mortifies us to the extreme." The Republican convention at Ripon was still two years away.

Garrison clung tenaciously to his refusal to acknowledge political action. His conclusions, given his premises, were logical if not encouraging. In his view, only the strictest of abolitionists could qualify for office, and such men would never be elected. William Goodell's candidacy for the Presidency in the campaign of 1852 he called "a farce in one act." His mood at the time of the passing of the Nebraska Act was summarized in his resolution offered to the annual meeting of the American Society declaring that "the one great issue to be made with the Slave Power, is, THE DISSOLUTION OF THE EXISTING AMERICAN UNION."

The week of May 24, 1854, was anniversary week, when all the benevolent societies as well as the Massachusetts Anti-Slavery Society and the Woman's Rights conventioneers crowded into Boston. On the evening of the twenty-fourth, Anthony Burns, a Negro employee of a Brattle Street clothing store owner, was seized on his way home from work and arrested on a trumped-up robbery charge. Taken to the Court House, he was accused of being an escaped slave and arrested on a fugitive slave warrant issued by United States Commissioner Edward G. Loring.

That evening Burns was visited in his cell by Colonel Charles F. Suttle of Alexandria, Virginia, his former master, and William Brent, the colonel's agent. The two men extracted a confession from Burns, and when Parker and Phillips visited him the following morning, he told them of his damaging admission. "I shall have to go back," he sighed. "Mr. Suttle knows me — Brent knows me. If I must go back, I want to go back as easy as I can." His counsel — Dana once more, along with the able Negro lawyer Robert Morris — secured a postponement, but they knew that the legal case was hopeless. The disposition of Burns would rest with the citizens of Boston. Two plans were now set in motion, the first a protest meeting at Faneuil Hall, the second a wild and dangerous plan of Higginson's to use the momentum of the meeting to effect a rescue. Let everything be made ready, he explained, by posting a body of men outside the Court House. Then send some loud-voiced speaker — preferably Phillips — to the Faneuil Hall meeting and at the right moment let him give the word that a mob was already attacking the Court House and send the crowd pouring into Court Square to bring out Burns.

Higginson's scheme failed only because of faulty timing. He and his followers, armed with axes and meat cleavers, rushed the door of the Court House while the crowd was still listening to Phillips in Faneuil Hall. They were met by fifty of the marshal's men, one of whom was killed in the rush. Higginson was wounded on the chin, and, dripping with blood, he fell back with his men. They were still milling around in front of the building when the mob arrived from Faneuil Hall. Among the new arrivals was Bronson Alcott, who strolled up to Higginson and with orphic innocence asked, "Why are we not within?" Informed that the first attack had failed, Alcott nodded, turned, and marched slowly up the steps, paused while bullets whistled past his head, and then, realizing that no one had followed him, calmly descended. Finally reinforcements from the police arrived and the rescuers wandered off.

Abolitionist arrangements to buy Burns's freedom were broken off when District Attorney Benjamin Franklin Hallett intervened, and after a full week's deliberation Commissioner Loring pronounced his verdict for Suttle. Then came a wire from President Pierce authorizing Hallett to incur any expense in executing the law. While surly crowds hooted and jeered, police and militia cleared the streets from the Court House to Long Wharf, where a revenue cutter waited to carry the fugitive back to Virginia. The marshal's posse, led by an artillery battalion and a platoon of United States Marines and followed by mounted dragoons and lancers, marched Burns between rows of special police who held back the fifty thousand spectators. As Burns remarked to the sheriff, "There was lots of folks to see a colored man walk down the street."

Phillips, Parker and Higginson were indicted, but after months of legal skirmishing the case was dropped. Burns, who had been sold on the return voyage, was purchased from his new master by the Boston philanthropists and packed off to Oberlin to study for the ministry. Commissioner Loring, Judge of Probate and lecturer at the Harvard Law School, did not fare so well. The women of Woburn sent him thirty pieces of silver, his students refused to attend his lectures, the Board of Overseers at Harvard declined to reappoint him, and a petition with twelve thousand signatures demanded his removal from office. He was finally removed by the legislature in 1858 and given an appointment by Buchanan.

Garrison added the final touch to the case of Anthony
Burns. At an open-air celebration of the Fourth of July in
Framingham Grove he solemnized the end of the Union in
a religious rite. First he read the usual passage from the
Scriptures. After laying his Bible down he spoke to the
crowd in measured and familiar tones, comparing the Declaration of Independence with the verdict in the Burns case.
Then, as a minister might announce the taking of the sacra-
ment, he told his listeners that he would now perform an
action which would be the testimony of his soul. Slowly he
lighted a candle on the table before him, and, picking up a
copy of the Fugitive Slave Law, touched a corner of it to
the flame and held it aloft, intoning the words "And let the
people say, Amen." "Amen," echoed the congregation. Next
he burned Loring's decision and Judge Curtis's charge to
the jury. Each time he repeated the incantatory phrase, and
each time his followers murmured the response. Finally, he
raised a copy of the "covenant with death," the United
States Constitution itself, and as it burst into flames pronounced judgment. "So perish all compromises with tyranny!
And let the people say, Amen!"

As the communicants repeated the word for the last time,
he stood before them arms extended. The verdict had been
pronounced, he was finished. It was at once the most calculated and the most dramatic action of his life, more impressive even than Burns's march through the city, more
electrifying than Phillips's speech in Faneuil Hall. His faithful
were pathetically few, but that did not matter any more.
Now the whole country would know of the burning of their
Constitution.

17

Secession

ON THE EVE of the Presidential election of 1856 Horace Greeley published an open letter to "W. L. Garrison" in the *Tribune* demanding to know his views of the three candidates. Greeley had followed Garrison's career from the beginning and thought he knew the extent of his "no-government" heresies. He assumed as a matter of course that the *Liberator* would be hostile to John C. Frémont as well as to Buchanan and Millard Fillmore, that is, until he read an editorial of Garrison's that changed his mind. "As against Buchanan and Fillmore," Garrison had written, "it seems to us the sympathies and best wishes of every enlightened friend of freedom must be on the side of Frémont; so that if there were no moral barrier to our voting, and we had a million votes to bestow, we should cast them all for the Republican candidate."[1]

Now Greeley knew an endorsement when he saw one, and he asked Garrison if he meant what he said in announcing his preference for Frémont and claiming to speak for the "universal feeling" of the ultra-abolitionists. In his reply Garrison explained that he favored the Pathfinder because Frémont was "for the non-extension of slavery, in common with the great body of the people of the North."[2] His remark signaled a retreat from perfectionism and nonresistance, a strategic withdrawal that ended in a rout four years later when he and his followers decided to prevent the national division they had long predicted.

By all rights Garrison should have treated Republicans to the same scorn he had bestowed on the Free Soilers and the Liberty Party. He did criticize their ideas as "feeble and indefinite" and their stand on slavery as "partial, one-sided, geographical," but these shortcomings he now forgave in the hope that new leadership would strengthen the party's moral fiber.[3] "In general intelligence, virtuous character, humane sentiment, and patriotic feeling — as well as in the object it is seeking to accomplish — it is incomparably better than the other rival parties; and its success, *as against those parties*, will be a cheering sign of the times."[4] His gradual drift from principles to personalities and a growing inclination to make political choices while eschewing politics began to confuse his followers and eventually drove them into the Republican camp carrying with them, so they thought, their leader's blessing.

Wendell Phillips remained loyal to moral suasion, but for every Phillips there were ten Sumners and Wilsons determined to build their careers on an anti-slavery platform. Garrison retained the loyalty of a few partisans whom he praised for having "the same estimate of men and institutions" as he did, but their number grew less each year and their usefulness questionable. He had demanded conformity too long to change now: his disciples were still expected to study the gospel according to Saint Liberator. The instincts of a patriarchal despot continued to make cooperation with him hazardous and usually impossible. Ten years after his quarrel with Frederick Douglass he still refused to appear on the platform with him. Gerrit Smith, a perennial victim of his wrath, complained more than once of Garrison's rudeness to a man who had praised him at home and abroad. But Garrison had a long memory for slights and snubs. Smith, he recalled, had supported both Lewis Tappan and his clique and Douglass himself. "I must say," he sniffed, "he has a singular method of praising and vindicating me."[5] No man could endorse "malignant enemies" and retain the respect of William Lloyd Garrison!

The old Garrisonians were dying off — Ellis Gray Loring, Charles Hovey, Arnold Buffum, and Effingham Capron. Hovey, a twenty-year veteran, left a forty-thousand-dollar trust fund that kept the destitute state society alive until the war. In 1857 Birney died, and Garrison grudgingly admitted than once long ago he had served the cause of the slave well. Other of his old co-workers had retired, Weld and his wife and sister-in-law to found a school, Stanton and Leavitt to join the Republicans. Garrison still quarreled with those who were left. One such wrangle arose out of his unfortunate attempt at humor in publicly referring to Abby Kelley Foster's "cracked voice and gray hairs." Abby bridled at such ungenerous treatment and demanded an apology. Garrison refused — "because I do not see or feel that I have been a wrong-doer." Abby accused him of belittling her efforts in behalf of the slave. "Not so," he retorted. "I believe you to have always been actuated by the highest and purest motives, however lacking in judgment or consistency."[6] Letters packed with recrimination and righteousness shuttled back and forth as Abby refused to forget his ungentlemanly behavior and he declined to apologize.

This aggressive self-righteousness, tightening as the years passed, was slowly twisting Garrison's reform impulse into a philosophy of obedience. His philosophy he summarized in the phrase "loyalty to man," but his old concern with worthiness betrayed an underlying anxiety. The loyalty of the reformer, he explained, comprises, first of all, loyalty to himself, striving to keep himself pure from sin and in progress toward holiness, and next, to his fellow men. "We cannot bestow anything upon God. But if we love Him, and wish to manifest our love, the very best way is to *obey* Him; and every possible mode of obedience to Him is contained in these two — improving ourselves, and helping our fellow men."[7] The order of duties was significant. Only when a reformer met his personal obligation to God was he free to impeach, admonish, rebuke, and, finally, "having done all, TO STAND."[8]

To stand where? It was all very well to insist that his view of reform was not "partial" but "complete," yet it was difficult to see how the peaceful secession of Northern purists would bring about the "immediate, total and eternal overthrow of slavery." Garrison seemed more and more occupied with the role of Hebrew prophet. "One thing is very palpable — our likeness as a people to the Jews of old."[9] The ancient Jews were not ashamed, neither did they blush, and their fate had been decreed by an angry God. America, hear the word of the Lord and tremble! Jehovah would soon exact full repentance for the sin of disobedience. Already the people of Kansas were reaping the whirlwind, and their trials foreshadowed greater ones to come. The image of the avenging destroyer, the God of wrath whose retribution is imminent, began to haunt him. To hasten the day of reckoning he called a delegated convention of the free states "for the purpose of taking measures to effect a peaceable withdrawal" from the Union. The Disunion Convention, as it was optimistically called, was held in Worcester in January, 1857.

The Worcester Convention turned out to be "nothing more than a Garrisonian meeting" with none but diehard disunionists on hand.[10] Political abolitionists were unwilling to involve themselves in such an unpopular affair. Henry Wilson and Charles Francis Adams sent disapproving letters, as did Amasa Walker and Joshua Giddings, rejecting what Adams termed Garrison's "mistaken theory of morals." His Worcester Convention applied this theory with customary thoroughness by voting the inevitable resolutions calling for Northern secession. In his defense of the resolves Garrison gave one of the most effective speeches of his career. "My reasons for leaving the Union," he told his handful of diehard disunionists, "are, first, because of the nature of the bond. I would not stand here a moment were it not that this is with me a question of absolute morality — of obedience to 'higher law.' By all that is just and holy, it is not optional whether you or I shall occupy the ground of Disunion." The problem was not one of expediency or the incompatibility of Northern and Southern interests. It was a question of *complicity* — of Massachusetts allied with South Carolina, Maine with Alabama, Vermont with Mississippi, in condoning wickedness. His own difficulty, he said, was wholly a moral one centered on the unmistakable fact that the Union was based on slavery. "I cannot swear to uphold it. As I understand it, they who ask me to do so, ask me to do an immoral act — to stain my conscience — to sin against God. How can I do this?"[11]

At the end of his speech he dismissed Southern secession threats with the observation that there was not a single intelligent slaveholder who favored the dissolution of the Union. "I do not care how much they hate the North, and threaten to separate from us; they are contemptible numerically, and only make use of these threats to bring the North down on her knees to do their bidding, in order to save the Union. Not one of them is willing to have the cord cut, and the South permitted to try the experiment." The time was still 1857, and as long as Southern threats need not be taken seriously, it was safe to preach disunion.

It may have been safe to advocate Northern secession, but it was decidedly unpopular. Garrison's renewed agitation plunged his organization into disaster. Wherever he lectured — Montpelier, Vermont; Salem, Ohio; Northampton, Massachusetts; Syracuse, New York — people were hostile and audiences nonexistent. Despondently he admitted that his old friends were almost entirely discouraged as to the cause. "The love of some has waxed cold; some have moved away; some have failed in business; some have been drawn into politics; and hardly any are left to sympathize with and sustain our radical position."[12] In Altoona, Pennsylvania, twenty-five people attended his lecture, the smallest audience he ever addressed. In Cortland, New York, a "mass convention" turned out to be an unenthusiastic crowd of women. He stuck to his disunion guns, blasting away at church and state, and at one lecture had the grim satisfaction "of seeing that my shots took effect by several wounded birds flying from the room." He never stopped hoping that some good would come of his lectures "beyond what is apparent."[13]

All that was apparent in the autumn of 1857 when he planned a national disunion convention was the pathetically small number of his followers. The call for the national meeting was signed by only 4200 men and 1800 women, most of them from Massachusetts and Ohio. They believed, in the words of the call, that when a majority of people in the North joined with them, they would "settle this question of slavery in twenty-four hours."[14]

The National Disunion Convention was never held, although a small group of Ohio disunionists finally met in Cleveland against their leader's advice. Beginning in the summer of 1857 a financial panic paralyzed American benev-

olence along with the business of the country and gave
Garrison his excuse to postpone what could only have been
a fiasco. The panic itself he first explained as God's judgment
on a "fast people." In a more reflective mood he attributed
it to the unregulated circulation of paper money and the
foolish speculative practices of the people. "The great majority
of the people are still in leading-strings — ignorant, credulous,
unreflecting — the victims of demagogueism [sic] or financial
swindling — though assuming to hold the reins of government
in their own hands. They are blind to their own interests, and
on the whole prefer to be adroitly cheated, rather than honestly dealt with."[15] Beneath the surface of his Christian egali-
tarianism there lurked the old Federalist arrogance and
contempt of the masses.

The Panic of '57 stirred the ashes of religious revival which
flared intermittently during the next year. Garrison scoffed
at it. A genuine revival, he sneered, would scare James
Buchanan so he could not sleep o' nights and drive the South
to lynch its preachers. All this talk of coming to Christ,
however, was just so much empty wind. It defined nothing,
failed to reach the heart, and was wholly destitute of moral
courage. If the history of religious awakenings was any indication, the revival of 1858, he predicted, would promote
meanness rather than manliness, delusion instead of intelligence.[16]

His new emphasis on the secular gave a revolutionary edge
to his disunionism. Abolitionists, he now believed, needed no
Scriptural proof for their convictions; they did not need to
go to the Bible to prove their right to freedom. The very
thought was absurd. "How dare you make it a Bible question
at all?" he demanded. The Declaration of Independence pre-
cluded all appeals to parchment, logic, or history; liberty
needed no Biblical sanction. At last the American Revolution

and the rights of the Negro stood free from the coils of
scriptural precedent.

There was poetic justice in the fact that while the North
overwhelmingly rejected Garrison's plea for peaceful secession, developments in Kansas made his predictions of violence
come true. In the first place, the Dred Scott decision appeared to support his pro-slavery interpretation of the Constitution. The majority decision, which he called "undeniably
a party one," appeared to lead the North either to war or
secession. Reports from Kansas in the summer of 1857 showed
how ill-equipped the Free Soil Republicans were to deal with
demon Democracy. Here was a territory where Free Soilers
outnumbered the border ruffians five to one, and what did
they have to show for their numbers? The Lecompton Constitution. "The people of that territory are as completely
subjugated as the populace of France or Italy. . . . What
hope is there for Kansas?"[17] Kansas, he declared, needed
"repentance and a thorough reformation." What kind of
reformation — whether the strong hand of Jim Lane or the
angry one of John Brown — he did not say. To demand as he
did that the North stand "boldly and uncompromisingly"
was to call it to action, and a call to action required a plan.
His lack of a plan precipitated the major crisis in his life.

The crisis began at a meeting of the society he had founded
in 1832, and it came from his old radical confederates the
Fosters. Abby and Stephen Foster had labored in the rocky
vineyard of Garrisonism for fifteen years, but lately they had
begun to watch political developments closely and particularly the rapid growth of the Republican Party. They concluded that the North was no longer to be aroused by preaching, and they chose the occasion of the annual meeting of
the Massachusetts Society in January, 1858, to tell Garrison
so. Foster admitted that the time was when moral suasion

had done great work in the land, but he pointed to the small audience before him as evidence that the old ways were outmoded. "Our people believe in a government of force; but we are asking them to take an essentially non-resistant position which is wholly inadequate to the exigencies of the case. They wish to vote." Up jumped Higginson to agree. "The *moral* position of this society," he told Garrison, "is the highest and noblest possible, but their practical position does not take hold of the mind of the community." Whether abolitionists ought to join the Republicans or strike out on their own he did not know, but the Fosters were in favor of a new anti-slavery party. The general discontent was unmistakable as Garrison's colleagues sat awaiting his reply.

His answer was hardly reassuring. He told his abolitionists that they were not responsible for the way in which the people received their warnings. "It is my duty to warn them," he said fixing his eye on the Fosters. "It is *not* my duty to contrive ways for men in Union with slavery, and determined to vote without regard to the moral character of their act, to carry out their low ideas, and I shall do no such work."[18] He had shown Massachusetts her shame and demanded that she renounce her compact with death. Was not this work and work enough? Clearly in 1858 it was not. Although he still controlled enough votes to defeat Foster's bid for a political party, the meaning of the revolt was not lost on him. Foster was asking him to choose between perfectionism and abolition, between religion and reform, and behind the demand lay the failure of a thirty-year experiment to unite them. He was pondering the dilemma when John Brown, taking the law into his own hands at Harpers Ferry, suddenly showed him the logical consequences of his doctrine of conscience.

He had first met John Brown at Theodore Parker's home

in January, 1857. While Parker and the other guests sat listening, Brown matched his New Testament pacifism with dire prophecies from the Old. Two years later Brown attended the New England Anti-Slavery Convention, where after a full day of speeches he was heard to mutter that "these men are all talk; what is needed is action — action!" His own brand of action forced Garrison to reconsider and then abandon his peace principles.

Garrison never doubted that Brown believed himself divinely commissioned to deliver the slave or that the old man and his sons were brave and heroic men. Yet he could not help thinking him misguided and rash, "powerfully wrought upon by the trials through which he has passed." By the standards of Bunker Hill, Brown died a patriot and a martyr. But by the standard of peace? Was there a place in history for the Gideons, the Joshuas and Davids? He did not know.[19]

The question of Brown's guilt continued to plague him until finally he too capitulated to the need for violence. At a memorial meeting held in Tremont Temple he read Brown's address to the court and then requested permission to comment on it. Then he asked how many nonresistants there were in the audience, and when only a single voice cried out, he paused a moment and then said that he too was a peace man who had labored unremittingly to effect the peaceful abolition of slavery.

Yet, as a peace man — I am prepared to say: 'Success to every slave insurrection at the South, and in every slave country.' And I do not see how I compromise or stain my peace profession in making that declaration. Whenever there is a contest between the oppressed and the oppressor, — the weapons being equal between the parties, — God knows that my heart must be with the oppressed and always against the oppressor. Therefore, whenever commenced, I cannot but wish success to all slave insurrections. I thank God when men who believe in the right and duty of wielding carnal weapons, are so far advanced that they will take those weapons out of the scale of despotism, and throw them into the scale of freedom. *It is an indication of progress and positive moral growth; it is one way to get up to the sublime platform of non-resistance; and it is God's method of dealing retribution upon the head of the tyrant. Rather than see men wearing their chains in a cowardly and servile spirit, I would, as an advocate of peace, much rather see them breaking the head of the tyrant with their chains. Give me, as a non-resistant, Bunker Hill, and Lexington, and Concord, rather than the cowardice and servility of a Southern slave-plantation.*[20]

Free at last from his pacifist scruples, he readily became reconciled to the Republican Party. Though he still spoke of it as a "time-serving, a temporizing, a cowardly party," he hoped that his renewed disunionist agitation might yet save it. Secretly he hoped that the Republicans, short of disunion, might check the spread of slavery by a show of strength. Publicly he declared that they could "create such a moral and religious sentiment against slavery as shall mould all parties and sects to effect its overthrow." If Republicans wondered why he still refused to vote, he answered that it was because the greater included the less, that the immediate abolition of slavery was incomparably more important than preventing its extension. His refusal to vote, however, signified no lack of interest in the coming Presidential campaign, "for in the various phases of that struggle, we recognize either an approximation to, or receding from, the standard of equal justice and impartial freedom which we have so long advocated."[21]

From moderate support to outright enthusiasm was only a step, and this step he took early in the election year of 1860.

He discerned a marvelous change in Northern opinion: the battle of free speech had been won and the conflict between freedom and slavery was now agreed to be irrepressible — "not of man's devising, but of God's ordering." It was deepening every day in spite of political cunning and religious sorcery. "The pending Presidential election," he wrote in September, "witnesses a marked division between the political forces of the North and of the South; and though it relates, ostensibly, solely to the question of the further extension of slavery, it really signifies a much deeper sentiment in the breasts of the people of the North, which, in process of time, must ripen into more decisive action."[22] That action, whatever it might be, awaited the outcome of the election.

He had fully expected that Seward would be nominated and was prepared to oppose him because of his seemingly rapid retreat from the irrepressible conflict. He despised Seward as the incarnation of political trickery. What the Republicans needed was a man with heart as well as intelligence. Abolishing slavery would prove no mere holiday recreation, "something that will lead on to fame and popularity, to office and power." It meant a willingness to sacrifice all these things for the sake of the slave. There appeared to be very few leaders of the right caliber in the Republican Party, and he was sure that Lincoln was not one of them.

Garrison's initial reaction to the nomination of Lincoln, though unfavorable, hardly matched the outraged cries of Wendell Phillips. In an editorial unusually vituperative even for him, Phillips labeled Lincoln the "Slave Hound of Illinois" and singled out his 1848 proposal for the return of fugitive slaves from the District of Columbia as positive proof of his pro-slavery intentions. Garrison at first refused to print the libel and accepted it only when Phillips agreed to sign his initials to it. Soon, however, he joined his friend in berating Lincoln as a slavocrat in disguise. Was a man who in one breath demanded the rendition of fugitive slaves and in the next professed to hate slavery — was such a man worthy of confidence and support? "Such a man shall never have my vote, either to occupy the Presidential chair, or any other station."[23] Lincoln might be six feet four inches tall, but he was a mental dwarf.

Their denunciation of Lincoln did not prevent Phillips and Garrison from hailing his election as a triumph of justice. "Babylon is fallen, is fallen!" cried Garrison, and Phillips announced cryptically that though Lincoln was in place, Garrison was in power. Nothing could have been further from the truth. In the great battle against institutions Garrison had lost nearly all the ground he formerly held. His advocacy of Northern secession had burgeoned into an act of defiance, a challenge to the South to answer "our great, magnificent, invincible North." From the arid heights of perfectionist anarchy he was descending to the plain of power politics. "Give me the omnipotent North," he told his society, "give me the resources of the eighteen free States of our country, on the side of freedom as a great independent empire, and I will ask nothing more for the abolition of slavery."[24]

He flatly refused to take Southern threats of secession seriously, since he was convinced that the South's fear of Lincoln only showed how desperate she had become. Whom the gods would destroy they first make mad. How far would Southern rabble-rousers go? Would they secede? "Will they jump into the Atlantic? Will they conflagrate their own dwellings, cut their own throats, and enable their slaves to rise in successful insurrection? Perhaps they will — probably they will not! By their bullying and raving, they have many times frightened the North into a base submission to their demands — and they expect to do it again! Shall they succeed?"[25]

These assurances of Southern pusillanimity failed to tally with his frequent references to the "brutal, demented, God-defying oppressors" or with his conviction that the South was one vast Bedlam full of lunatics. Eagerly he awaited the results of Lincoln's election. It had been a long, desperate struggle with the most satanic despotism on earth, but though the end was not yet, it could not be far distant — "all signs of the times are indicating that a great revolution is at hand." Of course, Southerners talked treason, but they were careful not to commit any acts which might endanger their necks. "Hence, all their blustering and vaporing amounts to treason, in spirit, language, and possible design, but not to anything tangible."[26]

When South Carolina provided the tangible evidence in December, he was willing to let the "errant sister" withdraw peacefully. "In vain have been, and will be, all compromises between North and South," he told his readers. "All Union-saving efforts are simply idiotic."[27] As one by one the Southern states left the Union, however, what had once been sheer rodomontade suddenly loomed ominously as acts "purely factious and flagrantly treasonable." The rebellion of the South was not revolution in the spirit of '76, but treachery of the deepest dye. The North, he insisted, should accept the inevitable, form a convention of free states and band together. The Union had been an insane attempt to unite hostile interests, hostile ideas and principles — two Gods, one for liberty, the other for slavery, two Christs, one for white men and the other for black. Let the new North organize an independent government and say to the slave states, "Though you are without excuse for your treasonable conduct, depart in peace!"[28] Strained to the breaking point by the secession of the South, Garrison's patience did not snap until Southern guns at Fort Sumter taught him the folly of peaceful secession.

In January, 1861, the Massachusetts Society met without its leader for the first time in its history. Confined to his bed by one of his intermittent fevers, Garrison heard how Phillips and Emerson had been shouted down by rowdies who whistled, stamped, hurled cushions and bottles, and finally paraded onto the stage, where they were beaten back by Phillips's armed bodyguard. Phillips obviously enjoyed his notoriety and had taken to carrying a pistol. Asked by one of his many feminine admirers whether he would use it, he replied with a flourish, "Yes, just as I would shoot a mad dog or a wild bull." His casual remark was an index of abolitionist militance in the new year.

As April grew near Garrison suddenly became convinced of Lincoln's soundness. He now saw in the President a "rare self-possession and equanimity" which he never knew he possessed. If war came — and it seemed likely that it would — he decided to give all his support to the administration. He still hoped it possible for Lincoln to accept separation in the spirit of Abraham and Lot, to leave the South to her own dreadful devices. Slavery would soon collapse and a new Union of North and South would emerge stretching from the Atlantic to the Pacific, "one in spirit, in purpose, in glorious freedom, the bitter past forgotten, and the future full of richest promise."[29] He was still savoring this dream of the birth of a true national vocation when the firing on Fort Sumter supplanted it with the nightmare of civil war.

Lincoln's call for volunteers thrust upon Garrison the choice he had avoided for thirty years. His losing struggle with the problem of reconciling pacifism and abolition is documented in four long editorials written after the fall of Sumter. In the first of them he reversed his position on secession and flatly denied that he had ever granted the right of the South to secede. "Certainly it is not a doctrine that has ever been advocated or countenanced by us; and we believe it wholly indefensible. . . . we deny that, between what the perfidious secessionists have done, and what we have urged upon the North to do in general, there is any point of comparison." In a passage which must have given sour satisfaction to the political abolitionists he admitted that the right of secession made a mockery of the Union. How could there be a *right* to perpetuate slavery? "Whence does such a 'right' originate? What 'sovereignty' is competent to exercise it? And if the abolitionists use their right 'for the destruction of slavery,' does it follow that the slaveholders have an equal right to seek the perpetuity of 'the sum of all villainies'? Is there no confusion of ideas here?"[30]

Indeed there was. The confusion lay in his attempt to make the right of revolution contingent upon civil liberties. He was saying, in effect, that there were "good" and "bad" revolutions, that good revolutions freed slaves and hence were justifiable but bad revolutions were wicked and unjustifiable.

He devoted a second editorial to clarifying the problem, and the result was confusion worse confounded. First of all, he declared, he had never granted any state the right to secede "*ad libitum.*" The Declaration of Independence provided no *carte blanche* for would-be revolutionists. The slaveholding South long ago had lost its claim to the Jeffersonian heritage and the Declaration of Independence. Where was the long train of abuses, the denial of life, liberty, or the pursuit of happiness? Northern disunionists, that intrepid band of true anti-slavery heroes, presented a different case altogether. The difference lay in their principles, in their reverence for higher law and their ideals of "eternal justice" and "unswerving rectitude." Northern secession was based on "the eternal fitness of things, and animated by a noble, disinterested, and philanthropic spirit," whereas Southern secession was "the concentration of all diabolism."[31] As his self-assurance dimmed, his prose acquired an incantatory quality, as though he thought that by repeating the formula he might come to believe it.

Civil war might have been avoided, he wrote in a third editorial, by the simple expedient of proclaiming liberty to the captives. We have healed Babylon, but Babylon is not healed. "No other alternative is left the Government, therefore, than either to be driven from the Capital, or to maintain unflinchingly its constitutional sovereignty." He welcomed the change in Northern opinion which he called "total, wonderful, indescribable." Under these circumstances who could doubt the outcome? The South lacked numbers, resources, energy, courage, and valor. Let there be no more treasonable talk of compromise or concession, but in humbling the Southern conspirators let the government immediately use the war power to proclaim universal and immediate emancipation![32]

It remained only to bury the peace cause as decently and quickly as possible, and this disagreeable chore he performed in the final editorial of the series, "The Relation of the Anti-Slavery Cause to the War." First he corrected the "widely prevalent but mistaken opinion" as to the pacific principles of the abolitionists. "They are generally supposed or represented to be a body of non-resistants, who cannot consistently, therefore, do otherwise than condemn or deplore the present clashing of arms in deadly strife." It was true that abolitionists had promised not to stir up slave rebellions and that as Christians they opposed the use of force generally. "But, as individuals, acting on their own responsibility, while largely imbued with the spirit of peace, they have never adopted the doctrine of non-resistance, with a few exceptional cases." About his own case he said nothing but passed quickly on to the question of the causes of the war. "The one great cause of all our national troubles and divisions is SLAVERY: the removal of it, therefore, is essential to our national existence." From the beginning abolitionists had predicted the consequences of slaveholding in the South. "Now that their predictions have come to pass, are they to indulge in morbid exclamations against the natural law of immutable justice, and to see in it no evidence of the growth of conscience, the power of truth, or the approach of the long-wished for jubilee?"[33] To his friends he added, "Let us *all* stand aside, when the North is rushing like a tornado in the right direction."[34]

Garrison's final estimate of the cause of the Civil War was essentially correct — it *was* slavery which disrupted the business of government, broke down the two-party system, made every foreign and domestic problem an insoluble one, and finally forced the South to secede. Even if the question of slavery in the territories was abstract and hypothetical (a debatable assumption at best), it was nonetheless real. It was precisely the abstract quality of the slavery problem that made it so real. The war did not come through any expressed desire of the American people in either section of the country or because their leaders blundered. Had a plebiscite been held in April, 1861, an overwhelming majority of Americans would have voted against war. But what does this prove? That history does not always follow the dictates of majority will. The story of the decade that ended with the firing on Fort Sumter reveals the power of abstractions to disrupt the normal course of events and distort normal political vision. Americans first tried to avoid the moral dilemma of slavery and then to deal with it at a distance as a territorial problem. They ended by going to war.

The rapidity with which the political crisis enveloped the country ought to have warned the anti-slavery men of the explosive power of their ideas. Abolitionists in general and Garrison in particular should have known where their kind of moral agitation would lead — had to lead. Since 1829 he had preached the incompatibility of slavery and democracy. He had used every weapon, framed every indictment, coined every phrase he could find to prove that the two ways of life were irreconcilable. Now he had to face the charges of contemporary "revisionists" who accused him of recklessly fostering a spirit of violence.

The question naturally arises [he wrote in 1858], — How is this astonishing change in Southern feeling and opinion to be accounted for? 'It is owing to the fanatical course pursued by the Abolitionists,' will be the reply of their traducers universally. 'If they had not created such an agitation and thereby alarmed and excited the South, slavery would ere this have been abolished in Maryland, Virginia, Kentucky, and other States. By their fierce anathemas and their outrageous measures, they have retarded the emancipation of the slaves at least half a century.' In some cases, such talk as this is the product of honest misconception and utter ignorance; in others, of short-sightedness and inattention; but generally of pro-slavery malignity and desperation. What an idiotic absurdity it is to say that earnest, persistent, uncompromising moral opposition to a system of boundless immorality is the way to strengthen it, and that the way to abolish a system is to say nothing about it![35]

The abolitionists did not cause the Civil War, but they played an indispensable part in precipitating the crisis that led to war. By identifying abolition with the cause of free society and dramatizing their fight as a struggle between an open community with a free intellectual market and a closed society afraid of ideas, they showed their generation the terrible discordance between their ideals and their behavior. They raised the Jeffersonian model for re-examination and with it the whole revolutionary tradition. They manufactured the myth of the Slave Power Conspiracy and capitalized on the Southern disposition to act as though it were fact. They protested the closing of the mails, the denial of free speech and the right of assembly in both sections of the country. They turned the United States out of its course and forced it to confront a moral question.

Garrison sensed, however dimly, that a healthy society must tolerate the agitation of unpopular opinion. He believed that there are certain situations in which compromise is undesirable if not impossible. The Civil War was such an instance. The obvious fact that no one wanted a war hardly alters the equally compelling fact that the abolition of slavery required an appeal to force. If such situations do occur — and in his soul Garrison was convinced that they did — then it is a moral failure and unpardonable folly to deny that the organized use of force may become necessary.[36] Garrison denied it as long as he could. He knew that the South had been given its chance to abolish slavery and that most Southerners never had any intention of abolishing it. He also knew that to defend the institution the South had rejected democracy. Had he faced the issues squarely, he should have known, probably by 1854, certainly by 1857, that slavery would have to be abolished by force. Finally, he should also have known that the freedom of the Negro was worth the risk of war because without it American democracy was a sham. In some such recognition lay the ability to meet the crisis when it came with rationality and courage. Garrison not only lacked a tragic sense of history, he failed in honesty to himself.

The tragedy of the Civil War was not that it was "repressible" and "needless," but that it was fought without any clear sense of purpose. For this tragic lack of direction the abolitionists, and chief among them Garrison, must bear a large share of the blame. Garrison's great failing was not the inciting of an unnecessary war but the lack of intelligence to direct it for moral ends.

18

Armageddon at Last

IN 1863, the midstream of the Civil War, Garrison wrote a patriotic poem for his readers depicting the savagery of their enemies.

> Satan seceded, and he fell,
> In chains and darkness doom'd to dwell
> With other traitors who rebel,
>   In act, and word,
> Because he'd rather reign in hell
>   Than serve the Lord
> Who guards us with his flaming sword.[1]

The demonic figure of the Southern rebel and his Northern accomplice, the Copperhead, governed Garrison's imagination through four years of civil war. Sometimes it brooded just over the horizon, a nameless threatening shape. More often it assumed the form of Jefferson Davis or Clement Vallandigham, Fernando Wood or Horatio Seymour. Whether treason stalked the West with the Knights of the Golden Circle or wandered through Washington corridors or drifted over the battlefields of Fredericksburg or rode with Grant through the Wilderness, it was an ever-present specter in Garrison's mind, portentous and fiendish. The Christian anarchist in him yielded to the super-patriot who discovered traitors and treason everywhere. His philosophy of minority rights crumbled before reason of state, liberty capitulated to authority, and Garrison joined the ranks of the demagogues.

He welcomed the war as the only means of freeing the slave. At times during the four years of fighting he seemed to understand what the war meant and what kind of America peace would bring. In the summer of 1862 he was invited to speak at Williams College and explain the abolitionists' relation to the war. He began by pointing out that true democracy had never been practiced in America, that the first American Revolution had not been the glorious struggle for human rights annually invoked by Fourth of July orators but only a colonial rebellion against the mother country. Americans, however, had justified their rebellion with a document that far transcended their immediate aims. "The Declaration of Independence still remains true, in spite of our recreancy to it." Against it the Confederacy opposed a medieval absurdity. Jefferson Davis told his soldiers that they were fighting the tyranny of numbers. What was this but "toryism run to seed," a return not simply to the rule of kings but to the feudalism of the dark ages? There were no "people" in the South, he told the students, nor any democracy in the true sense of the word. There was only a slave oligarchy, a class of depressed poor whites, and the slaves. The first were desperate men, Miltonic fallen angels who would rather rule in hell than serve in heaven. The poor whites were mere tools of the masters, "demoralized, benighted and barbarous." The Negroes offered the only hope for the South, for they were *"the only class at the South to constitute a basis for civilization, by their deep religious nature, by the aptitude to learn, by their aspiration for a higher destiny, and thus, with a large infusion of Northern brains and muscles, to make the unity of the republic a possible and permanent event."*[2]

It was a picture of social revolution engineered by the

North and the Negroes which he painted for his audience, a class upheaval bringing the end of feudalism and the beginnings of industrial democracy, a second American Revolution. Unfortunately this vision quickly faded and in its place there emerged the simpler and sterner motif of Republican rule. If the Civil War failed to achieve the kind of egalitarian justice of which he dreamed, it nonetheless changed his whole world. It disrupted the religious movement he had created and destroyed his philosophy of moral reform. It released a chauvinistic urge formerly confined by pacifist scruples. It shattered his friendship with Wendell Phillips, the one man who might have clarified his idea of racial equality. It altered his view of England and English reformers. Finally, the war replaced his stable New England civilization with the raw society and irresponsible power of the Gilded Age.

The war brought out his latent loyalty to the Union, which he explained as "the paramount duty of the citizen . . . to the government." "Theoretically and practically, its preservation is of paramount importance to that of any local institution under it," he announced, "hence, its right to destroy such institutions, root and branch, is unquestionable, when bloody rebellion is seen to be its all-controlling spirit."[3] Then the war power became competent for all activities of government, but this power was not despotic, he told his readers, because it rested on popular will and functioned as the organ of "THE PEOPLE." To leave the South free to settle the slavery question meant casting off the duties and responsibilities assigned by Providence in delivering the slave out of bondage. As a corrective measure for those of his old disunionists who persisted in citing the Declaration of Independence to justify Southern secession he recommended a thorough reading of the fifty-eighth chapter of Isaiah.

For the converted patriot the first two years of the war

were trying indeed. With increasing disgust he found the
government "blind" and its leaders "stumbling, halting, pre-
varicating, irresolute, weak, besotted."[4] Nor did the rest of
the world, British abolitionists included, seem to understand
the dangers of Southern nationalism. "How can we let them
go in peace," he demanded of George Thompson, "they want
to spread slavery over the whole country."[5] Political abolitionists had been asking the same question of him for twenty-
five years.

Bowing to the demands of war, he subjected anti-slavery
to a searching reappraisal which resulted in a "Restatement
of the Principles, Measures, and Object of the American
Anti-Slavery Society," a three-column editorial in the *Liberator* for October 4, 1861. The abolitionists, his editorial
pointed out, had worked under the original Declaration of
Sentiments for nearly ten years before adopting the motto
NO UNION WITH SLAVEHOLDERS. They had turned to the disunionist slogan only to secure a hearing from the American
people; they never had been and were not now disloyal to
the Union. The federal Constitution protected the rights of
free speech and a free press, and these rights were all that
the Garrisonians had ever claimed. "Distinguished for their
pacific sentiments, they have discountenanced all violence and
disorder, and sought their ends only through a rectified public sentiment, by the power of truth." From Christian anarchy
Garrisonism had been miraculously converted into a respectable theory of constitutional reform!

As soon as the Union Army entered its first summer campaign, he hailed it as God's machine for dispensing retribution. The whole land would be scourged and there would be
desolation and death, weeping and mourning, but then with
the slave freed the land would have rest and the waste places
be restored. Confederate shells at Bull Run exploded this

prediction along with the confidence of the North and left frightened politicians and bewildered generals gasping for an explanation. Garrison quickly exonerated the Northern troops. As soon as war was declared he had predicted that "demoniacal acts" would be perpetrated by the "Southern Sepoys," and now in the aftermath of battle he told of wounded Union soldiers "thrust through and through with bowie-knives and bayonets and otherwise mangled — in some instances their bodies quartered, and in others their heads cut off, and made footballs of by their fiendish enemies."[6] He began to hope for a huge slave rebellion and promised that when it came "as non-resistants, we shall give the slaves our warmest sympathies." At the same time he stepped up his attack on the "treasonable" Democratic Party, accusing it of giving aid and comfort to the rebels.

He boasted that his peace principles were as beneficent and glorious as ever, "neither disproved nor modified by anything now transpiring in the country." If the American people had accepted them long ago, there would have been no slavery and no war. Since war had come, however, he supported it because there was no wrong or injustice on the side of the Union while there was nothing but lynch law and diabolism on the side of the secessionists. In upholding the Union he did not compromise his pacifist beliefs in the least. "On the contrary, we wish all the North were able to adopt those principles, understandingly, heartily, and without delay; but, according to the structure of the human mind, in the whirlwind of the present deadly conflict, this is impracticable."[7]

Lincoln's policies during the first two years of the war gave the abolitionists scant encouragement. His annual message in December, 1861, contained no suggestion that he was seriously considering a general emancipation. "What a wishy-washy message from the President!" Garrison complained. "It is more and more evident that he is a man of a very small calibre, and had better not be at the head of a government like ours, especially in such a crisis."[8] Perhaps Phillips was right after all in denouncing Lincoln as a man without a single generous sentiment. The President was obviously paralyzed by his fear of losing the loyalty of the border states. He was fully equipped by the war power to proclaim an emancipation — what was he waiting for? If the providential opportunity were allowed to pass, there could only come heavier judgments and bloodier results. The time for an emancipation proclamation was right now!

Garrison did not misrepresent the President's attitude toward the Negro: Lincoln hated slavery, but he was not an abolitionist. He declared himself naturally opposed to slavery and believed that if it was not wrong nothing was wrong. At the same time he held that a statesman could not allow his private judgments to determine his policy and that it was particularly inexpedient, as he put it, "to practically indulge . . . abstract judgment on the moral question of slavery."[9] The result was a policy shaped largely by force of circumstances. Though he hated slavery, he did not believe in racial equality. In the summer of 1862 he held a conference at the White House with a group of prominent Negroes hoping to get their approval for his plan of gradual emancipation. In terms reminiscent of Jefferson's *Notes on Virginia* he explained to them how both the black and the white race suffered from close contact and how the Negroes could never hope to attain equality. In the whole country, he said, not a single Negro was considered the equal of the white. No one could change a condition that lay in the nature of things. His solution, to which he clung until his death, consisted of a scheme of gradual manumission coupled with

colonization or, his own ugly word for it, "deportation."
Already he was considering the project of a group of land
speculators for developing the Chiriqui plantation near
Panama with a consignment of free Negroes; and later in the
war he actually contracted with the promoters of a Haitian
plan to relocate freed slaves on the Ile à Vache. After a year
on the island, during which a third of their number died, the
deportees were returned to the United States.

Neither Lincoln nor Congress satisfied Garrison's demands
for a general emancipation policy. A confiscation act of
August 6, 1861, made slaves captured while working for the
enemy forfeit but not free, and a later act made the escaped
slaves of traitors "forever free of their servitude." Congress
also abolished slavery in the District of Columbia, but a
general emancipation proclamation awaited the President's
initiative. The first move came instead from the anti-slavery
generals — Benjamin Butler and David Hunter — who issued
emancipation proclamations of their own. These Lincoln
quickly revoked, and there matters stood until September,
1862.

Garrison naturally applauded Frémont's "wise, beneficent
and masterly procedure" in Missouri and accused Lincoln of
a serious dereliction of duty in failing to extend emancipation
under martial law. He hastened to counter Lincoln's plan
for gradual manumission with the demand for "immediate
and unconditional emancipation." By immediate emancipation he meant, now as he always had, "the recognition and
protection of his [the Negro's] manhood by law — the power
to make contracts, to receive wages, to accumulate property,
to acquire knowledge, to dwell where he chooses, to defend
his wife, children and fireside."[10] Significantly, he ignored the
question of the franchise: in his mind emancipation did not
include the right to vote.

Lincoln's deportation plan revived Northern interest in the old colonization schemes which Garrison had assailed three decades before. One of these renewed projects involved a group of Boston philanthropists and industrialists who were interested in the development of Haiti. They arranged a meeting and timorously asked him to speak; but Garrison, though he admitted that the colonizationists were acting in good faith, attacked their scheme as an escape from the duty of assimilating the Negro into American life. He spoke, instead, to the colored people of Boston urging them to have nothing to do with the plan. It might be that they would suffer from race prejudice for some time to come, he told them, and no doubt the temptation to go where they would not be proscribed was a strong one. Yet the noblest work they could do was stand in their lot and, if need be, suffer. "Before God, I do not see how this nation can be really civilized and Christianized if you go. You are needed to make us Christians, to make us understand what Christianity means."[11] If they stayed the day could not be far off when the last vestige of caste would disappear and blacks and whites would live harmoniously as one people.

Garrison's faith in Lincoln's leadership grew stronger as the military crisis deepened. He instructed abolitionists to stand aside and let Northern patriotism do its work. Skeptical as he was of the President's ideas on emancipation, he felt a new responsibility toward him and cautioned his followers to avoid any harsh criticism of his administration. Never was it so important as now for abolitionists to weigh their words carefully and avoid needless persecution. Instructions went out to subordinates to quit their unpopular agitation. "I have always believed that the Anti-Slavery cause has aroused against it a great deal of uncalled for hostility," he wrote to Oliver Johnson in complete seriousness, "in consequence of extravagance of speech and want of tact and good judgment, on the part of some most desirous to promote its advancement."[12] He had conveniently forgotten his old role of agitator.

He undertook to defend Lincoln against the increasingly sharp attacks of Phillips and the Fosters, who withheld their support until the government freed the slave. Suppose, Garrison asked, that Lincoln were given a chance to answer his critics, would he not say something like this? " 'Gentlemen, I understand this matter quite as well as you do. I do not know that I differ in opinion from you; but will you insure me the support of a united North if I do as you bid me? Are all parties and all sects at the North so convinced and so united on this point that they will stand by the Government? If so, give me the evidence of it, and I will strike the blow.' "[13] The evidence, Garrison noted, was still lacking.

Such doubts did not deter Wendell Phillips and Stephen Foster from denouncing Lincoln unsparingly. At the annual meeting of the Massachusetts Society in the spring of 1862 Garrison fended them off with a resolution declaring the government "wholly in the right," but the question of emancipation remained. When Miller McKim, acting for Garrison, resigned as secretary of the American Anti-Slavery Society later that spring, stating that the abolitionists' work was done, Foster and Pillsbury denied that the work of the society was anywhere near finished and demanded that the government take immediate action. Although Garrison narrowly defeated resolutions holding Lincoln "culpable," he knew that his control over his societies had been seriously weakened. Loss of power mattered less to him now that the war had curtailed almost all anti-slavery activity and Lincoln seemed the abolitionists' only hope.

Yet the President's delay in emancipating the slave stretched

Garrison's forbearance to the limit. In March, 1862, while the *Liberator* prepared to defend Presidential moderation, Lincoln outlined his plan for gradual, compensated emancipation in an overture to the border states. Even Garrison admitted that the plan in effect offered a bounty to states in rebellion and that there was no emergency warranting such an extraordinary proposal. In view of the resolutions before Congress calling for unconditional emancipation Lincoln's plan looked like a decoy. Either the President was empowered to abolish slavery everywhere, he insisted, or the war power was a fiction. Then Lincoln vetoed General Hunter's emancipation proclamation, and a few months later held his fateful conference with the Negro delegation, a "spectacle," Garrison cried, "as humiliating as it was extraordinary."[14] Could anything be more absurd and untimely? Negroes might be banished by Presidential edict but they could never be coaxed into emigrating. The President, Garrison was forced to conclude, was "wholly destitute" of sympathy for the slave.

Then came September and the preliminary Emancipation Proclamation. The pressure generated by Hunter's and Frémont's edicts had gradually increased until Lincoln felt the need to act. Garrison had expected a dramatic gesture, an "Ithuriel spear" that would transform every "pseudo-loyal toad" it touched into a "semi-rebellious devil."[15] Though he admitted that the proclamation marked Lincoln's new freedom from treasonable advisers, he was disappointed in its narrow compass and hesitant language. It postponed emancipation in the rebel states for three months, and though it committed the government to emancipation, it failed to provide a practical program. The document only proved that Lincoln would do nothing directly for the slave but worked "only by circumlocution and delay."[16]

In December, when Lincoln explained his emancipation

program in his annual message, Garrison rejected it as a plan
for buying Southern treason "in lots to suit the purchasers."
Instead of proclaiming the need of prosecuting the war with
renewed vigor and suppressing the South, the President went
into a homily about the evils and disadvantages of disunion,
and treated the war as a matter of dollars and cents. Like
Rip van Winkle, Lincoln had been sleeping for the last thirty
years oblivious to everything going on in the country. His
scheme bordered on lunacy — "it would in our judgment,
warrant the impeachment of the President by Congress as
mentally incapable of holding the sacred trusts committed to
his hands."[17] His blistering editorial, which foreshadowed
his support of the Republican radicals in the days of Reconstruction, marked the point of greatest alienation from the
President. Suddenly Lincoln looked like Phillips's first-rate
second-rate man, a reluctant leader without courage. "A
man so manifestly without moral vision, so unsettled in his
policy, so incompetent to lead, so destitute of hearty abhor-
rence of slavery, cannot be relied on in an emergency."[18]
Then came January 1, 1863, and the final Emancipation
Proclamation.

Garrison was sitting in the balcony of the Music Hall
listening to Beethoven's Fifth Symphony when the message
arrived that Lincoln's proclamation had just come over the
wire. The triumphal music was interrupted while the audience gave nine ringing cheers for Lincoln and three for
Garrison and the abolitionists. From that day Garrison became a "tenacious Unionist" and ardent defender of the
President. The proclamation which he had dismissed as in-
effective he welcomed as a great historic event, and he praised
Lincoln for acting in a "cautious" and "considerate" manner
with due respect for the "obligations and prerogatives of
government." Now the President had only to "finish what

he has so largely performed." "Thirty years ago," he told his Massachusetts Society a few days later, "it was midnight with the anti-slavery cause; now it is the bright noon of day with the sun shining in his meridian splendor."[19]

Thus the year 1863, the midpoint of the war, saw Garrison give his full support to Lincoln and his administration at a time when the President needed all the approval he could get. The Republicans had nearly lost control of Congress in 1862, when five of the states which had elected Lincoln fell to the Democrats. The Emancipation Proclamation and the resurgence of the Democratic Party furnished two good reasons for upholding the President, but even more important was Garrison's growing awareness of the dimensions of political leadership. All his life he had sought the components of the great man — in Timothy Pickering, Harrison Gray Otis, Lyman Beecher, Daniel Webster — only to be disillusioned by his hero's flaws or baffled by his own fear of authority. Now in the midst of civil war he suddenly realized that for all his failings Lincoln was a great leader and a great man. A year that witnessed Burnside's costly blunder at Fredericksburg and Hooker's mistake at Chancellorsville, draft riots in New York, and the rapid growth of Congressional opposition to the President also saw the education of Garrison in the ways of democratic leadership. In view of the continued obstructionist tactics of his followers his decision to stand by Lincoln required intelligence and courage.

The alternative to Lincoln's policy of moderation was the Carthaginian peace advocated by the Radicals in Congress and by Wendell Phillips. The Radicals were determined to secure freedom for the Negro, confiscate the estates of the rebels and distribute them among their former slaves, disfranchise the masters, and rule in the name of Northern righteousness. Phillips took the lead in denouncing Lincoln for his "heartlessness, and infamous pandering to negro-phobia," his "senile lick-spittle haste" in following the directives of disloyal Northerners. "The President and the Cabinet are treasonable," he told a Republican audience in 1862. "The President and the Secretary of War should be impeached." To a Cooper Union crowd he said that the President never professed to be a leader. "He wants to know what you will allow and what you demand that he shall do." Privately he told Sumner, "Lincoln is doing twice as much today to break this Union as Davis is. We are paying thousands of lives and millions of dollars as penalty for having a timid, ignorant President all the more injurious because he is honest."[20] On the other hand, unlike Garrison, Phillips knew what emancipation and the return of peace must bring — food and housing for the Negro, access to the land, education and welfare legislation, and the key to all these, the right to vote. Garrison was hampered by his refusal to consider a social revolution. He opposed giving the Negro the franchise and remained wholly ignorant of the conditions in the South which demanded social legislation. The differences between the two men, which were magnified in the years to come, originated in the clash between a romanticized evangelical Christianity and the skeptical, secular outlook of a professional reformer.

Despite his defense of Lincoln, Garrison did not intend to relinquish all right to criticize the administration. When Lincoln issued his reconstruction plan in December, 1863, he joined Phillips in condemning it. Lincoln hoped to reestablish the state governments in the South with one-tenth of the voters who would take an oath of allegiance to the Union and agree to make temporary arrangements for the apprenticeship of former slaves. Garrison complained of the excessive lenience of the President's plan, which allowed the rebels to vote and disfranchised a whole body of loyal freemen.

"It opens the way for duplicity and perfidy to any extent, and virtually nullifies the confiscation act of Congress, a measure next in importance to the abolition of slavery."[21] As yet he was not prepared to face the possibility of a head-on conflict between the President and Congress over reconstruction; he only knew that Lincoln's magnanimity was a weakness.

At the same time he closed the columns of the *Liberator* to his old pacifist friends. What would peace gain if men who fought for other things would not fight for liberty? "The way to peace, permanent peace, as things are now is manifestly for the conflict to go on, until liberty shall become universal. When we get this liberty, we shall have peace."[22] The pacifists tried to press the peace question on him only to be told that "this is not the best period for an abstract ethical discussion of the question of Non-Resistance."[23]

He still held that private scruples need not prevent the exercise of public duty and that the accommodation of peace principles to the realities of war did not invalidate them. He asked the principal of the Boston Latin School to excuse his son Frank from military drill, but the problem of the draft he met with a piece of rationalization. The true nonresistant, he said, should refuse to serve and also decline to hire a substitute, though he might submit in good conscience to the fine exacted by the government for failure to serve. When his Quaker friends refused to accept this line of reasoning, he avoided further argument and cheerfully suggested that "everyone will do well, *and best*, to be fully persuaded in his own mind."[24]

This was the advice he gave to his oldest son George, who did not share his pacifist beliefs and succumbed to the patriotic fervor of the recruiters. Much to his disappointment George accepted a commission as a second lieutenant in the

Fifty-fourth Massachusetts Regiment, the first Negro outfit in the Union Army. Garrison begged George to reconsider, but when the young man refused, he reluctantly accepted his decision. When George marched down State Street with his regiment on his way to the Carolinas, Garrison stood watching at the corner of Wilson's Lane, where twenty-eight years earlier a mob had dragged him unresistingly toward the Court House.

I miss you by my side at the table, and at the printing-office [he wrote George], and cannot get reconciled to the separation. Yet I have nothing but praise to give you that you have been faithful to your highest convictions, and, taking your life in your hands, are willing to lay it down . . . if need be, in the cause of freedom, and for the suppression of slavery and the rebellion. True, I could have wished you could ascend to what I believe a higher plane of moral heroism and a nobler method of self-sacrifice; but as you are true to yourself, I am glad of your fidelity, and proud of your willingness to run any risk in a cause that is undeniably just and good.[25]

In December, 1863, Helen Garrison suffered a stroke which left her partially paralyzed for the rest of her life. The shock of his wife's illness nearly prostrated Garrison, who now that the children had grown up was more than ever dependent on her. He spent most of his time at home now, nursing Helen, doing small chores about the house, and poring over his list of exchanges. He still attended the conventions and the meetings, but with less and less enthusiasm. He admitted that he was tired — tired of making speeches, tired of the constant friction with younger and more impetuous abolitionists. For the first time in his life he was willing to leave the arguments and the bickering to others. As it happened, they were unwilling to accept his offer of peace.

At the annual meeting of the Massachusetts Society in

1864 Phillips accused the government of a readiness "to sacrifice the interest and honor of the North to secure a sham peace." Garrison bridled. "Now, sir," he said patiently to Phillips, "I do not believe a word of it, and I cannot vote for it." There was a time, perhaps, when he had had little confidence in Lincoln, but since the Emancipation Proclamation he had changed his mind. True, the President was slow in making decisions and needed spurring on, but no one could really believe that he was ready to make a sham peace. "This is a very grave charge."[26] But Phillips had the votes: Garrison's amendment to his resolution was beaten and the society went on record as opposing Lincoln's administration. From that moment Garrison lost interest in the organization he had founded and began to concentrate on re-electing Lincoln.

As early as January, 1864, the *Liberator* was broadcasting its editor's opinion that the re-election of Lincoln would be the wisest and safest course. Lincoln had his faults, but these and "a thousand incidental errors and blunders" might easily be excused in a man who had freed the slaves. Besides, the fewer the differences among loyal Northerners the less chance that the Democrats, who were "essentially, brutally, persistently pro-slavery," would strike hands with the rebels.[27]

He clashed with Phillips a second time at the American Anti-Slavery Society meeting that spring, when Phillips charged Lincoln with refusing to give the vote to the Negro. Garrison had hoped to avoid this question, which he called "a new issue," but Phillips insisted that Negro suffrage was the final goal toward which abolitionists were bound to advance. Once more Garrison's resolutions defending the President were defeated and his explanations rejected. At first, he was surprisingly tolerant of his friend and protégé. He admitted that Phillips was "brilliant and eloquent" and hoped that their disagreement would not alter their friendship, yet the fact that Phillips now controlled all that was left of his anti-slavery movement inevitably brought their friendship to a breaking point. Henceforth Garrison was convinced of his old friend's poor judgment and overriding ambition.

Following their disagreement in New York the two men went their separate ways, Phillips to Cleveland with the wild notion of securing Frémont's nomination, Garrison to Baltimore to attend to the re-election of Lincoln. In rejecting Frémont, Garrison displayed the political acumen worthy of a ward boss. General Frémont, he reminded Phillips, lacked popular support. Even with his strong anti-slavery record, how could he defeat the Copperheads? "If I were speaking on a moral issue, I should speak in a very different manner . . . for the man who stands alone in a moral cause, though all the world be against him if God be for him, stands in a majority, and is conqueror. *But when you come to politics*, that is another sphere. Then you must have votes, then you must have men and money; then you must have political influence and respectability."[28] Civil war had taught him politics as the art of the possible.

From Baltimore he went directly to Washington for a meeting with Lincoln at the White House, where the President received him cordially and invited him to return the next day. Garrison told him of the enthusiastic Republican Convention and of his search for the old Baltimore Jail, which had since been torn down. The President chuckled, remarking that times had certainly changed — once he couldn't get out of jail and now he couldn't get in. Then Lincoln introduced him to his other guests. "I was at once surrounded with a larger group of persons than even himself," he wrote to Helen with pardonable pride.[29] Chase was out of the city, but he found Stanton in his office and after an hour's chat announced himself pleased with the Secretary's "thoroughgoing anti-slavery spirit." Blair and Seward he ignored. His friends Sumner and Wilson invited him to sit with them in the Senate and introduced him to their Radical colleagues, whom he would soon join in defeating executive reconstruction. The Massachusetts Senators even managed to find him a hotel room in the crowded city and were otherwise "exceedingly marked in their attentions." On the following day he had a second meeting with the President, also "a very satisfactory one indeed." "Mr. Lincoln," he began, "I want to tell you that for every word I have ever spoken in your favor, I have spoken ten in favor of General Frémont . . . but, Mr. President, from the hour that you issued the Emancipation Proclamation, and showed your purpose to stand by it, I have given you my hearty support and confidence." Lincoln spoke of his plans for reconstruction — of the oath of allegiance and his promise of executive recognition to those states where one-tenth of the voters took the oath and established governments without slavery. He would need all the support the abolitionists could give him. Garrison promised to do his part. The President's candor won him over completely, and he returned to Boston ready for another campaign in which the *Liberator* would confute error, rebuke wrong, unmask dissimulation, condemn guilt, and see to it that Abraham Lincoln was re-elected.[30]

Phillips soon saw that though he now controlled both the national and state societies, he had no way of making either Johnson's *Anti-Slavery Standard* or the *Liberator* support the cause of John C. Frémont. Both editors continued to hymn Lincoln's praises as before. Phillips remonstrated with Garrison for his unfair tactics. "Of course, an earnest conversation, though a brief one, ensued between us," Garrison reported blandly, "in which I told him he had in every instance compelled a fair and friendly defense of the President by his partisan appeals for Frémont, and his unjust and sweeping accusations." He warned Johnson that Phillips was bent on controlling the *Standard* and that there were "breakers ahead." "I fear P. has made up his mind to leave us; but time must determine. He is evidently in a heated state."[31]

Indeed Phillips was so irate that he sent off instructions to Henry Bowditch, the treasurer of the national society, not to pay a cent more out of the coffers to the *Standard*. Garrison intervened and called a meeting of the Executive Committee. Phillips claimed that he had committed the society to Frémont not once but three times and that the *Standard* ought to conform to its decision. "I fear he may take with him a majority of the Executive Committee," Garrison wrote wistfully, "but whether the majority be on one side or the other, it looks as if we are to be rent asunder, and our organized operations brought to an immediate close."[32] The dissolution of the anti-slavery organization, however, awaited the end of the war.

As a campaign sheet for Lincoln the *Liberator* had few peers. Garrison imperturbably announced that "if to give the weight of our sympathy and influence to Mr. Lincoln's re-election makes us recreant to anti-slavery principles," then he was pro-slavery. He accused Frémont of pursuing a "distracting course" and continually urged him to step aside. He minimized the administration's failings and asked his readers to take a "telescopic" rather than a "microscopic" view of the war, and "instead of dwelling upon and magnifying to huge dimensions those incidental errors and outrages which are inevitable in the midst of such awful civil war, and which are sure to be corrected, fix your gaze upon those sublime and glorious acts of President Lincoln's administration, whereby slavery has received its death warrant, and the haughty Slave Power been laid low in the dust."[33] He singled out the

New York newspapers — the *World, News, Express,* and
Journal of Commerce — as "treasonable journals" worthy of
suppression. In an editorial entitled "Where Lies the Danger,"
on August 19, 1864, he demanded vigorous action against
any citizen suspected of harboring "treasonable designs." "A
timid, half-way policy will not discourage but rather em-
bolden and stimulate sedition. Open-mouthed conspirators,
who possess any influence, should be promptly arrested; and
every traitorous gathering should be summarily dispersed by
the strong arm of military authority. . . . By their own Constitution THE PEOPLE have provided for the exercise of this
summary power in times like these, as a matter of self-preservation; and, unless they have ceased to believe in the right of
expediency of upholding the Constitution, they will stand
by its enforcement to the extremest needs."[34] Not since the
campaign of 1828 had he engaged in such free-wheeling partisan journalism, and not since the Federalist editorial experiments of his youth had the profile of his authoritarian personality seemed so sharp.

In September the Frémont boom collapsed and Sherman's
march to the sea disposed of McClellan and the Chicago
Platform. Frémont withdrew from the race, thus saving himself, Garrison wrote, "from the shame and calamity of a
copperhead triumph." Once Lincoln was safely elected by a
majority of four hundred thousand, Garrison anticipated a
quick end to the war. With the inverse logic of the innocent
he read Lincoln's re-election as a mandate for the Republican
Radicals, as if totally unaware of the power struggle already
being waged in Washington for the control of the government. In fact, his own ideas on reconstruction reflected the
mood of Congress rather than the Presidential temper. He
agreed that there must be no recognition of the rebel states
as legal entities. They were in a state of "misrule, anarchy,

chaos" out of which new constitutional status would be evolved by Congress, which alone had the power to determine their existence. No amnesty of Lincoln's could transform rebellious states into loyal ones. It was for Congress to decide upon the necessary military control, direct the occupation, and determine the time and conditions of re-entry into the Union. "No other course can give repose or security, or make atonement for the horrible excesses of those revolted portions of the country."[35]

While his general views on the treatment of the rebels coincided with those of the Congressional Radicals, his ideas on rehabilitating the Negro were hazy and confused. Like Lincoln, he knew that emancipation would find the slaves where slavery had left them, in need of Northern help; and he saw an immense field in the South for philanthropic and missionary effort. As the various freedmen's organizations emerged in the last year of the war, he hailed them as "trustworthy mediums" of restoration, but of their scope and function, the nature of their aims he knew next to nothing. The end of the war found him with only a general sympathy for the Negroes overshadowed by his towering hatred of their former masters.

On April 8, 1865, the federal steamship *Arago* cleared New York Harbor for Charleston, South Carolina. On board were Garrison and George Thompson along with General Robert Anderson, Henry Wilson, the Henry Ward Beechers, and a boatful of political generals and minor government officials. They were on their way to Fort Sumter to watch General Anderson raise the flag over the fort he had been forced to surrender four years ago. George Garrison had been granted a furlough to join his father, who was anxious for the first glimpse of his son in nearly a year.

The voyage through the calm seas of a warm spring proved

a pleasant diversion from the war. Garrison wrote daily to his invalid wife describing in detail his triumphal visit to the home of rebeldom. The invaders stopped for a short while in once beautiful Savannah, now "a city of mingled gentility and squalor." Charleston Harbor was crowded with masts flying the Union flag. Before the ceremonies he traveled out to Mitchelville, the first self-governing town of freedmen in the South. The inhabitants welcomed him rapturously, packed the local church to hear him talk, and serenaded him with "The Day of Jubilee" as he drove off. To ensure the proper spirit of jubilation at the flag-raising ceremony itself, a Union naval captain had collected over two thousand newly emancipated slaves of all ages and sizes whose joy at being guests of the government was unbounded. The ceremonies went off in stirring fashion: Anderson raised his flag and Beecher's speech was properly pontifical. In the evening a banquet was held at the Charleston Hotel at which Garrison commented solemnly on South Carolina's fall from grace. "She has been brought down from her pride of place. The chalice was put to her lips, and she drank it to the dregs." He said that he had never been the enemy of the South, only a friend who had tried to save her from this "great retribution demanded in the name of the living God." To the victorious Union and loyal Southerners he offered the toast which he called the governing passion of his soul: "Liberty for each, for all, and for ever." Before he retired for the night he visited the office of the *Charleston Courier*, the old antagonist of the *Liberator*, where he picked up the type stick and set a paragraph of Beecher's speech. Before him on the compositor's slab lay tangible proof of his triumph.

The next day he stopped at the tiny cemetery beside St. Philip's Church, where he meditated at the grave of Calhoun and pronounced the death verdict on slavery. "Down to a deeper grave than this slavery has gone, and for it there is no resurrection." Then from graveyard musings to a huge gathering of the freedmen in Zion's Church to listen to endless eulogies and accept bouquets of spring flowers. Just before he rose to speak three little girls approached him and placed in his lap a floral wreath. He explained to the congregation the purpose of his visit to Charleston and his reasons for undertaking the cause of their freedom. "It was not on account of your complexion or race, as a people, that I espoused your cause, but because you were children of a common Father, created in the same divine image, having the same inalienable rights, and as much entitled to liberty as the proudest slaveholder that ever walked the earth." The Union, he promised them, would stand by them to establish their freedom — "the Government has its hold upon the throat of the monster Slavery, and is strangling the life out of it."

Whatever his audience in Zion's Church thought, back in Boston there were those of his colleagues who doubted that the government would give the Negro his rights. The assassination of Lincoln seemed to them to presage a tragic retreat from the ideals of the war, and they determined to wrest full control of the old American Anti-Slavery Society before Garrison disbanded it and to continue the fight to secure for the Negro the vote. They were waiting for him when he returned from Charleston.

The dispute at the annual meeting of the American Anti-Slavery Society inevitably turned on the issue of Negro suffrage. Garrison knew that he lacked the votes to dissolve the society, but with a flash of the old combative spirit he threw down the gauntlet by moving to disband. "The point is here," he explained. "We organized expressly for the abolition of slavery; we called our Society an *Anti-Slavery* Society. The other work (Negro suffrage) was incidental. Now, I

believe, slavery is abolished in this country, abolished constitutionally, abolished by a decree of this nation, never, never
to be reversed, and, therefore, that it is ludicrous for us, a
mere handful of people with little means, with no agents in
the field, no longer separate, and swallowed up in the great
ocean of popular feeling against slavery, to assume that we
are of special importance, and that we ought not to dissolve
it."[36] Since the government would necessarily guarantee the
freedmen their civil liberties by force of arms, the abolitionists were now superfluous.

Phillips proceeded to demolish Garrison's argument. The
Thirteenth Amendment had not yet been ratified, he pointed
out, and the South remained unconverted. "You cannot kill
off all the white men who cherish a hatred toward democratic
institutions. You can only flank them, as Grant flanked Lee —
flank them by democratic elements — Yankee commerce,
black suffrage, divided lands." Slavery was stunned perhaps,
but not dead. "Prejudice is rife. All over the country, the
colored man is a Pariah."

PHILLIPS: Now, friends, my abolitionism, when I pledged my
faith to that Declaration of Sentiments and Constitution of the
American Anti-Slavery Society, was, 'Absolute equality before
the law; absolute civil equality,' and I never shall leave the
Negro until, so far as God gives me the power to do so, I
achieve it.

GARRISON: — Who proposes to do so? . . . I think I am competent
to interpret the language of the Declaration of Sentiments [of
1833] if any man living be. I was the author of it; and unless
I have grown demented, I ought to know what I meant, and
what this Society meant in using that language. This Society
is 'The American *Anti-Slavery* Society.' That was the object.
The thought never entered my mind then, nor has it at any
time since, that when slavery had received its death wound,

there would be any disposition or occasion to continue the Anti-Slavery Society a moment longer . . .

PHILLIPS: — I do not know what Mr. Garrison meant when he wrote the Declaration of Sentiments, and the Constitution of the American Anti-Slavery Society —

GARRISON: — I do.

PHILLIPS: — Of course he does, and his construction is sufficient for his guidance, but not for mine or yours.

When Pillsbury and Foster entered the fray, personal animosities flared. Foster regretted that the "old" and "tired" members felt disposed to quit. Garrison accused Phillips of making "unjust and unfounded allegations." George Thompson used the old Garrisonian trick of citing earlier remarks of Phillips and appealed "from Phillips drunk to Phillips sober." Garrison recalled that in 1861 Phillips said that slavery had been dealt its deathblow. "Can I not grow wiser?" Phillips asked.

Garrison's views on the question of Negro suffrage had grown steadily more conservative. Personal freedom was one thing, he now felt, the vote another. He granted that in the course of their fight the abolitionists had often turned aside to agitate for enfranchisement of free Negroes in various parts of the North, but he emphatically denied that the ballot was ever an essential part of their program. "In enumerating the grievances under which the slaves of the South have been crushed so long, no abolitionist has ever alluded to their exclusion from the ballot-box as in that category." Then what was the sense of freeing the slave? Phillips wanted to know. Garrison's editorial reply summarized his interpretation of the history of the anti-slavery crusade and, in a larger sense, his whole conservative philosophy. "Of course, there was no dif-

ference of opinion as to the fact, that, inasmuch as slavery
was the extinction of every natural right, so its abolition
would open the way for *ultimate* social, civil and political
equality; but this through industrial and educational development and not by any arbitrary mandate." Simply because
ignorant white men were allowed to vote there was no reason
to enfranchise millions of ignorant blacks. When in history
had emancipation ever been accompanied by a recognition of
political equality?

Chattels personal may be instantly translated from the auction-
block into freemen; but when were they ever taken at the same
time to the ballot-box, and invested with all political rights and
immunities? According to the laws of development and progress,
it is not practicable. . . . Nor, if the freed blacks were admitted
to the polls by Presidential fiat, do I see any permanent advantage
likely to be secured by it; for submitted to as a necessity at the
outset, as soon as the State was organized and left to manage its
own affairs, the white population with their superior intelligence,
wealth, and power, would unquestionably alter the franchise in
accordance with their prejudices, and exclude those thus summarily brought to the polls. Coercion would gain nothing. In
other words . . . universal suffrage will be hard to win and to
hold without a general preparation of feeling and sentiment. But
it will come . . . yet only by a struggle *on the part of the disfranchised,* and a growing conviction of its justice 'in the good
time coming.' With the abolition of slavery in the South prejudice or 'colorphobia,' the natural product of the system, will
naturally disappear.[37]

Here was the conservative message he had spent his whole
life preaching — slavery was a moral rather than a political
issue, immediate emancipation meant gradual rehabilitation,
not social revolution.

He was willing to put his belief in moral reform to the

test by moving the dissolution of the society and watched sadly as one by one the members voted against him.[38] Once again as it had for twenty-two years, the Nominating Committee reported his name for re-election as President. Gravely he declined. Phillips was elected in his place and submitted a tribute to the retiring president in the form of a resolution which was adopted with a rising vote. In his farewell speech he accepted Phillips's eulogy gracefully and mocked the funereal mood of the members, calling on them to celebrate the day of jubilee, the resurrection from the dead.

Slavery is in its grave, and there is no power in this nation that can ever bring it back. I thank you, beloved friends, who have for so many years done me the honor to make me the President of the American Anti-Slavery Society. I never should have accepted that post if it had been a popular one. I took it because it was unpopular; because we, as a body, were everywhere denounced, proscribed, outlawed. To-day, it is popular to be President of the American Anti-Slavery Society. Hence my connection with it terminates here and now, both as a member and as its presiding officer. I bid you an affectionate adieu.

If it was popular to be an abolitionist in the spring of 1865, it was especially satisfying to be the retired leader of a vindicated and now glorious cause. In stepping down Garrison simply abandoned the dusty forum of the abolitionists for the legislative halls of the Republican Party. The tragedy was that to the citizens of the North who were finally ready to listen to an anti-slavery hero he had nothing to say.

19

Reconstruction and Redemption

NEAR MIDNIGHT on December 29, 1865, Garrison sat at his office desk hurriedly composing his "Valedictory" and handing each paragraph as he finished it to the printers who waited at his elbow. This was the way he had worked for thirty-five years, dashing off editorials at the last minute and inserting them just before the paper went to press. Now he was putting the *Liberator* to bed for the last time. Having finished, he laid down his pen, walked to the composing bench, set the final paragraph himself and locked it in. Then, saying goodnight to the printers, he went home to Helen.

For a valedictory his editorial was neither sentimental nor self-righteous. He sounded no trumpets, he said, made no parades. "The object for which the *Liberator* was commenced — the extermination of chattel slavery — having been gloriously consummated, it seems to me especially appropriate to let its existence cover the historical period of the great struggle; leaving what remains to be done to complete the work of emancipation to other instrumentalities (of which I hope to avail myself), under new auspices, with more abundant means, and with millions instead of hundreds."[1]

Leaving the freedmen to millions, however, meant abandoning them to a Northern majority who had no clear sense of purpose. So Phillips argued when he refused to disband the

American Anti-Slavery Society or close down the *Standard*. Edmund Quincy, Henry Wright and Samuel May, Jr., retired from the society with Garrison. The new Executive Committee refused to vote a resolution of thanks to the retiring editors of the *Standard*, Johnson and Quincy; and when it finally made a reluctant acknowledgment of their services, they refused to accept it. Hostility between Phillips and Garrison continued to mount. Garrison accused Phillips of ingratitude, Quincy openly snubbed him, and the old cordiality of the clique died. "We don't see any of them," Ann Phillips said of the Garrison family now, "for they feel very unkindly towards us."[2] Phillips admitted sadly that half the men he had worked with for thirty years would not speak to him on the street.

Garrison was irked by Phillips's reminder that the work of rehabilitating the Negro had just begun and bridled at his "unjust imputations upon his old associates." As for the remnants of the society he himself had founded, "of course, as the whole thing is a farce, I care nothing for it."[3] He wrote a long and virtriolic letter to the *Independent*, the religious weekly edited by Theodore Tilton in New York, denouncing Phillips as an opportunist who sought to make political capital out of the black man. Undoubtedly Phillips would take the letter as a "mortal affront," he told Johnson. "But I can stand anything but an imputation upon my fidelity to the colored race; and I know not why he should be allowed to hold us all up to view as hauling down our flag, and beating a hasty retreat, without being strongly rebuked for it."[4] Diehard supporters of Phillips declared that for the last two years they had thrown the *Liberator* away in disgust. What more proof, he asked Helen, was needed of the evil influence wrought by Phillips? Thus Garrisonism died as it had been born, in the midst of recrimination and rancor.

In 1864 Garrison had moved his family from Dix Place to a rambling frame house in Roxbury. Set high above the road on ledges and surrounded by an orchard, his new home was only a half-hour from the city but secluded enough to be a little lonely now that the children had grown up and left home. After a Harvard education financed by Phillips, his son Wendell married Miller McKim's daughter Lucy and joined E. L. Godkin on the *Nation*. Fanny found her match in the aggressive Henry Villard and set out to help him carve his fortune out of American railroads. The older boys, William and George, had gone into business after the war. Young Frank, whose adolescent aimlessness disturbed his father, drifted between the Villard home and Roxbury. Helen, though confined to the house, was as cheerful and uncomplaining as ever, but without his family the big, high-ceilinged rooms seemed strangely empty. "Harry will forgive me if, occasionally, I involuntarily sigh to think that you have been taken away from our household," he wrote to Fanny, "of which you were its light and joy; yet to wish it otherwise were selfish indeed."[5] Most of his time now he spent in his study rummaging through old newspapers and clipping articles for his anti-slavery history.

His Republican prejudices were strengthened by a visit to Washington in February, 1866, where he saw Sumner and Wilson again and discussed Andrew Johnson's faults with Ben Wade and Thad Stevens. He attended the debates over the President's veto of the Freedmen's Bill and interviewed General Oliver O. Howard, who asked his help in establishing the Freedmen's Bureau. All of his acquaintances ridiculed Johnson and spoke of the need for new congressional leadership to counter his despotic policies. Garrison gave two addresses in Washington, both to small audiences, in which he added his own warnings of executive tyranny. On his way home he stopped with Theodore Tilton in Brooklyn, where he lectured at the Academy of Music. At the end of his speech he used some of the new information gleaned from the Radicals to inform his audience of an impending revolution which Johnson was plotting with the aid of the Democratic Party. "What I said was quite impromptu," he wrote to Fanny, "but I am more and more convinced that Pres. Johnson will attempt a *coup d'état* against Congress by the time summer is upon us. He will do it 'constitutionally' and 'to preserve the Union' and put down Northern 'conspirators.' The elements of violence are gathering for the onslaught. Tell Harry his 15,000 loyal men in Washington will be needed."[6] Home once more in Roxbury, he decided to uphold the Republicans in their fight against executive usurpation.

He missed the editorial routine and was often at a loss to fill the time. "I am, as yet, uncertain what to do," he confided to Henry Wright. "But I must try to find some employment soon, as my candle is burning at both ends."[7] He told Wendell that the "price of family living," which was "enormous," would soon force him to seek steady employment. For this and other reasons he began to consider writing a multivolume history of anti-slavery. His family and friends urged him to begin work right away, and Ticknor & Fields promised to underwrite it. Fanny, who knew how much her father missed the *Liberator*, suggested that he sign a contract immediately. "Be merciful!" he begged. "It is a matter requiring the gravest deliberation before I actually commit myself one way or another."[8] Vague doubts held him back, something told him he was not "competent" to write either an autobiography or a history of abolition. It was much easier to accept Oliver Johnson's invitation to write occasional articles for the *Independent*. Free-lance journalism, he concluded, suited his talents better than excavating in dusty anti-slavery archives.

His financial worries were relieved by news of a plan to raise fifty thousand dollars for him as a national testimonial. At first he doubted whether it would succeed, remembering that similar testimonials for George Thompson and John Brown's widow had proven "slumps." "I have seen so many similar attempts end in miserable failures, that I shall not be disappointed if this shall meet with the same fate. . . . But whether it shall succeed or not, I shall none the less be grateful to those who have set it on foot. Of course, it is for us as a family to say little or nothing about it to others at present."9 Yet he could not help inspecting the project periodically and watching closely as the figures climbed toward the thirty-thousand mark. He even suggested to the committee names of possible contributors who had not yet been approached. In March, 1868, the committee presented him with a check for thirty-one thousand dollars and a ringing testimonial to "the leader and inspirer of the movement against American slavery." Their tribute he acknowledged with gratitude if not in strictest truth. "Of this testimonial I may be permitted to say, that none was ever more unsought or more unexpected; none more spontaneous or more honorable was ever proffered."10

In the spring of 1866 he sprained his arm badly, and the electrical treatments in which he had so much faith improved it no more than they had his wife's paralysis. He used his disability as an excuse for postponing the history. Frank and Wendell kept sending documents and clippings with the repeated suggestion that he begin compiling a collection of anti-slavery source materials. "I am obliged to Wendell for his suggestions about 'extracts,' etc.," he wrote to Frank, "but to be of any value as a book of references he must remember that something more than my *ipse dixit* will be necessary in the way of impeaching and arraigning Church and State. But it will be a difficult thing to decide how much or how little of evidence to present to sustain the needed allegations."[11] He was occupied with these perplexing thoughts when the Radical attack on President Johnson called him to his post.

From the outset the Republican Radicals were bent on dismantling the executive machinery under the guise of saving the country from tyranny. Since Lee's surrender events in the South appeared to give credence to their fear of reaction. Far from granting civil rights even to a minority of the qualified Negroes, the Southern states erected Black Codes designed to keep the freedmen in a state hardly distinguishable from slavery. By December, 1865, every former Confederate state had complied with the Lincoln-Johnson plan for readmission; they had drafted new constitutions and elected state legislatures, repudiated the Confederate debt, and ratified the Thirteenth Amendment. In his annual message to Congress Johnson announced that the Union had been restored. Senators and Representatives from the South arrived in Washington to await congressional approval of their credentials.

It suddenly seemed to Garrison and the Radicals that their war had been fought for nothing, that Johnson working with their enemies had nearly achieved a restoration of the old order. Quickly they set their machinery in motion. The Joint Committee of Fifteen replied to Johnson's message by declaring that the rebel states had committed suicide and therefore fell under the complete jurisdiction of Congress, which would prescribe the terms for their readmission. Then began a struggle for control which ended fifteen months later with the Tenure of Office Act, an attempt to alter

permanently the balance of power within the federal government in favor of Congress.

Garrison's assault on Johnson gathered momentum in the
spring of 1866. The North had won the war; he would not
let it lose the peace. On the first anniversary of his trip to
Charleston he confided his fears to Wendell. "How sad and
shocking was the assassination of President Lincoln! And how
sad and shocking to have such a perfidious successor as President Johnson! Who can tell what another year will bring
forth?"[12] Unable to attend the first meeting of the Sumter
Club, he sent a proclamation of his new alliance with the
Radicals.

Andrew Johnson might have placed his name high on the roll of
the illustrious and world-renowned benefactors of the human
race; but, by his evil and treacherous course, his usurping and
despotic policy in the interests of those who are still rebels in
spirit and purpose, his perfidy as their *soi-disant* "Moses" toward
the liberated bondmen of the South, he seems bent upon sending
his name down to posterity along with those of Benedict Arnold
and Judas Iscariot. . . . Allow me, therefore, to offer you the
following cold-water sentiment: *The speedy impeachment and
removal of Andrew Johnson from the office he dishonors and
betrays.*[13]

In April, Congress passed the first Civil Rights Act. Johnson vetoed it, and it was re-passed over his veto. In June, the
Joint Committee presented Congress with the Fourteenth
Amendment. During the spring and summer there were race
riots in New Orleans, Memphis and Norfolk, which fed
Garrison's fear of a Southern counterrevolution directed by
Johnson, "the guiltiest man in the nation."[14] He was afraid
too that the President's Swing around the Circle, that "dis-
graceful tour" of "a blackguard," might detach Northern

loyalties from the congressional plan of reconstruction. By October it was clear that the South had no intention of ratifying the Fourteenth Amendment. He was puzzled by the fact that Phillips and Sumner also opposed the amendment because it did not give the Negro the vote. He could not understand such reasoning. "I mean to be careful not to find myself in agreement with the South in regard to any measure relating to her despised and injured freedmen. At least, hitherto, I have always found reason to approve what she specially detests, and vice versa, and I still think it a very safe rule."[15] He was not alone in refusing to recognize the importance of the Negro ballot for Republican rule: with the exception of Phillips few politicians in the North in 1866 saw its significance. It took the election of Grant to teach Republicans the usefulness of a quarter of a million black votes.

As the Radicals prepared to impeach Johnson, Garrison's calculations matched those of the congressional leaders. "Without the President is impeached," he wrote to Frank, "I do not see how any plan of reconstruction by Congress can be made available."[16] In January, 1867, he compiled a long article on impeachment for the *Independent*. When a people are prevented from calling their leader to account by their veneration for his office, he wrote, it is a sure sign of democratic degradation. Why did Northerners shrink from impeachment? Why wait until Johnson multiplied his wicked designs? Congress, aware of the dangers of executive tyranny, was ready to act. "Happily, that body, as now constituted, is eminently loyal and patriotic, and represents no political party in the old sense of party — only the PEOPLE, lifted above selfish consideration, and intent on saving the Republic from disruption." In attempting to be fair and just to the President, Congress had already carried magnanimity to questionable limits. As for Johnson, "there he sits, grasping unconstitutional power, bidding defiance to the popular will, recreant to his oath of office, determined to rule or ruin, contemptuous and hostile toward Congress, applauded and upheld by all that is treasonable in the land, detested and feared by all that is loyal, and with vast powers to carry out his desperate purposes." Two more years and who could predict the violence and blood he would bring on the land?[17]

Behind the President, Garrison saw demon Democracy breathing fire and brandishing the slave whip, a party of barbarism and brutality at war with God and nature, with Christ and freedom. "It is a party to be as much denounced as any combination of conspirators against God and the right that was ever organized on earth."[18] This year of impeachment might have been 1828 and his words those of the young Federalist editor of the *Journal of the Times*. Forty years had not changed his fear of power.

Before he died Lincoln had nearly fulfilled Garrison's unformulated ideal of the great man. His candor and tact, his uncanny political sense combined with a humanity and power for growth made him, both for Garrison and the people of the North, a national father, righteous, compassionate, friendly, wise and strong. Though he struggled against the magnetic force of Lincoln's personality, Garrison ended by succumbing to it. Lincoln's death removed the one hero in his life and replaced him with a lesser man who invited the kind of criticism at which he excelled. Andrew Johnson released the destructive energy in him that Lincoln had been able to channel. Even before Lincoln's assassination Garrison was shifting his allegiance to the side of the Radicals, but he never understood the confused motives of the congressional leaders, either the honest fanaticism of Stevens and Wade or the political designs of George Julian or Henry Wilson. He only sensed that their attack on Johnson stemmed from an urge to tear down the executive power, and he joined in attempting to demolish the office of President for the same reason he had fought authority all his life. The Radicals discovered his fear of power and used it for their own ends. Without Lincoln's guidance, and left to make his own way through the maze of Reconstruction politics, Garrison wandered aimlessly, willing to dynamite Johnson's road to reunion but unable to cut his own path to social equality. After twisting and turning, his devious route brought him to the great barbecue of the Gilded Age.

In May, 1867, he sailed for Europe to join Fanny and Harry at the International Exposition in Paris. They returned to London in June for a public breakfast given in his honor by Bright, Buxton, Lord Houghton, John Stuart Mill, Earl Russell, Herbert Spencer, Thomas Huxley and three hundred men of affairs who united in paying honor to the "great Champion" of American freedom. Then back to Paris for the International Anti-Slavery Conference and two days of speeches in a language he could not understand. Paris fairly overwhelmed him, "the central point of the world for all that is splendid, fashionable, sensual, and frivolous." Like Henry James's Americans, he approached the "spectacle" of Paris with caution. "It is 'Vanity Fair,' on a colossal scale," he reported to Helen, "as described by Bunyan in 'Pilgrims' Progress,' and full of temptations and allurements to those who think only of present enjoyments, and forget all that relates to the immortal life."[19] Even he found it difficult to be spiritually minded in Elysium.

From Paris he set out on a tour of Switzerland and Germany, an American innocent's excursion with no causes or conventions to interfere with the pleasure of sight-seeing. He stopped at Interlaken and Lucerne, "charming places both";

Zurich, "delightfully situated"; and Constance, "a remarkably quaint old town." At the gambling casinos outside of Hamburg he watched the fashionable players hovering around the tables "spell-bound and greedy of gain. . . . It was to me an astounding spectacle, and most instructive and admonitory to watch the changing countenances of the players. It is among the most terrible of all human passions." In Heidelberg he roamed through old castles and along the battlements, but confessed to his wife that he much preferred Frankfurt, "the best we have yet seen, and the most American."[20]

In London he went to hear Gladstone and Bright debate the Electoral Reform Bill of 1867 and lunched with John Stuart Mill. There were visits to Birmingham, Sheffield, and Leeds, where he was welcomed enthusiastically. "I am repeatedly told . . . that I do not appear to have grown a day older. . . . But it is my baldness, however, that looks as young as it did twenty-one years ago; 'only this, and nothing more.' " Newspapers in London, Edinburgh, Glasgow and Birmingham carried accounts of his anti-slavery exploits, and everywhere he went there were eager crowds and public entertainment. "If I had not long ago crucified myself to the opinions of men, I might be in peril of slumbering on enchanted ground for the rest of my life."[21] November saw him back in Boston.

The nomination of Grant, a military leader with a supposed weakness for alcohol, hardly won Garrison's enthusiastic support, but the thought of Horatio Seymour at the head of a resurgent Democratic Party was enough to drive him into the general's camp. He tried to look beyond the candidates to the parties and human rights, the Republicans pledged to protect these rights, the Democrats determined to kill them. In the old days before the war it had been a question of banks, tariff, or free trade, but now Christianity itself was at stake and the witnesses for God had to speak out.

RECONSTRUCTION AND REDEMPTION

Four years of corruption altered this view not at all. When Sumner indicted Grant for condoning financial scandals and protecting his friends, Garrison dismissed his charges as enormously exaggerated, the kind of rumor that could only give comfort to rebels and Copperheads. Nor did he consider Grant's nomination for a second term a poor choice. "On the contrary," he told Wendell, "I deem it immensely important to the welfare and repose of the country, in view of the impending crisis. As for Greeley and his Tribune, there is no language to describe their folly and baseness."[22] This time he did not hesitate to come out strongly for Grant. He warned Sumner that he must not be surprised "if a general belief obtains that you have unfairly availed yourself of opportunities to work division in the Republican ranks." He promised to speak to the Negroes "with equal plainness" and urge them "by every consideration of their safety and happiness" to re-elect Grant.[23]

As the financial scandals of Grant's second term mounted, he flatly refused to believe the Republicans guilty of logrolling or dishonesty. When the Belknap scandal broke, he announced that "a score of Belknaps will not make me believe that the Republican party means to connive at official corruption."[24] The Republican Party was God's means of punishing the South. He gave Hayes his support in 1876 and never doubted that he had been honestly elected. Of the politics of Redemption he knew no more than he had about Jackson's war on the bank or Polk's Manifest Destiny.

If he failed to understand postwar politics, he also took a narrow and astigmatic view of the Negro problem. The key to a general rehabilitation of the South he found in reeducation "from primary school to college." To lift the South from moral degradation was the sublime mission of the North. "Cursed by her old slave system beyond all that imagination can depict or language express, she is both morally and intellectually incapable of self-recovery, and needs help in every way and of every kind."[25] Yet when Lee was made President of Washington College, Garrison objected strenuously to this kind of self-help. Was Lee converted by General Grant at the time of his surrender, he asked? Was Saul among the prophets?

Out of the welter of confused opinions and misunderstandings there stood the irrefutable fact of his racial tolerance. In supporting the Civil Rights Act he protested against the omission of the clause ensuring integration of the public schools.

The common schools [he wrote in his finest editorial statement after the war] must be open to all and for all, whether white or black, whether native or foreign. Those who, for any reason, do not choose to avail themselves of its benefits, may consult their own choice or prejudice, as the case may be; but they must not make it subservient to their exclusiveness. To gratify them in this respect would be to lay the axe at the root of our free institutions and to engender animosities that no community can afford to tolerate.[26]

The words have a clarity and force which he seldom achieved and a logic hardly improved by the judicial opinions of another age.

He pursued his various reform interests until the end of his life. In 1871 he voted for the first time since 1834, against the granting of liquor licenses. Phillips's Prohibition Party, however, held no appeal for him; he saw no use in "a third wheel to the Mill" when there was scarcely enough moral power to turn the wheels of the two major parties. Nor did he agree with Phillips that labor was the problem of the hour. He scoffed at the notion of the toiling masses exploited by irresponsible capitalists. "What have they to complain of in regard to constitution and laws for which they are not directly responsible? . . . Is not the government of them, by them, and for them (ostracized womanhood excepted), to be moulded as they shall judge best? Or, if in any case it is not for them, upon whom rests the responsibility but themselves? . . . Our danger lies in sensual indulgence, in a licentious perversion of liberty, in the prevalence of intemperance, and in whatever tends to the demoralization of the people."[27] No reform issue was strong enough to draw his support away from the Republican Party.

The woman's rights movement divided in 1869 when Susan B. Anthony and Elizabeth Cady Stanton, having failed to secure the vote in Kansas by constitutional amendment, decided to enter politics and chose the mountebank George Francis Train as their candidate for President. Train's antics and unsavory reputation drove the more moderate feminists, led by Julia Ward Howe and Lucy Stone, to form the non-political American Woman Suffrage Association under the aegis of Henry Ward Beecher. Garrison accepted a vice-presidency in the new society and helped launch the *Woman's Journal*. He also served as president of the Massachusetts Woman's Suffrage Association, attended its conventions, and gave lectures throughout New England on the need to "restore to woman that share of power . . . which has been wrested from her." With him it was still a question of male tyranny. Who gave men the authority to deny women the vote? By what right did they withhold it? Against the unreasoning power of the male sex women would inevitably triumph. "No matter how many stubborn or stupid men may resist, no matter how many weak-minded or timorous women say nay, it will nevertheless be triumphant, adding new lustre to the nineteenth century."[28]

A lingering interest in free trade led him to accept an office in the American Free Trade League and to help organize the Revenue League of Boston. He readily admitted that he was only "a novice" at the "details and statistics" of business, but hastened to add that the mysteries of government and finance were only the clever contrivances of "usurpers and demagogues." "There is nothing intricate in freedom, free labor, free institutions, the law of interchange, the measure of reciprocity."[29] It was simply class interest and human greed that confused the general welfare with selfish gain. In his mind the rules of political economy and the precepts of Christian charity were still identical.

This same Christian universalism sustained his last crusade — against the Chinese Exclusion Bill, in which he found "essentially the old anti-slavery issue in another form." In a letter to the *New York Tribune* written just before his death he explained for the last time the simple faith in racial equality and toleration that had been the central theme in his long career. "The Chinese are our fellow-men, and are entitled to every consideration that our common humanity may justly claim. . . . Such of them as are seeking to better their condition, being among the poorer classes, by coming to these shores, we should receive with hospitality and kindness. . . . It is for them to determine what they shall eat, what they shall drink, and wherewithal they shall be clothed; to adhere to their own customs and follow their own tastes as they shall choose; to make their contracts and maintain their own rights; to worship God according to the dictates of their own consciences, or their idea of religious duty. . . . This is not a personal controversy . . . but a plea for human brotherhood as against all caste assumptions and clannish distinctions."[30] The letter was a fitting epilogue to the anti-slavery drama.

In 1876 Helen died. Desolate and ill, Garrison was unable

to attend the funeral services conducted by Phillips, whose gesture of reconciliation touched him deeply. His own health was failing, and his friends, hoping that a sea voyage might improve it, suggested travel. Accompanied by Frank, he spent the summer of 1877 in England but came home saddened by a last visit with George Thompson and the prospects of a lonely life in Roxbury. He attended séances regularly now, communing with the spirits of his wife and his old colleagues, whose messages he faithfully recorded for his children. His greatest pleasure came when Fanny brought her children to visit or he spent the holidays with them in New York.[31] Fanny took him to see Edwin Booth in *Richelieu* and Modjeska as Adrienne. A performance of *Mignon* only convinced him of the decline of American musical taste. He much preferred the songs and hymns which his grandchildren sang. At home he busied himself with his still voluminous correspondence and projects for aiding the Negroes against the Southern Redeemers. In 1878 he made a last trip to Newburyport to visit the office of the *Herald*, where he set three sonnets with a dexterity that amazed the young apprentices who gathered around to watch. He still enjoyed the beauty of clean copy.

He was busy raising money to relocate Negroes in Kansas when he fell ill in April, 1879. Fanny found him wasted and despondent when she came to take him home with her to Union Square in New York. There it was evident that he would not recover, and his family gathered at his bedside. In the evenings they would stand outside his door singing the old hymns he had taught them while he beat time feebly with his hand. On the night of May 22 the doctor, noticing a wave of his hand as if in dismissal, asked him what he wanted. "To finish it up!" he whispered. On the next day he fell into a coma and twenty-four hours later he died.

Epilogue

WHEN GARRISON DIED in 1879, Reconstruction had already ended with Northern assent to the subordination of the Southern Negro. Slavery was dead, but racial inequality and the belief in the inferiority of the black man lived on. The Civil War had proved a limited victory that preserved the Union but intensified race conflict, freed the slaves but returned them to the management of their former masters. Beset by the new doubts of a Darwinian age, the postwar generation began to reassess the idea of human perfectibility and the message of liberation it had taught. Gradually the simple, buoyant faith in the perfectibility of man was giving way to a more sophisticated theory of evolution. Yet it was this belief in natural moral goodness — perfectionism — which had formed the credo of ante-bellum America, provided the driving force of the anti-slavery movement, and sustained the pitch of Garrison's reform. It had also caused a war.

All Americans before the Civil War shared in the perfectionist dream in some way, for perfectionism promised the country a perpetually renewable innocence and vigor. Perfectionism meant freedom — freedom from sin and guilt, freedom from the past and the burdens of history, freedom from institutions and power. What had Europe with its decadence and corruption to teach a young America? Left alone to flourish, the New World would produce a new race of men strong in their natural goodness and their commitment to total freedom. Perfectionism verified the American belief in the second chance.

The signs of this perfectionist faith were everywhere in ante-bellum America: in the physical fact of the frontier; in the Jacksonian bias against institutions and corporate power; in the pervasive sense of the civilizing mission of Americans; in the concept of nature as a regenerative experience; in the legends and folklore of the people. There were two principal sources of American perfectionism: the Enlightenment tradition of the American Revolution and the pietism of evangelical religion, the first a secular belief in progress transplanted from Europe, the second a millennial expectation at the heart of American revivalism. Combined, these two powerful ideals of infinite progress and the equality of souls made an explosive compound of moral idealism. It was this idealism which the abolitionists discovered they shared with the people and which gave their argument its peculiarly effective appeal.

The anti-slavery movement itself sprang from a religious impulse and advanced with the Second Great Awakening; that is, it originated in a religious revival and remained primarily a religious crusade. Since it was chiefly Christian in its emphasis, it was subject to the two great polar forces in Christian thought – the pull of pietism and the stress of social ethics. Pietism emphasizes the devotional ideal of religion, the desire for salvation and the achievement of holiness. Christian ethics, on the contrary, postulates a community and the good life to be lived within it. Pietism tends to be sectarian, mystical, perfectionist. It concentrates on the regenerative relation between God and the individual, on the inner experience of divine power. Thus it tends to be anti-institutional and ascetic. By stressing the role of the individual conscience and making obedience to it the highest form of duty, it gives the true believer a new freedom from the rules and regulations of the world; but in stressing the idea of purity it is apt to be rigoristic and exclusive. The idea of a social ethic is in many ways its exact opposite — adaptable, humanistic, inclusive, an ideal of Christian life that takes account of organization and power.

Both of these forces were at work within the anti-slavery movement from the beginning. The abolitionists knew very little about the institution of slavery. They approached the problem from the direction of regenerative experience through the avenue of conversion. Their strong Protestant individualism led them to treat slavery not simply as an inefficient labor system but as a betrayal of Christian values. They believed that slavery was inhuman because it denied God to the black man. They viewed slavery as a moral problem. It was not long, however, before some of them discovered the institutional complexities of the slavery problem. There were those like Garrison and his followers who persistently ignored these questions, but there were also those abolitionists like Birney, Stanton, and Leavitt who recognized the need for organization and policy. As the anti-slavery enterprise grew it was exposed to the same tension between piety and ethics as its parent Christianity.

The original American Anti-Slavery Society was both a sect and a church, a closed society of faithful saints and a wider community embracing all the people. Garrison's Declaration of Sentiments exemplified the underlying ambiguity of the anti-slavery program: it promised political action but enjoined moral reform; it demanded immediate emancipation but failed to define it; it preached pacifism but appealed to passion. Within a decade these twin forces had produced divergent strains of anti-slavery, one based on political action, the other on moral preaching. Both groups of abolitionists claimed that their program was the only true one, and each accused the other of abandoning the slave. Both were wrong. In reality, each group embodied an aspect of the abolitionist temperament and the religious mind, and each in its own way illustrated the problems of religious idealism and defined the limits of Christian reform.

Both of these Christian strains found expression in William Lloyd Garrison. He wanted to abolish slavery and make a better world, but even more he wanted to avoid contamination by keeping his own hands clean. In the face of mounting evidence to the contrary he clung to the illusion that anti-slavery and pacifism were not merely compatible but complementary. Most of the abolitionists had indulged in this hope in the beginning, but it did not take long to undeceive them. Garrison, however, refused to give up the fiction of peaceful revolution. Until the actual outbreak of war he declined to admit that a situation might arise which would require him to choose between peace and freedom for the slave. The Civil War may not have been inevitable, but after the Compromise of 1850 a peaceful solution to slavery grew less likely each day. It was just this fact that his critics tried to tell him — that the pressure of events operating independently of the will of the majority of Americans was dividing the country and making his prophecy of disunion come true. Garrison failed to understand the very forces he had let loose. For thirty years he cried havoc, and when it came, he refused to credit it and contented himself with his prophet's role, rousing the emotion of Northerners and Southerners yet disavowing their actions, creating an atmosphere of unreason and ignoring the consequences. In his uncompromising stand against both slavery and politics he personifies the great strength and the equally great weakness of radical reform.

The radical reformer in American politics has been something of a split personality, a nonconformist with authoritarian leanings who presents the community with a dilemma by recalling it to its ideals and rejecting its arguments for order and stability. In the strength of his nonconformity Garrison contributed significantly to an American tradition concerned with the integrity of minorities and the protection of civil liberties. His anti-slavery career illustrates the importance of minorities in a free society, the need to withstand the pressure for conformity exerted by society and the willingness to be beaten rather than give hostages to majority opinion. Garrison believed that in the long run respect for law mattered less than concern for right. He considered politics dirty business and looked on the man of average goodness as an enemy in disguise. With his convictions of racial equality, his iron determination in the face of overwhelming opposition, and his insistence on the right to hold and preach unpopular opinions he has a strong claim on the American liberal tradition.

Nonconformity, however, is only one aspect of the radical temperament, and it was only a part of Garrison's mind. The other was distinctly authoritarian. Impulsive yet distrustful, seeking support but rejecting it when given, aggressive and undisciplined, demanding obedience but unable to accept it, he lacked the knowledge of men and the world that makes for leadership. His organization suffered grievously from his failings. When he did not try to do everything himself, he grudgingly delegated a task to a follower and then treated him as a threat to his ascendancy. His societies remained small because he refused to share power and tolerate possible rivals. Because he also lacked any administrative sense he convinced himself that it was unnecessary. His meetings and conventions were like religious revivals, spontaneous and disorganized, and the *Liberator* especially suffered from his lack of method. The man who demanded order and authority in the new world he was making could not find it in his own life. His view of the world as a vast arena for the struggle between God and the devil, his tenacious anti-intellectualism, and above all, his vision of a perfect and self-regulating society of saints disclosed the longings of an authoritarian mind concerned with getting and using power over others.

Inevitably the contradiction in Garrison's personality colored the cause to which he gave himself. Orestes Brownson, a tireless joiner of causes in his own right but also a shrewd observer, identified this contradiction when he noted that Garrison and the anti-slavery men had no just claim to the American civil rights tradition. "Moreover," he added, "the abolitionists do not, properly speaking, discuss the subject of slavery. Nay, it is not their object to discuss it. Their object is not to enlighten the community on the subject, but to agitate it. . . . *When men have made up their minds,* when the epoch for deliberation has gone by, and that for action has come, when their object is less to convince than it is to rouse, to quicken, to inflame; then proceedings like those of the abolitionists are very appropriate."[1]

The abolitionists *had* made up their minds; they never doubted for a moment that slavery was wrong. Despite the complaints of Brownson and other critics, they succeeded in identifying their cause with the life of free society. They were the carriers, however unworthy at times, of perfectionism and the ideals of democracy. They invoked the freedoms guaranteed by the Constitution and demanded that the people honor them and listen to their arguments. Yet their arguments, as Brownson quite rightly pointed out, were not the kind that could be discussed dispassionately. Their ideas were packed with high explosive and eventually destroyed a community based on slavery. The abolitionists found the majority wrong and demanded the liberty to say so. The liberty that Garrison and his followers dreamed of, however, was an absolute liberty, a freedom that was neither brotherly nor Christian. It was this subversive ideal of liberty which, despite their professions of peace and Christian love, led logically to war and the overthrow of slavery.

This contradiction in the anti-slavery attitude was expressed on a higher level in the changes Garrison and the abolitionists made in the doctrine of natural law. As they received it from the Declaration of Independence and first invoked it in self-defense, natural law meant a body of rights pragmatically determined and consonant with what was believed to be the nature of man. In the course of their fight against slavery the abolitionists changed the content while keeping the concept. Natural law, as Garrison came to use it, meant metaphysical truth, a divine spirit hovering over humanity. For the pragmatic Aristotelian they substituted a Christian faith in a universally valid spiritual criterion. Drained of its pragmatic content, natural law came to mean, as Justice Holmes once observed, anything that people are willing to fight for. The Civil War proved that the American people were willing to fight over slavery.

The anti-slavery persuasion was marked by a final contradiction which was the source of the abolitionists' great strength and tragic weakness. Their courage and their fierce sense of freedom blinded them to the realities of the power struggle and the consequences of freeing the slave. The very intensity of their belief prevented them from understanding fully what it lay in their power to do for the Negro. They welcomed emancipation, but they were not ready for it and did not know how to use it. With the actual freeing of the slave their lack of understanding became increasingly apparent until finally anti-slavery radicalism broke down.

If Garrison personifies the contradictions of American

radical reform, his anti-slavery career illustrates the continuing problem of moral absolutes in a democracy. A free society needs radicals with their moral absolutes just as antebellum Americans needed the abolitionists to tell them that slavery was wrong. But perfectionism — the dream of a perfect society of regenerate men — which sustained Garrison and his followers, rejected democratic politics and the idea of compromise, ignored programs and plans. By concentrating almost exclusively on the moral issue, appealing directly to individuals, and demanding immediate and wholesale change, it eliminated the very possibility of controlled change. Without radicals to criticize it a democracy is not really free; with them it maintains a precarious existence. If it cannot afford to silence its critics, neither can American democracy ignore the dangers to its stability inherent in their insistent demand for a better world.

"In every great fluctuation that takes place in human society," John Jay Chapman wrote of Garrison and the Civil War, " — whether it be a moral, a political, or even an industrial phenomenon, — force converges upon some one man, and makes him the metaphysical center and thought-focus of the movement." Chapman was not equipped to probe the collective mind of ante-bellum America: the grandson of an abolitionist, he was too close temporally and temperamentally to the Emersonian Representative Man to see Garrison as he was. Garrison was not a heroic figure but, rather, Emerson's sufficient man, "an officer equal to his task." He knew the contradictions of his age experientially, which is to say that his weakness was in a sense an American weakness. He lacked the power of a leader and the sureness to shape his feelings and give direction to his beliefs. Not a Representative Man, he was yet a representative figure of American society before the Civil War whose single great achievement and equally great failure testify to the tragic meaning of history.

Notes

1: NEWBURYPORT BOYHOOD

1. William Lloyd Garrison to Theodore Weld *et al.*, March 17, 1873, Garrison Papers, Boston Public Library.
2. W. P. Garrison and F. J. Garrison, *William Lloyd Garrison: The Story of His Life as Told by His Children*, 4 vols. (New York, 1885–1889), I, 12. (Hereafter cited as *Life*.)
3. Contract between Joseph Garrison, William Saunders, and the firm of Simonds & White, November 10, 1772, quoted in W. O. Raymond, "Selections from the Papers and Correspondence of James White, Esquire, A.D. 1762–1783," New Brunswick Historical Society *Collections*, I, 3 (1897), 310. Simonds and White were Newburyport merchants who played a leading part in opening the Saint John country.
4. Andrew Lloyd and his wife, Mary Lawless Lloyd, are listed as indentured servants in the journal of Captain William Owen, R.N., the founder of the settlement at Campobello where the Lloyds lived for a time after their arrival. See W. F. Ganong, "The Journal of Captain William Owen, R.N., During his Residence on Campobello in 1770–1771," New Brunswick Historical Society *Collections*, I, 2 (1896), 194.
5. For the story of the Nova Scotia revival see Maurice W. Armstrong, *The Great Awakening in Nova Scotia* (Hartford, Conn., 1948).
6. Frances L. Garrison to her daughter, Maria Elizabeth Garrison, May 24, 1820, quoted in *Life*, I, 39.
7. Abijah Garrison to Frances L. Garrison, April 22, 1804, Garrison Papers, Houghton Library.
8. Abijah Garrison to his parents, April 4, 1805, Garrison Papers, Houghton Library.
9. Abijah Garrison to Susannah Palmer, July 27, 1814, Garrison Papers, Houghton Library.
10. Frances L. Garrison to Mrs. Martha Farnham, April 5, 1814. The letter is in the possession of Mr. Walter McIntosh Merrill. Parts of it are reprinted in his *Behold Me Once More: The Confessions of James Holley Garrison* (Cambridge, Mass., 1954), 10–11, fn.
11. Frances L. Garrison to William Lloyd Garrison, August 29, 1817, quoted in *Life*, I, 33.
12. *Behold Me Once More* (see note 10), 8.

13. Frances L. Garrison to William Lloyd Garrison, March 24, 1823, quoted in *Life*, I, 48–49.
14. *Behold Me Once More* (see note 10), 18.
15. Frances L. Garrison to Mrs. Martha Farnham, April 18, 1816, quoted in *Life*, I, 32.
16. William Lloyd Garrison to Frances L. Garrison, May 26, 1823, quoted in *Life*, I, 49–50.
17. William Lloyd Garrison, Address to the Franklin Club of Boston, October 14, 1878, Boston Public Libary.

2: THE YOUNG CONSERVATIVE

1. Manuscript letter from Joseph B. Morss to Francis Jackson Garrison and Wendell Phillips Garrison and quoted by them in *Life*, I, 55. Morss was a fellow apprentice on the *Herald*.
2. Manuscript of Charles J. Brockway quoted by the sons in *Life*, I, 56, fn. Brockway, two years younger than Garrison, took part in the debates of the Franklin Club.
3. The quotation is taken from the last of a series of three editorials written by Garrison for the *Herald* in support of the gubernatorial candidacy of Harrison Gray Otis in 1823. See the *Newburyport Herald*, April 23, 1823.
4. Timothy Pickering to Rufus King, March 4, 1804, quoted in Henry Adams, ed., *Documents Relating to New England Federalism, 1800–1815* (Boston, 1877), 351.
5. Timothy Pickering to George Cabot, January 29, 1804, in Adams, *New England Federalism*, 340.
6. Such was Garrison's description of Pickering in a letter to the *Salem Gazette*, June 29, 1824.
7. *Newburyport Herald*, May 21, 1822.
8. *Newburyport Herald*, May 31, 1822.
9. William Lloyd Garrison to Frances L. Garrison, May 31, 1823, quoted in *Life*, I, 49–50.
10. *North American Review*, October 1820.
11. Frances L. Garrison to William Lloyd Garrison, May 12, 1820, quoted in *Life*, I, 38.
12. *Newburyport Herald*, July 19, 1823.
13. Garrison's editorials appeared under the title "Our Next Governor" in the *Newburyport Herald*, March 14, April 1, and April 3, 1823.
14. Frances L. Garrison to William Lloyd Garrison, June 3, 1823, quoted in *Life*, I, 51.
15. William Lloyd Garrison to Ephraim Allen, July 7, 1823, quoted in *Life*, I, 52.
16. *Salem Gazette*, July 27, 1824.
17. *Newburyport Herald*, May 17, 1825.
18. *Essex Courant*, March 16, 1826.
19. *Newburyport Free Press*, March 22, 1826.
20. *Free Press*, March 22, 1826.
21. *Free Press*, April 13, 1826.
22. *Free Press*, July 27, 1826.
23. *Free Press*, June 8, 1826.

24. *National Philanthropist*, April 11, 1828.
25. *Free Press*, July 13, 1826.
26. *Free Press*, September 21, 1826.
27. *Free Press*, September 14, 1826.

3: BOSTON

1. Lyman Beecher, *Autobiography*, 2 vols., ed., Charles Beecher, 2nd ed., (New York, 1886), I, 43.
2. *Journal of the Times*, January 30, 1829.
3. *Liberator*, 1:92, quoted in *Life*, I, 81. Garrison's sons, working from complete files of the paper, cited the volume and page number but not the date.
4. *Boston Courier*, July 14, 1827.
5. *National Philanthropist*, January 18, 1828.
6. *National Philanthropist*, March 7, 1828.
7. *Journal of the Times*, December 26, 1828.
8. *National Philanthropist*, June 13, 1828.
9. *Genius of Universal Emancipation*, October 23, 1829; *National Philanthropist*, May 30, 1828.
10. *National Philanthropist*, May 23, 1828.
11. *National Philanthropist*, January 25, 1828.
12. *National Philanthropist*, March 14, 1828.
13. *National Philanthropist*, February 1, 1828.
14. *National Philanthropist*, February 29, 1828.
15. *National Philanthropist*, May 16, 1828.
16. *National Philanthropist*, February 8, February 29, 1828.
17. *National Philanthropist*, April 18, 1828.
18. *National Philanthropist*, January 25, 1828.
19. *National Philanthropist*, June 13, 1828.

4: BENJAMIN LUNDY

1. *National Philanthropist*, January 11, 1828.
2. *National Philanthropist*, March 21, 1828.
3. For King's speech see *Annals of Congress*, 16 Cong., I Sess., 380ff.
4. Edward Brown, *Notes on the Origin and Necessity of Slavery* (Charleston, 1826), 6, quoted in W. S. Jenkins, *Pro-Slavery Thought in the Old South* (Chapel Hill, 1935), 73.
5. "Address to the Legislature of South Carolina by Gov. Stephen D. Miller," printed in the *Charleston Courier*, November 28, 1829, and quoted in Jenkins, *Pro-Slavery Thought*, 76–77.
6. *National Philanthropist*, July 4, 1828.
7. Garrison's speech at the annual meeting of the American Anti-Slavery Society in 1864. See *Proceedings of the American Anti-Slavery Society at its Third Decade* (New York, 1864), 121.
8. *Journal of the Times*, October 3, 1828.
9. *Journal of the Times*, October 3, 1828.
10. *Journal of the Times*, February 27, 1829.
11. *Journal of the Times*, October 17, 1828.
12. *Journal of the Times*, January 30, 1829.

13. *Journal of the Times,* February 20, 1829.
14. *Journal of the Times,* October 10, 1828.

5: THE ROAD TO PRISON

1. William Lloyd Garrison to Jacob Horton, June 27, 1829, quoted in *Life,* I, 124–126.
2. *Idem.*
3. Thomas Jefferson, *Notes on Virginia* in *Basic Writings of Thomas Jefferson,* ed. Philip S. Foner (New York, 1944), 144–148.
4. See Joseph Tracy, "Historical Discourse," *Memorial of the Semi-Centennial Anniversary of the American Colonization Society* (Washington, D.C.), 66.
5. See H. N. Sherwood, "The Formation of the American Colonization Society," *The Journal of Negro History,* II, 3, 221–222.
6. Clay's speech was reported in the *National Intelligencer,* January 2, 1817. See also Archibald Alexander, *A History of Colonization on the West Coast of Africa* (Philadelphia, 1849), 77–82.
7. Randolph's speech is quoted in Joseph Tracy, *A View of Exertions Lately Made for the Purpose of Colonizing the Free People of Color in the United States* (Washington, 1817), 4ff.
8. American Colonization Society *First Annual Report,* 8, quoted in Sherwood, "Formation of the American Colonization Society," *The Journal of Negro History,* II, 3, 213.
9. Robert Goodloe Harper, speech at the Seventh Annual Meeting of the American Colonization Society, *Seventh Annual Report* (1823).
10. The figures are given in Early Lee Fox, *The American Colonization Society, 1817–1840* (Baltimore, 1919), 89.
11. The text of the Park Street address is given in the Old South Leaflets (General Series, v. 8, No. 180).
12. *Genius of Universal Emancipation,* September 2, 1829.
13. *Genius of Universal Emancipation,* October 30, 1829.
14. George Bourne, *The Book and Slavery Irreconcilable* (Philadelphia, 1816), quoted in Alice Dana Adams, *The Neglected Period of Anti-Slavery in America* (Boston, 1908), 81.
15. *Genius of Universal Emancipation,* October 9, 1829.
16. *Genius of Universal Emancipation,* December 4, 1829.
17. *Genius of Universal Emancipation,* October 9, 1829.
18. *Genius of Universal Emancipation,* October 23, 1829.
19. *Genius of Universal Emancipation,* November 20, 1829.
20. *Genius of Universal Emancipation,* March 5, 1830.
21. *Idem.*
22. William Lloyd Garrison to Harriet Farnham Horton, May 12, 1830, Garrison Papers, Boston Public Library.
23. Arthur Tappan to Benjamin Lundy, May 29, 1830, quoted in *Life,* I, 190–191.

6: LAUNCHING THE LIBERATOR

1. For the story of Arthur Tappan's part in the American reform movement see Lewis Tappan, *The Life of Arthur Tappan* (London, 1870).

2. Tappan, *Arthur Tappan*, 127–128.
3. Arthur Tappan to William Lloyd Garrison, September 12, 1831, quoted in *Life*, I, 237, fn.
4. Arthur Tappan to Lewis F. Laine, Secretary of the Andover Theological Seminary Anti-Slavery Society, March 26, 1833, quoted in Tappan, *Arthur Tappan*, 128–130.
5. Tappan, *Arthur Tappan*, 163.
6. "Proposals for Publishing a weekly periodical in Washington City, to be entitled The Public Liberator and Journal of the Times," quoted in *Life*, I, 199–202.
7. For a discussion of the Hicksite schism see Bliss Forbush, *Elias Hicks, Quaker Liberal* (New York, 1956).
8. The sermon is quoted in L. C. M. Hare, *The Greatest American Woman* (New York, 1937), 61. See also Otelia Cromwell, *Lucretia Mott* (Cambridge, Mass., 1958), ch. X.
9. *Liberator*, 19: 178, quoted in *Life*, I, 204.
10. *Memoir of Samuel Joseph May*, ed. T. J. Mumford (Boston, 1873), 143.
11. Samuel J. May, *Recollections of Our Anti-Slavery Conflict* (Boston, 1869); *Memoir*, 147–148.
12. "To the Public," *Liberator*, January 1, 1831.

7: FANNING THE FLAMES

1. William Lloyd Garrison to Samuel J. May, February 14, 1831, Garrison Papers, Boston Public Library.
2. *Idem.*
3. *Liberator*, 1:145, quoted in *Life*, I, 236–237.
4. *Liberator*, 1:49, quoted in *Life*, I, 227.
5. *Liberator*, 1:145, quoted in *Life*, I, 235.
6. *Liberator*, 1:139, quoted in *Life*, I, 235.
7. William Lloyd Garrison to Henry Benson, October 19, 1831, Garrison Papers, Boston Public Library.
8. "Universal Emancipation," *Liberator*, January 8, 1831.
9. David Walker, *Appeal* (Boston, 1829), 30–35.
10. *Genius of Universal Emancipation*, January 15, 1830.
11. William Lloyd Garrison to LeRoy Sunderland, September 8, 1831, Garrison Papers, Boston Public Library.
12. Otis's letter first appeared in the autumn of 1833 in the *Boston Advertiser;* see also *Niles Register*, September 14, 1833, and *Life*, I, 242–244.
13. *Liberator*, October 28, 1831.
14. See *Life*, I, 247–248.
15. *Liberator*, 1:207, quoted in *Life*, I, 249.
16. William Lloyd Garrison to Henry Benson, September 26, 1831, Garrison Papers, Boston Public Library.
17. William Lloyd Garrison to Henry Benson, November 12, 1831, Garrison Papers, Boston Public Library.
18. *Liberator*, 2:25, quoted in *Life*, I, 279.
19. William Lloyd Garrison to Ebenezer Dole, June 29, 1832, Garrison Papers, Boston Public Library. Dole was a minister in Hallowell, Maine, and an early supporter of the *Liberator*.
20. *Idem.*

21. William Lloyd Garrison to Henry Benson, July 21, 1832, Garrison Papers, Boston Public Library.
22. William Lloyd Garrison to Henry Benson, May 12, 1832, Garrison Papers, Boston Public Library.
23. *Liberator*, July 9, November 19, 1831.
24. *Address before the Free People of Color*, June, 1831 (Boston, 1831), 3.
25. William Lloyd Garrison to Henry Benson, July 30, 1831, Garrison Papers, Boston Public Library.
26. *Thoughts on African Colonization* (Boston, 1832), 2. G. H. Barnes holds that Garrison's pamphlet derived chiefly from Charles Stuart's tracts, *Is Slavery Defensible from Scripture?* (Belfast, 1831) and *The West India Question*, which first appeared in the *British Quarterly Magazine and Review* for April, 1832, when Garrison had nearly completed his *Thoughts*. *The West India Question*, however, ran through several editions on both sides of the Atlantic, and Garrison read it thoroughly. In a letter to Theodore Weld, Elizur Wright, then Professor of Mathematics at Western Reserve College in Hudson, Ohio, refers to a copy of Stuart's *West India Question* received from Garrison. "Today I am obliged to you for another, the West India Question. It is very seasonable, for a copy of the same, which I received from Mr. Garrison some time since, has quite worn itself out with hard service." Wright also credits Garrison's *Thoughts* with converting William Goodell to immediatism. G. H. Barnes, D. L. Dumond (eds.), *The Weld-Grimké Letters* (New York, 1934), 2 vols., I, 102–103. In addition to the two tracts mentioned above Stuart wrote several other anti-colonization pamphlets: *Remarks on the Colony of Liberia and the American Colonization Society* (London, 1832); *A Letter on the American Colonization Society* (Birmingham, 1832); *Prejudice Vincible* (London, 1832); *Liberia, or the American Colonization Scheme Further Unravelled* (Bath, n. d.). It is difficult to believe that any of Stuart's work published in England in 1832 arrived in this country in time to influence the preparation of *Thoughts*, which was in its final stages by April of that year. Moreover, if my reading of Garrison's Park Street address is correct, the question of priority (for what it is worth) would seem solved. After the publication of *Thoughts* Garrison became thoroughly familiar with all of Stuart's work as well as with the man himself, whom he found eccentric but well-meaning. During one of his absences from Boston he attempted to interest Stuart in managing the *Liberator*, but Stuart refused. Garrison was inclined to dismiss Stuart's lectures as of less value than his writings.
27. *Thoughts*, 8.
28. *Thoughts*, 149. The italics are Garrison's.
29. *Thoughts*, 8.
30. *Thoughts*, 118.
31. *Thoughts*, 119.
32. William Lloyd Garrison to Reverend Ebenezer Dole, Hallowell, Maine, June 29, 1832, Garrison Papers, Boston Public Library. Garrison objected, however, to the bright-colored clothes and jewelry worn by the Negroes. "I regret to say that it is too true that a passion for gaudy finery is too prevalent among our colored population; but this is naturally created and inflamed by their degraded situation, which leads

them to imitate and surpass in folly those who are on a higher level than themselves. This is another reason why prejudice should expire, and slavery be abolished; for as soon as they are enlightened, and made virtuous, they will despise that in which they now take the most delight." Letter to his wife, May 30, 1839.

33. *Thoughts,* 79.
34. *Thoughts,* 80.
35. William Lloyd Garrison to Robert Purvis, December 10, 1832, Garrison Papers, Boston Public Library.
36. William Lloyd Garrison to Henry Benson, July 21, 1832, Garrison Papers, Boston Public Library.

8: TRIUMPH AND DOUBT IN 1833

1. William Lloyd Garrison to Miss Harriet Minot, April 22, 1832, Garrison Papers, Boston Public Library.
2. William Lloyd Garrison to Isaac Knapp, April 11–17, 1833, quoted in *Life,* I, 341–42.
3. *Liberator,* 3:39, quoted in *Life,* I, 329.
4. *Abolitionist,* I, 88–89, quoted in Barnes, *Anti-Slavery Impulse,* 220–221.
5. Garrison published an account of the testimonial breakfast given to him by his English friends. The pamphlet, *London Breakfast to William Lloyd Garrison,* contains the anecdote of his meeting with Buxton (p. 38) which is also given in *Life,* I, 351.
6. New England Anti-Slavery Society *Second Annual Report* (Boston, 1833), 44.
7. *Second Annual Report,* 47.
8. Quoted in Barnes, *Anti-Slavery Impulse,* 221.
9. The Exeter Hall address appeared in the *Liberator,* the *London Patriot,* and selections from it in several New York papers. The letter to the *London Patriot* is the first of two letters dated July 22 and August 6, and is quoted in Oliver Johnson, *William Lloyd Garrison and His Times* (Boston, 1885), 2nd ed., 132.
10. He published Macaulay's letter in the *Liberator* immediately upon his return. See *Life,* I, 377–378.
11. See Charles Grandison Finney, *Lectures on Revivals* (New York, 1835), 275–276. The best discussion of Finney's theology is William G. McLoughlin, *Modern Revivalism* (New York, 1959), chs. I–II.
12. Wright's letter to Garrison was published in the *Liberator,* January 5, 1833.
13. Elizur Wright to Theodore Weld, December 7, 1832, *Weld-Grimké Letters,* I, 94–96. The effects of Garrison's arguments in the *Liberator* on Green and Wright are seen in the account Wright furnishes of Green's lectures. He continues: "From the first he [Green] derived the doctrine that philanthropists should base their efforts on a clear distinction between *right* and *wrong:* from the second, that every succeeding generation that copies the sins of its predecessors becomes more guilty in the sight of God: and from the third, that when men seek their own will, their judgment is worthy of little confidence, or in other words that prejudice unfits a man to testify or decide concerning the character of another." It is clear that Wright, Storrs, and Green converted Weld to

anti-slavery using Garrison's arguments which they read in the *Liberator*. A month before he visited Hudson in the fall of 1832 Weld wrote to James Birney that he was "ripe in the conviction that if the Colonization Society does not dissipate the horror of darkness which overhangs the southern country, we are undone. *Light breaks in from no other quarter*." Weld to Birney, September 27, 1832, Dwight L. Dumond ed., *Letters of James Gillespie Birney, 1831–1857* (New York, 1938), 2 vols., I, 27.

14. Wright to Weld, December 7, 1832, *Weld-Grimké Letters*, I, 96.
15. Theodore Weld to William Lloyd Garrison, January 2, 1833, *Weld-Grimké Letters*, I, 97–99.
16. Garrison collected the unfavorable notices of his return to New York and printed them in the *Liberator*, 3: 161. See *Life*, I, 380–382.
17. *Liberator*, 3: 63, quoted in *Life*, I, 387–388.
18. *Liberator*, 3: 179, and preface to the pamphlet *Speeches in Exeter Hall* (Boston, 1833), quoted in *Life*, I, 388–390.
19. William Lloyd Garrison to George W. Benson, November 2, 1833, Garrison Papers, Boston Public Library.
20. Circular of the Friends of Immediate Emancipation in Boston, Providence, New York and Philadelphia, signed by Arthur Tappan, Joshua Leavitt, Elizur Wright, calling a convention in Philadelphia for December 4, 1833, to form a national society. A copy of the circular which was mailed to Weld is reprinted in the *Weld-Grimké Letters*, I, 117–118.
21. Elizur Wright, Jr. to Theodore Weld, November 2, 1833, *Weld-Grimké Letters*, I, 119.
22. Lewis Tappan's remarks were published in the *Abolitionist*, I, 181, and excerpted in *Life*, I, 402–405.
23. Samuel J. May, *Recollections*, 86ff.
24. The story of Garrison's debt is told in Barnes, *Anti-Slavery Impulse*, 56–57.
25. William Lloyd Garrison to Henry Benson, February 26, 1834, Garrison Papers, Boston Public Library.
26. William Lloyd Garrison to Henry Benson, September 12, 1834, Garrison Papers, Boston Public Library.
27. William Lloyd Garrison to Henry Benson, February 26, 1834, Garrison Papers, Boston Public Library.

9: MOBS AND MARTYRS

1. The courtship correspondence is part of the Villard Papers in the Houghton Library collection. See also Walter McIntosh Merrill, "A Passionate Attachment," *New England Quarterly*, XXIX, 2 (June, 1956), 182–203.
2. William Lloyd Garrison to Helen Eliza Benson, March 25, 1834.
3. Helen Eliza Benson to William Lloyd Garrison, March 21, 1834.
4. William Lloyd Garrison to Helen Eliza Benson, March 25, 1834.
5. William Lloyd Garrison to Helen Eliza Benson, March 26, April 24, April 25, 1834.
6. Helen Eliza Benson to William Lloyd Garrison, May 3, 1834.
7. William Lloyd Garrison to Helen Eliza Benson, June 2, 1834.
8. Helen Eliza Benson to William Lloyd Garrison, quoted in Walter Mc-

Intosh Merrill, "A Passionate Attachment," *New England Quarterly*, XXIX, 2, 200.

9. William Lloyd Garrison to Anna Benson, October 9, 1834, Garrison Papers, Boston Public Library.

10. In April, 1834, Garrison and Knapp published a pamphlet, *Shall the Liberator Die?* explaining their financial situation and appealing for funds.

11. Henry Ware to Samuel J. May, October 15, 1834, in *Memoir of Henry Ware*, quoted in *Life*, I, 462.

12. Elizur Wright, Jr. to Theodore Weld, September 5, 1833, *Weld-Grimké Letters*, I, 114–117.

13. When Stuart visited the Benson household in the late spring of 1834, Helen reported her conversation with him in a letter to Garrison, June 23, 1834. Villard Papers, Houghton Library.

14. The announcement of the Amherst Society was printed in the *Liberator*, August 3, 1833.

15. *Liberator*, 4:207, quoted in *Life*, I, 458–462.

16. *Weld-Grimké Letters*, I, 260–262.

17. *Liberator*, August 15, 1835.

18. Prudence Crandall to William Lloyd Garrison, January 18, 1833, quoted in *Life*, I, 315–316.

19. William Lloyd Garrison to Isaac Knapp, April 11, 1833, Garrison Papers, Boston Public Library.

20. William Lloyd Garrison to George W. Benson, March 8, 1833, Garrison Papers, Boston Public Library.

21. William Lloyd Garrison to George Benson, June 16, 1834, Garrison Papers, Boston Public Library.

22. Garrison reprinted Arthur Tappan's letter in the *Liberator*, January 31, 1835.

23. Lewis Tappan's letter, dated January 26, 1835, appeared with his brother's in the *Liberator*, January 31, 1835.

24. *Liberator*, July 4, 1835.

25. *Liberator*, August 29, 1835.

26. *Liberator*, 5:139, quoted in *Life*, I, 503.

27. *Liberator*, July 25, 1835.

28. William Lloyd Garrison to Henry Benson, September 3, 1835, quoted in *Life*, I, 516.

29. The best account of the Boston mob which incorporates the several eye-witness reports is in *Life*, I, ch. XIV; II, ch. I.

30. "Picture of the American Mind in 1835," *Liberator*, November 14, 1835.

31. "William Lloyd Garrison," in *The Selected Writings of John Jay Chapman*, ed. Jacques Barzun (New York, 1957), 54–55.

10: "OUR DOOM AS A NATION IS SEALED"

1. William Lloyd Garrison to Anna Benson, November 27, 1835, Garrison Papers, Boston Public Library.

2. William Lloyd Garrison to Samuel May, December 26, 1835, quoted in *Life*, II, 66.

3. *Liberator*, February 27, 1836.

4. Amos A. Phelps to William Lloyd Garrison, December 10, 1835, quoted

in *Life*, II, 62–63. Garrison was prepared to condemn Channing's book before he read it. "Well, it is announced that the great Dr. Channing has published his thoughts upon the subject of slavery! of course, we must now all fall back, and 'hide our diminished heads.' The work I will not condemn until I peruse it; but I do not believe it is superior either in argument or eloquence to many of our own publications. . . . The hosts of abolitionists in Great Britain and this country have spoken and written in vain — but now Dr. Channing speaks, listen ye heavens! and give ear, oh earth! It was not in the power of Jesus Christ, but it is in the power of Dr. Channing, to rebuke sin and sinners, without exciting their 'bad passions'! Wonderful!" Letter to Samuel J. May, December 5, 1835, Garrison Papers, Boston Public Library.

5. Garrison's speech was reported in the *Liberator* and is quoted in *Life*, II, 104.
6. *Liberator*, April 16, 1836.
7. *Liberator*, December 20, 1834.
8. *Liberator*, December 27, 1834.
9. *Liberator*, December 20, 1834.
10. William Lloyd Garrison to David Lee Child, August 6, 1836, Garrison Papers, Boston Public Library.
11. William Lloyd Garrison to George Benson, April 10, 1836, quoted in *Life*, II, 82, fn.
12. *Liberator*, October 29, 1836.
13. William Lloyd Garrison to Henry Benson, January 16, 1836, quoted in *Life*, II, 84–85.
14. William Lloyd Garrison to Geoge Benson, January 11, 1836, Garrison Papers, Boston Public Library.
15. *Liberator*, July 23, 1836.
16. William Lloyd Garrison to Effingham L. Capron, August 24, 1836, Garrison Papers, Boston Public Library.
17. William Lloyd Garrison to Samuel J. May, September 23, 1836, Garrison Papers, Boston Public Library.
18. William Lloyd Garrison to Henry Benson, December 17, 1836, Garrison Papers, Boston Public Library.
19. For Noyes's own account of his religious experiences and an exposition of his theological as well as his social doctrine see *Religious Experiences of John Humphrey Noyes*, ed. George Wallingford Noyes (New York, 1923), chs. VII–XV.
20. The quotation and the ones that follow are from Noyes's letter to Garrison, March 22, 1837, quoted in *Life*, II, 145–148.
21. William Lloyd Garrison to Henry C. Wright, April 16, 1837, Garrison Papers, Boston Public Library.
22. *Liberator*, July 28, 1837.
23. Garrison's poem, "True Rest," appeared in the *Liberator*, August 25, 1837. The quotations that follow are from the *Liberator*, June 23, 1837.

II: A WOMAN IN THE PULPIT

1. Sarah Grimké to Theodore Weld, June 11, 1837, *Weld-Grimké Letters*, I, 401.
2. *Liberator*, June 9, 1837.

3. *Liberator*, June 23, 1837.

4. *Idem.*

5. Sarah Grimké to Theodore Weld, June 11, 1837, *Weld-Grimké Letters*, I, 401.

6. Angelina Grimké to Theodore Weld and John Greenleaf Whittier, September 20, 1837, *Weld-Grimké Letters*, I, 428.

7. Theodore Weld to Sarah and Angelina Grimké, August 26, 1837, *Weld-Grimké Letters*, I, 434.

8. Sarah and Angelina Grimké to Henry C. Wright, September 27, 1837, *Weld-Grimké Letters*, I, 438.

9. Sarah Grimké to Henry C. Wright, August 12, 1837, *Weld-Grimké Letters*, I, 420.

10. The Pastoral Letter was published in the *Liberator*, August 11, 1837.

11. The "Clerical Appeal" first appeared in the *New England Spectator* and was reprinted in the *Liberator* with the Pastoral Letter. Two of the ministers, Charles Fitch and Joseph Towne, published a second appeal, "Protest of the Clerical Abolitionists," which Garrison printed in the *Liberator*, September 8, 1837.

12. *Liberator*, August 18, 1837.

13. Woodbury's letter appeared in the *New England Spectator*, August 17, 1837.

14. *Liberator*, September 1, 1837.

15. Henry B. Stanton to James G. Birney, September 1, 1837, *Letters of James Gillespie Birney, 1831–1857*, ed. Dwight L. Dumond, 2 vols. (New York, 1938), I, 420–423.

16. Lewis Tappan to William Lloyd Garrison, September 21, 1837, quoted in *Life*, II, 163–166.

17. Birney published his views on the affair of the clerical appeal in Gamaliel Bailey's *Philanthropist*, September 15, 1837, copied in the *Liberator*, 7:161. See *Life*, II, 166, fn. Privately Birney wrote to Lewis Tappan, "I greatly lament the course Mr. Garrison seems to be taking. I have been disappointed in him. In the emergency he may bring upon us, the Ex. Com. must not only be prudent but firm. I considered the matter over, and thought it well to publish in relation to the Boston controversy what you will see in the next Phil'st. It will have a tendency if any thing that I can say will, to mitigate his fury, and keep the other party from rash action. I have chosen this course, in preference to writing to the latter individually, as I could not do it, under the pressure of my preparations for removal in the manner I wished. (Inter nos) I have no expectation that G. can be reduced to moderation, and I am not prepared to say, that his departure from us may not be the best thing he could do for the cause of Emancipation." September 14, 1837, *Birney Letters*, I, 425. Birney's letter in the *Philanthropist* marked the beginning of his feud with Garrison. Garrison commented on Birney's letter in the *Liberator*, October 20, 1837.

18. Garrison quoted Wright's letter in his own letter to George Benson, September 23, 1837, the full text of which appears in *Life*, II, 167–170. Wright sent Garrison a second letter in which he criticized his perfectionist views. ". . . I have never yet met with a man who was free from sin. I am obliged to reject your own claim to sinlessness. Your very letter refutes it. Hence I am obliged to reject your theory, or to believe

that the gospel has never done its appropriate work within the range of my observation." Wright to Garrison, November 6, 1837, quoted in *Life*, II, 178–181. As soon as she read the clerical appeal, Maria Weston Chapman dashed off a letter to Wright informing him of "the *absolute necessity* of holding by Garrison with a giant grasp." Wright refused to take sides. "Nor can I see," he added, "how Garrison stands in any need of our aid — for he seems to have left his enemies thrice dead behind him, even if he has not killed some of his friends. The truth is that as much as I regretted and abominated the 'appeal' — and I did so most cordially — I was sorry to see Garrison & Phelps expend upon it those annihilating batteries which ought to have been directed to another quarter. . . . We gain nothing by stopping to punish 'traitors' much less vacillating and cowardly friends." Mrs. Chapman's letter is undated. Wright's reply is dated September 15, 1837. Weston Papers, Boston Public Library.

19. William Lloyd Garrison to George W. Benson, September 23, 1837, quoted in *Life*, II, 167–170.
20. Theodore Weld to Sarah and Angelina Grimké, August 26, 1837, *Weld-Grimké Letters*, I, 434.
21. *Liberator*, December 15, 1837.
22. Angelina Grimké to Weld and John Greenleaf Whittier, September 20, 1837, *Weld-Grimké Letters*, I, 430. Sarah agreed. "I must confess my womanhood is insulted, my moral feelings outraged when I reflect on these things, and I am sure *I know just* how the free colored people feel towards the whites when they pay them more than common attention; it is *not paid as a* RIGHT, but *given as a* BOUNTY on a *little* more than *ordinary* sense. There is not one man in 500 who really understands what kind of attention is alone acceptable to a woman of pure and exalted moral and intellectual worth." Letter to Theodore Weld, September 12, 1837, *Weld-Grimké Letters*, I, 415.

12: THE POLITICS OF PERFECTION

1. *Liberator*, November 24, 1837.
2. "Prospectus for Volume Eight," *Liberator*, December 15, 1837.
3. William Lloyd Garrison to Helen Garrison, September 21, 1838, Garrison Papers, Boston Public Library.
4. The full text of the Declaration of Sentiments appears in *Life*, II, 230–234.
5. Edmund Quincy to William Lloyd Garrison, September 21, 1838, quoted in *Life*, II, 234–236.
6. William Lloyd Garrison to Samuel J. May, September 24, 1838, quoted in *Life*, II, 236–237.
7. *Liberator*, October 12, 1838.
8. Ladd's letter to Garrison appeared in the *Liberator*, November 23, 1838. Garrison commented, "Mr. Ladd is content to stop at the millennium! So are we — and at nothing short of it."
9. Scott's first letter to Garrison was printed in the *Liberator* along with Garrison's reply on October 26, 1838.
10. Scott's rejoinder and Garrison's second reply appeared in the *Liberator*, November 16, 1838.

11. *Liberator*, December 7, 1838.
12. William Lloyd Garrison to George Benson, January 5, 1839, Garrison Papers, Boston Public Library.
13. These resolutions were first introduced by Alanson St. Clair and Nathaniel Colver at Fitchburg on January 3, 1839. Garrison published them in the *Liberator*, January 11, 1839.
14. William Lloyd Garrison to George Benson, January 14, 1839, Garrison Papers, Boston Public Library.
15. The account of the annual meeting is given in the report edited by Maria Weston Chapman under the title *Right and Wrong in Massachusetts, 1839*. The most devoted of Garrison's followers, Mrs. Chapman edited the entire series of *Right and Wrong* reports (1836–1840).
16. Henry B. Stanton to James G. Birney, January 26, 1839, *Birney Letters*, I, 481–483.
17. William Lloyd Garrison to Mary Benson, March 3, 1839, quoted in *Life*, II, 281.
18. William Lloyd Garrison to George Benson, March 26, 1839, Garrison Papers, Boston Public Library.
19. *Proceedings of the Sixth Annual Meeting of the American Anti-Slavery Society* (New York, 1839), 30.
20. *Proceedings*, 40.
21. See the account of the New England Convention in the *Liberator*, June 7, 1839.
22. James G. Birney, *A Letter on the Political Obligations of Abolitionists . . . With a Reply by William Lloyd Garrison* (Boston, 1839).
23. *Liberator*, September 13, 1839.
24. The circular was first printed in the *Emancipator*, July 24, 1839. Garrison published it in the *Liberator*, August 2, 1839.
25. Wright's letter, written from Dorchester on October 12, 1839, was finally published in the *Abolitionist* after the Massachusetts Abolition Society had disavowed it. In the *Liberator* of November 29 Garrison demanded that Wright publish it, and he himself reprinted it on December 6.
26. *Liberator*, December 13, 1839.

13: TRIUMPH OF THE SAINTS

1. William Lloyd Garrison to George Benson, September 30, 1839, quoted in *Life*, II, 329.
2. William Lloyd Garrison to Helen Garrison, May 19, 1840, quoted in *Life*, II, 357–358.
3. William Lloyd Garrison to Elizabeth Pease, May 15, 1842, quoted in *Life*, II, 331–332.
4. William Lloyd Garrison to George Benson, January 4, 1840, Garrison Papers, Boston Public Library.
5. Henry C. Wright to William Lloyd Garrison, February 20, 1840, quoted in *Life*, II, 339–340.
6. See the account of the meeting in the *Liberator*, March 20, 1840.
7. The quotation is from the *Philanthropist*, May 5, 1840. Earle replaced LeMoyne who had declined the Warsaw nomination.
8. *Liberator*, February 14, February 21, 1840.
9. Garrison printed the "Address" in the *Liberator*, February 28, 1840.

10. *Liberator*, March 13, 1840.
11. *Liberator*, March 27, 1840.
12. *Liberator*, April 3, 1840.
13. *Liberator*, April 10, 1840.
14. *Liberator*, April 17, 1840.
15. Garrison's account of the trip appeared in the *Liberator*, May 15, 1840.
16. See Garrison's account of the meeting, *Liberator*, May 15, May 22, 1840. The figures are his.
17. William Lloyd Garrison to Helen Garrison, May 15, 1840, Garrison Papers, Boston Public Library.
18. Lewis Tappan to Theodore Weld, May 26, 1840, *Weld-Grimké Letters*, II, 836.
19. William Lloyd Garrison to Helen Garrison, May 19, 1840, quoted in *Life*, II, 357–358.
20. See Lucretia Mott's diary of her visit, *Slavery and "The Woman Question,"* ed. Frederick B. Tolles (London, 1952), 29–31.
21. See Garrison's and Rogers's accounts in the *Liberator*, August 14, August 21, 1840.
22. William Lloyd Garrison to Helen Garrison, June 29, 1840, quoted in *Life*, II, 381–382.
23. James Birney to Lewis Tappan, July 23, 1840, *Birney Letters*, II, 584.
24. William Lloyd Garrison to Helen Garrison, June 29, 1840, Garrison Papers, Boston Public Library.
25. William Lloyd Garrison to Helen Garrison, July 23, 1840, quoted in *Life*, II, 397.
26. Garrison did not publish an account of the meeting until December 18, 1840, when a Scotch Chartist named Charles McEwan wrote an open letter to him warning him not to imitate abolitionists in Scotland "who neglect their own country and attend to strangers." Garrison replied to McEwan in the same issue of the *Liberator* and again made the distinction between slavery as a legal institution and incidental economic injustices.
27. William Lloyd Garrison to Henry Wright, December 16, 1843, Garrison Papers, Boston Public Library.
28. William Lloyd Garrison to Samuel J. May, September 6, 1840, Garrison Papers, Boston Public Library.
29. William Lloyd Garrison to Elizabeth Pease, September 30, 1840, Garrison Papers, Boston Public Library.
30. John A. Collins to William Lloyd Garrison, September 1, 1840, quoted in *Life*, II, 414.
31. *Liberator*, November 6, 1840.
32. William Lloyd Garrison to John A. Collins, October 16, 1840, Garrison Papers, Boston Public Library.
33. *Liberator*, October 30, November 13, 1840.
34. "The Chardon Street Convention," *Collected Works* (Boston, 1833) X, 371–377.
35. The call was printed in the *Liberator*, October 16, 1840.
36. William Lloyd Garrison to George Benson, November 1, 1840, quoted in *Life*, II, 423–424.
37. *Liberator*, February 5, 1841.
38. Such at least was Emerson's conclusion.

14: "NO UNION WITH SLAVEHOLDERS"

1. *Writings of Nathaniel P. Rogers,* quoted in *Life,* III, 22.
2. Edmund Quincy to Richard D. Webb, June 27–July 26, 1843, quoted in *Life,* III, 82–83.
3. Sidney H. Gay to Edmund Quincy, August 21, 1844, Garrison Papers, Boston Public Library. A young man of thirty at the time, Gay was a member of an old Boston family and a friend of Phillips and Quincy. When the Childs resigned from the *Standard,* he took over as editor along with Quincy and Mrs. Chapman.
4. William Lloyd Garrison to Helen Garrison, November 27, 1842, quoted in *Life,* III, 67–71.
5. Edmund Quincy to William Lloyd Garrison, November 6, 1843, quoted in *Life,* III, 84–87.
6. John A. Collins to William Lloyd Garrison, December 7, 1840, Garrison Papers, Boston Public Library.
7. *Liberator,* January 5, 1844.
8. The constitution of Hopedale appeared in the *Liberator,* February 26, 1841.
9. *Liberator,* October 28, 1843. "The formation of the various reformatory associations of the day," he wrote in 1841, "notwithstanding we may gladly hail their appearance, must be looked upon with a feeling of sadness, as furnishing so many proofs of the spurious character of American Christianity. Genuine Christianity would require no special effort — no separate organization, to carry out the principles of anti-slavery, or of any other moral or social reform; for it would make clean work of everything which is offensive to God, or injurious to man." *Liberator,* August 11, 1841.
10. William Lloyd Garrison to George W. Benson, January 7, 1841, quoted in *Life,* III, 25, fn.
11. *Liberator,* January 5, 1844.
12. *Liberator,* November 19, 1841.
13. *Liberator,* February 10, 1843.
14. For Garrison's exegesis of the phrase "this generation," see the *Liberator,* January 12, 1844. His sobering second thoughts on Noyes and his Putney experiment, particularly his ideas on marriage, are found in the *Liberator,* November 27, 1841. For his estimate of Father Miller see the issue for February 10, 1843.
15. *Liberator,* July 30, 1841.
16. Nathaniel P. Rogers to Richard D. Webb, February 20, 1842, Garrison Papers, Boston Public Library.
17. William Lloyd Garrison to Helen Garrison, November 27, 1842, quoted in *Life,* III, 69. For the story of Foster's career see Parker Pillsbury, *Acts of the Anti-Slavery Apostles* (Concord, N.H., 1883), chs. VII–XII.
18. Stephen Symonds Foster to William Lloyd Garrison, February 20, 1841, Garrison Papers, Boston Public Library.
19. *Liberator,* 12: 95, quoted in *Life,* III, 28.
20. Wendell Phillips to Richard D. Webb, July 27, 1841, Garrison Papers, Boston Public Library.
21. The height of Garrison's campaign against the Liberty Party came in

1841–1842. See, for example, editorials in the *Liberator*, January 1, April 16, August 12, 1841, from which the quotations are taken.

22. James C. Jackson, a political abolitionist from Massachusetts, called Garrison an abstractionist; and Alvan Stewart, a Liberty Party organizer in New York, concluded his letter of criticism to Garrison with the lament that "such supreme folly should have entered this world." *Liberator*, August 4, 1843.

23. *Liberator*, October 1, 1841.

24. "When a nation is to be reformed, the first thing *in order*, is to arouse it from its slumber of moral death; and when this is accomplished — when the trump of reformation has startled every sleeper and agitated every bosom — the reformation may be said to have made a mighty stride onward." *Liberator*, January 28, 1842.

25. "Voting for Liberty men is the end of the law of righteousness. . . . Here we have the cloven foot of political selfishness revealed without disguise. Here, too, we see of what elements the Liberty Party is composed. In order to secure votes, that party must disclaim all action against slavery except in a political form, and then only so far as to prevent the North from being unjustly overborne by the South. It must eschew the word abolitionism — discard every feature that would serve to identify it with the original anti-slavery movement — operate mainly on the selfish principle — welcome all to its ranks who will, in its terms, subscribe to 'the Declaration of Independence and the Constitution,' not of the Anti-Slavery Society, but of the United States. They who are disposed to join it are assured that they need not be abolitionists at all, unless they choose. . . . Our opposition to the Liberty Party does not arise from our unwillingness to see a political change effected in favor of universal emancipation in our country. Far from it. . . . It is as impossible for men to be moral reformers and political partisans at the same time, as it is for fire and gunpowder to harmonize together. Change the religious sentiment of the North on the subject of slavery, and the political action of the North will instantly co-operate with it. With this religious sentiment, — now thrown into the scales of slavery — the Liberty party has no conflict. It seeks to effect political reform independently of religious reform." *Liberator*, November 11, 1842.

26. Beriah Green in a letter of complaint which Garrison published, *Liberator*, September 2, 1842.

27. *Liberator*, March 11, 1842.

28. *Liberator*, September 2, 1842.

29. Abby Kelley (Foster) to William Lloyd Garrison, September 6, 1843, Garrison Papers, Boston Public Library.

30. *Liberator*, November 26, 1841.

31. *Liberator*, 12: 18, quoted in *Life*, III, 46.

32. William Lloyd Garrison to George Benson, March 22, 1842, Garrison Papers, Boston Public Library.

33. *Liberator*, September 13, September 20, 1844.

34. Edmund Quincy to Richard D. Webb, January 29, 1843, quoted in *Life*, III, 88–89.

35. Edmund Quincy to Richard D. Webb, June 27–July 26, 1843, Garrison Papers, Boston Public Library.

36. *Acts and Resolves of Massachusetts*, 1843, ch. 19, 69, n.d.

37. *Acts and Resolves of Massachusetts,* 1845, 598–599.
38. *Liberator,* October 31, 1845.

15: COMPROMISE

1. Caroline Weston to Anne Warren Weston, June 13, 1846, Weston Papers, Boston Public Library.
2. William Lloyd Garrison to Helen Garrison, August 4, 1846, Garrison Papers, Boston Public Library.
3. William Lloyd Garrison to Helen Garrison, August 18, 1846, Garrison Papers, Boston Public Library.
4. William Lloyd Garrison to Elizabeth Pease, April 1, 1847, Garrison Papers, Boston Public Library.
5. William Lloyd Garrison to Richard D. Webb, July 1, 1847, Garrison Papers, Boston Public Library.
6. "Next to a fort, arsenal, naval vessel, and military array, I hate a customhouse — not because of the tax it imposed on the friendly Scottish gift, but as a matter of principle." Garrison to Mrs. Louisa Loring, July 30, 1847, quoted in *Life,* III, 179.
7. William Lloyd Garrison to Elizabeth Pease, July (?), 1847, Garrison Papers, Boston Public Library.
8. William Lloyd Garrison to Richard D. Webb, March 1, 1847, Garrison Papers, Boston Public Library.
9. Wendell Phillips to Francis Jackson, January, 1847, Garrison Papers, Boston Public Library.
10. *Liberator,* July 2, 1847.
11. William Lloyd Garrison to Helen Garrison, August 9, 1847, Garrison Papers, Boston Public Library.
12. "Address to the Friends of Freedom and Emancipation in the United States," written by Garrison and issued by the Executive Committee of the American Anti-Slavery Society. The address was printed in the *Liberator,* 14: 86–87 and is quoted in *Life,* III, 107–110.
13. *Liberator,* May 7, 1847.
14. William Lloyd Garrison to Helen Garrison, August 28, 1847, Garrison Papers, Boston Public Library.
15. William Lloyd Garrison to Helen Garrison, September 18, 1847, Garrison Papers, Boston Public Library.
16. William Lloyd Garrison to Helen Garrison, October 20, 1847, Garrison Papers, Boston Public Library. Douglass finally selected Rochester as the site of his paper which he called the *North Star.* The first issue was published on December 3, 1847. Garrison and Douglass continued to meet at anti-slavery conventions, but their relationship was no longer cordial. The breach finally came at the annual meeting of the national society in Syracuse in 1851, when Douglass refused to accept Garrison's pro-slavery interpretation of the Constitution.
17. Theodore Parker to William Lloyd Garrison, January 9, 1848, quoted in *Life,* III, 220.
18. Edmund Quincy to Richard D. Webb, March 9, 1848, quoted in *Life,* III, 218–220.
19. *Liberator,* February 25, 1848.
20. *Liberator,* 18: 186, quoted in *Life,* III, 145–147.
21. *Liberator,* March 10, 1848.

22. *Liberator*, 18:134, quoted in *Life*, III, 235.
23. *Boston Recorder*, quoted in the *Liberator*, February 9, 1849.
24. William Lloyd Garrison to Edmund Quincy, n.d., quoted in *Life*, III, 235.
25. *Congressional Globe*, 31st Cong., 1st Sess., Vol. XXII, Part 1, 646ff, 476ff.
26. *New York Herald*, May 6, May 7, 1850.
27. The annual meeting was reported in the *New York Herald*, May 8–9, 1850, and more fully in the *Liberator* and *Anti-Slavery Standard*. See *Life*, III, ch. X.
28. *Philadelphia Ledger*, May 14, 1850.

16: THE GREAT SLAVE POWER CONSPIRACY

1. *Liberator*, 21:19, quoted in *Life*, III, 319.
2. J. Miller McKim to Sarah Pugh, November 1, 1852, Garrison Papers, Boston Public Library.
3. Edmund Quincy to Samuel May, Jr., June 10, 1851, Garrison Papers, Boston Public Library. Samuel May, Jr., was the nephew of Garrison's old colleague and for many years the General Agent of the Massachusetts Society.
4. For Garrison's opinions of Father Mathew see the issues of the *Liberator* for August and September, 1849. Garrison's original letter to the priest requesting his support for anti-slavery appears in *Life*, III, 248–250.
5. *Liberator*, March 30, 1849.
6. See Garrison's editorial in the *National Anti-Slavery Standard*, October 25, 1856 in which he censures the "proscriptive and pro-slavery" spirit of the American Party. In 1854, however, he was forced to admit that the Know-Nothing legislature of Massachusetts was one of the most democratic in the history of the state, but attributed this to the fact that "the aristocratic element was completely exorcised out of it." *Liberator*, 25:86, quoted in *Life*, III, 414, fn.
7. *Liberator*, July 6, 1849.
8. *Liberator*, 21: 203, quoted in *Life*, III, 345.
9. *Liberator*, August 24, 1849.
10. Francis Bowen, "The War of Races in Hungary," and "The Politics of Europe," *North American Review*, LXX (1850), 78–100, 499–520.
11. Garrison's speech at the preliminary woman's rights meeting in June, 1850, is quoted in *Life*, III, 309–312.
12. *Liberator*, 22:74, quoted in *Life*, III, 375–376. "I am a firm believer in the reality of those spiritual manifestations, after the many things I have witnessed, and the various tests I have seen applied; yet I am not a credulous man, nor at all given to the marvellous, and seldom exercise my ideality." Garrison to Lydia Maria Child, February 6, 1857, Garrison Papers, Boston Public Library.
13. Andrew Jackson Davis, "A Psychometric Examination of William Lloyd Garrison," *The Penetralia: Being Harmonial Answers to Important Questions* (Boston, 1856).
14. *Liberator*, 21:114, quoted in *Life*, III, 368.
15. "The Function and Place of Conscience in Relation to the Laws of Men: A Sermon for the Times, Preached at the Melodeon on Sunday,

September 22, 1850," *Collected Works of Theodore Parker*, ed. F. D. Cobbe, 14 vols. (London, 1863–1874), vol. V, 138–139.
16. Parker's remark is quoted in Henry Steele Commager, *Theodore Parker: Yankee Crusader*, 2nd ed. (Boston, 1960), 215.
17. Charles Francis Adams, Jr., *Richard Henry Dana*, 2 vols. (Boston, 1890), I, 216–217.
18. *Liberator*, February 18, 1851.
19. Samuel J. May to William Lloyd Garrison, December 6, 1851, Garrison Papers, Boston Public Library.
20. *Liberator*, March 26, 1852. Garrison nevertheless was concerned with the problems of the Underground Railroad and noted a passage in Sunderland's *Spiritual Philosophers* on the ability of Australian bushmen to travel without compasses. "The method is to 'turn very gradually around while the chin is rather depressed upon the cravat,' and, at the same time to repeat, rapidly and continually, the hissing sound *sh*, till the breath spontaneously stops, and thereby indicates that you are facing the magnetic North, the magnetic East, or the Magnetic West — ... the experimenter may know he is facing magnetic *North*, by this test; that when he is actually facing the magnetic North, the hissing breath will *not* be suspended, by facing exactly 'to-the-right-about.'" Manuscript marked "Not for Publication," and dated March 3, 1851, Garrison Papers, Boston Public Library.
21. Garrison's speech in Westchester, Pennsylvania, was delivered on October 26, 1852, and is quoted in *Life*, III, 365.
22. *Liberator*, 24: 82, quoted in *Life*, III, 409.
23. George Murray McConnel, "Recollections of Stephen A. Douglas," *Illinois State Historical Society Transactions* (Springfield, 1901), 48 et. seq., quoted in George Fort Milton, *The Eve of Conflict: Stephen A. Douglas and the Needless War* (Cambridge, Mass., 1834), 121.

17: SECESSION

1. *Liberator*, 26: 142–146, quoted in *Life*, III, 443. Another of Garrison's editorials saluted the Republican Party as the "legitimate product of the *moral* agitation of the subject of slavery for the last quarter of the century." *Liberator*, 26: 166.
2. *Liberator*, 26: 174, quoted in *Life*, III, 447.
3. Resolutions presented by Garrison and passed by the New England Anti-Slavery Convention, May 27, 1856.
4. *Liberator*, 26: 166, quoted in *Life*, III, 444.
5. William Lloyd Garrison to Samuel J. May, September 14, 1857, Garrison Papers, Boston Public Library.
6. William Lloyd Garrison to Abby Kelley Foster, September 14, 1859. See also letters of his to Mrs. Foster dated July 22, July 25, September 8, 1859, Garrison Papers, Boston Public Library.
7. *Liberator*, September 4, 1857.
8. *Liberator*, 26: 166, quoted in *Life*, III, 444–446.
9. *Liberator*, July 10, 1857.
10. Garrison's own admission in the *Liberator*, January 22, 1857.
11. Garrison's speech was printed in the *Liberator*, January 22, 1857.
12. William Lloyd Garrison to Helen Garrison, February 14, 1858, Garrison Papers, Boston Public Library.

13. William Lloyd Garrison to Helen Garrison, October 29, 1858, Garrison Papers, Boston Public Library.
14. The call for the Disunion Convention was published in the *Liberator*, September 25, 1857.
15. *Liberator*, November 20, 1857.
16. *Liberator*, April 30, May 21, 1858.
17. *Liberator*, July 31, 1857.
18. Debates of the Massachusetts Anti-Slavery Society, 1858, reported in the *Liberator*, February 5, 1858.
19. For Garrison's editorials on John Brown see the *Liberator*, November, December, 1859, January 13, 17, 1860.
20. Speech at the John Brown Memorial Observance Day held at the Tremont Temple, November 2, 1859. See *Liberator*, December 9, 1859. Italics mine.
21. *Liberator*, 29: 18, quoted in *Life*, III, 483; *Liberator*, September 7, 1860.
22. *Liberator*, September 7, November 9, 1860.
23. Garrison's Fourth of July speech at Framingham Grove published in the *Liberator*, July 20, 1860. After the election, however, he complimented Lincoln on his "dignity and self-respect" and his decision to give "no countenance to any of the compromises that have yet been proposed."
24. Garrison's speech at the annual meeting of the American Anti-Slavery Society, May, 1860, reported in the *Liberator*, June 1, 1860.
25. *Liberator*, November 16, 1860.
26. *Liberator*, January 6, November 23, 1860.
27. *Liberator*, January 4, 1861.
28. *Liberator*, April 12, February 15, 1860.
29. *Liberator*, March 8, 1861.
30. *Liberator*, April 12, 1861. Garrison's new patriotism antedated the bombardment of Fort Sumter by a month. "Look at the present state of the country! The old Union breaking up daily, its columns falling in every direction — four Southern States already out of it, and all the others busily and openly preparing to follow — the national Government paralyzed through indecision, cowardice, or perfidy — the national flag trampled upon and discarded by the traitors, and a murderous endeavor on their part, by firing heavy shot, to sink a Government vessel entering the harbor of Charleston upon a lawful errand, compelling her to flee in disgrace . . . treason and traitors everywhere, in every slave State, in every free State, at the seat of Government, in both Houses of Congress, in the army and navy, in the Executive department, at the head of the press, audacious, defiant, diabolical." *Liberator*, March 8, 1861.
31. *Liberator*, April 19, 1861.
32. *Liberator*, April 26, May 3, 1861.
33. *Liberator*, May 10, 1861.
34. Garrison explained his view on the peace cause in a series of letters to Johnson, Edward Davis, Miller McKim, *et al.*, May–December, 1861, Garrison Papers, Boston Public Library.
35. *Liberator*, April 23, 1858.
36. Yet as late as May 28, 1860, Garrison complained that "the war spirit is evidently on the increase in this country, and next to nothing seems to be doing directly for the promotion of peace. . . . We think the Peace

Society itself, in evading the Anti-Slavery issue of the times has been signally untrue to its object — blindly overlooking the great obstacle existing to the achievement of that object."

18: ARMAGEDDON AT LAST

1. "The Copperhead," *Liberator*, July 30, 1863.
2. Garrison's speech was printed in the *Liberator*, August 29, 1862.
3. *Liberator*, June 27, September 26, 1862.
4. *Liberator*, July 25, 1861.
5. William Lloyd Garrison to George Thompson, February 21, 1862, printed in the *Liberator* of the same date.
6. *Liberator*, July 26, 1861.
7. *Liberator*, June 7, 1861.
8. William Lloyd Garrison to Oliver Johnson, December 6, 1861, Garrison Papers, Boston Public Library. "If there be not soon an 'irrepressible conflict' in the Republican ranks, in regard to his course of policy, I shall almost despair of the country." *Liberator*, December 6, 1861.
9. *The Complete Works of Abraham Lincoln*, ed. J. G. Nicolay, John Hay, and F. D. Tandy, 12 vols. (New York, 1905), X, 65.
10. William Lloyd Garrison to James Redpath, an open letter published in the *Liberator*, December 7, 1860.
11. Garrison's speech was reported in the *Liberator*, August 9, 1861.
12. William Lloyd Garrison to Oliver Johnson, September 9, 1862, Garrison Papers, Boston Public Library.
13. Garrison's speech to the Massachusetts Anti-Slavery Society, quoted in *Life*, IV, 43–45. Garrison could still be sharply critical of Lincoln's policy decisions. When the President appointed Halleck and McClellan as general-in-chief and commander of the Army of the Potomac, Garrison called him a "wet rag" and his decision "as near lunacy as any one not a pronounced Bedlamite" could make. "The satanic democracy of the North, and the traitorous 'loyalty' of the Border States, have almost absolute control over him, and are industriously preparing the way for the overthrow of his administration, and the inauguration, if not of a reign of terror, at least one that will make terms with Rebeldom, no matter how humiliating they may be." Garrison to Oliver Johnson, September 9, 1862, Garrison Papers, Boston Public Library.
14. *Liberator*, August 22, 1862. See also Garrison's editorial in the *Liberator*, March 21, 1862.
15. *Liberator*, October 3, 1862.
16. William Lloyd Garrison to Frances Garrison, September 25, 1862, Garrison Papers, Boston Public Library.
17. *Liberator*, December 5, 1862.
18. *Liberator*, December 25, 1862.
19. See the *Liberator*, January 16, January 30, February 6, 1863.
20. Excerpts from Phillips's Boston speech at a Republican rally and the Cooper Union speech are quoted in Ralph Korngold, *Two Friends of Man* (Boston, 1950), 297, 321–322.
21. *Liberator*, 33: 202, quoted in *Life*, IV, 85 fn.
22. *Liberator*, June 5, 1863.
23. "Especially do we consider it very unfortunate for any one, claiming to

be a Non-Resistant, who so enforces the doctrine as to give 'aid and comfort' to traitors and their copperhead sympathizers at this particular crisis." *Liberator*, July 31, 1863. To Oliver Johnson he wrote, "Ardently as my soul yearns for universal peace, and greatly shocking to it as are the horrors of war, I deem this a time when the friends of peace will best subserve their holy cause to wait until the whirlwind, the fire and the earthquake are past, and then 'the still small voice' may be understandingly and improvingly heard." Garrison to Oliver Johnson, July 5, 1863, Garrison Papers, Boston Public Library.

24. William Lloyd Garrison to Alfred H. Love, November 9, 1863, Garrison Papers, Boston Public Library.
25. William Lloyd Garrison to George Garrison, August 6, 1863, quoted in *Life*, IV, 83–84.
26. Garrison's speech at the annual meeting of the Massachusetts Society was reported in the *Liberator*, 34: 22, and is quoted in *Life*, IV, 94–97.
27. *Liberator*, 34:23, quoted in *Life*, IV, 104.
28. Garrison's speech at the New England Convention, reported in the *Liberator*, 34: 94, quoted in *Life*, IV, 111. Italics mine.
29. William Lloyd Garrison to Helen Garrison, June 8, 1864, Garrison Papers, Boston Public Library.
30. William Lloyd Garrison to Helen Garrison, June 9–11, 1864, Garrison Papers, Boston Public Library; *Liberator*, 34: 99, quoted in *Life*, IV, 117.
31. Copy of a letter from Garrison to Oliver Johnson, June 17, 1864; Garrison to Johnson, June 20, 1864, Garrison Papers, Boston Public Library.
32. William Lloyd Garrison to Samuel May, Jr., June 17, 1864, Garrison Papers, Boston Public Library.
33. *Liberator*, July 22, 1864.
34. *Liberator*, August 19, 1864.
35. "Reconstruction," *Liberator*, December 2, 1864.
36. Debates of the Annual Meeting of the American Anti-Slavery Society, May 9–10, 1865, reported in the *Liberator*, 35: 81, and quoted in *Life*, IV, 158–159.
37. *Liberator*, January 13, 1865; *Liberator*, 34: 118, quoted in *Life*, IV, 123–124.
38. The vote, 118 to 48 against disbanding the American Anti-Slavery Society, was an index of abolitionist strength in 1865.

19: RECONSTRUCTION AND REDEMPTION

1. *Liberator*, December 29, 1865.
2. Ann Phillips to Henry C. Wright, December 7, 1868, Weston Papers, Boston Public Library.
3. William Lloyd Garrison to Frances Garrison Villard, January 27, 1866, Garrison Papers, Boston Public Library.
4. William Lloyd Garrison to Oliver Johnson, February 11, 1866, Garrison Papers, Boston Public Library.
5. William Lloyd Garrison to Frances Garrison Villard, April 2, 1866, Garrison Papers, Boston Public Library.
6. William Lloyd Garrison to Frances Garrison Villard, March 3, 1866, Garrison Papers, Boston Public Library.

7. William Lloyd Garrison to Henry C. Wright, February 9, 1866, Garrison Papers, Boston Public Library.
8. William Lloyd Garrison to Wendell P. Garrison, March 25, 1866, Garrison Papers, Boston Public Library.
9. William Lloyd Garrison to Helen Garrison, April 6, 1866, Garrison Papers, Boston Public Library.
10. The letter of the Testimonial Committee to Garrison and his reply are quoted in *Life*, IV, 183–188.
11. William Lloyd Garrison to Francis J. Garrison, April 12, 1866, Garrison Papers, Boston Public Library.
12. William Lloyd Garrison to Wendell P. Garrison, April 10, 1866, Garrison Papers, Boston Public Library.
13. Draft of a letter to the Sumter Club, April 13, 1866, Garrison Papers, Boston Public Library.
14. William Lloyd Garrison to Frances Garrison Villard, August 11, 1866, Garrison Papers, Boston Public Library. Garrison's fear of a *coup d'état* lingered until December. In September he warned of the "conflict" that "yet remains to be fought with the dragon of slavery." Garrison to Samuel May, September 18, 1866. In October he wrote to Frank that he still thought "the President means to make, if need be, a forcible issue with Congress in December." Garrison to Francis J. Garrison, October 26, 1866. Finally in December in another letter to Frank he admitted that Johnson's annual message was "subdued and measured in its tone, though still stubbornly bent on the policy of reconstruction marked out by its upstart author! . . . It is manifest, already, that Congress is bent on carrying out its program, conscious that the people will expect nothing less, and perhaps will insist on something more. The popular feeling is cheering." December 7, 1866, Garrison Papers, Boston Public Library.
15. William Lloyd Garrison to Frances Garrison Villard, September 21, 1866, Garrison Papers, Boston Public Library.
16. William Lloyd Garrison to Francis J. Garrison, January 18, 1867, Garrison Papers, Boston Public Library.
17. "The Duties of the Hour," *Independent*, January 17, 1867.
18. William Lloyd Garrison to Henry C. Wright, January 11, 1868, Garrison Papers, Boston Public Library.
19. William Lloyd Garrison to Helen Garrison, May 24, 1867, Garrison Papers, Boston Public Library.
20. Garrison to Helen Garrison, October 3, October 12, 1867; Garrison to Frances Garrison Villard, October 4, 1867, Garrison Papers, Boston Public Library.
21. Garrison to Oliver Johnson, July 30, 1867; Garrison to Helen Garrison, July 16, 1867, Garrison Papers, Boston Public Library.
22. William Lloyd Garrison to Wendell P. Garrison, July 25, 1872, Garrison Papers, Boston Public Library.
23. Open letter to the Hon. Charles Sumner, *Boston Journal*, August 3, 1872.
24. William Lloyd Garrison to Wendell P. Garrison, March 10, 1876, Garrison Papers, Boston Public Library.
25. *Independent*, April 2, 1868.
26. *Independent*, April 16, 1874.

27. William Lloyd Garrison to W. G. H. Smart, 1874, quoted in Korngold, *Two Friends of Man*, 365.
28. William Lloyd Garrison to Henry Ward Beecher, May 10, 1870, quoted in *Life*, IV, 244–245.
29. Letter to the *Boston Journal*, April 21, 1869.
30. Letter to the *New York Tribune*, February 27, 1879. See also his letters to the same paper, February 17, February 25, 1879.
31. Garrison was the most tolerant of grandparents. When Fanny complained of her children's behavior, he reassured her with permissive advice. "That they will have their wayward turns, like other children, we expect, and shall appreciate them none the less." Fanny's little girl Helen was his favorite. "I mean to be very impartial, but if I shall lean a little more toward Helen, her sex must be my apology! The very delicacy of her nature and the nervous susceptibility of her constitution draw her very closely to my heart. Treat her, always, with great tenderness." Garrison to Frances Garrison Villard, April 3, 1874, Garrison Papers, Boston Public Library.

EPILOGUE

1. Garrison printed Brownson's article, "The Abolitionists — Free Discussion" in the "Refuge of Oppression" column of the *Liberator*, October 19, 1838. Italics mine.

Bibliography

MANUSCRIPTS

American Anti-Slavery Society Agency Committee Minutes, 1833–1840.
American Anti-Slavery Society Executive Committee Minutes, 1837–1840.
James G. Birney Papers. William L. Clements Library, University of Michigan.
Maria Weston Chapman and Henry G. Chapman Papers. Boston Public Library.
Lydia Maria Child and David Lee Child Papers. Boston Public Library.
Edward M. Davis Papers. Houghton Library, Harvard University.
Mary A. Estlin Papers. Boston Public Library.
Abby Kelley Foster Papers. Worcester Historical Society.
William Lloyd Garrison Papers. Boston Public Library.
William Lloyd Garrison Family Papers. Sophia Smith Collection, Smith College.
Samuel May, Jr. Papers. Boston Public Library.
Theodore Parker Papers. Massachusetts Historical Society.
Amos Phelps Papers. Boston Public Library.
Quincy–Webb Correspondence. Boston Public Library.
Gerrit Smith Papers. Syracuse University.
Lewis Tappan Papers. Manuscript Division, Library of Congress.
Henry Villard Papers. Houghton Library, Harvard University.
Theodore Weld, Angelina Grimké Weld, and Sarah Grimké Papers. William L. Clements Library, University of Michigan.
Weston Family Papers. Boston Public Library.
Elizur Wright, Jr. Papers. Manuscript Division, Library of Congress.

REPORTS, PROCEEDINGS, PLATFORMS

American Anti-Slavery Society, Declaration of Sentiments, 1833.
Annual Report of the American Anti-Slavery Society, 1834–1839, 1855–1861.
Annual Report of the Massachusetts Anti-Slavery Society, 1836–1853.
Annual Report of the New England Anti-Slavery Society, 1833–1835.
Annual Report of the New England Anti-Slavery Convention, 1836, 1838.
Proceedings of the American Anti-Slavery Society, 1833, 1853, 1863.
Proceedings of the New England Anti-Slavery Convention, 1834, 1836.
Proceedings of the Massachusetts State Disunion Convention, 1857.

NEWSPAPERS

African Repository (Washington, D.C.)
Emancipator (New York and Boston)
Free Press (Newburyport, Mass.)
Friend of Man (Utica, N.Y.)
Genius of Universal Emancipation (Baltimore, Md.)
Herald of Freedom (Concord, N.H.)
Independent (New York)
Journal of the Times (Bennington, Vt.)
Liberator (Boston)
Massachusetts Abolitionist (Boston)
National Anti-Slavery Standard (New York)
National Philanthropist (Boston)
Newburyport Herald (Newburyport, Mass.)
Pennsylvania Freeman (Philadelphia)
Philanthropist (New Richmond, Cincinnati)

GARRISON'S WRITINGS AND SPEECHES

Address at Park Street Church, Boston, July 4, 1829. Old South Leaflets (General Series, vol. 8, No. 180).
An Address delivered before the Free People of Color, in Philadelphia, New York, etc. Boston, 1831.
An Address on the Progress of the Abolition Cause. Boston, 1832.
Address delivered in Boston, New York, and Philadelphia before the Free People of Color. New York, 1833.
Slavery in the United States of America, an Appeal to the Friends of Negro Emancipation Throughout Great Britain. London, 1833.
A Selection of Anti-Slavery Hymns, for the Use of the Friends of Emancipation. Boston, 1834.
Shall the Liberator Die? Boston, 1834.
Juvenile Poems for the Use of Free American Children, of Every Complexion. Boston, 1835.
An address in Marlboro' Chapel. Boston, 1838.
An Address at the Broadway Tabernacle, New York . . . in commemoration of the Complete Emancipation of 600,000 Slaves . . . in the British West Indies. Boston, 1838.
A Letter on the Political Obligations of Abolitionists by James G. Birney: with a Reply by William Lloyd Garrison. Boston, 1839.
Sonnets and Other Poems. Boston, 1843.
Address on the Subject of American Slavery. London, 1846.
Selections from the Writings and Speeches of William Lloyd Garrison. Boston, 1852.
To Kossuth. Boston, 1852.
Principles and Modes of Action of the American Anti-Slavery Society. London, 1853.
No Compromise with Slavery. New York, 1854.
West India Emancipation. Boston, 1854.
The "Infidelity" of Abolitionism. New York, 1860.
The New Reign of Terror. New York, 1860.

The Loyalty and Devotion of the Colored Americans in the Revolution and War of 1812. Boston, 1861.

Spirit of the South towards Northern Freemen and Soldiers defending the American Flag Against Traitors of the Deepest Dye. Boston, 1861.

The Abolitionists and Their Relations to the War. New York, 1862.

Southern Hatred of the American Government, the People of the North, and Free Institutions. Boston, 1862.

"Introduction" to *Joseph Mazzini, His Life, Writings, and Political Principles.* New York, 1872.

Letters of William Lloyd Garrison, Wendell Phillips, and James G. Blaine . . . for All Who are Interested in the Approaching Election . . . Concord, N.H., 1872.

Helen Eliza Garrison: A Memorial. Cambridge, Mass., 1876.

The Nation's Shame: Sonnets. Boston, 1899.

CONTEMPORARY BOOKS, PAMPHLETS, SERMONS, BIOGRAPHIES, AND COLLECTIONS

Adams, Charles Francis, ed. *The Memoirs of John Quincy Adams.* 12 vols. Philadelphia, 1874–1877.

Adams, Nehemiah. *A Southside View of Slavery.* Boston, 1855.

Bacon, Leonard. *Slavery Discussed in Occasional Essays from 1833–1846.* New York, 1846.

Ballou, Adin. *History of the Hopedale Community . . .* Lowell, Mass., 1897.

Beecher, Charles. *The Autobiography and Correspondence of Lyman Beecher.* 2 vols. New York, 1865.

Birney, J. G. *The American Churches, the Bulwarks of American Slavery.* Newburyport, Mass., 1834.

———. *Letter on Colonization . . .* New York, 1836.

Bourne, George. *The Book and Slavery Irreconcilable.* Philadelphia, 1816.

Bowditch, William I. *The Rendition of Anthony Burns.* Boston, 1854.

———. *Slavery and the Constitution.* Boston, 1849.

Channing, William Ellery. *Slavery.* Boston, 1836.

Child, Lydia Maria. *Anti-Slavery Catechism.* Newburyport, Mass., 1836.

Clarke, James Freeman. *Anti-Slavery Days.* New York, 1883.

Collins, John A. *Right and Wrong Amongst Abolitionists in the United States.* Glasgow, 1841.

Crallé, Richard, ed. *The Works of John C. Calhoun.* 6 vols. New York, 1853–1855.

Dresser, Amos. *The Narrative of Amos Dresser, with Stone's Letters from Natchez.* New York, 1836.

Earle, Thomas. *The Life, Travels and Opinions of Benjamin Lundy.* Philadelphia, 1847.

Finney, Charles G. *Lectures on Revivals.* Sixth edition. New York, 1835.

Fitzhugh, George. *Sociology for the South.* New York, 1854.

Foster, Stephen S. *The Brotherhood of Thieves, a True Picture of the American Church and Clergy.* Boston, 1843.

Garrison, William Lloyd. *Thoughts on African Colonization . . .* Boston, 1832.

Garland, H. A. *The Life of John Randolph of Roanoke.* 2 vols. New York, 1856.

Goodell, William. *An Account of Interviews which took place . . . be-*

tween a Committee of the Massachusetts Anti-Slavery Society and the committee of the legislature . . . Boston, 1836.

————. *Come-outerism: the Duty to Secede from a Corrupt Church.* New York, 1845.

————. *A Full Statement of the Reasons which were in part offered to the Committee of the Legislature* . . . Boston, 1836.

————. *Slavery and Anti-Slavery.* New York, 1852.

————. *Views of American Constitutional Law, in its Bearing on American Slavery.* Utica, N.Y., 1844.

Green, Beriah. *Sketches of the Life and Writings of James Gillespie Birney* . . . Utica, N.Y., 1844.

————. *Things for Northern Men to Do.* Whiteside, N.Y., 1836.

Grimké, Angelina. *Letter to Catherine Beecher* . . . Boston, 1838.

Helper, H. R. *The Impending Crisis in the South: How to Meet It.* New York, 1859.

Hemmenway, John. *The Apostle of Peace: Memoir of William Ladd.* Boston, 1872.

Higginson, Thomas Wentworth. *Contemporaries.* Boston, 1899.

Hosmer, William. *The Higher Law in its Relation to Civil Government.* Auburn, N.Y., 1852.

Jay, William. *An Inquiry into the Character and Tendencies of the American Anti-Slavery Society.* New York, 1835.

————. *Miscellaneous Writings on Slavery.* Boston, 1853.

Johnson, Oliver. *William Lloyd Garrison and His Times.* Boston, 1879.

Livermore, George. *An Historical Research Respecting the Opinions of the Founders of the Republic on Negroes.* Boston, 1862.

Lovejoy, J. C. and O. *Memoir of the Reverend Elijah P. Lovejoy.* New York, 1838.

Lowell, James Russell. *The Anti-Slavery Papers of James Russell Lowell.* 2 vols. Boston, 1902.

May, Samuel. *Some Recollections of Our Anti-Slavery Conflict.* Boston, 1869.

Merrill, Walter McIntosh, ed. *Behold Me Once More: The Confessions of James Holly Garrison.* Cambridge, Mass., 1954.

Mumford, Thomas J. *Memoir of Samuel May.* Boston, 1873.

Noyes, John Humphrey. *History of American Socialisms.* Philadelphia, 1870.

Parker, Theodore. *The Dangers from Slavery.* Boston, 1854.

————. *The New Crime Against Humanity* . . . Boston, 1854.

————. *The Trial of Theodore Parker.* Boston, 1855.

Phelps, Amos. *Lectures on Slavery and its Remedy.* Boston, 1834.

Phillips, Wendell. *The Constitution a Pro-Slavery Compact.* New York, 1856.

————. *Speech* . . . *at the Worcester Disunion Convention.* Boston, 1857.

————. *Speeches, Lectures, and Letters.* Boston, 1870.

Pierpont, John, ed. *A Collection of the Newspaper Writings of N. P. Rogers.* Concord, N.H., 1847.

Pillsbury, Parker. *Acts of the Anti-Slavery Apostles.* Concord, N.H., 1883.

————. *The Church as It Is.* Boston, 1847.

Rankin, John. *Letters on American Slavery.* Boston, 1833.

Seward, W. H. *The Irrepressible Conflict.* Albany, 1860.

Smith, Gerrit. *The Crime of the Abolitionists*. Peterboro, N.Y., 1835.
————. *Sermons and Speeches*. New York, 1861.
Spooner, Lysander. *The Unconstitutionality of Slavery*. Boston, 1847.
Stevens, Charles E. *Anthony Burns, A History*. Boston, 1856.
Stowe, Harriet Beecher. *Uncle Tom's Cabin*. Boston, 1852.
Stuart, Charles. *Is Slavery Defensible from Scripture?* Belfast, 1831.
Sumner, Charles. *Recent Speeches and Addresses*. Boston, 1856.
Tappan, Lewis. *Address to the Non-Slaveholders of the South on the Social and Political Evils of Slavery*. New York, 1833.
————. *The Life of Arthur Tappan*. London, 1870.
Tolles, Frederick B., ed. *Slavery and "The Woman Question," Lucretia Mott's Diary of her Visit to Great Britain to Attend the World's Anti-Slavery Convention of 1840*. Haverford, 1952.
Tracy, Joseph. "Historical Discourse," *Memorial of the Semi-Centennial Anniversary of the American Colonization Society*. Washington, D.C., 1867.
Walker, David. *Appeal in Four Articles Together with a Preamble to the Colored Citizens of the World, but in Particular, and Very Expressly, to those of the United States of America*. Boston, 1829.
Wayland, Francis, and Fuller, Richard. *Domestic Slavery Considered as a Scriptural Institution* . . . New York, 1845.
Weld, Theodore. *American Slavery as It Is*. New York, 1839.
————. *The Bible Against Slavery*. Pittsburgh, 1864.
————. *A Statement of the Reason which Induced the Students of Lane Seminary to Dissolve their Connection with that Institution*. Cincinnati, 1834.
Wilson, Henry. *Rise and Fall of the Slave Power in America*. 3 vols. Boston, 1872–1877.
Wright, Elizur, Jr. *The Sin of Slavery and its Remedy*. New York, 1833.

SECONDARY WORKS

Adams, Alice D. *The Neglected Period of Anti-Slavery*. Boston, 1908.
Adams, Henry, ed. *Documents Relating to New England Federalism*. Boston, 1877.
Annan, Noel. *Leslie Stephen*. London, 1951.
Aptheker, Herbert. *American Negro Slave Revolts*. New York, 1943.
————. "Militant Abolitionism," *Journal of Negro History*, XXVI (Oct., 1941), 438–445.
Armstrong, Maurice W. *The Great Awakening in Nova Scotia*. Hartford, Conn., 1948.
Barnes, Gilbert H. *The Antislavery Impulse*. New York, 1933.
Barnes, Gilbert H., and Dumond, Dwight L., eds. *The Letters of Theodore D. Weld, Angelina Grimké Weld, and Sarah Grimké*. 2 vols. New York, 1934.
Bemis, Samuel Flagg. *John Quincy Adams and the Union*. New York, 1956.
Bentley, George R. *A History of the Freedmen's Bureau*. Philadelphia, 1955.
Birney, Catherine H. *The Grimké Sisters*. Boston, 1885.
Birney, William. *James G. Birney and His Times*. New York, 1890.

Bodo, John R. *The Protestant Clergy and Public Issues.* Princeton, 1957.
Brebner, John B. *The Neutral Yankees of Nova Scotia.* New York, 1937.
Brown, Arthur. *Always Young for Liberty: A Biography of William Ellery Channing.* Syracuse, 1956.
Buckmaster, Henrietta. *Let My People Go: The Story of the Underground Railroad and the Growth of the Abolition Movement.* New York, 1941.
Chapman, John Jay. *William Lloyd Garrison.* New York, 1913.
Cole, Arthur C. *The Irrepressible Conflict.* New York, 1934.
————. "Lincoln and the American Tradition of Civil Liberty," *Illinois State Historical Society Journal,* XIX (Oct. 1926–Jan. 1927), 102–114.
Cole, Charles C. *The Social Ideas of the Northern Evangelists, 1826–1860.* New York, 1954.
Commager, Henry Steele. *Theodore Parker.* Boston, 1936.
Coupland, Reginald. *The British Anti-Slavery Movement.* London, 1933.
Craven, Avery O. *Civil War in the Making.* Baton Rouge, 1959.
————. *The Coming of the Civil War.* 2nd ed., Chicago, 1957.
————. "The Coming of the War Between the States, An Interpretation," *Journal of Southern History,* II (Feb.–Nov. 1936), 303–323.
————. *The Growth of Southern Nationalism* (*A History of the South,* edited by Wendell H. Stephenson and E. Merton Coulter, vol. VI), Baton Rouge, 1952.
————. *The Repressible Conflict.* Baton Rouge, 1939.
Cromwell, Otelia. *Lucretia Mott.* Cambridge, Mass., 1958.
Cross, Whitney R. *The Burned-Over District.* Ithaca, 1950.
Curti, Merle Eugene. *The American Peace Crusade, 1815–1860.* Durham, 1929.
Donald, David. *Charles Sumner and the Coming of the Civil War.* New York, 1960.
————. *Lincoln Reconsidered: Essays on the Civil War Era.* New York, 1956.
Donald, Henderson H. *The Negro Freedman: Life Conditions of the American Negro in the Early Years After Emancipation.* New York, 1952.
Dorris, Jonathan T. *Pardon and Amnesty Under Lincoln and Johnson: The Restoration of the Confederates to their Rights and Privileges, 1861–1898.* Chapel Hill, 1953.
Dumond, Dwight L. *Antislavery Origins of the Civil War.* Ann Arbor, 1939.
———— ed. *The Letters of James G. Birney.* 2 vols., New York, 1938.
Eaton, Clement. *Freedom of Thought in the Old South.* Durham, 1940.
————. "The Jeffersonian Tradition of Liberalism in America," *South Atlantic Quarterly,* XLIII (Jan., 1944), 1–10.
————. "The Resistance of the South to Northern Radicalism," *New England Quarterly,* VII (June, 1935), 215–231.
Filler, Louis. *The Crusade Against Slavery, 1830–1860.* New York, 1960.
Fish, Carl R. *The Rise of the Common Man, 1830–1850.* New York, 1927.
Fladeland, Betty. *James Gillespie Birney: Slaveholder to Abolitionist.* Ithaca, 1955.
Fletcher, Robert S. *A History of Oberlin College.* 2 vols., Oberlin, Ohio, 1943.
Foner, Philip S. *Business and Slavery.* Chapel Hill, 1941.

————. *The Life and Writings of Frederick Douglass.* 4 vols., New York, 1950–1955.

Forbush, Bliss. *Elias Hicks, Quaker Liberal.* New York, 1956.

Forster, E. M. *Marianne Thornton.* New York, 1956.

Fox, Early Lee. *The American Colonization Society, 1817–1840.* Baltimore, 1919.

Franklin, John Hope. *The Militant South, 1800–1861.* Cambridge, Mass., 1956.

Fuess, Claude M. *The Life of Caleb Cushing.* 2 vols., New York, 1923.

Hare, L. C. M. *The Greatest American Woman.* New York, 1937.

Harlow, Ralph Volney. *Gerrit Smith, Philanthropist and Reformer.* New York, 1939.

Hart, Albert B. *Slavery and Abolition.* New York, 1906.

Hofstadter, Richard. *The American Political Tradition and the Men Who Made It.* New York, 1948.

Jackson, Russell Leigh. "History of Newburyport Newspapers," *Essex Institute Historical Collections,* LXXVIII (April, 1952), 103–137.

James, Joseph B. *The Framing of the Fourteenth Amendment.* Urbana, Ill., 1956.

Jenkins, W. S. *Pro-Slavery Thought in the Old South.* Chapel Hill, 1935.

Klingberg, Frank J. *The Anti-Slavery Movement in England: A Study in English Humanitarianism.* New Haven, 1926.

Korngold, Ralph. *Two Friends of Man: The Story of William Lloyd Garrison and Wendell Phillips and their Relationship with Abraham Lincoln.* Boston, 1950.

Krout, John Allen. *The Origins of Prohibition.* New York, 1925.

Lloyd, Arthur Y. *The Slavery Controversy, 1831–1860.* Chapel Hill, 1939.

Locke, Mary S. *Anti-Slavery in America from the Introduction of African Slaves to the Prohibition of the Slave-Trade, 1619–1808.* Boston, 1910.

Malin, James C. *The Nebraska Question, 1852–1854.* Lawrence, Kansas, 1953.

Mathieson, William Law. *British Slavery and Its Abolition, 1823–1838.* London, 1926.

McLoughlin, William G. *Modern Revivalism: Charles Grandison Finney to Billy Graham.* New York, 1959.

Mead, Sidney Earl. *Nathaniel William Taylor.* Chicago, 1942.

Merrill, Walter McIntosh. "A Passionate Attachment," *New England Quarterly,* XXIX, 2, 182–203.

Milton, George Fort. *The Eve of Conflict: Stephen A. Douglas and the Needless War.* Cambridge, Mass., 1934.

Moore, Glover. *The Missouri Compromise.* Lexington, Ky., 1953.

Morison, Samuel Eliot. *The Life and Letters of Harrison Gray Otis.* 2 vols., Boston, 1913.

————. *The Maritime History of Massachusetts.* Boston, 1921.

Meyers, Marvin. *The Jacksonian Persuasion.* Stanford, 1957.

Nevins, Allan. *The Emergence of Lincoln.* 2 vols., New York, 1950.

————. *Ordeal of the Union.* 2 vols., New York, 1947.

Nichols, Roy Franklin. *The Disruption of American Democracy.* New York, 1948.

Noyes, George Wallingford, ed. *Religious Experience of John Humphrey Noyes.* New York, 1923.

Nye, Russel B. *Fettered Freedom: Civil Liberties and the Slavery Controversy, 1830–1860.* East Lansing, 1949.

————. *William Lloyd Garrison and the Humanitarian Reformers.* Boston, 1955.

Phillips, Ulrich B. *American Negro Slavery.* New York, 1918.

————. *Life and Labor in the Old South.* Boston, 1929.

Potter, David M. *Lincoln and His Party in the Secession Crisis.* New York, 1942.

Pressly, Thomas. *Americans Interpret Their Civil War.* Princeton, 1954.

Quarles, Benjamin. *Frederick Douglass.* Washington, D.C., 1948.

————. *The Negro in the Civil War.* Boston, 1953.

————. "Sources of Abolitionist Income," *Mississippi Valley Historical Review,* XXXII (June, 1945), 63–87.

Randall, J. C. *Lincoln, the President.* 4 vols., Vol. IV completed by Richard N. Current. New York, 1945–1955.

Shepard, Odell. *Pedlar's Progress: The Life of Bronson Alcott.* Boston, 1937.

Sherwin, Oscar. *Prophet of Liberty: The Life and Times of Wendell Phillips.* New York, 1958.

Siebert, W. H. *The Underground Railroad from Slavery to Freedom.* New York, 1898.

Simms, Henry H. "An Analysis of Abolition Literature, 1830–40," *Journal of Southern History,* VI (Aug. 1940), 368–439.

————. *A Decade of Sectional Controversy.* Chapel Hill, 1942.

Smith, Theodore C. *The Liberty and Free Soil Parties in the Northwest.* New York, 1897.

Smith, Timothy L. *Revivalism and Social Reform in Mid-Nineteenth Century America.* New York, 1957.

Stampp, Kenneth M. *And the War Came: The North and the Secession Crisis, 1860–1861.* Baton Rouge, 1950.

————. "The Fate of the Southern Antislavery Movement," *Journal of Negro History,* XXVIII (Jan. 1943), 10–23.

Thomas, Benjamin P. *Theodore Weld, Crusader for Freedom.* New Brunswick, N.J., 1950.

Tuckermann, Bayard. *William Jay and the Constitutional Movement for the Abolition of Slavery.* New York, 1893.

Turner, Frederick Jackson. *The Rise of the New West.* New York, 1906.

Tyler, Alice Felt. *Freedom's Ferment.* Minneapolis, 1944.

Wesley, Charles H. "The Participation of Negroes in Anti-Slavery Political Parties," *Journal of Negro History,* XXIX (Jan. 1944), 32–74.

Whitridge, Arnold. *No Compromise! The Story of the Fanatics Who Paved the Way to the Civil War.* New York, 1960.

Wilson, Janet. "Early Antislavery Propaganda," *More Books: Bulletin of the Boston Public Library,* XIX (Nov.–Dec. 1944), 343–361, 393–406; XX (Feb. 1945), 31–52.

Wolf, Catherine H. *On Freedom's Altar: The Martyr Complex in the Abolition Movement.* Madison, Wis., 1952.

Woodward, C. Vann. *Reunion and Reaction: The Compromise of 1877 and the End of Reconstruction.* Boston, 1951.

Wright, Benjamin F., Jr. *American Interpretations of Natural Law: A Study in the History of Political Thought.* Cambridge, Mass., 1931.

Bibliographical Note

THE PRINCIPAL MANUSCRIPT SOURCE for Garrisonian anti-slavery is the collection in the Boston Public Library: the Garrison Papers presented by the sons; the Weston Papers; the Chapman Papers; the Phelps Papers; the Child Papers; the Papers of Samuel May, Jr.; the Estlin Papers and the May–Estlin Correspondence; and the Quincy–Webb Correspondence. In addition to twelve volumes of the *Liberator* accounts, the collection includes two volumes of manuscript minutes, the American Anti-Slavery Society's Agency Committee Minutes, 1833–1840, and the Minutes of the Executive Committee, 1837–1840. Other important sources for New England abolitionism are the Garrison Papers in the Houghton Library at Harvard, the William Lloyd Garrison Family Papers in the Sophia Smith Collection at Smith College, the Foster Papers at the Worcester Historical Society, and the Theodore Parker Papers at the Massachusetts Historical Society.

The extensive activities of the Western branch of the abolitionist movement are reported in the Weld–Grimké Papers and the James G. Birney Papers in the Clements Library at the University of Michigan, one of the most valuable anti-slavery collections in the country. A two-volume selection from the Weld–Grimké Papers edited by G. H. Barnes and a second two-volume selection from the Birney Papers edited by Barnes and Dwight L. Dumond give detailed accounts of Weld's and Birney's conversion to anti-slavery, the organization of the Seventy, and their troubles with the Garrisonians. The Lewis Tappan Papers and the Elizur Wright Papers in the Library of Congress, together with the Gerrit Smith Collection at Syracuse, chronicle the rise of political abolition, the schism of 1840, and the inglorious history of the American and Foreign Anti-Slavery Society.

The Annual Reports and Proceedings of the American Anti-Slavery Society and the Massachusetts Anti-Slavery Society, carefully edited and wrapped in the heavy prose of the abolitionists, tell only part of the internal political history of the anti-slavery movement. Garrison's accounts of the various meetings and conventions of his followers are even less trustworthy although the *Liberator* usually gave them full publicity.

Anti-slavery newspapers vary in quality as well as perspective. The *Liberator* (Boston, 1831–1865) is essential for an understanding of the anti-slavery movement and humanitarian reform. Carelessly edited and belligerent in tone, it nevertheless covers almost every aspect of the abolitionist crusade as its editor interpreted or misinterpreted it. Nathaniel Rogers's *Herald of Freedom* (Concord, N.H., 1835–1844) generally follows the Garrison line, but on perfectionism takes an independent and radical stand. The *National Anti-Slavery Standard* (New York, 1840–1870) is most informative under the management of David and Lydia Child; subsequent editors proved too dull for their readers' tastes or too independent for Garrison's. The *Emancipator* (New York, Boston, 1832–1844) covers the activities of the national society throughout the thirties but is less valuable after the schism of 1840. The *Massachusetts Abolitionist* (Boston, 1838–1841) demonstrates the difficulties of conducting an editorial war with Garrison. The *Philanthropist* (New Richmond, Cincinnati, 1836–1843) under James G. Birney and then Gamaliel Bailey reports

Western anti-slavery and offers trenchant criticism of Garrison. John Greenleaf Whittier's *Pennsylvania Freeman* (Philadelphia, 1838–1844) has none of the Quaker fire of Lundy's *Genius of Universal Emancipation* (Baltimore, 1827–1833). William Goodell's *Friend of Man* (Utica, N.Y., 1836–1842) documents the rise of political abolition and, after 1840, provides a running commentary on Garrison's foibles. The *African Repository* (Washington, D.C., 1825–1844) is valuable chiefly as a source of lingering colonizationist sentiment.

Index